Lee M. Allen
Marc G. Pufong

GEORGIA
STATE POLITICS
The Constitutional Foundation
Seventh Edition

Kendall Hunt
publishing company

Cover images: © Shutterstock, Inc.

Kendall Hunt
p u b l i s h i n g   c o m p a n y

www.kendallhunt.com
Send all inquiries to:
4050 Westmark Drive
Dubuque, IA 52004-1840

Printed in the United States of America

We dedicate this 7th edition first, to all teachers who tirelessly impact civic knowledge through their steady commitments to teaching and enhancing civic education as the most effective vehicle to secure and preserve democratic ideals. Second, to our respective families, the eternal sources for unwavering love, the sustenance of our sense of purpose for the continued yearning for knowledge and truth. For Lee M. Allen are Joyce D. Allen and Su-Zan. For Marc G. Pufong are Irene K. Pufong, Eloui-Jospin, Kelog-Pier, and Cerry-Klaire.

Contents

1 Introduction to Georgia Politics   1

2 Georgia Civil Rights and Civil Liberties   17

3 Political Participation in Georgia   43

4 The Legislative Branch   65

5 The Plural Executive of Georgia   87

6 Administration and Agencies   111

7 The Georgia Judiciary   127

8 Budgeting and Finance   161

9 State Education Policy   181

10 Local Government   205

11 The State Constitution   225

List of Photos and Figures

List of Cartoons

List of Tables

Preface to the 7th Edition

Continuity and Change

Adding structural *depth to past editions,* we believe a *new edition* echoing Jefferson's admonition bear our continued commitments for a stable curriculum, especially one which fosters the importance of civic education and values. We take all these to mean the understanding of our state government on its own terms.

It is our sincere belief that textbooks designed to promote citizenships must make explicit a steady commitment to foster a pledge to promote civic knowledge through teaching and learning. By embracing the primacy of education as the most effective vehicle to secure and preserve democratic ideals, Thomas Jefferson gave a remarkable voice to Freedom, one which cherished the absence of restraint on Liberty. People, he observed, were the ultimate source of government powers.

It is no doubt, Jefferson was the first American leader to suggest the creation of a public supported school system, an idea which led to the founding of the University of Virginia. That was and is also a vivid illustration how his foresight on education would impact the formation of the development of many state educational systems in nineteenth-century America. Among them was the State of Georgia which went on to establish public support for primary and secondary education, a system of governance of its public colleges and universities when few people wanted to make it a trumpet of their own views.

As a required part of the 1983 Constitution, Georgia law requires that "all persons receiving a degree from an institution within the Georgia University System show proficiency in the Constitutions of the United States and Georgia." To help students understand their civic responsibilities and task to maintain the freedoms acquired by their forebears, most often at heavy cost, academicians must take care to provide suitable textbooks, and make them accessible. Our text can lay such a claim. We believe that consistent with the Jeffersonian conceptions of education as an instrument to promote assurances for responsible citizenships, textbooks must bear commitments, implicit or otherwise explicit, to a stable curriculum that foster those values.

With the ubiquity of the Internet today, several such publications exist at various scales which may call to question their coherence and efficacy.

Our book, *Georgia State Politics: The Constitutional Foundation* is time tested and fills that gap. Our theoretical approach is Constitutional, yet framed within the Georgia State's evolving *traditional, individualistic,* and *moralistic* political culture of two desirable outlooks, namely, change and continuity. In one instance it may mean continuity and change that manifest *adaptability.* In another situation, it may mean a call for a fusion of *activism* and *restraint,* and yet in other cases they may call for innovations.

Georgia's political culture therefore allows us to trace and assess the various forms of expectations of continuity and change in the development of the various Constitutions of Georgia and its people. It also allows us to link those developments to current trends in the newest or frequent amendments to the Constitution, the dynamic of Georgia's institutions of governance and the general needs, aspirations, and expectations of the people of Georgia as manifested in their politics. It is possible that, depending on the possible trigger of expectations recent Constitutional changes and amendments may or may not lend themselves to explanations supplied by elements of Georgia's traditional political culture. The answer to why this might be the case may lie squarely in Georgia complex politics of the time. So the question for us is not necessary whether Georgia changes, but why it changes and by how much?

In the end while any attempt to understand the necessary give and take of democratic politics in American Government can be a difficult project, we believe that using this book will make it easier because of its specific focus on Georgia's politics and political culture. Several features are designed to increase interest and readability, but the present authors are primarily dedicated to tracing the continuing threads of political continuity and modern change wherever possible among Georgia's many communities, local governments, and enduring state institutions.

The Organization of the 7th Edition

The 7th edition of *Georgia State Politics: The Constitutional Foundation* retains the same structure, the same order and number of chapters as those of the edition that precedes it. Content-wise however, every chapter has been updated and remains comprehensive in the examination of legal and political authorities that are constitutionally driven. The chapters are written and illustrated to be brief enough to remain interesting, and long enough to provide the reader with a solid understanding of contemporary Georgia State government, the Constitution and politics.

The target audience remains the same. The book remains very useful to those to whom Georgia's politics and the Constitution is required or expected as part of their civic education; and to all those who merely seek to gratify further knowledge or the continued appraisal of how state government fulfills their constitutional responsibilities. This book is designed to be used either as a stand-alone text for the study of *Georgia State Politics and Constitution,* or as a compatible text for a joint Georgia State Politics and American Government course. It can also be put to use in comparative political studies of American States. In sum, this revised 7th edition provides added depth while keeping the comprehensive framework of past editions. It preserves the same numbers of chapters and continues with the same themes and doing so while also maintaining the specific insight on Georgia's civic and political culture. These attributes, we deem, continue to set this book apart from most other textbooks written and illustrated on State government or comparative state politics.

This edition also welcomes at the helm Dr. Marc G. Pufong, a Professor of Political Science and Public Law at Valdosta State University, who along with Dr. Lee M. Allen serve as coauthors. A contributor in the previous 6th edition, Professor Pufong is the lead author beginning with the new 7th edition.

As in the past, Chapter 1 continues to serve as a compass that points to what we propose to do, the objectives we seek to accomplish and, more specifically, it sets into perspective the theoretical foundation of the book. It introduces Georgia politics, the political values and conceptions that underlie its government and people. As in the past, Chapter 1 continues to invite discussions that surround Georgia's politics, its practices and constitutional basis and scope of powers of Georgia government as well as present a general outline of this latest version of Georgia's State Constitution.

Chapter 2 presents the Civil Rights and Liberties of the citizens of the State of Georgia. Updated by Marc G. Pufong, it includes modification from previous editions that account for recent amendments to the Georgia Constitution. This, for example, allows noting changes such as the retraction of the previously included definition of marriage and the prohibition of same sex marriages. While maintaining the past structure, the updates and modifications also include the historical background of Georgia's Bill of Rights which traces its origins from the first Constitution of 1777 through the full and comprehensive treatment in 1861 to subsequent versions, including the Constitution of 1983.

Chapter 3 focuses on political participation and attendant activities that facilitate and foster participation in the democratic process in the State of Georgia. This too has been updated in the 7th edition by Lee M. Allen. Divided into three broad sections, updates have been made with new and updated charts and tables provided to include political linkages and participation. Specifically, citizen's activities and links to the two political parties and interest groups demonstrate their ability to influence local politics and Georgia State politics at large.

In Chapter 4, Professor Allen presents needed updates of the Georgia Legislature and the legislative process. Presented in three parts, the updates made cover the discussions of (a) the legal process governed by constitutional and statutory mandates such as the requirements that appropriations and tax measures originate in the lower House, etc; (b) the parliamentary process, and rules and procedures that specify how legislation is considered in each House; and lastly (c) the political process where legislators and non-legislators (including the governor) compete for power and advantages that shapes lawmaking in the Georgia Assembly.

Chapter 5 is also an update by Lee M. Allen from the previous edition on Georgia's *plural executive*. The plural executive structure means that a variety of separately elected officials, each supported by independent bureaus, act in concert with the Governor and an additional large variety of appointed administrators, to collectively execute public policies in the State of Georgia. While basically that structure remains unchanged, Professor Allen provides recent updates in this to demonstrate how evolving changes affect the powers of the various entities that make up the pluralistic administrative structure as set forth by the State Constitution of 1983. From a few political perspectives, this hampers unified political control, and so may be referred to as a *bureaucratic* constitution.

Chapter 6, on the administrative apparatus of state government, has also been updated for this edition of the book by Professor Lee M. Allen. As in the past editions, the original focus of the chapter has been retained while showing how it allows modern modifications, thus demonstrating the flexibility inherent in Article IV of the Georgia Constitution which provides for an administrative branch of government. In light of these evolving changes in government operations, much diligence has been devoted to reassessing the functions, duties, and responsibilities of Georgia's administrative state to include changes in some of the major administrative organs, and especially how they fit into the overall governing system.

Chapter 7, on the Georgia Judiciary, has been modified significantly for this 7th edition by Marc G. Pufong. It presents an overview of the Georgia Court System with discussions that situate the role of Georgia courts as they act within the broader Georgia traditionalistic political culture. A careful overview of the courts, their jurisdictions, procedures, and functions are presented with new illustrations of Georgia's judicial institutions to ease understanding of this limited and yet intriguing branch of government.

Chapter 8 has also been modified by Lee M. Allen and is by far the most significantly updated chapter in this 7th edition. This section focuses on Georgia's budgeting process during a single year, to show how unrealized expectations can lead to the need for corrections in the anticipatory budgets. Given the changing nature of politics and budgeting, especially during the *Great Recession*, such an update was very necessary. Budgetary politics often involve a fierce struggle over who really gets what, and who pays as provided by law in Georgia. Thus, the people of Georgia provide in their Constitution a complex array of checks and balances designed to ensure that the powers of the state are used effectively only to benefit the health and well-being of all of its citizens, especially in times of fiscal crisis. A detailed overview of these and other assessments that include numerous tables and figures are included in this new update.

Chapter 9 on Educational Policy includes significant updates by Marc G. Pufong who reviewed and updated major educational policies, institutions, and structures, their goals and policies, and more importantly, their finances and administrative support. They also examined the state of education within the current financial constraints in light of serious overall cuts in budgets in the last few years. This is especially so in light of the fact that Georgia continues to devote almost half of its entire budget each year to primary, secondary, and higher education.

Chapter 10 on Local Government has been updated by Marc G. Pufong with the intent to preserve the notion that states and communities in America and in Georgia in particular, play an important role in the political life of the nation and people. While the overall posture of the chapter has been maintained, some substantive changes have been made in the chapter to keep up with changes in local governance in the state, especially in the City of Atlanta and surrounding areas, in light of their immediate and primary responsibility to the people. Consistent with the current financial crisis since the Great Recession of 2008, many cities are significantly affected and therefore scaling down and tightening existing services, while opposing plans for new services.

Chapter 11 on the State Constitution has been updated by Professor Marc G. Pufong to include the changes incorporated from recent amendments to the Georgia State Constitution. As in past editions, this chapter continues to provide details of the Georgia Constitution and does so with the focus that explains how the Georgia system of government reflects the will of the people to help modernize the State of Georgia. Alternatively, even if prescriptive and descriptive in presentation, it reflects on the varied desires and policy preferences of many different groups of people, illustrating how multiple wills and desires, along with different ideas, can be incorporated into one government and one Constitution.

Overall, the new 7th edition in our view represents continuity rather than a break away from the past and previous editions. As we started in the last edition, we continue to provide a list of key words and essay questions at the end of each chapter to help stimulate learning and classroom discussions. A significantly modified multiple choice question bank is provided at the end of the book for each chapter for both the instructor and student examinations. Equally, a test bank and answers is available online from the publisher to instructors who adopt this edition of the book. Starting with this edition of Georgia State Politics detail Power Point lectures for all 11 chapters are being developed as part of comprehensive teaching ancillary package to facilitate teaching objectives and learning while using this book.

It is our utmost hope that this book's new packaging will continue to open new landscapes to instructors who adopt and use this book in their courses as well as to readers who like to better their understanding of Georgia State Politics and the Constitution.

Acknowledgments

We are indebted to our many disciplinary colleagues over the years for their advice, suggestions, and occasional contributions to *Georgia State Politics: The Constitutional Foundation*. These include teachers and professors from many institutions, all sharing the same passion and commitment to teach and to promote democracy and a republican form of government. We especially thank colleagues who worked or provided feedback on this or in previous editions of this book. In this vain we particularly thank Dr. Richard T. Saeger, a past contributor, Dr. Mandy B. Bailey and Professor Kendra A. Hinton also as past contributors for their invaluable input along with comments and suggestions and from many colleagues and students here and around the state. A word of special thank you to Verna Harvey, DPA for her insightful and detailed feedback that facilitated our revision of this edition of the book.

We also must acknowledge the support and assistance offered by the staff and administration of Valdosta State University. We are indebted to the Deans of the College of Arts and Sciences and the Honors College for their recognition, support, and encouragement. We are grateful to many of our students for offering their perspectives and continued frank comments over the years. In this vain, appreciation is extended to the spring 2016 American Government Honors class at Valdosta State University for their invaluable feedback on draft copies of this new edition. Lastly, our gratitude is extended to the professional staff at Kendall Hunt Publishing Company for their assistance in the preparations of this edition. Connor Schreck, the author account manager and Brenda Rolwes, the project coordinator, both offered invaluable stylistic and organizational suggestions that impacted this edition. In fact, it was at the prompting of Mr. Schreck which got this project underway in the first place. Most of all we thank our families, whom over the years have encouraged and supported our educational endeavors.

Of course, we accept all the blame for any errors of omission and commission which may appear herein. There are a few differences on matters of fact and interpretation which may have been compromised, or left vague so that the readers would supply their own interpretations. The thematic outlook of the book is framed on *continuity* and *change* in Georgia State Politics and constitutional foundation. We invite you to offer suggestions and opine where necessary and continue to look forward to all views.

In the end, we believe we have written a useful book for a variety of audiences, both in Georgia and in other states, and as always, welcome comments for betterment.

Lee M. Allen and Marc G. Pufong
April 20, 2016

Figure 1.1   Monument to Governor James Oglethorpe
Courtesy of Lee M. Allen

1

Introduction to Georgia Politics

Introduction to Georgia Politics

Georgia is the largest state east of the Mississippi River. It contains 58,977 square miles of land area, which ranges from the Appalachian Mountains of the Northwest region to the rolling hills and plains of the Piedmont and its great pine forests, and down to the fertile river deltas and the Savannahs, the coastal beaches and the lush off-shore islands. This area is drained by two watersheds, one leading to the Mississippi River and then to the Gulf of Mexico; the other leading south and east, ending in the Atlantic Ocean. Georgia was founded in 1733 by 114 European colonists, led by James Oglethorpe, who came on the good ship Anne (Spalding and Jackson, 1988, 1989).

Today the modern state of Georgia is inhabited by an estimated 10 million people, both rural and urban dwellers of diverse backgrounds and is considered by some estimates as the eighth most populous state in the United States. Named after King George II of Great Britain, the capital city is Atlanta. Georgia was the fourth state to ratify the U.S. Constitution on January 2, 1788. Georgia is known as *the Peach State* for which the fruit was made the official fruit of the state in 1995. Georgia is also known as the *Empire State of the South*, a name so highly contested that it is beginning to lose its aura (see Table 1.1).

Structurally, Georgia's government includes legislative, executive, and judicial branches. Executive authority in the state rests with the governor. Most of the executive officials who comprise the governor's cabinet are elected rather than appointed by the governor. Georgia has two members of the U.S. Senate and a total of 14 members in the U.S. House of Representatives, a seat more after the 2010 decennial census and reapportionment. Georgia was the fourth state to ratify the U.S. Constitution. Since 2012, Georgia has 16 representatives to the US Congress, 14 in the House of Representatives (10 Republicans, 4 Democrats) and 2 in the House of Senate both of which are Republicans. There is no female congressional representative from the State of Georgia. The State House of Representatives has 180 members and 56 members in the State Senate or a total of 236 members in the Georgia legislature (see Table 1.2).

Table 1.1 Georgia State Basics 2016	
Motto	*Wisdom, Justice and Moderation*
Capital	Atlanta
Popular names	Peach State and The Empire State of the South
Area of state	59.425 sq. miles
Population—2015	10,097,348
Population in 1890 (US Census)	82,548 (inclusive of all persons)
Admitted to U.S statehood	1788
First Constitution	1777*
Number of Constitutions since 1777	10
Current Constitution	1983
Number of Amendments in GA	70
Number of GA Ruling Document	12 since colonial charter issued in 1732
Interim Rules Prior to 1777 GA Constitution	1776 Rules & Regulation of the Colony of GA**

* Georgia's first Constitution in 1777 was followed by updated versions in 1789 and 1798. A new Constitution was adopted at the beginning of the Civil War in 1861, and at the end of the war in 1865. Another new Constitution was adopted soon after the beginning of Reconstruction in 1868 and at its end in 1877. There have been three Constitutions in the modern era—in 1945, 1976, and the current Constitution of 1983.
** Adopted by "Georgia's Provincial Congress in April 1776," served as a temporary Constitution for Georgia's revolutionary government. Based on the concept of popular sovereignty, the rules are considered by some to be Georgia's first Constitution.
Source: By authors Georgia State Politics from Various Sources

The Importance of State Government

The late U.S. Senator Everett McKinley Dirksen of Illinois used to complain that the way things were going, pretty soon the only people who would care about state boundaries would be Rand-McNally (the mapmakers). That was well before the Internet but what Senator Dirksen was lamenting was the transfer of *too much power* from the states to the national or federal government. The Senator's complaint was that states were losing power, their very reason for existence. If the state simply let go of powers by allowing or encouraging the national government to become involved in more than is necessary in State legitimate areas of public policy, then there is a misunderstanding of our federal system. To be sure, the states have given up a great deal of their power to the national government.

Table 1.2	Georgia Congressional Representatives by Districts & Party Affiliation—2016–2018		
Johnny Isakson	Since 2005	Senator State-wide	Republican
David Perdue	Since 2015	Senator State-wide	Republican
Buddy Carter	Since 2015	District 1	Republican
Sanford Bishop	Since 1993	District 2	Democrat
Lynn Westmoreland	Since 2007*	District 3	Republican
Hank Johnson	Since 2007	District 4	Democrat
John Lewis	Since 1987	District 5	Democrat
Tom Price	Since 2005	District 6	Republican
Rob Woodall	Since 2011	District 7	Republican
Austin Scott	Since 2011	District 8	Republican
Doug Collins	Since 2013	District 9	Republican
Jody Hice	Since 2015	District 10	Republican
Barry Loudermilk	Since 2015	District 11	Republican
Rick Allen	Since 2015	District 12	Republican
David Scott	Since 2003	District 13	Democrat
Tom Graves	Since 2010	District 14	Republican

*Set for retirement in 2016
Source: Compiled and designed by authors: Georgia State Politics

Since the 1930s, the relationship between the national government and the states has become much more cooperative, replacing the competitive federalism (the relationship between the national government and the states is known as federalism) that existed before President Roosevelt's New Deal (the name for the programs that F.D.R. proposed to get the nation out of the Great Depression). This cooperation frequently takes the form of the national government's identifying a problem, passing legislation to address that problem, and providing carrots (inducements often in the form of money) or sticks (threats to withhold money if the states don't comply) to tackle the problem. Normally, the states do not have the option of choosing to do nothing. Cooperation, then, really becomes coerced cooperation.

To draw the conclusion that this transfer of power to Washington has left the states powerless would be to go far beyond what the facts warrant. In fact, this is an error of thinking which assumes that there is a finite amount of power and that if one side gains power, then the other side must lose power. This is a zero sum fallacy. In fact, the power of all governments to regulate their citizens, and to control nature and improve living conditions has grown tremendously over the years. The states are hardly powerless; they just don't have the same kinds of power they used to have in relation to the national government. The national government started off small but has grown very large in recent years, in our complex federal system. Many people believe that the federal government has become *too* large, and much of its power should devolve to the states. The watchword of the Republican *revolution* that captured control of the 104th Congress in 1994 was, in fact, *devolution*.

Also, other levels of government operate in the United States and Georgia, such as international treaties and organizations, multistate agencies, and sub-local neighborhood compacts, which work together well. The unity of federalism has been highlighted by studies which stress the increasing vertical bureaucratization of programs in the United States, created by the lobbying of special interest groups (Beer, 1978). In fact, every policy and program exists at every level, administratively integrated, with costs shared by all three levels.

State government entities may no longer officially discriminate on the basis of race. They may, however, enact affirmative action guidelines that exceed federal guidelines. States cannot pollute the environment. They may, however, pass environmental protection laws that exceed the national pollution standards. States have lots of powers. What they lack is the power to deprive their citizens of the equal protection of the laws, or to subject their citizens to unreasonable dangers. In other words, the states' power to do evil is curtailed; their power to do good is limitless.

We look to state governments to provide us with education, with transportation, with police protection, with health care and sanitation, with jobs and economic development, with recreation, and with justice. The national government cooperates with the states in all of these areas. States, however, bear most of the responsibility. States then, are not merely important; in the areas that affect us most directly, states are the most important tier of our governments. And their strength is a protection against factions and special interest groups that dominate the nation (Madison, 1961).

The Constitutional Basis of State Government

Because some state governments existed prior to the writing of the Constitution of the United States, the national Constitution could not be said to have created the states. Nor did the states create the national government; rather, the people created both levels of government. And although each level of government has its own powers, ultimately some political authority has to decide which level has which powers. Article VI of the U.S. Constitution contains the "Supremacy Clause" which states that "This Constitution . . . the laws . . . and all treaties . . . of the United States, shall be the supreme law of the land." Therefore, any state constitution or state law (states can make treaties or compacts only with congressional approval) that contravenes the U.S. Constitution, federal law, or a U.S. Treaty is unconstitutional on the face of it.

If Georgia wanted a state constitutional provision or a law establishing a state church, the state could not do so because it would violate the federal laws, particularly the Establishment Clause of the First Amendment of the U.S. Constitution. If Georgia wanted to reestablish slavery, the Thirteenth Amendment to the U.S. Constitution would preclude the state from doing so. And if Georgia wanted a law prohibiting interracial marriage (in fact, such a law existed until fairly recently), provisions of the U.S. Constitution and federal law would invalidate such a blatant violation of personal freedom. In short, states are free to exceed federal constitutional protections; they are not free, however, to supersede those protections. They are not free to deny, disparage, or abuse peoples' rights. Thus states sometimes offer greater protections to its citizens than does the federal government to the national population.

Sometimes government agencies or overzealous bureaucrats, both state and federal, do *ride roughshod* over rights and must be ordered to stop. Frequently, it is a state's Attorney General who offers the opinion that an action, law, or constitutional provision is legally unenforceable. Occasionally, it is the state courts which rule that a law violates the state Constitution or that a state law or the state Constitution violates federal law or the U.S. Constitution. On even rarer occasions, it is a federal appellate court, exercising the power of judicial review (determining whether a law is consonant with the Constitution) that holds some state law or constitutional provision to be in violation of federal laws and the U.S. Constitution. Regardless of which legal authority reviews it, they all agree that the hierarchy of law in the United States is in the following order: (1) the U.S. Constitution; (2) Federal laws; (3) Treaties of the United States; (4) State Constitutions; (5) State laws; (6) Local (City and County) Ordinances. Each must be consistent with all the laws above it.

Relationships among the various levels of government in the United States are not always about power or high principles. Sometimes mundane business matters and strategies of economic growth at the local government level take center stage. In the Five Points Neighborhood in the City of Atlanta, the federal government proposed to operate a new office complex, the Atlanta Federal Center and to relocate about 8,000 workers to that facility (land and building would be owned by the city). The consolidation would allow federal employees to work together with associated savings in amenities such as a cafeteria, day-care center, and a clinic. One impact study estimated that the entire project would add $68.6 million to the local economy (Salter, 1993, p. C7).While the merchants in the area were optimistic about the proposed project, other merchants and politicians worried that the relocations and changes in work habits and transportation would injure existing businesses (Parker, 1993, p. C7).

In a democracy such as ours, politicians are always in the market for new ideas to impress the voters and to inspire other politicians to close ranks and pursue a mutually beneficial program. Such was the necessity facing Governor Zell Miller at the beginning of the 1994 legislative session. Although his previous legislative agenda, *Georgia Rebound,* could be considered a success (the economy did improve afterward), every program has its critics and naysayers. Yet, at least theoretically, new programs have one outstanding advantage: they lack a track record to be attacked by opponents during the heat of an election campaign. Usually the flag, mom, and apple pie are good old standbys, but in Georgia, the issues of the flag (confederate symbol or historical tradition?) and mom (affected by the gay rights problem) were tarnished; and apple pie is not a top priority in the Peach State.

Governor Miller had been burned pretty badly during the flag controversy, so he needed some new issue. Ah, how about anti-crime and educational issues? So suddenly there was a new agenda for the 1994 legislative session, a package the people purportedly wanted and needed, and that Miller could tie into the traditional conservative values of the state, and so he and his fellow Democrats could face the strengthening Republican party candidates in the following fall election with a politically popular platform. In fact, this strategy worked so well that Miller would continue to employ it throughout the rest of his second term. Roy Barnes, his successor, followed much the same strategy, but without the same level of success; and, in fact, his stances on the old standby issues became so unpopular and for that reason on November 5, 2002, he lost his own bid for a second term, when the electorate elected Sonny Perdue in a historically significant change of party loyalty.

Sonny Perdue became the first Republican elected as Governor of the State of Georgia since the Reconstruction Era of the 1870s. Today, all but two of Georgia's elective offices who represent the people of this State in Washington are Democrats (see Table 1.2).

State Constitutions

Although the theory of constitutional government has a long history, real constitutions were first created by colonists in North America. In addition to the national Constitution, every one of the fifty states has a Constitution. To a significant extent all are modeled on American revolutionary ideas and reflect a common pattern. They all reflect a belief in popular sovereignty and democracy; they all contain preambles which state the basic purposes of the state government. They all have bills of rights, which largely mimic the original Virginia Bill of Rights written by Thomas Jefferson, although most expand on it. They all have articles outlining the organization, powers, and selection procedures for the three branches of government—legislative, executive, and judicial. They all spell out the methods of selection for these branches.

But beyond these similarities there are also significant differences. One such difference is length. The U.S. Constitution is short, containing only about 8,700 words. State Constitutions tend to be much longer (averaging 26,000 words), although the newer ones are much shorter than the older ones. One reason why they are longer is because they usually have articles pertaining to the specific duties of the state government. For example, they contain articles on taxation, boards and commissions, education, the environment, licensing, transportation, etc. Another reason why they are longer is that they tend to be amended more often. The U.S. Constitution has only 27 amendments. Alabama's has had over 700.

Even though Georgia modernized its Constitution in 1983, it has been amended scores of times since then. The last chapter details these more recent changes. Since voters can only ratify state amendments in statewide elections, and since Georgia does not have statewide elections in odd-numbered years, a new crop of potential amendments may be ratified in 2016.

Georgia's Constitution

The Constitution of the State of Georgia, unlike the national Constitution, begins with a Bill of Rights. Georgia's Bill of Rights emphasizes the power of the people to alter or reform government, and it is often used. In fact, Georgia is second only to Louisiana in terms of the number of Constitutions enacted. Louisiana has had 11 since 1812; Georgia has had 10 since 1777. Nineteen states still operate with their original Constitution, much amended. And one state, Massachusetts, still uses its colonial charter. In Georgia, the political tradition has been more dynamic, calling for periodic revisions to meet the needs of a changing society.

Georgia's 10 Constitutions reflect this alert response. Political changes at the national level justified new Constitutions in 1777 and 1789. Popular dissatisfaction led to a new Constitution in 1798, and the turmoil of the Civil War produced several controversial new Constitutions; the Secession in 1861, the Lincoln Plan in 1865, the Reconstruction Era in 1868, and the Bourbon Coup or Restoration Constitution of 1877. More recently, the pressures of modern life led to Executive Reform in 1945, an Interim Constitution in 1976, and the contemporary Bureaucratic Constitution which went into effect on July 1, 1983.

Figure 1.2   The Voice of the People
Courtesy of Lee M. Allen

In comparison, the federal Constitution has been amended (but not revised) over a dozen times during the same period, substantially altering the federal relationship and the tax structure between 1965 and the present. In another decade or two, new problems will probably result in a call for another modernization of the Constitution of the State of Georgia. Some critics say the people are apathetic and powerless. In Georgia, the people are like a slumbering giant; when they are jolted awake by scandals or hard times, the political system takes notice. Our state's people shape the Constitution to their needs. In Georgia, the people rule.

The 1983 Constitution reflects the modern trend in state Constitutions: it is short (only 25,000 words); is less specific and much less legalistic in the use of language. It consists of a preamble and 11 articles. The preamble is similar to that of the U.S. Constitution except that Georgia's invokes divine protection and guidance. In that sense, the Georgia Constitution embraces a common feature of preambles to state Constitutions. As noted in this Chapter as well as in Chapter 11, between 1983 and 2014, well over ninety-six (96) amendments were proposed to the Georgia Constitution with seventy-seven (77) adopted, and nineteen (19) rejected.

The people of the State of Georgia enjoy the protection of a Bill of Rights which is in many ways more libertarian than that of the federal document. The Georgia Bill of Rights is in Article One, Section One of the state Constitution, and included within it are several provisions which provide protections beyond those of the federal government. Paragraph VI expressly allows us to assert *truth* as a defense against charges of libel; paragraph XII is the right to prosecute or defend lawsuits in person (although lawyers are recommended); and in paragraph XIV we find the right to an attorney whenever charged with a criminal offense. The Georgia Bill of Rights also, in paragraph XXVI protects the separate property of spouses, a modern note of gender sensitivity. And finally, the Constitution of Georgia, like that of the United States, has a reserve clause which protects the inherent rights of the people even if those rights have not been articulated, like the penumbral right of privacy. The Georgia Bill of Rights is more extensive than the federal provisions.

While few persons will deny or protest that the civil liberties movement (limiting government encroachment on all citizens' lives) is alive and growing in Georgia, the area of Civil Rights (whether different people have the same rights) continues to be contentious and provocative. Should minors be allowed to drink alcohol, or ex-convicts be allowed to vote, or homosexuals be allowed to marry? Among these groups, the National Gay and Lesbian Task Force is one of the most active in attempting to change political and cultural beliefs and customs. On the other side of the issue are political entities like conservative Cobb County, which passed legislation saying *"homosexuality* is *incompatible with community standards"* (Watson, 1993, p. 3A). The issue was highlighted as both sides moved in a series of demonstrations and marches to take advantage of the spotlights thrown on Georgia when the national media converged on the state for the 1996 Olympic Games.

Article II continues the theme of popular sovereignty, by providing for voting and elections and detailing procedures for suspension and removal of public officials. This section also provides for secret ballots, first used in Australia. Article III is the legislative article, its position in the Constitution reflects the legislative primacy established after the Revolutionary War. This illustrates the importance of the representatives of the people in framing title laws of the state. The Third Article describes the composition of the legislature, called, in Georgia, the General Assembly; it also identifies title officers of the General Assembly, and outlines its organization, procedures, and its powers.

Georgia does not have a unitary chief executive like the presidency of the federal government. Instead, it has a complex array of independent agencies and a plural executive. Indeed, the increasing complexities of modern life have led to a strengthening of bureaucratic structures. This is reflected in the Fourth Article, dealing with constitutional boards and commissions, some of which are elected by the people, one of which (the State Transportation Board) elected by the members of the General Assembly, and some of which are appointed by the Governor, subject to confirmation by the State Senate. The relationship between the Governor and the state bureaucracy is often subtle, held together as much by personal charisma and by politics as by formal Constitutional provisions.

Article V describes the executive branch per se; the administrative agencies (or the bureaucracy, as it is called by those who don't like it). Unlike

Article II of the U.S. Constitution, which is the federal executive article, and which describes the methods of election (the Electoral College) and the powers of the Chief Executive officers (the President and Vice-President), Georgia's Constitution addresses the election and powers of Georgia's various separately elected executive officers. Most states have more than two popularly elected executive officers. Georgia has eight, which places it in the middle range of states in terms of the number of independently elected executives required. These executive officers in Georgia include the Governor, the Lieutenant Governor, the Secretary of State, the Attorney General, State School Superintendent, Commissioner of Insurance, Commissioner of Agriculture, and Commissioner of Labor. All these independently elected constitutional officers are known as a plural executive.

Article VI completes the establishment of the major officials of the state, by outlining the judicial branch of government. It also identifies the types of courts, their jurisdiction, and the procedures for selection of judges, their compensation, and discipline. The article creates a network of specialized courts to deal with the complex problems presented to a modern society. It also includes district attorneys, who are major players in the legal system. And as foreshadowed in Article I of the Constitution, the state courts are specifically given the authority of judicial review over legislative acts.

Just as the creation of a national income tax required a separate federal Constitutional Amendment (the 16th Amendment), Georgia also deals with taxation policy at the constitutional level. Article VII is the taxation article, granting the power to tax, the power to exempt from taxation, and discusses the purposes for which debt may be incurred. Since education is the most important function of state government, it has its own article in the State Constitution. Thus Article VIII is the public education article, providing for the governance, bureaucratic structure, and for the financial support of education at the elementary, secondary, and college levels.

Local city governments do not merit mention in the national Constitution; these governments lack sovereignty and are creatures of the states. Because counties and cities derive their powers from the state, a separate article is necessary to address the legal status and duties of substate governments. Article IX of the Georgia Constitution describes the structure, powers, and governance of city and county governments. It also concerns the many special districts, and relations among these and between the state and its substate governments.

Article X is the amending article. It allows amendments to the Constitution to be proposed either by the General Assembly or by a constitutional convention. It is based on the Madisonian idea that frequent elections to facilitate change are superior to suppressing dissent and risking violent change. It provides for amendments to be submitted to the voters, with a majority of those voting necessarily for ratification. Finally, Article XI is the implementing article. That is, it provides for the effectuation of the Constitution, concluding in Paragraph VI: "this Constitution shall become effective on July 1, 1983; and except as otherwise provided in this Constitution, all previous Constitutions and all amendments thereto shall thereupon stand repealed."

Georgia's Politics

Georgia's government is based on its Constitution which delegates and limits powers. Understand that Constitution is a necessary condition for understanding the Peach State's government. But it is not a sufficient condition. To truly understand its government, one must examine Georgia politics. To understand the political system, that is the operation of political parties, belief systems, and patterns of political participation, we must understand the political culture of the state. Of course, the complex economic system and the variety of ethnic and racial groups in Georgia means that there are lots of different perspectives in the state. But there is a pattern, a political culture defined as the general collection of political beliefs, practices, and behaviors of a people.

The dominant political culture in Georgia can be described as traditionalistic. Political scientist Daniel Elazar has identified three major patterns of political culture in the United States. These are the traditionalistic, individualistic, and the moralistic cultures. He describes Georgia's political culture as a blend of traditionalistic and individualistic, with a trace of the moralistic political culture in the mountains of north Georgia. The individualistic and traditionalistic political cultures are alike in that persons active in politics are expected to benefit personally from their activity, although not necessarily by direct pecuniary gain (Elazar, 1984, pp. 118–119).

> The traditionalistic political culture accepts government as an actor with a positive role in the community, but it tries to limit that role to securing the continued maintenance of the existing social order. To do so, it functions to confine real political power to a relatively small and self-perpetuating group drawn from an established elite who often inherit their right to govern through family ties or social position. . . .

> The individualistic political culture emphasizes the conception of the democratic order as a marketplace. In this view, government is instituted for strictly utilitarian reasons, to handle those functions demanded by the people it is created to serve. A government need not have any direct concern with questions of the good society, except insofar as it may be used to advance some common conception of the good society . . .

> The moralistic political culture emphasizes the commonwealth conception as the basis for democratic government. Politics, to the moralistic political culture, is considered one of the great activities of humanity in its search

for the good society . . . Good government . . . is measured by the degree to which it promotes the public good and in terms of the honesty, selflessness, and commitment to the public welfare of those who govern (Elazar, 1984, pp. 115–119).

An understanding of Georgia's political culture as being traditionalistic helps us to understand why Georgia for so long had a one-party system, why voter turnout in Georgia is among the lowest in the nation, and also why Georgia has had so many Constitutions in her history. It also helps to explain Georgia's political conservatism. That conservatism is also explained, in part, by ethnicity, which is tied closely to political culture. Indeed, as political scientist Thomas R Dye captures and adds insight too as he writes:

The location of . . . political subcultures throughout the American states is largely determined by the migration patterns of different ethnic and religious groups . . . it appears that the *moralistic* subculture is a product of northern European, English, and German liberal Protestantism; the *individualistic* subculture is a product of southern and eastern European and Irish Catholicism; and the *traditionalist* subculture is a product of fundamentalist white Protestantism in potential conflict with large black populations (Dye, 1997, p. 10).

The Constitution of 1983

Georgia is governed constitutionally. Although common today, constitutional government is a recent innovation in human civilization. It grew out of British social contract theory, which asserts that government rests on the consent of the governed, evolving to cope with the conflicts and tensions that arose among the various ethnic groups and political factions within those small but energetic island nations. The theory of a government of laws, instead of a government of autocratic monarchy, took root in the British colonies, and has become a venerable tradition in the area now known as the State of Georgia. In the new American nation, the older idea of Parliamentary supremacy became the normal standard instead of deviation from monarchical rule, and legislative government came into its own. In the new world, Constitutional government is limited government, a restraint on politicians, bureaucrats, and special interest groups.

Modern Georgia began as a tiny colony of the United Kingdom on the southwestern fringes of the British Empire seagoing trade; near rival Spanish Florida. The new arrivals brought a highly productive food production system, and the literary heritage of the old world. Because their crops, livestock, and technology were geographically suited to the new temperate conditions, the European colonists prospered (Spalding and Jackson, 1988, 1989). The new land of Georgia, and its sister colonies, eventually grew industrially, socially, and politically, far beyond the wildest dreams of its founders, due in large part not only to their technology, but also to the flexibility and fairness of constitutional government, part of the heritage of Western civilization. This limited government framework still governs Georgia today.

By convention, the original operating British charters are not thought of as constitutional *per se,* but they served the same purpose: a fundamental outline of official powers and official limits. Thus the 1732 Charter of the Colony of Georgia, a Grant of George II, was the first legal organic act of the new colony. Scholars differ on whether Georgia and the other colonies became independent nations after the Revolutionary War. But by the simple language of the Articles of Confederation, succeeding states claimed themselves to be sovereign, and Georgia's first Constitution was, from that perspective, a national one. However, after Georgia joined the Union in 1788, with its broadened constitutional system, claims of sovereignty became muted for a while, and finally almost ceased entirely a hundred years later, but only after violent conflict. While the people of the United States as a whole have adopted only two Constitutions since the Revolutionary War, the people of the State of Georgia have adopted ten. These ten Constitutions can be divided into three groups: the founding era, the federalizing era, and the modern era; these are displayed in Table 1.3.

In the founding era, legislative primacy was the rule of the day, and constitutions adopted in that period reflected the common revolutionary bias against the excesses of monarchical or executive rule. At both the national and state level, constitutions exalted the representative legislature. During the federalizing era, regional and ethnic strife mingled with bitter

Table 1.3   Georgia Constitutional Systems
Founding Era
Legislative Primacy Constitution (1777) Union Constitution (1789) Reform Constitution (1798)
Federalizing Era
Confederal Constitution (1861) Reconciliation Constitution (1865) Reconstruction Constitution (1868) Restoration Constitution (1877)
Modern Era
Executive Reform Constitution (1945) Interim Constitution (1976) Bureaucratic Constitution (1983)
Source: Compiled by authors, Georgia State Constitution.

debate over the extent and legitimacy of states' rights, and the great amount of constitutional revision of that time period shows the stresses and strains of the Civil War era.

Going into modern times, the executive branch has seen a revival of its historic strength, but the most modern trend endangers the chief executive system itself, with the burgeoning growth of modern bureaucracy eclipsing its powers someways. Accordingly, some scholars, are lamenting that the world is experiencing an emerging bureaucratic government (Nachmias, 1980, p. 14). Georgia seemingly is going along with this general trend. In 1945, Georgia Governor Ellis Arnall sponsored constitutional reforms, including a new Article Three insulating the Public Utilities Commission from interference by political hacks (Pound & Saye, 1971, pp. 55–56).

The latest Georgia Constitution, adopted in 1983, continued to follow the emerging global pattern, and created a large number of independent commissions, agency boards, and local authorities that largely operate outside of the formal control of the chief executive. A notable feature was the independence of educational institutions. In Georgia, the modern trend toward bureaucratic government has blended nicely into the state's traditionalistic and individualistic culture. The feudal plantation systems of the past have evolved into the functional fiefdoms of the present. The result is a continuation of a venerable way of life, localistic and decentralized.

Key Terms

Competitive Federalism
Cooperative Federalism
Devolution
Evolution
Individualistic Political Subculture
Moralistic Political Subculture
Political Culture
Daniel Elazar
Thomas R. Dye
Traditionalistic Political Subculture
The Constitution of 1983
The Founding Era
The Federalizing Era
The Modern Era

Essay Questions

1. Arguably the national government has become more powerful leaving the states powerless. What is the reasoning behind this argument? Is the argument true?

2. Explain the basis for various state constitutions in the United States Constitution.

3. State constitutions may vary considerably. In what ways are state constitutions similar? How does the Georgia State Constitution com pare to constitutions adopted in other states?

4. Why is the United States Constitution more concise (brief) than the Georgia State Constitution (as well as other state constitutions)?

5. How does the latest Georgia State Constitution follow theemerging global pattern?

6. List and carefully discuss the three groups that define the various Constitutions of the State of Georgia.

Figure 2.1   Martin Luther King, Jr.
Library of Congress

Georgia Civil Rights and Civil Liberties

Civil rights and civil liberties are too often understood more for their historical struggles than for the rights and liberties attained or for the actual gains made for the rights achieved. It is therefore not surprising that they are also too often spoken about in *activism* and *movement* terms emphasizing instead their reactions to unjust laws, successes and failures. Stephen Tuck's latest update and account on the "Civil Rights Movement" in New Georgia Encyclopedia (2016) is a classic example. It hail the civil rights movement in the American South as "one of the most significant and successful social movements in the modern world." That statement place emphasis more to Black Georgians civil participation as part of the Southern black struggle for full civil rights and part of a wider national struggle for racial equality than to the achievements and gains made. By documenting the struggles for equal rights from post-Civil War to post World War II and the gains achieved in the late 1940s, 1950s and 1960s, much is left unstated about State denial of legal rights to vote, force legal segregation in most areas of daily life, and the persistent discrimination, all of which amounted to Sate violence.

For civil rights achievements made, Tuck (2016) point instead activism: the movements, legal challenges and mass demonstrations to strikes and self-defense mechanisms. However, there is not account of State retreat. In fact, federal laws, not state laws brought about sweeping civil rights legislation of the late 1950 and 1960 even if these challenges took place within states and against state laws. Federal legislation prohibited segregation and discrimination by providing for the rights to vote and non-discriminations in housing, etc. In Georgia, all these efforts ushered a new phase of race relations which bolstered Jimmy Carter's election with black votes to the governor's office in 1971, and ultimately to the presidency in 1976.

This chapter discusses civil rights and civil liberties in the state of Georgia as intertwined within the State's political and constitutional history. First, it presents the historical background of Georgia's Bill of Rights. It does so by tracing its origins from the first Constitution in 1777 to its full and comprehensive treatment in the Constitution of 1861 through subsequent versions, and onto the last Constitution in 1983. Second, it frames the focus of the Bill of Rights in four parts. Section I on the Rights of Persons focusing primarily on the Civil Rights and Liberties of citizens in the State of Georgia.

Section II covers the Origin and Structure of Government of Georgia. In Sections III it covers the General Provisions, and lastly in Section IV is the Marriage Provision. This provision, of course, became obsolete after 2015 U.S. Supreme Court decision in *Obergefell v. Hodges*.

Historical Background

The Georgia Bill of Rights was ratified, along with the Constitution of the State of Georgia in 1861, soon after the State of Georgia seceded from the Union on January 18, 1861. The reasons for the emergence of a bill of rights at this point in history of the state has been the object of much debate but it is important to observe that between the enactment of the first Georgia Constitution in 1777 and 1861 while Georgians lived under four constitutions, these constitutions did not contain a comprehensive bill of rights. To be sure, these constitutions did protect a few individual liberties; these included the freedom of religion and the press, the right to trial by jury, and the all-important *writ of habeas corpus*. And all of these are still protected by the Georgia Constitution's Bill of Rights today. A common historical justification for their inclusion during this period seems to be because the British were the most likely to violate these rights, a factor that had also led to the initial Revolutionary War in 1775–1783 (Bratcher, 2005).

Written by Thomas R. R. Cobb in 1861, the Georgia Bill of Rights, as commonly known today, was known then as the *Declaration of Fundamental Principles*. These principles added many rights to the Georgia State Constitution, which included all of the rights then provided for by the Constitution of the United States, as well as some original provisions. In addition to the rights enumerated, the Constitution of 1861 explicitly provided for judicial review and forcefully stated that "the enumeration of those rights shall not be construed to deny other inherent rights of citizens." In subsequent versions (such as the Georgia Constitution of 1865) the prohibition against servitude was added to the Bill of Rights. This was at the end of the American Civil War, which saw the abolition of slavery with the passage and inclusion of the 13th Amendment of the US Constitution.

The Georgia Constitution of 1868, adopted during Reconstruction (1867–76), included Georgia's version of the federally mandated Equal Protection Clause and added several protections, including the prohibition of whipping as the punishment for a crime. Also added to the Bill of Rights in the old Georgia Constitution of 1877 was the prohibition against banishment of criminals. In 1945, a few notable changes were also made to the Georgia Constitution. In 1976, two provisions were added. First, certain properties were exempted from levy and sale, and second, in recognition of the progress of women's rights, a provision protecting separate spousal property was included in that Constitution. All of these historical developments were brought forth into the 1983 Georgia Bill of Rights. While most of the enumerated rights in that version have their origins in the Constitution of 1861, some can be traced as far back as the first Georgia Constitution of 1777. Some have been lost. Alas, banishment has also practically been re-established in Georgia, and even people of minor crimes can be instructed not to return to their home counties.

There is consensus among scholars that the 1861 liberties have proven remarkably stable. Both Dorothy T. Beasley, 1985 article "The Georgia Bill of Rights: Dead or Alive?" and Robert N. Katz, 1986 article "The History of the Georgia Bill of Rights," makes stronger cases for this stability (Beasley, 1985; Katz, 1986). So far since 1861, Georgia has adopted six new Constitutions, all basically with the same listed rights brought forth into each new version of the Constitution, in essentially the same form, but with a few modifications to keep up with contemporary usage and understandings. In our modern world of developing new technologies, constitutions have to be living documents to allow society to adapt. We should expect that the Georgia Bill of Rights will continue to provide these historical protections, while remaining adaptable to the recognition of new liberties and rights when demanded by new social circumstances. From a constitutional point of view, some facets of civil rights and liberties have always been a steady feature of the Constitution of the State of Georgia. But whether those rights have in fact been similarly enjoyed by its citizens is an entirely different question, and the actual implementation of the law for everyone is harder to assert.

Civil Rights and Civil Liberties

Our civil rights and civil liberties are two of the most fundamental features of Georgia's State Constitution. After all, the original purpose of the new Georgia colony was to provide a haven for people in debt and for the unemployed poor, although in fact the majority of the actual settlers were ordinary working people. Our civil rights and civil liberties include such important political values as our religious liberty, the popular rights of free speech, free press, freedom of assembly, and the freedom from imprisonment for debt (except for child support). Both the eighteenth century founder and proprietor James Edward Oglethorpe and the twentieth century civil rights leader Martin Luther King Jr. worked to support these efforts.

A common understanding is that civil rights are positive acts because it obligates the government to protect persons against arbitrary or discriminatory treatment by the government or by other people. Similarly, civil liberties may be viewed as negative rights because they impose constraints by refraining government from abridging liberties such as the freedom of speech, press, and the related rights of assembly and association, and the exercise of religion. So, for example, Paragraph V of the Georgia Bill of Rights which guarantees the freedom of speech and of the press states that "No law shall be passed to curtail or restrain the freedom of speech or of the press. . . ." Negatively phrased rights also include the right to bear arms, the freedom from violent crime, and from involuntary servitude (except for conviction of crimes).

Many other rights and privileges are part of the traditional political culture of the state, rooted in a historical tradition that dates back over 250 years. This makes Georgia one of the leading developers of democracy at a time when monarchy and elite privilege was the rule in most of the world. While this chapter focuses on describing the scope and extent of the Georgia's Bill of Rights per se, the various civil liberties and civil rights enjoyed by the citizens of the State of Georgia's student readers are advised to read the exact wording of the Constitution after they have read this chapter.

A Bill of Rights enumerates certain individual liberties and protects those liberties from governmental intrusion, unless there is sufficiently compelling justification for governmental action. All of the rights protected by the U.S. Constitution are also protected under the Georgia Bill of Rights. The first article of the Georgia State Constitution, the Georgia Bill of Rights, has four parts. These parts are the Rights of Persons, the Origin and Structure of Government, the General Provisions, and lastly, Marriage (yet to be formally repealed in light of the 2015 *Obergefell v. Hodges* decision). The *first* part, focusing on the rights of persons, describes and enshrines some of our most basic civil liberties and civil rights. This part has 28 paragraphs with focus on individual liberties (as noted above, civil liberties and civil rights are two different concepts).

Many of these rights are similar to the rights listed in the United States Bill of Rights. Yet, there are some big differences. For instance, the Georgia Bill of Rights lists among its freedoms the Freedom of Conscience, which is the *natural and inalienable right to worship God, each according to the dictates of that person's own conscience* without interference, and adds the right to religious opinion along with freedom of religion. The second part explains the primary conception of the origins and purposes of popular government. In so doing it describes the origin and foundation of government, the object of government, the separation of powers, and the superiority of civil authority over military authority. Also, this section explicitly describes the separation of church and state and set forth other provisions which control the structure and operation of the state and its political institutions. The third part is the general provision which cover imminent domain and private ways rights, and tidewater titles. And lastly, the last part dealt with specification and definition of marriage to a specific understanding exclusive to a union between a man and a woman. Again, as noted above the last part is yet to be formally repealed in light of the

2015 *Obergefell v. Hodges* decision. In summary, these provisions include those that impose limitations on official powers, the basic patterns of intergovernmental relationships among state institutions, and protection for private property rights.

Courts and the Bill of Rights

Within Georgia, the courts play the role of final arbiter as to the meaning of the Georgia Constitution. As a result, some provisions of the Georgia Bill of Rights, as interpreted by the state courts, are more protective of individual liberty than textually similar provisions of the Constitution of the United States. It should be observed that as a general rule, state constitutions can and should provide more, *not* less, protection to individual liberty than the Constitution of the United States. Thus, the Georgia Constitution includes some liberties that are simply not mentioned by the federal Constitution. For example, the Georgia Constitution protects "freedom of Conscience," that is the natural and inalienable right to worship God; the right not to be abused during arrest or imprisonment, and forbids whipping as a form punishment for crimes.

However, pending the United States Supreme Court's ruling on these matters, some States through their constitutions or amendments can and do deny its courts the power to decide cases in some areas of Civil Rights even if such prohibition may be presumptively unconstitutional under the United States Constitution. In November 2004, Georgia voters passed a new constitutional **amendment** to include one of those time-tested amendments with the clear intent to prohibit marriages between persons of the same sex in the State of Georgia. Specifically, in that new addendum, Article I, Section IV, paragraph I (a) provided that "Marriages between persons of the same sex are prohibited in this state" and in furtherance to that prohibition in paragraph I (b) of the same Section also stated that "No union between persons of the same sex shall be recognized by this state as entitled to the benefits of marriage." This state, the Section IV paragraph stated further, "shall not give effect to any public act, record, or judicial proceeding of any other state or jurisdiction respecting a relationship between persons of the same sex that is treated as a marriage under the laws of such other state jurisdiction." Lastly, paragraph I (b) directing commands to the courts of the State of Georgia stated that *"the courts of this state shall have "no jurisdiction" to grant a divorce or separate maintenance with respect to any such relationship or otherwise to consider or rule on any of the parties' respective rights arising as a result of or in connection with such relationship."*

The June 15, 2015, United State Supreme Court decision in the case of *Obergefell v. Hodges* set aside this provision of the Georgia Constitution while also disabling similar provisions in 30 states' constitutions which in

Figure 2.2 Attorney General Olens' Statement on Supreme Court Marriage Ruling *Obergefell v. Hodges*
"Today the Supreme Court of the United States ruled the Constitution requires a state to license a marriage between two people of the same sex and to recognize a marriage between two people of the same sex when their marriage was lawfully licensed and performed out of state. It does not permit bans on same-sex marriage. In our system of government, the Supreme Court bears the ultimate responsibility for determining the constitutionality of our laws. Once the Supreme Court has ruled, its Order is the law of the land. As such, Georgia will follow the law and adhere to the ruling of the Court."
Source: Attorney General Olens' Statement on Supreme Court Marriage Ruling, June 26, 2015

1992 visited the same restrictions on civil rights of their citizens. Specifically, the Court held that same-sex couples have a constitutional right to marriage under the Fourteenth Amendment of the *United States Constitution*. In so doing, the Supreme Court did more. Its *Obergefell decisions* effectively reinstated the powers of the courts in these jurisdictions that were previously restricted by law to treat equally anyone whose civil rights to marry was denied under the color of the laws of the United States. In the State of Georgia, to render clear the impact of the US Supreme Court decision and Georgia's own position on this matter, on June 26, 2015, the Office of the Attorney General of the State of Georgia issued the statement in the above capsule in a state-wide memorandum (see Figure 2.2 above). Figure 2.3 on page 23 invites you the reader to consider and weigh in about who needs civil rights protection and why? Is the Governor correct and if so why?

Civil Liberties

Section One of Article One of the Georgia Constitution contains 28 different paragraphs, of which the great majority concentrates on protection of our liberty. Civil liberties issues focus on the question of the general degree and limits of freedom allowed by society, and whether or not some types of activities will be forbidden to everyone. Twenty-one of the paragraphs, as described below, detail the liberties enjoyed by the people of the State of Georgia. Another four paragraphs discuss libertarian topics as well as civil rights issues. In civil liberty issues the concern is over the limits on liberty and the boundaries between our freedom and the power of government.

The first paragraph of Article One guarantees that no Georgian shall be deprived of three of the most important possessions of a free citizen: life, liberty, or property; unless a government agency deliberately (and properly)

> **Figure 2.3**   Can a bill that allows discrimination give rise to a state-sanctioned discrimination?

Responding yes to this question on Monday, March 28, 2016, Governor Nathan Deal announced that he will veto HB 757, a legislation that enumerates certain actions religious leaders, faith-based organizations and people of faith shall not be required to take or perform. He will exercise the veto a day after this announcement. While the governor claimed he had no objection to the general objectives of the *Pastor Protection Act* especially the version that was passed by the Georgia House of Representatives; he was displeased with the final version of the bill because it contained language that could give rise to a state-sanctioned discrimination.

The Governor continues, ". . . I appreciate the efforts of the General Assembly to address these concerns and my actions today in no way disparages the motivations of those who support this bill. Their efforts to purge this bill of any possibility that it will allow or encourage discrimination illustrate how difficult it is to legislate on something that is best left to the broad protections of the First Amendment of the United State Constitution . . ." ". . . If indeed our religious liberty is conferred by God and not by man-made government, we should heed the 'hands-off' admonition of the First Amendment to our Constitution. When legislative bodies attempt to do otherwise, the inclusions and omissions in their statues can lead to discrimination, even though it may be unintentional. That is too great a risk to take."

". . . In light of our history, I find it somewhat ironic that some in the religious community today feel that it is necessary for government to confer upon them certain rights and protections." ". . . If indeed our religious liberty is conferred upon us by God, and not by man-made government, perhaps we should simply heed the hands-off admonition of the First Amendment to the United States Constitution. . . ." ". . . Some of those in the religious community who support this bill have resorted to insults that question my moral convictions and my character. Some within the business community who oppose this bill have resorted to threats of withdrawing jobs from our state. I do not respond well to insults or threats..."

". . . The people of Georgia deserve a leader who will make sound judgments based on solid reasons that are not inflamed by emotion. That is what I intend to do . . . " ". . . As I've said before, I do not think we have to discriminate against anyone to protect the faith-based community in Georgia . . ." My decision regarding HB 757 is not just about protecting the faith-based community or providing a business friendly climate for job growth in Georgia . . ."

"... This is about the character of our state and the character of its people. Georgia is a welcoming state filled with warm, friendly and loving people. Our cities and countryside are populated with people who worship God in a myriad of ways and in very diverse settings. Our people work side-by-side without regard to the color of our skin, or the religion to which we adhere ..." Lastly, Governor Deal surmised "... We are working to make life better for our families and our communities. That is the character of Georgia. I intend to do my part to keep it that way. For that reason, I will veto HB 757...."

Source: By author, drawn from the Office of the Governor of the State of Georgia, *"Transcript of Gov. Nathan Deal's remarks regarding HB 757, delivered at a news conference on March 28, 2016."* https://gov.georgia.gov/press-releases/2016-03-28/deal-veto-hb-757, *March 28, 2016*

acts to deprive a person of these things. These freedoms are also explicitly provided for in the national Constitution. But if the government perceives a need to act in such a fashion, it must move carefully, by an official and formal proceeding marked by all of the requirements of due process of law. Due process of law usually requires that a person be notified in advance of the intended action, that an official public hearing shall be held, and that the person shall have an opportunity to dispute the state's action, including calling witnesses and having the benefit of legal counsel during the process.

Another civil liberty is found in the third paragraph, which provides for freedom of conscience and guaranteeing that each person has the natural and inalienable right to worship God in her own way, and that no human authority should control or interfere with anyone's right of conscience. Similarly, the next paragraph guarantees that we all shall enjoy freedom of speech and of the press. So in Georgia, every person may speak, write, and publish sentiments on all subjects. But of course everyone shall be responsible for the abuse of that liberty, such as inciting to riot or falsely shouting "fire" and thus threatening the lives and safety of other citizens.

Another new problem in modern Georgia concerns the rapidly evolving technologies of electronic computing, data collection and storing of information about citizens, and censorship and regulation of public access to various websites. Government at all levels in the world today has of course an interest in electronic monitoring of communications lines. Both the national government and the state governments are properly concerned with the vast communication network and its influence with a perpetual War on Terror; the state and local governments are interested in taxation of sales taxes across state lines; and of course parents are often interested in limiting their children's access to depictions of pornography and violence. In addition, the new interactive capabilities of cable TV allow commercial cable firms and their sponsors to monitor the programs and frequency of our daily television viewing. In Georgia, where the Bible belt brand of morality is exceptionally strong, questions are raised about the extent to which these doubtful channels and websites can be censored by families.

We are living in a world that has shrunk to a global village owing to the advent of rapid connectivity technology. Social networking sites have paved the way of getting people's messages across to their own kind; thus mankind's motivation to take action against some hegemonic tyrannies has been enhanced. This is a factor not only increasing the will and power of the people who fueled the regime change protests as most recently during Arab Spring protests but also of protestors in the United States and Georgia. This empowerment has made citizens of all countries better able to speak up and declare their desire to claim freedom as their birth right. The shots heard around the world continues to reverberate in the new Global Era.

Views on the cost and benefits of this evolving technology no doubt are varied. Some people say that the Internet is like traveling. They say each trip is like a new journey and they never know where they are going to be taken to. But a new problem is that some spend so much time on the Internet that they withdraw from regular society. They escape reality into a realm with no real boundaries or existence. While lost in the cyber world for long periods of time, they are neglecting other important activities like time with the family, socializing, work, and health concerns. Internet addiction has been cited as a contributing factor in the disintegration of marriages and families, and the collapse of promising careers. And the loss of personal interaction has led to a great increase in incivility generally, and particularly in the realm of political compromise.

In the 2011 uprisings in Tunisia and Egypt, new social media such as Facebook and Twitter helped dissidents rise up against the government. When Tunisian protestors took to the street and toppled the government of Zine El Abidine Ben Ali, social media tools like Facebook and Twitter helped organize the protests. When the government realized this, officials began to covertly and slyly attack the Facebook users. So while the new techno community arguably makes it possible for people to communicate despite the power of repressive governments and its leaders, new counter strategies are also evolving. Humans are defined by their ability to use complex language to communicate, and thereby to establish a community. Nevertheless, when communication is suppressed for the majority of the people of a nation, the pattern of revolution is ultimately inevitable. Facebook, Twitter, and other social networking are the latest form of technology facilitating confrontation over serious issues across traditional lines of authority.

What if you call someone a thief, and that person says you are lying? Well, paragraph six covers that situation, under the provision governing libel lawsuits. In all civil or criminal actions for libel, the defendant may

Figure 2.4 The Internet: A New Social Problem
Courtesy of Lee M. Allen

offer evidence that the matter is true, and if a trial determines that the matter charged as libelous is in fact true, then the defendant shall be discharged. Of course citizens are well advised to be soft spoken, and not to *shoot off their mouths* unless they are prepared to back up everything they say with hard evidence.

One of the most controversial liberties possessed by all Americans is the right to keep and bear weapons, including firearms. Currently it is disputed whether this right belongs to each individual citizen or only to organized and approved militia companies. It is clear that this right originated as a result of the successful American Revolution against the tyrannical British government. These revolutionaries in Georgia and the other 12 colonies insisted on their right to use weapons to protect themselves. But nowadays some political action groups think that times have changed, and that since the problem of controlling violent criminals is greater than problems of abusive government, the liberty should be re-interpreted and severely restricted. Currently, the right of the people to keep and bear arms remains intact, subject to the power of the General Assembly to proscribe the manner in which arms may be bought and sold, carried and used. Today firearms of all types are closely regulated.

The ninth and tenth paragraphs describe some relatively non-controversial liberties. These include the rights of people to assemble in groups, and to circulate petitions calling for redress of their public grievances. The people have the right to assemble peaceably for their common good or pleasure, and to sign petitions to send to officials of their government so that their problems can be attended to. Sometimes laws do not attract attention simply because they are good laws and are working well. Examples of this are found in the next paragraph, which prevents several of the most favorite abuses by bad governments. These include bills of attainder (legislative targeting of individuals) and ex post facto laws (punishing someone for something he or she did which was legal at the time), also known as retroactive laws. This section also prohibits any laws impairing the obligation of contract, or voluntarily surrendering or recanting any of their special privileges or immunities.

The Jury System

Paragraph 11 focuses on the important matter of citizen juries. It is a prime tenet of our culture that when the government accuses people of crimes they should be tried by a jury of the citizen peers, and not by a government official. It specifies that the right to trial by jury shall remain inviolate, except perhaps where a jury is not demanded in writing by either party. But in all criminal cases, defendants are guaranteed the right to a public and speedy trial by an impartial jury; and the jury shall be the judges of the law and the facts. While in extremely rare cases a judge may set aside a jury verdict, the system of review by higher courts and public opinion ensures that this possibility is not abused.

Usually a trial jury will consist of 12 persons, especially in important felony cases. However, to save time and money the General Assembly may prescribe any number, not less than six, to constitute a trial jury in the smaller courts of limited jurisdiction and in the state superior courts in misdemeanor cases. The General Assembly regulates by law for the selection and compensation to persons to serve as grand jurors and trial jurors. The monetary compensation for jury duty is not very high; the major reward for citizens comes in the satisfaction of knowing that they have helped to maintain our rights and liberties.

Paragraph 12 of the Georgia Constitution makes sure that all Georgians have full and unrestricted rights of access to the state courts. More specifically, it provides that no person shall be deprived of the right to prosecute or defend his or her legal causes, either in person or by representation by an attorney. It would be unfair if a person was not allowed to defend himself if charged with a crime. Our continued liberty depends on being able to defend ourselves in such circumstances. This concern is also the subject of the next constitutional paragraph, which limits the government's use of searches, seizures, and warrants. The people have a right to be secure in their persons, houses, papers, and effects against unreasonable searches and seizures. Generally a state judge or magistrate will issue a search warrant only if witnesses make an oath or affirmation asserting that there is probable cause to suspect criminal activity, and if the warrant particularly describes the place or places to be searched by the official officers, and if it also specifies the persons or things to be seized.

Paragraph 14 outlines the rights and liberties that people have if they are charged with an offense against society, a crime or other risk to their freedom such as imprisonment for contempt of court. These include having the benefit of a defense lawyer, which is almost essential if a person is to be able to defend herself in a modern court of law. Other elements of this section include being furnished with a copy of the accusation or indictment and, on demand, with a list of witnesses on whose testimony such charge is founded. Accused persons also have the right to use compulsory process (the power to subpoena) to obtain the testimony of their own witnesses; and the right to be confronted with the witnesses testifying against such person.

In our modern society, two new issues have arisen which have caused considerable debate over our cherished right to be confronted by our accusers. First, society's mounting concern over child abuse cases and the sensitivity of underage witnesses to intimidation have raised questions of the right of confrontation in those kinds of cases. Prosecutors will sometimes demand that a child's testimony be pre-recorded, and that cross-examination will not be conducted in open court. Also, sometimes an agency will leak accusations against persons to the mass media, and in effect conduct a trial that leaves persons unable to defend themselves against supposition, rumors, and innuendo. Under these conditions, innocent people may be fired from their jobs, turned out by their families, and sometimes hounded by their neighbors.

In modern Georgia, few if any people have been secretly thrown in jail without a public trial, but that used to be a real problem in historical times. The remedy for this abuse of government power was for someone to go to a regular judge and seek a writ of *habeas corpus*, which is an order to the jailer to produce the prisoner and to show proof that the person was being lawfully detained. This protection is provided in paragraph 15 of the first Article of the Georgia Constitution. It is still used often today however, as a procedure where a defendant can claim that there was some serious defect in his original trial, and to request an appeals court to let him have another chance to demonstrate his innocence. The Constitution provides that this *writ of habeas corpus* shall not be suspended unless the public's safety may require it, as in the extremely unlikely event of rebellion or invasion. Of course, rebellion is unlikely in our democratic society where people are free and realize the fact. It is only when people are severely mistreated by their government and their leaders that they begin to think about using force and violence to secure their liberty. Ever since the days of Spartacus in ancient Rome, even tyrants learned not to push people too far.

The next two paragraphs in Article I, Section I provide further protections for persons accused of crimes. Because we disapprove of torture, and because we know that persons can sometimes be forced to confess to crimes that they did not commit, the Georgia Bill of Rights ensures that no person shall be compelled to give testimony tending in any manner to be self-incriminating. Furthermore, the Constitution provides that excessive bail shall not be required, nor excessive fines imposed, nor cruel or any unusual punishments inflicted; nor shall any person be abused in being arrested, while under arrest, or in prison. While there are occasional reports of such abuses occurring, the criminal justice system is closely watched, and proven incidents of beating of inmates will result in the punishment of the guards and officials involved.

Paragraph 18 ensures that no persons shall be put in jeopardy of life or liberty more than once for the same offense. There are exceptions however, such as when a new trial has been granted after conviction, or in case of mistrial. Because of the overcrowding of our prison systems in Georgia, it has become common for prosecutors to charge defendants with every possible offense arising from a criminal activity. Thus, someone who hits a victim several times might be charged with several counts of battery. Faced with the prospect of several trials and several possible convictions, many criminals may plea bargain; plead guilty to one charge in return for less time in jail. In some states, prosecutors may even have the right to appeal a jury verdict of not guilty, and try a defendant again for the very same crime!

The next section, paragraph 19, concerns the rare problem of someone accused of treason against the State of Georgia. Treason against the State of Georgia is defined as insurrection against the State, adhering to the State's enemies, or giving them aid and comfort. No person shall be convicted of treason except on the testimony of two witnesses to the same overt act or confession in open court. Many government officials and state agency employees are required to take a loyalty oath asserting their allegiance to the State of Georgia.

The consequences of being convicted of a crime in Georgia are described in the next few paragraphs, limiting the kinds and effects of punishment. Number 20 guarantees that no conviction shall work corruption of blood (punishing a criminal's relatives as well as the criminal), or allowing the courts to engage in forfeiture of a criminal's estate (although stolen property, or property used for criminal activity, or purchased with tainted funds can and will be confiscated). Paragraph 21 forbids using banishment and whipping as punishment for crime. The next paragraph provides that there shall be no involuntary servitude within the State of Georgia except as a punishment except for crime after legal conviction thereof or for contempt of court. This outlaws slavery within the State of Georgia. Similarly, number 23 prohibited imprisonment for debt but federal law and interstate compacts regarding parents who fail to pay their child support obligations can be jailed until they pay up. And paragraph 24, the last of the sections dealing with civil liberties per se, guarantees that no person shall be compelled to pay costs in any criminal case except after conviction on final trial.

Georgia thus has a long list of guarantees for persons which prevent many of the old abusive actions that historically were used to limit the liberties of the people. However, there are some civil liberties which exist in some states, but not in Georgia. Of these, perhaps the most significant is whether citizens have the right to initiate new laws and policies without the approval of the state government. In some states, such as California, the people have the liberty to circulate petitions for new laws which, if signed by a sufficient number of voting citizens, puts the proposed new laws directed on the ballot for popular approval, completely bypassing the ordinary legislative role in enacting new laws. While the Georgia Constitution does permit ballot initiatives in some local government matters, it is not as liberal as California. Civil liberties, protections against overzealous government officials, are traditionally important and protected elements of our state constitutional system.

Civil Rights

Civil rights are closely related but still a different concept. Civil rights focus on egalitarian issues. In other words the question is whether or not all people are treated equally by the government. Interest and participation in the full extent and scope of civil rights is arguably among the most controversial issues in any democratic society, including Georgia. The major questions sparking our lively debates include asking about the distribution of rights of equality and privilege among the people. Should all citizens have exactly the same rights and opportunities under government and its agencies? Does discrimination exist and when should the powers of government be used to ensure that no one has unfair advantages under the policies and the operations of state government? Arguably, the civil rights movement in the American South, and definitely including Georgia, was one of the most significant and successful social movements that help to bring about some modern changes (Tuck, 2004, 2016).

Black Georgians accordingly formed part of this Southern movement for full civil rights and the wider national struggle for racial equality. What followed is that all ethnic groups are now guaranteed equal opportunity, the right to vote, and both genders are also provided with equal treatment in educational and occupational settings. The Georgia Constitution addressed these important civil rights matters.

The political culture of Georgia has often supported advances in civil rights. Perhaps the most significant inequality in human history has been the different treatment of men and women. Perhaps in early history primitive conditions made it advisable for society to channel women into domestic servant roles, with low status. But the modern technological revolution, and its requirements for a highly trained intelligent work force, does not allow us to exclude fifty percent of our human resources from full access to skilled employment opportunities. Georgia has been a leader in women's rights. For example, in 1802 Georgian Sarah P. Hillhouse became the first woman to own and edit a newspaper. And Wesleyan College in Macon, in 1836, became the first college in the world to be chartered to confer degrees to women. Similarly, in 1866 Georgia became the first to allow women to have full property rights, and in 1922 Georgia choose Rebecca Felton as the first elected United States Senator. Civil rights and equal opportunity is as important to Georgians as making sure that government does not infringe on our liberties.

The second paragraph of Article One provides protection to persons and their property by guaranteeing equal protection under the law. It proclaims that protection to persons and property is the paramount duty of government, and that the state government shall be impartial in its administration of the laws. In Georgia no person shall be denied equal protection of the laws. No individual or group can be denied rights which are granted to other citizens. Similarly, paragraph four specifically orders that no inhabitant of this state shall be molested in person or property or be prohibited from holding any public office or trust on account of religious opinions. However, it takes the precaution of ensuring that the right of freedom of religion shall not be constructed as to excuse acts of licentiousness or justify practices inconsistent with the peace and safety of the state.

Echoing the national Constitution, the Constitution of the State of Georgia in paragraph seven proclaims that all citizens of the United States, resident in this state, are hereby declared citizens of this state; and that it shall be the affirmative duty of the General Assembly to enact such laws as will protect them in the full enjoyment of the rights, privileges, and immunities due to such citizenship. And paragraph 24 was inserted to make sure that the social status of any citizen shall never be the subject of legislation. This reflected the national Constitution, which prohibits the federal government from proclaiming any elite individuals being granted any title of nobility. Thus Georgia cannot declare that anyone is either a peasant or an aristocrat. And, in line with modern practice to guarantee that women are treated equally, the state Constitution prohibits the practice of putting wives and their property under the control of their husbands. Paragraph 27 says that the separate property of each spouse shall remain the separate property of that spouse, except as may otherwise be provided by the laws of the state, such as prenuptial agreements, contracts, and divorce decrees.

One major reason for the adoption of the present Georgia Constitution was disenchantment with the antebellum treatment of the issue of civil rights, particularly freed slaves, in many states following reconstruction. Civil rights are always the subject of debate and controversy, partly because of prejudice and partly because social progress creates new inventions and customs which raise or revive questions of claims for privilege for the elite few. During the turmoil of the 1960s civil rights movement in Georgia, great pressure grew to modernize the constitutional wording to reflect the new social and political conditions of the twentieth century. During the political struggles that ensued, the Reverend Martin Luther King, Jr. became the leader of the civil rights movement in the 1960s.

Case Study: Martin Luther King Jr.

Individuals participate in politics or seek political careers for many reasons, and sometimes they may become great leaders who effect great changes in politics and society. One such individual was the Reverend Martin Luther King Jr. Probably nothing makes people more active and politicized than being subjected to bias and discrimination, especially when it interferes with their rights and opportunities, or results in being treated as second-class citizens. Following the Second World War, an increased sensitivity to equality and equal rights resulted in the great civil rights movement that culminated in an end to official racial segregation and Congressional passage of important civil rights acts. Martin Luther King Jr. grew up in Atlanta, Georgia, and became the leader of the civil rights movement in the 1960s. His dedication and sacrifice to that cause has earned him recognition as one of the most important and progressive American figures of the twentieth century. His "I have a dream" speech will long be remembered as one of the most eloquent statements of human civil rights.

Both Liberty and Rights

Some sections of the Georgia Bill of Rights concern issues which touch on both civil rights and on civil liberties. For example, Paragraph 11 covers the operation of the state's jury system. This portion of the law is devoted to making sure that civil liberties and civil rights are not just handled by government officials, who may have institutional agendas, but rather by ordinary citizens chosen at random. The jury system in Georgia is therefore designed to make sure that people have the maximum certainty that their cases will be decided by a jury of their peers. Thus, felony trials always require a jury of 12 persons. And further protections against arbitrary government actions specifies that grand jurors, who issue complaints charging people with crimes and the trial jurors who decide guilt, will operate separately. Yet, according to a 1999 Associated Press reporting based on information obtained from the Georgia State Board of Pardons and Paroles (GSBPP) one out of every ten Georgians will likely serve time in a state jail or prison; and studies showed that the odds were worse for black males.

Paragraph 26 of the Georgia Bill of Rights covers the homestead exemption. The basic idea is that an elderly person's home should not be taken away just because she owes a lot of money and cannot repay it in a timely fashion. A homestead exemption was set at not less than $1,600.00; and it also gives the General Assembly the authority to define when or if any additional exemptions shall be allowed and to specify the amount of such exemptions. The state assembly is also required to provide for the manner of exempting such property and for the sale, alienation, and encumbrance thereof; and it should be noted that the law actually provides for the waiver of the homestead exemptions by a debtor. So if people want to waive their homestead exemptions, to obtain a mortgage loan for example, they can do so, if they want to take the risk. Today, unfortunately, the *Great Recession of 2008* and its attendant revenue shortfalls for the state coffers, has led the legislature to almost eliminate the homestead exemption in many local cases.

Finally, the last part of Section One of Article One, paragraph number 28, has a reserve clause for civil liberties and civil rights. It provides that the enumeration of the rights described above shall not be interpreted as meaning that there is an automatic denial of other rights. The enumeration of rights herein contained as a part of this Constitution shall not be construed to deny to the people any inherent rights which they may have hitherto enjoyed. To use a somewhat silly example, suppose that our legislature imposed a tax on the air we need to breathe. Under the reserve clause, a citizen could go to the courts for a ruling that the new tax violated our inherent right to use the atmosphere.

Automatic Restoration of Rights

In the State of Georgia, one loses their civil rights if they are convicted of a "felony involving moral turpitude" or if they have been judicially determined to be mentally incompetent. This is provided under the Georgia Constitution, Article II, Section 1, III items (a) and (b). However, the rights to vote, for example, are restored automatically upon completion of an imposed sentence. As an example, a convicted person may not hold public office "unless their civil rights have been restored and at least ten years have lapsed from the date of the completion of the sentence as long as there is no subsequent conviction for another crime that involves moral turpitude." According to a Georgia Attorney General opinion on this matter, to regain the right to sit on a jury, either a pardon or the restoration of one's civil rights is necessary (Georgia Opinion of the Attorney General #69, No. 83-33, 1983). In particular cases, an official Opinion of Attorney Generals in the State of Georgia may be very important in clarifying some points of Georgia law before a particular court may ever get to decide that law in an actual case or controversy.

Other opinions have involved state constitutional prohibitions against felony offenders holding an appointment of honor or trust, such as the position of deputy sheriff, a peace officer, except where they have been pardoned. However, one Attorney General took the position that because those appointments are precisely to positions of honor and trust, it does not prevent the state General Assembly from acting to increase the onus of these offenses, and making convictions an absolute prohibition to the qualification for those positions. As opined by that Attorney General's opinion, this is the case because the General Assembly is authorized by law to provide even much higher qualifications for the officers under Georgia law [see Georgia Code Annotated Section 92A-2108(d)].

Discretionary Restoration of Rights

In the State of Georgia, as in many other states, the power to pardon and to remove disabilities from prior conviction is vested on a State Board of Pardons and Paroles. However, the board may be prohibited from issuing a pardon and its powers may be superseded by the legislature; as in the cases involving recidivists and persons serving life sentences (see Georgia Constitution Article IV, Section 2, Para. II). Although the Governor appoints the members of the State Board of Pardons and Paroles, the law prohibits the Governor from exercising power or any authority whatsoever over Pardon and Paroles administration and processes (see Georgia Code Annotated Section 42-9-56). In addition to issuing pardons and sentence commutations, the Board may issue "Restoration of Civil and Political Rights" to felony offenders including those from out-of-state and federal convictions (See Board instructions, at http://pap.georgia.gov/pardons-restoration-rights).

For the restoration of civil rights, more specifically, a petitioner must have completed his or her sentence including the payment of fine with no impending charges, if applicable, and lastly, two years must have lapsed without any criminal activity (after the completion of the initial conviction). For a full pardon, the petitioner must have completed a five-year waiting period after the completion of the sentence without any criminal activity.

However, waivers can be extended to those petitioners who can show that the five-year waiting period would be detrimental to their livelihood. For example, if a petitioner can show that the five-year waiting period would impact upon their qualification for employment in their chosen profession they might be extended a waiver. Finally, Georgia law also extends and makes the restoration of rights to federal and out-of-state offenders living within the state of Georgia.

In the end, it is important to understand that the restoration of rights only affect people's basic civil rights (i.e., the right to jury and access to public office, because even a full pardon does not always imply complete innocence). For example, a pardon does not restore a convicted felony offender to a public office he or she was forced to relinquish as a result of a conviction (see *Morris v. Hartsfield*, 197 S.E. 251) (Ga. 1938). What a pardon is and what it really does is that it relieves the burden of civil and political disabilities imposed by a conviction (see Georgia Code Annotated Section 42-9-54 and Georgia compilation of the Rules and **Regulations** (475-3)).

ARTICLE I–SECTION II

Origin and Structure of Government

The second section of Article One, concerning the origin, foundations, and structure of government, focuses on the basic political concepts underlying our state government. Paragraph one proclaims our fundamental belief that all government, of right, originates with the people, is founded upon their will only, and is instituted solely for the good of the whole. Public officers are considered to be the trustees and servants of the people and must at all times be answerable to them. The second paragraph concerns the object of government. It reflects our value system, asserting that the people of this state have the inherent right of regulating their internal government. Government is instituted for the protection, security, and benefit of the people; and at all times they have the right to alter or reform the same whenever the public good may require it.

Paragraph III concerns the separation of legislative, judicial, and executive powers. The legislative, judicial, and executive powers are intended to forever remain separate and distinct; and no person discharging the duties of one shall at the same time exercise the function of either of the others except as herein provided. As we see in following paragraphs, the Constitution puts particular limits on the powers of the government institutions by what can be called a check and balance system. In paragraph IV, the power of the courts to punish for contempt shall be limited by legislative acts. As detailed in paragraph V, if the General Assembly enacts legislation in violation of this Constitution or the Constitution of the

United States, the judiciary branch shall be required to declare them void. And paragraph six declares that the civil authority shall be superior to the military.

The next two paragraphs deal with narrower topics. Paragraph seven prevents the government from trying to favor the establishment of a religion. It definitely asserts that no money shall ever be taken from the public treasury, directly or indirectly, in aid of any church, sect, cult, or religious denomination or of any sectarian institution. And paragraph eight deals with gambling and lotteries, contains amendments to the constitution, and supersede the previous ban on gambling. Prior to 1991, all gambling and lotteries were prohibited in Georgia. But due to budgeting problems, the State Constitution was amended to permit gambling and lotteries as long as the proceeds were used for the purposes of education (e.g., funding public kindergartens and Hope Scholarships). Certainly, what the legislature giveth, it could also take away, and the Georgia Lottery could be abolished by a subsequent constitutional amendment. But after more than a decade, the lottery remains a popular institution with many Georgians. Thus, the likelihood that it would be abolished is slim, and the fact that its originally publicized purpose, to support education, is ensconced in the Constitution makes it doubly secure.

Under the old British system of monarchy, the King could do no wrong, and therefore people could not sue the King for any misdeeds; there was sovereign immunity. But in our democracy, it is understood that state government may sometimes inadvertently injure someone, and that person should be able to sue for compensation. Lawsuits filed to get repayment for injuries are called tort actions, and we believe that everyone should have the right to sue anyone who injures them. Accordingly, paragraph nine provides that the General Assembly may waive the state's sovereign immunity from suit, and that the General Assembly may provide by law for procedures for the making, handling, and disposition of actions or claims against the state and its departments, agencies, offices, and employees.

There are other limitations designed to protect the state treasury. The General Assembly is allowed to provide by law for the processing and disposition of claims against the state which does not exceed certain maximum amounts. And the state's traditional defense of sovereign immunity is also generally waived for the breach of any valid written contract entered into by the state or its departments and agencies. So for example, state agencies are required to honor their contracts with citizens and businesses. Thus, unless otherwise stated or provided for by law by the General Assembly, all officers and employees of the state or its departments and agencies may be subject to suit and may be liable for injuries and damages caused by their negligent performance of, or even of a negligent failure to perform, their official functions.

And state employees may be personally liable for injuries and damages if they act with actual malice or with actual intent to cause injury to persons during the performance of their official functions. But otherwise, with some exceptions, officers and employees of the state or its departments and agencies are not subject to suit or liability, and no judgment shall be entered against them, merely because someone is injured or doesn't like the approved actions or duties of these government officials. The provisions are further strengthened by other parts of the state constitution, which students are advised to read in their entirety.

ARTICLE I–SECTION III

General Provision

In our capitalist society, the lure of wealth and the acquisition of private property is used to encourage people to work hard to create new inventions and in so doing, in general, improve the general economy. But sometimes to develop public good requires that the government, in the name of the people, take or damage private property. Some examples of these occur when building roads or bridges. The third section of Article I sets out some basic rules controlling such state action. Generally, the state is allowed to appropriate property, but it is required to pay people for their property. The first paragraph of this section sets out in some detail-this complicated area of private property rights.

When a government body asserts its right to take property, the legal term used may be *eminent domain* or *condemnation*. The first paragraph states that except as otherwise provided . . . , private property shall not be taken or damaged for public purposes without just and adequate compensation being paid first. However, the second part says that when private property is taken or damaged by the state, county, or municipality for public roads or streets, or for public transportation, or for any public purpose as determined by the General Assembly, just and adequate compensation will *not* be paid until the terms have been fixed and provided by law. When the terms of *just and adequate* compensation is fixed by law, it shall then be paid in preference to all other state obligations *except* bonded indebtedness.

This means that when the government takes or damages private property under that paragraph and is certified by the legislature, those who suffer such loss are paid before those who lend money to the public body. Of course, the fiscal system in the State of Georgia is very well administered. However, there remain the very remote chance that Georgia may fail to repay its debts and its creditors are exacted the force of Article I, Section III (b) of the Georgia Constitution. Paragraph (c) affords a favorable protection to those whose property is condemned. It states that the General Assembly may by law require the condemner, for example, a local government, to make prepayment against adequate compensation as a condition precedent to the exercise of the right of eminent domain. This is to make sure that all parties with claims to the property are protected. And in furtherance, paragraph (d) provides that the General Assembly may provide by law for the payment by the condemnor of reasonable expenses, including attorney's fees, incurred by the property owner in determining just and adequate compensation.

Anticipating other problems that might happen to people whose property has to be taken for the public good, under the power of eminent domain, the framers of the Constitution of the State of Georgia laid down an answer. Paragraph (e) provides that notwithstanding any other provision of the Constitution, the General Assembly may provide by law for relocation assistance and payments to persons displaced through the exercise of the powers of the government and that tax money may be spent for that purpose. In practice this provision was inadequate in providing protection to the little guy, the private property owners. The alarming trend has been that of allowing wealthy developers who persuade local officials to condemn small properties for forced consolidation, new economic development, and thus a larger tax base. A 2005 United States Supreme Court decision gave heads up to this practice. In *Kelo v. City of New London,* the Court held that governmental taking of property from one private owner to give to another in furtherance of economic development constitutes a permissible *public use* under the Fifth Amendment. Put simply, according to the Supreme Court, the use of eminent domain for economic development did not violate the public use clauses of the state and federal constitutions. Accordingly, if a legislative body has found that an economic project will create new jobs, increase tax and other city revenues, and revitalize a depressed urban area (even if that area is not blighted), then the project serves a public purpose, which qualifies as a public use. The court also ruled that the government's delegation of its eminent domain power to a private entity was constitutional under the Connecticut Constitution.

As expected, Georgians, as did citizens in several other states, reacted angrily by amending their State Constitution to the toll of 44 state actions by 2012 so as to shout: "not here." In 2006 Georgia voters overwhelmingly voted (by 83.4%) to place restrictions on the power of eminent domain by providing for a constitutional amendment. Under this amendment, local governments cannot now easily allow private developers to condemn private property for their own, or ostensibly for public use. Prior to the *Kelo* decision in 2005, only eight states specifically prohibited the use of eminent domain for economic development *except* to eliminate blight: Arkansas, Florida, Kansas, Kentucky, Maine, New Hampshire, South Carolina, and Washington. As of June 2012, 44 states enacted some type of reform legislation in response to the *Kelo* decision. Of those states,

22 enacted laws that severely inhibited the brand of takings allowed by the Kelo decision, while the rest enacted laws that place some limits on the power of municipalities to invoke eminent domain for economic development. Today, only six states have not passed laws to limit the power of eminent domain for economic development.

The last two paragraphs under Article I, Section III anticipates and provides legal answers *private ways* and *tidewater titles* problems. First is the solution when the government is called upon to settle disputes between two private landowners, most particularly, if one property is surrounded by another person's property. If a court or a government agency determines that one owner should have a right to go across someone else's private property, then Paragraph II of this last section of Article I, Section III provides a solution to that problem. Specifically, Paragraph II on "Private Ways" states that in case of necessity, private ways may be granted, but only if *just and adequate compensation* is first paid by the applicant.

Second is a problem which is all too common for those who are owners of property that are near or that border the ocean. Because the State of Georgia borders on the Atlantic Ocean, there have been disputes about the ownership of beachfront properties and to be expected, throughout history there have also been a lot of different laws about the ownership of waterfront property. In some countries, private citizens are forbidden to own any property near the ocean. In the United States, citizens are allowed to own such property, and sometimes even to build houses right next to the water. But on oceanfront property, the tides move in and out, and the land between high tide and low tide may be considerable. State laws vary on the subject. In California, property can only be owned to the high tide level, and ordinary citizens are allowed to walk on the low areas left above the water line. In Texas, property may be privately owned down to the low tide mark. In Georgia, however, Paragraph III of Article I, Section III provides Georgia's own answer to the title problem. It provides that the Act of the General Assembly, approved back in December 16, 1902, which extends the title of ownership of lands abutting on tidal water to the low water mark, is ratified and confirmed by the Constitution of Georgia. So in Georgia, a property owner has a right to prevent citizens from walking along the beach at low tide or to prevent citizens from beach combing for shells and driftwoods.

Conclusion

In summary, this chapter focuses primarily on Article I of the Constitution of the State of Georgia which provides for the Bill of Rights.

Civil Liberties as outlined in the Bill of Rights of the State of Georgia and US Constitution guarantees the protection of persons, expressions, and property from the arbitrary interference of government officials. In this State, there are no special classes of citizens with superior rights. Civil rights pertain to positive acts of government which may be designed to subject citizens to arbitrary or discriminatory treatment by government or individuals; these are prohibited by the Constitution. The modern Georgia State Constitution emphasizes the importance of civil rights and civil liberties, as should be expected given the State's history and traditions. Georgia's civil rights focus on the people's belief that everyone should be treated equally whenever possible, and equally, its civil liberties reflect the people's determination that government should not be abusive or tyrannical.

As modern effectuations of our traditional beliefs, both values of civil rights and civil liberties have made Georgia one of the leading developers of democracy. Arguably, this started well over 200 years ago when monarchy and privilege elites dominated governments throughout the world and continues today in what mostly is a cultural diverse and pluralist model of governance. Generally, in order to ensure that our liberties and rights are protected, today's democratic institutions and governmental bodies are designed to protect these values that are inclusive of our liberties and inalienable rights. Beside our governing institutions exemplified by the legislative and executive branches of government, are the many different organized economic and cultural interest groups in Georgia that typify our modern cultural diverse and pluralist model of participatory democracy. These interest groups, competing for influence, promote their agendas in our free speech, free press, and eventually through the elections of leaders of the various political parties. This is in agreement with the pluralist view of democracy which sees the government by the people as operating through competing interest groups.

As described further in Chapters 3 and 4, the average citizen of the State of Georgia has many avenues to participate in politics and in political activities that matter most to their lives.

Key Terms

Bill of Attainder
Civil Liberties
Civil Rights
Eminent Domain
Ex Post Facto Laws
Freedom from Imprisonment for Debt
Freedom of Assembly
Freedom of Conscience to Worship
General Provisions
Homestead Exemption

Prohibition against Ex Post Facto Laws
Right to Trial by Jury
Social Media and Evolving Technologies
Sovereign Immunity
Twelve-person Jury System

Essay Questions

1. What is the difference between civil rights and civil liberties?

2. What are the constitutional safeguards provided by the Georgia Constitution to protect someone who is accused from the trial and sentencing phase of a criminal proceeding?

3. In what ways has the political culture in Georgia supported advances in civil rights?

4. List and discuss in the correct order the hierarchy of law from top to bottom as provided in Chapter 1.

5. Explain why the authors of this text in Chapter 2 assert almost emphatically that while the constitution is a necessary condition for understanding the Peach State government, it is not a sufficient condition.

Figure 3.1   The Historical Legislative

Source: Courtesy of Georgia State Department of Archives and History

3
Political Participation in Georgia

Citizenship and Participation

The guarantee of a republican form of government based on the rule of elected officials supposes that the people have ultimate power. This comes too close to pure democracy. Because the strength of that form of government relies on citizen participation, the degree to which the people are active in their governments is extremely important. That is, the extent to which citizens participate in decisions that govern their lives vindicates the essence of that form of governance functionally, as a democracy.

We define political participation generally as actions through which citizens seek to influence or support government policy outputs that benefit, affect, or impact their lives. This definition accepts both the participatory and representative notions of democracy. We see citizen actions that constitute participation as taking many forms and notable among them are voting in a free election, joining a political party, standing as a candidate in an election, joining advocacy groups, or participating in a demonstration.

Citizen–State Contestations

In 1873, Susan B. Anthony seems to query the very premise and meaning of the fundamental right to participate in self-governance and the State's own role in it as she quipped in the following sentence: "Here in the first paragraph of the Declaration [of Independence], is the assertion of the natural right of all to the ballot; for how can "the consent of the governed" be given, if the right to vote be denied?" Apparently, she saw in political participation what most democratic theorists such as Robert Dahl (2000) also hold to be an accurate view of participation—among which is the fundamental right to partake in self-governance. As a matter of right, political participation is derived from the freedom to speak out, assemble, and associate or the ability to take part in the conduct of public affairs at all levels of government explicitly and implicitly. These rights are registered in the State and national Bill of Rights which imposes obligations on the government to ensure those rights. An interesting question implicit in the examination in this chapter is whether the State of Georgia has more or less advanced political participation among its citizens.

Although the degree of political participation in Georgia politics is not as widespread as many desire, the fact is that for centuries the voting franchise has been enlarged time and time again. The most significant development was undoubtedly achieved when women were officially given the right to vote. This of course happened not because of the good will of the majorities but after serious episodes of status quo challenges and contestations. Popular participation in politics and government is essential to each and every successful democracy.

But because of the dangers of overbearing majorities, we prefer a representative system instead of a pure democracy. And by creating a complex network of local, state, and federal governing bodies, in the end we maximize, at the expense of individual citizens access to power, the routes that interest groups can use to gain access and to influence public policy.

This is not to suggest that voting barriers do not exist in states such as Georgia. The most controversial barrier of all is known as the *no match, no vote*, identification restrictions. Framed in positive phrases such as *voter security* and *anti-voter fraud*, these measures limit voter registration, turn voters away from polling places, and cast doubt on the validity of ballots. In the 2005 session of the Georgia General Assembly, the new Republican majority passed legislation that amended a previous 1997 law. This new amendment required voters to produce a photo identification card and proof of citizenship in order to vote (see OCGA 21-2-417, 2005). In a lawsuit challenging this legislation, Democrats argued that the law was aimed instead at reducing minority voter participation, which tends to be Democratic. Republicans claimed that they were not trying to discourage minorities from voting, instead they were concerned about voter fraud.

Enjoining the enforcement of the 2005 Georgia Voter ID law, a federal district court judge held in *Common Cause/Georgia v. Billups* (N.D.Ga. 2005) that the ID law was tantamount to a poll tax, prohibited by the 24th Amendment to the U.S. Constitution. The district court's argument was that forcing citizens to obtain a photo ID is akin to forcing them to pay for the privilege of voting. In response to this ruling, the Georgia General Assembly again introduced another identical bill that required a photo ID, but this time paid for by the state, not out of the voter's own pocket (see OCGA Sec 21-2-417-1, 2006). Again, the significant distinction between the 2005 Act and the 2006 Act is that under the 2006 law, the fee requirement for the State Voter ID card was eliminated.

In 2011, after several years of legal challenges (see *Common Cause/Georgia v. Billups* II and III, IV and a denial of certiorari by the U.S. Supreme Court in 2009,) the Supreme Court of the State of Georgia upheld the constitutional validity of the Georgia Voter ID law. Summing its ruling on the

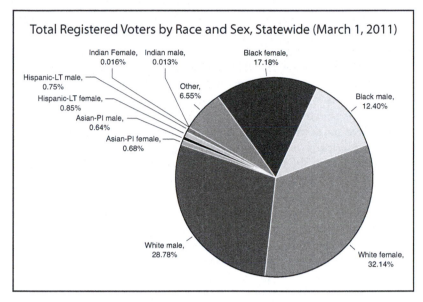

Figure 3.2   Georgia Registered Voters 2011
Source: Georgia Secretary of State website,
http://sos.ga.gov/elections/VRStats/voter_registration_history.pdf

matter the Court held that "[W]hen a state election law provision imposes only 'reasonable, nondiscriminatory restrictions' 'the State's important regulatory interests are generally sufficient to justify' the restrictions." ". . . Accordingly, the trial court properly discharged its obligation by reviewing the evidence in accordance with the burdens placed on each respective movant and correctly declined to find that the 2006 Act violates Georgia's equal protection clause" (*Democratic Party of Georgia, Inc. v Perdue*, 2011).

Beyond the state powers is the power of national government. Decisions concerning political participation, particularly voting, including the setting of times for elections, the eligibility of voters, and the offices to be filled by elections have traditionally been considered state and local governmental prerogatives. However, the national government has been gradually encroaching on this territory. The Fifteenth Amendment to the United States Constitution prohibited states from denying anyone the right to vote "on account of race, color, or previous condition of servitude," although many states, including Georgia, found numerous ways to evade those prohibitions.

For example, the Nineteenth Amendment guaranteed to women the right to vote, although in many states, again including Georgia, that right was not exercised by women nearly to the same extent as it was by men (until recently). The Twenty-sixth Amendment to the U.S. Constitution gave

18-, 19-, and 20-year-olds the right to vote in all elections. But this merely did for the nation what Georgia had been doing since 1943, when it granted people in that age group the right to franchise.

Federal statutes as well as Constitutional Amendments require States to alter their electoral procedures, where procedures and laws may have the effect of discriminating against local minorities. The Voting Rights Act of 1965, as extended in 1982, requires Georgia and other so-called Section Five states (those with a history of racial discrimination against African Americans or other minorities, e.g., Mexicans in Texas) to seek preclearance from the Civil Rights Division of the U.S. Department of Justice or from the Federal District Court for the District of Columbia before they are allowed to make any change in voting districts or voting procedures. Even if such a change might purport to enhance rather than dilute minority voting strength, such as changing city council or county commission elections from an at-large to a ward or district basis, federal approval must still be sought and granted.

Article II of the Georgia Constitution addresses the matter of voting and elections. It requires voting to be by secret ballot and to be open to all persons over the age of 18 who meet certain residency requirements, and who are neither convicted felons involving a crime of *moral turpitude* nor mental incompetents. Owing in large part to its long existing one-party tradition, Georgia requires candidates for public office to win a majority of the votes cast in a primary election. If no candidate does so, a run-off election between the top two vote-getters is provided for. Legislation passed by the Georgia General Assembly in 1998, however, required only a 45% plurality to win general elections. The Democratically-controlled legislature at that time calculated that the Libertarian party was more likely to take votes away from Republicans than Democrats, because of the similarity of Republican and Libertarian ideology, and that Democrats could easily win 45%, since Libertarians seldom got more than 2% or 3% of the votes in a general election. When Republicans captured control of the General Assembly, they repealed the 45% law.

The only constitutional restrictions placed on the right to run for public office are that candidates must be a registered voter and may not have been convicted of a felony involving moral turpitude, unless his or her rights have been restored. Of course, a candidate may have to have access to money, may have to have ideas, may have to have charisma (you can't make a silk purse out of a sow's ear), but those are political restrictions, not constitutional ones. Article II also requires candidates for local, state, or national office to resign their current offices, if any, "if the term of the office for which such official is qualifying for (sic) begins more than 30 days prior to the expiration of such official's present term of office."

Most of Article II deals with the dismissal or removal of public officials. Public officials may be recalled, meaning that the general assembly may enact a procedure whereby the people can remove an officeholder from office if they feel that he or she is not performing satisfactorily. An elected state official—Governor, Lt. Governor, Secretary of State, Attorney General, State School Superintendent, Commissioners of Agriculture, Insurance, and Labor, and members of the General Assembly—*can* be suspended from office if he or she is indicted for a felony. If he or she is convicted of a felony, that official *will be* suspended.

Linking People, Parties, and Groups

In democratic politics, is it a reasonable expectation that the will of the people, for the most part, determines the substantive policies and procedures of the State's business? This chapter focuses on the major political linkages between the participation of the citizens, the two political parties, and a wide variety of interest groups. In 1988, Georgia had the somewhat dubious distinction of ranking dead last among all 50 states in terms of voter participation in the presidential election held that year. Only about 38% of the eligible electorate turned out to cast its votes for either George Bush or Michael Dukakis. That was a fairly terrible statistic for what then was a Democratic state. It was a little better in 1992 but fell again in 1996. In 2000, Georgia voter turnout had increased to 43.8% (tied with Nevada), but only three states had worse voter turnout: Arizona, Hawaii, and Texas.

According to the Federal Election Commission, the independent regulatory agency found in 1975 by the United States Congress to regulate the campaign finance, the national average turnout in 2000 was 51.3% of eligible voters (http://www.fec.gov). In 2004, with voter turnout a record high across the nation in 36 years, Georgia slipped even further. While 49.6% of eligible voters in Georgia voted that year, only two states, Arizona and Hawaii were lower (Faler, 2004). The *Committee for the Study of the American Electorate* (2004) estimated that well over 120.2 million people cast ballots in November of 2004, a figure that translates into a 59.6% turnout rate nation-wide (https://www.gwu.edu/~action/2004/electrte. html).

Normally turnout in presidential elections is much higher than turnout in other elections where a presidential nominee does not head the ticket. This observation is true in Georgia, too. Sadly, the average person's lack of interest in national politics is generally surpassed only by apathy about international, state, and local politics. In the gubernatorial election of 1994, for example, voter turnout was only 29.9% of the eligible electorate, although it did rise to 31.6% in 1998, but in the hotly contested election of 2002, it rose to 53%. By Georgia standards, that is excellent turnout, but it did not last very long. In 2006, it had fallen again to just over 40% and recent years continue with the same trend. Why is the level of public interest and participation so poor in Georgia?

Political Participation in Georgia Politics

If by participation we mean voting only, participation *per se* is not as poor as it seems. In the United States we measure voter turnout according to the number of eligible voters, not by the number of registered voters. Registering to vote can be made easy or difficult. In Georgia, as in much of the United States, voting is a two-stage process—registering first and then actually voting—so that there are more obstacles in the U.S. than in other countries. If we were to measure voter turnout by the number of registered voters who vote, Georgia would be in the 60th, not the 40th, percentile. Compared to other countries and states, that is not good, but it is not as terrible as it looks at first blush.

The fact stands, however, that voting is the form of political participation engaged in most frequently by those who engage in any form of political participation. Activities such as running for public office, membership and participation in party activities and in political campaigns, giving campaign contributions, sporting a campaign button or a bumper sticker, or writing or calling a public official, are much less likely to attract participants than the act of voting.

People do not participate simply because it is easier not to do so. Often registration requirements, as noted above, still serve as an effective barrier to voter participation, even though national *motor voter* law now requires Georgia and other states to facilitate registration by allowing persons to register when they obtain or renew their drivers' licenses or when they visit the welfare office. Otherwise, one must present himself or herself at the county courthouse to register to vote. In some jurisdictions, voting registrars will travel to schools, colleges, senior citizen centers, and other locations to facilitate the registration process, but all such activities are optional. A birth certificate, or naturalization papers, or even a driver's license may be all the documentation required to prove citizenship and residency.

Since Georgia has permanent rather than periodic registration, once one is properly registered and votes at regular intervals, his or her name remains inscribed on the rolls. In contrast, a requirement for periodic registration means that rolls are regularly purged after a certain time whether the voter votes or not. In fact, where that is the procedure, such as in Texas, registration is far more of a barrier than it is in Georgia.

As discussed elsewhere in this chapter, with the 2011 Georgia Supreme Court decision in *Democratic Party of Georgia, Inc. v Perdue* (GA

Table 3.1   Georgia Active Political Parties
Constitution Party of Georgia
Democratic Party of Georgia
Georgia Green Party
Libertarian Party of Georgia
Georgia Republican Party of Georgia
By authors: Georgia State Politics

Sup. Ct., March 7, 2011), affirming Governor Perdue's position for Voter ID, Georgia now has both a permanent registration process and a Voter ID requirement for its citizens to vote. Of course this came about after several years of legal battle before the Georgia Supreme Court in 2011 held that the Republican majority initiated photo ID requirements in the 2006 state law was "a minimal, reasonable, and nondiscriminatory restriction which is warranted by the important *state* regulatory interests to prevent voter fraud." In the eyes of the Court therefore, when a state election law imposes only "reasonable, nondiscriminatory restrictions," its important mission for doing so is sufficient to justify the imposed restrictions.

Another reason for low levels of participation is that some people doubt that their vote will make a meaningful difference. When the winner is certain, or if competition for office is weak or non-existent, potential voters may remain non-voters. Thus, in states with weak interparty competition, voter turnout tends to be low, especially in general elections where the opposition party either runs no candidate at all or a mere token candidate. Often the quality of party competition depends upon the extent of cleavages within the community, based in turn on the degree of urbanization, income, education, and the percent of resident minorities (Hy & Saeger, 1976, p. 53). This may have been a factor in Georgia, which has for over a century traditionally been a one-party (Democratic) state. That is, until recently. For decades the Democratic Party, while seldom carrying the state in presidential elections, nevertheless won virtually all other elections. But Lyndon Johnson is said to have declared that the passage of the Voting Rights Act would cause the Democratic Party to lose their control of the Southern states. It took two generations for that to happen in Georgia, but happen it did.

Until 2003, Democrats controlled both houses of the General Assembly, controlled the Governor's office since the reconstruction era, and usually won nearly every other state executive office (only the Public Service Commission had seen Republicans among its members), and only five Republicans had been elected to Congress from Georgia between the end of Reconstruction (in 1876) and 1992. These were Mack Mattingly in the

Senate from 1981 to 1987; Howard (Bo) Callaway from 1965 to 1967; Ben Blackburn in the House from 1969 to 1975; Pat Swindall in the House from 1985 to 1989; and Newt Gingrich, who had served in the House since 1979.

The year 1992, however, was particularly fruitful for Republicans in Georgia. They gained 18 seats in the State House of Representatives, six seats in the State Senate, one U.S. Senate seat (Paul Coverdell) and three U.S. House seats (Reps. Linder, Kingston, and Collins). Many of these victories resulted, at least in part, from legislative redistricting, which could have been expected to benefit the Democrats, who controlled the General Assembly. While the result of a legislative redistricting effort is sometimes nullified by partisanship at the federal level, a statistical study of the federal review of Georgia's redistricting efforts hypothesized that the Department of Justice under the first Bush administration successfully pursued a Republican oriented strategy of packing a few legislative districts with a maximum number of voting age Black Americans to increase the potential number of Republican districts (Lauth & Reese, 1993, p. 3). The research supported the view that a federal Justice Department, dominated by Republicans, was able to use the Voting Rights Act to partisan advantage at the state level.

That partisan advantage bore precious fruit in the 1994 and 1996 congressional elections. Joining Gingrich, who would become Speaker of the U.S. House of Representatives following the Republican takeover of Congress in 1994, and Representatives Linder, Kingston, and Collins, were three newly elected Republican congressmen—Saxby Chambliss, Charlie Norwood, and Bob Barr—with Congressman Nathan Deal switching from the Democratic to the Republican Party. Republicans now hold a majority, controlling 8 of the 13 Georgia congressional seats. Interestingly, all Republicans incumbents are Whites.

In the 2002 election cycle, Linder, Kingston, Collins, Deal, and Norwood were all reelected. The polarizing Newt Gingrich had resigned earlier and been replaced by Johnny Isakson, who was also reelected. Barr had lost his seat in the August primary and two new Republican congressmen—Phil Gingery and Max Burns—joined their GOP colleagues. Saxby Chambliss moved on to the U.S. Senate after defeating Max Cleland in the general election. He joined former Governor Zell Miller there; Miller had been appointed by Governor Barnes to fill the vacancy created by the death of Paul Coverdell.

In 2004, Denise Majette, who had defeated McKinney in 2002, decided to run for the U.S. Senate, when Miller announced that he would not seek election, and she was defeated by Johnny Isakson; McKinney won the Democratic nomination, and regained her old seat, only to lose it to "Hank" Johnson, Jr. in the 2006 Democratic primary. Max Burns lost his seat to John Barrow. Mack Collins took on Isakson in the Republican primary and lost. Otherwise, all incumbents won reelection. And the biggest surprise of all was that Republicans also won control of the State House of Representatives by an overwhelming margin (they now hold 106 seats). The GOP also gained seats in the State Senate (now holding 34). And in the 2005 session of the Georgia General Assembly, Republicans were able to pass a redistricting plan that virtually guaranteed their domination of state politics in 2006 and beyond.

The critical point was reached in the 2010 election. A woman candidate for Governor, Karen Handel, won the primary election, but without a plurality, and former Congressman Nathan Deal came in second; leading to a run-off election which Deal won. By the end of the primary, Handel had taken a particularly bitter and aggressive tone, calling Deal, a former congressman, "a corrupt relic of Washington" and repeatedly pointing to a congressional ethics report that said he likely violated federal ethics rules. Deal at first refused to respond in kind, but in the final week or so lashed out at Handel for, among other things, having hedged on whether she once supported a gay rights organization. Handel dominated the Atlanta urban and suburban region, where the Republican electorate is both White and generally upper-middle-class, thus very keen on the low taxes message. The difference between Handel and Deal was only about 2,400 votes, but Handel quickly conceded and threw her support behind Deal in the November election against the Democratic Roy Barnes.

Figure 3.3 2010 Election Results

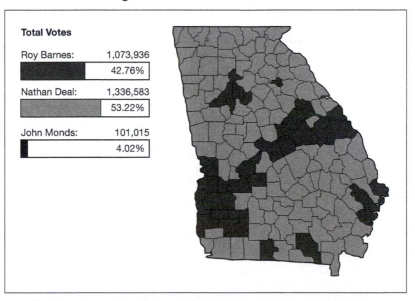

Total Votes		
Roy Barnes:	1,073,936	
	42.76%	
Nathan Deal:	1,336,583	
	53.22%	
John Monds:	101,015	
	4.02%	

This set up the general election battle between Republican Nathan Deal and Democratic candidate Roy Barnes. As can be seen from Figure 3.3, when Gov. Deal won the 2010 election he did so by carrying nearly every county in the state, apart from the urban areas surrounding Atlanta. In all, Deal won 120 of Georgia's 159 counties, while Democrat Roy Barnes won only 39, including Clayton, DeKalb, Fulton, and Rockdale. Deal also captured most of the counties below the so-called *gnat line* that separates metro Atlanta and North Georgia from Middle and South Georgia. Since then, Georgia has been dominated by the Republican Party. Of course, not everyone favors divisive politics or bitterly fought elections, especially when it involves the possibility of re-aligning elections. For example, when in Louisiana in the 1991 Governor's race between former Ku Klux Klansman David Duke and the Governor Edwin Edwards, the struggle was so very divisive that otherwise dormant voters had become more actively involved, thus swelling the turnout to extraordinary proportions; but at the cost of bitter feelings.

Conversely, much perceived apathy may in fact represent a basic contentment with the political status quo. Georgia, as one of the original thirteen colonies, was organized along small community circumstances without a lot of consolidation. So we still have a lot of government entities in the state. It has been said that all politics is local and if people are happy with their immediate circumstances as solidified in government structures there may be no perceived need for them to do anything else. Their satisfaction with over 1,000 government entities in Georgia may explain some of the non-participation.

On the other hand, the third reason why people do not participate is because they do in fact lack faith in the political system, or feel that it is too complex for them to understand. Ignorance of candidates, parties, or issues serves as a barrier to participation. Thus, turnout in states with low levels of educational attainment is usually quite low. Georgia is, unfortunately, such a state, ranking at or near the bottom of the list of states in terms of educational

Table 3.2 Government Entities in Georgia	
Government Units	**Number**
State Government	1
County Governments	159
School Districts	180
Special Districts	620
Municipal Governments	529

Sources: Compiled by authors, including Hepburn, Lawrence R. *"Politics and Government"* in *Contemporary Georgia* (Athens, Georgia: University of Georgia, 1987), and *"Georgia County Snapshots"* (Atlanta: Department of Community Affairs, 2006

attainment. The result for Georgians is high dropout rates, poor scores on standardized tests, poor performance on the Armed Forces Literacy Test, low percentages of students pursuing higher educational opportunities, and low voter turnout.

Several other factors positively associated with political participation include a high degree of urbanization, high median family incomes, and small percentages of disadvantaged minority groups. As a whole, Georgia strikes out on all three counts. Georgia is largely a rural state (some people count Atlanta as a separate state) still fairly poor in terms of income, especially outside the Atlanta metropolitan area, and has very high numbers of minority group members who have not been incorporated into the middle class. The largest minority group, Blacks or African Americans, constitute about 28% of the total population, and historically have not been able to achieve the economic or educational levels of other ethnic groups. The effect of these demographic factors is obvious. However, well-educated, well-to-do urban minorities actually participate more than do Whites from poor rural areas.

Thus, a large number of factors have a synergistic impact that dampens voter participation. As we have seen, however, this is not necessarily bad; our analysis suggesting that imaginative change-oriented people are the most active voters supports the idea that much perceived apathy in Georgia may in fact reveal basic contentment with the political status quo.

Moreover, voter turnout in Georgia is actually improving rather dramatically. Some of the improvement can be explained by falling turnout across the nation, so that Georgia does not look as bad as it used to. But there is also evidence that Georgia's voter turnout is improving absolutely as well as relatively. One study shows that from 1960 to 1996 the convergence of Georgia and national turnout in presidential election years has been nearly inexorable. That is, in nearly every year Georgia turnout improved in both absolute and relative terms, while national turnout declined in the same absolute and relative way (Ellinger, 1997).

Georgia's Political Party System

State party systems can be classified as two-party, modified one-party, or simple one-party structures, depending on the strength and number of victories the opposition party gets or the number of votes it usually gets. On this basis, Georgia has been classified as a noncompetitive one-party Democratic state. That means that the Democratic Party won virtually all of the elections in the state (except Presidential) and in fact won them by substantial margins, frequently by votes of more than 60% (Gray and Jacob 1996, p. 149). Why was this so? There are many reasons why any state has the party system it does. The history of a state or region often reveals the

Figure 3.4 Leading the Campaign
Courtesy of Lee M. Allen

significant factors, and in this context the Civil War continues to have an influence on Georgia's political parties.

With regard to political party affiliations, states tend to "vote as they shot." Along the eastern Atlantic seaboard, both the northern states, and the more southern states, established their prevailing political patterns more than a hundred years ago. All of the states of the southern Confederacy, except Florida, have had either one-party Democratic dominance or modified one-party Democratic systems. Georgia could be described as the most Democratic, or perhaps as the least Republican, of all of them.

However, there certainly were some Republican counties in Georgia. These mostly tend to be located in the north Georgia mountains, remnants of communities that opposed secession and have largely remained Republican since the Civil War days. In addition, there are other communities in Georgia which, influenced by economic growth, transportation corridors, federal military bases, or transplanted Yankee retirees, today tend to vote along Republican party lines.

Aside from historical events, population growth and migration patterns also offer significant explanations for any particular state's political party system. In addition to the "mountain Republican" counties, such as Catoosa, Fannin, and Whitfield, the other most important Republican strongholds in Georgia are found in the Atlanta metropolitan area and its surrounding counties, especially Cobb, Clayton, Cherokee, and Gwinnett—with large numbers of transplanted managers and professionals from northern and

Midwestern states who arrived in Georgia with Republican affiliations and have kept them intact.

Other urban counties, such as Bibb (Macon), Muscogee (Columbus), Chatham (Savannah), Richmond (Augusta), Lowndes (Valdosta), and more affluent counties—Glynn (St. Simons, Jekyll, and Sea Islands) have growing numbers of Republicans and have experienced the growth of a viable two-party system. There is a third group of Republicans in Georgia: Goldwater Republicans. These are former Democrats who so admired former Senator Barry Goldwater (Rep., Arizona) and his stand on the 1964 Civil Rights Act (he was one of the few non-southerners to vote against it) that when he became the GOP presidential nominee in 1964, they converted to his party. Thus ideology is also a reason for a state's party system being what it is.

But ideology is usually more significant a factor in presidential politics than it is in state or local politics. Georgia Democrats are quick to point out that they are just that: *Georgia* Democrats. The emphasis on "Georgia" is intended to let other people know that they do not necessarily approve of the national Democratic Party, or its leaders, its presidential candidates, and certainly not its liberal ideology. Georgia Democrats are conservative, both fiscally and socially, and are proud of it. They elect conservative Democrats to the U.S. Senate and to the U.S. House, to the General Assembly, to the Governor's mansion, to other state posts, to county commissions, to sheriff's posts, to city councils (even when they are officially non-partisan), and to virtually every other office filled by election. The relatively few Democrats in Georgia who are national Democrats are intellectuals or members of minority groups, residing usually in Atlanta. To some observers, Blacks outside Atlanta tend to be almost as conservative as their White counterparts.

The distinctive existence of the Georgia Democratic Party illustrates well the dictum uttered by Tip O'Neill, a former Speaker of the House of Representatives of the United States Congress: "all politics is local." In the United States, there really is not a unified national Democratic Party system, no real national Democratic party. What appears to be a national party system is really a collection of state party systems, and in turn what appears to be a state party system is actually little more than an amalgam of local (mostly county) party systems. In fact, the repeated use of the word "system" by the authors may be misleading. American party politics is a lot less than systematic.

Different authors use different typologies for classifying state party systems, but virtually all of them considered Georgia's party system as one-party dominant or as modified one-party Democratic, even in the late 1990s. However, most of those assessments were dated, even in those general State and Local Government texts published as late as 1998. The gains that Republicans have made in Georgia since 1994 are nothing short of phenomenal, culminating in the election of a Republican governor for the first time since Reconstruction in the 2002 election.

Owing to the defection of three Democratic senators following that election, the Georgia state senate also fell under Republican control for the first time since Reconstruction, and the GOP even managed to defeat the venerable Speaker of the House, Tom Murphy, in 2002. And, as we pointed out earlier in this chapter, in 2004 the State House of Representatives followed the State Senate into the Republican dominated ranks.

The state's constitutional officers were all Democrats before 1994. Then Republicans won elections for State School Superintendent and Insurance Commissioner, and with then Attorney General Michael Bowers' defection from the Democrats prior to the election and his victory as a Republican, half of the constitutional officers were members of the GOP. In 2006, owing to the choice of Secretary of State Cathy Cox and Lt. Governor Mark Taylor to challenge each other in the Democratic primary for governor, neither of these offices fielded an incumbent in the general election. Thus Cox, having lost the primary was out, and Taylor, having lost the general election, was out as well. Republicans then captured both of these constitutional offices. A runoff election resulted in the only Democratic-held seat on the Public Service Commission also going to the Republicans. Democrats now control only the constitutional offices of Attorney General, Labor Commissioner, and Agriculture Commissioner. All five of the Public Service Commission seats belong to Republicans.

Georgia's Party Organization

Both the Democratic and the Republican parties have state executive committees that meet periodically, and recommend policies and procedures for their respective parties. Members of these committees are chosen in local caucuses by their fellow partisans for long terms. The duties of these committees include fund-raising, policy-making, and approving choices for membership in the Electoral College (a reward for faithful service). Each of the state organizations elects officers, including a chairperson, a vice-chairperson, and an executive board. Each of the state party committees has a paid staff headed by an executive director who coordinates the day-to-day activities of the state party. Given the increasing candidates centeredness of political campaigns, the state executive committees have relatively little to do with directing campaigns. Moreover, while fund-raising may be numbered among the committee's duties, they never collect enough, and the resulting dearth of funds to distribute forces candidates to rely on their own devices to raise money.

If one were to think that the state executive committees were answerable to the Democratic and/or Republican National Committees, one would be making a natural mistake, but a mistake nonetheless. Samuel J. Eldersveld (1964, Chapter 5) described our party system as "stratarchical" not

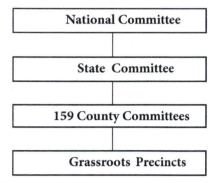

Figure 3.5   Political Party Organizations
Compiled by authors.

hierarchical, so as to emphasize that each stratum—federal, state, and local, is largely independent of the others. Thus the National Committees do not dictate to the state committees, and the state committees do not (although they may try) dictate to the various county committees. Insofar as there is any action in the party organization, the county organization is where the action is.

Perhaps the main reason for this local based party system is the fact that the vast majority of elected officials in the United States are locally based, paid, and organized. Although it varies somewhat from county to county in Georgia (and with 159 counties that is a lot of room for variation), Georgians elect the following officials to county offices: county commissioners and county sheriffs; judges of state and superior courts, probate courts, juvenile courts; magistrates and district attorneys; various clerks of the courts; school board members and school superintendents. While some of these— particularly the judges—are elected on nonpartisan ballots, the parties still play a role in endorsing them for office.

Each of the county committee members is elected in the primary elections, and each appoints a chairperson and such other officers as are called for in their party charters. The electoral base of all of this activity is the precinct. In a state-by-state ranking of the strength of local party organizations (basically the county committees), Georgia's Republican committees were the weakest of all 50 states, and the Democrats were not far behind; their rank was 46th in the nation (Gibson, 1985, pp. 154–155). It would appear, therefore, that local "party organization" in Georgia may be a bit of an oxymoron, a contradiction in terms; there is precious little organization in either of the two political parties ever, that too may be changing. While the Democratic Party organization appears to be somewhat demoralized and moribund, anecdotal evidence suggests that the Republican organization is optimistic and invigorated, sensing that majority party status is now within reach.

Figure 3.6	Georgia Congressional Representatives by Districts & Party Affiliation—2016–2018		
Johnny Isakson	Since 2005	Senator State-wide	Republican
David Perdue	Since 2015	Senator State-wide	Republican
Buddy Carter	Since 2015	District 1	Republican
Sanford Bishop	Since 1993	District 2	Democrat
Lynn Westmoreland	Since 2007*	District 3	Republican
Hank Johnson	Since 2007	District 4	Democrat
John Lewis	Since 1987	District 5	Democrat
Tom Price	Since 2005	District 6	Republican
Rob Woodall	Since 2011	District 7	Republican
Austin Scott	Since 2011	District 8	Republican
Doug Collins	Since 2013	District 9	Republican
Jody Hice	Since 2015	District 10	Republican
Barry Loudermilk	Since 2015	District 11	Republican
Rick Allen	Since 2015	District 12	Republican
David Scott	Since 2003	District 13	Democrat
Tom Graves	Since 2010	District 14	Republican

*Set for retirement in 2016
Source: Compiled and designed by authors: Georgia State Politics

Interest Groups in Georgia

Power abhors a vacuum. In states where political parties are weak, as in Georgia, political interest groups are strong (Froman, 1966, pp. 952–962). Variously called interest groups, special interest groups, or pressure groups, political interest groups are organized associations created to affect or effectuate public policy. They differ from political parties in that their members do not seek public office as such, but rather desire to influence policy outcomes and outputs. The more and varied the regions, industries, peoples, and purposes that a state government encompasses, the more and varied the interest groups will be. Georgia has a lot of such varied interests, and hence, a lot of interest groups.

In fact, reflecting its large size and diverse economy, Georgia has an awful lot of interest groups. They cannot all be described here, because even identifying the basic groupings would be a long list. Interest groups can be business associations and labor unions, farmers and fishermen, sportsmen, professional and trades groups; that is, they are often organized around the various occupational or economic groups found in Georgia. On the other hand, they can be established on the basis of achieved religious preferences such as the National Council of Churches (NCC); or ascribed racial groupings, such as the National Association for the Advancement of Colored People (NAACP).

Interest groups may be built up from shared experiences leading to a desire to participate in policy making. The League of Women Voters (LWV) and the American Legion (AL) are examples of such groups. Furthermore, ideological interest groups may organize to shape general policies; the liberal Americans for Democratic Action (ADA) or the conservative Eagle Forum (AF) are two such groups. Many interest groups represent recipients (or hopeful recipients) of government services, such as welfare, student loans, and business subsidies. Curiously, because of the complexities of the nearly 1,270 governments in the State of Georgia alone, the actual governments themselves, and their agencies and officials often find it necessary or expedient to try to lobby each other to influence the course of public policy in Georgia and in adjoining states, and across the nation. Groups of government entities band together for such purposes, such as the nationally based State Municipal Association, the National Association of Counties, and the National Association of Chiefs of Police (Dye, 1997, p. 107).

To determine which interest groups were the most powerful in Georgia Politics, Ronald J. Hrbenar and Clive S. Thomas asked knowledgeable persons both within and without the state to put together two lists of interest groups: the first identifying those which were consistently influential, and the second to list those which were either rising or falling in power, or which were only occasionally active (Gray & Jacob, 1996). On the second list were the Board of Regents of the University System, The Georgia Municipal Association, the Association of County Commissioners, and the Georgia Trial Lawyers Association. Influential Georgia organizations of the first rank are depicted on Table 3.3.

Table 3.3	Georgia Interest Groups
Bank of America	Medical Assoc. of Georgia
SunTrust Bank	Georgia Assoc. of Educators
Wachovia Bank	St. Dept. of Transportation
Coca Cola	Business Council of Georgia
Delta Airlines	Georgia Powers Employee Union

Assembled by the authors from various sources including Dye, Thomas R. *Politics in States and Communities,* 9th ed. (Englewood Cliffs, N.J.: Prentice- Hall, 1997), and Gray, et al., *Politics in the American States: A Comparative Analysis,* 5th ed. (Washington, D.C.: C.Q. Press, 1996).

In Georgia, and in much of the United States, business organizations certainly do dominate. They have both the means and the determination to influence policy to their advantage, or at least not to the disadvantage, of their interests. But the Georgia Association of Educators is also a force to reckon with. It represents a significant number of well-educated, well-informed professionals located in every state House and Senate District, who vote and who are largely united in their goals, objectives, and concerns. And that description is a formula for political success.

A number of factors affect the ability of an interest group to influence public policy. Former Georgia Southern University President Nicholas Henry, a political scientist, identifies seven such factors (Henry, 1987, pp. 65–68). These factors include not only the size of the membership and their financial wealth, but also intangibles such as leadership qualities and the effectiveness of their organization. The various factors are listed below in Table 3.4.

Based on results alone, the Georgia Association of Educators (GAE) appears to score highly on each of these factors. These factors, along with the importance of education for economic competitiveness, probably goes far to explain why the proportion of Georgia's state budget spent on education (over 50%) is as high as it is. Another highly rated group is the Medical Association of Georgia (MAG), which scores highly enough on these factors to cause its success rate to exceed its failure rate in its policy initiatives. In other words, what the MAG lacks in size it makes up for in other areas, particularly in money. And money, once described by Jesse Unruh, former speaker of the California House of Representatives as "the mother's milk of politics," can be influential indeed. Money alone is no substitute for all of the other factors, but in conjunction with the other factors it tends to give great power to those influential groups which have plenty of it to spare. In contrast, the organization calling itself Queer Nation/Atlanta ranks low on all of these factors and has correspondingly little influence in the State of Georgia.

Interest groups have two major political functions: lobbying and campaign financing. The term "lobbying" derives from the practice of

Table 3.4   Factors of Influence
1. The size of the group
2. The group's cohesiveness
3. Its geographical spread
4. Members' social status
5. Its leadership and organization
6. The features of its program
7. The political environment
Source: Compiled by authors: Georgia State Politics

interested parties contacting Members of the British Parliament (who had no individual offices) in the lobby of the Parliament Building (Westminster). The image evoked by the term is one of a petitioner sidling up to the very buttonholes of legislators to solicit support. While a bit simplistic today, the fundamental relationship described is still accurate. The variety of techniques interest groups use to influence government almost matches their variety of interests. Often, they conduct public relations campaigns to persuade the public to their points of view. In our representative system, if they can get the public on their side, the legislator will soon follow. In addition, they encourage, campaign for, and fund the campaigns of elected executive officials. They also pressure appointed bureaucrats, seeking special rules, regulations, and strict or lax enforcement of standards. Interest group lawyers threaten litigation in the courts, seeking and obtaining injunctions, mediation, settlements, decisions, and appeals. But most obvious of all, hundreds of their representatives, known as lobbyists, can be seen during each session of the General Assembly, and in smaller numbers at county commissions and city council meeting. They attempt to *buttonhole* legislative policy makers in the halls of government, and wine and dine our elected representatives in fancy restaurants and plush hospitality suites set up in hotels and at sporting arenas.

The reputation of lobbyists for bribing legislators is based partly on historical fact, the Yazoo Land Fraud, but it is not a particularly common practice in the modern era. For a number of reasons, attempts at bribery are chilled by fears of detection and the consequences of disclosure, leading to the lobbyist's loss of effectiveness and loss of office for the legislator. Indeed, legislators who pride themselves on their integrity are prone to *blow the whistle* on lobbyists who attempt to buy their votes.

What lobbyists really want is *access* to decision-makers, and today that access is *bought* with information, not with money. Faced with a dizzying array of issues, most beyond the comprehension of a single legislator, our representatives cry out for information about problems: what are the real goals of a bill, what effect will it have on the legislator's constituents, and how will it affect their own districts? The legislative committee system, the state bureaucracy, and the limited research facilities of the General Assembly all welcome lobbyists who have thoroughly studied a bill and who are in a position to explain it. Of course, the information provided by some may be biased, but it is a place to start, and by weighing it against other sources of information, often from opposing lobbyists, the legislators can make a more informed and better decision.

Sometimes it seems as if everyone is lobbying everyone else, especially during the annual sessions of the General Assembly. Actually, lobbying was illegal in Georgia before 1992. Under this quaint fiction, an ancient law made lobbying akin to bribery and a misdemeanor. Indeed, lobbyists were called *registered agents* in the State of Georgia and had to pay a $5.00 fee to the Secretary of State at the start of each legislative session. They were then free to go about their registered agent business, unhampered by any additional laws, rules, or regulations.

Prior to passage of the 1992 ethics legislation by the General Assembly, lobbyists in Georgia did not have to declare publicly which bills they were working to pass or defeat; nor did they have to report the amounts they were spending on their efforts. Nor did they have to report any meals, drinks, gifts, or entertainments they provided to their legislative friends, except for their formal monetary campaign contributions. The Secretary of State's Office received $5.00 from each of 1,229 individual registered agents for the 1990 legislative session, almost five for each legislator (Pettys, 1990, p. 2).

The 1992 ethics law was perhaps the most hotly debated issue at that session of the Georgia General Assembly. In its final form it made lobbying legal, but it actually regulated it much more closely than it had been before. Instead of a nominal one-time fee, lobbyists were required to pay an annual $200.00 registration fee to the State Ethics Commission plus an additional $15.00 for supplemental registration and a lobbyist identification tag. However, the fees were rescinded in 1994, although registration with the Ethics Commission was still required by law. All lobbying expenditures must be reported, along with the names of the legislators whom the lobbyists were trying to influence. The law sets a maximum of $1,000.00 that an interest group can give in campaign contributions for local offices and for the General Assembly seats, and, over a four-year election cycle $5,000 per primary, $5,000 per general election, and $3,000 per runoff to candidates for statewide office.

Perhaps the main reason why lobbyists don't have to illegally bribe legislators is that there are two perfectly legal ways to transfer money directly. In Georgia, legislators are allowed to engage in business ventures with lobbyists. However, the real return here is long-term future benefit. The other technique is quick up-front money, and is called a campaign contribution. The transfer is usually handled by specially created groups called political action committees (PACs). While these PACs are limited in the amount they can contribute to any one candidate (Pettys, 1990) there is no limit on the number of candidates they may contribute to, and more importantly there is no limit to the number of PACs that can be formed by any one interest group. As a result, PACs are becoming increasingly influential, especially as the costs of political campaigning escalate. With this complex system, a particular PAC will be unable to *buy* a legislator, but it can certainly get a legislator to return its telephone calls whenever it deems necessary. That's access. That's influence. That's power.

What about those who are not members of organized interest groups? Do they have access? Certainly they can write or call their legislators. They can attend the periodic town meetings and pre-legislative forums that some legislators hold. But unless they organize, their interests and concerns are unlikely to be heeded. People who lack the factors of political influence, and who are unable to create effective organizations to pursue their goals in the political system, have little or no influence (Parenti, 1988). Increasing the share of the state's budget, gathering more political influence, and changing the law and the state's Constitution are most effectively done by organized special interest groups. Georgia ranks 10th in the nation in terms of the number of interest groups it has. It also ranks as a dominant/complementary state in terms of the overall impact that interest groups have. That means that political interest groups are more powerful than political parties in the state, but the interest groups are not so powerful that they eclipse or subordinate the parties (Gray & Jacob, 1996). Considering the fact that in 1987 the Georgia General Assembly was ranked second in the nation in terms of its accountability to interest groups, or 49th in its accountability to the unorganized public, the Peach State seems to be becoming more democratic (the ideology) as it becomes less Democratic (the Party). That is, as party competition increases, interest group dominance decreases.

Key Terms

Access
Interest Group
Factors in Interest Group Formation
Local Politics
Lobbyist (Lobbying)
One-Party System
Party Organization
Party Fund Raising
Primary Elections
Run-Off Elections
Voting Rights Act
Voter Registration

Essay Questions

1. How do interest groups differ from political parties?

2. Why has Georgia traditionally been a one-party system?

3. Is there a relationship between the number of governments and the rate of political participation and voting?

4. Where does the Georgia State Constitution address removing public officials?

5. Who is responsible for recommending policies and procedures for the political parties in Georgia? What factors are involved?

Figure 4.1   The Georgia State Capitol Building
Courtesy of Lee M. Allen

The Legislative Branch

The State of Georgia, as all of the 49 other states of the United States, has a legislature that is made up of elected representatives. Their primary task is to consider matters brought forth by the governor or introduced by its members to create legislation that becomes law. That body also initiates articles of impeachment and try, when needed, officials of the State government charged with crime. That check is part of the system of checks and balances among the three State branches of government that mirrors the federal system and prevents any branch from abusing its power.

Unlike Nebraska which boasts only one state chamber in its legislature, the State of Georgia along with 48 other States has a bicameral legislature made up of two chambers: an upper house and a lower house. Both chambers make state laws and fulfill other aspects of state governing responsibilities for the State of Georgia. The upper chamber is known as the Senate, and its members generally serve longer terms, usually four years. The larger lower chamber is known in Georgia as the House of Representatives and its members serve shorter terms.

Article three of the Constitution of the State of Georgia governs the bicameral structure of the General Assembly, the way the two Houses operate, and describes the most important functions of the legislature, primarily those having to do with state finances and budgeting. These monetary processes have been part of Georgia's inherent political culture since the European Colonial Era, and date back to when the British barons forced King John to sign the Magna Carta. It has been truly said that the power of the legislature is the power of the purse. More is presented on complex topic in Chapter 5 on the Governor and Chapter 8: Budgeting and Finance.

As is traditional in polities tracing their heritage back to the days of opposition to executive tyranny, all bills for raising revenue, or appropriating money, originate in the most representative body of the legislature; in Georgia this is the House of Representatives. But the Senate also has a role to play—it has to put its seal of approval on an exact copy of the bill in its chamber. Together, the two Houses constitute the General Assembly.

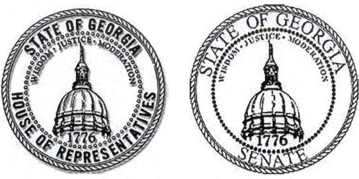

Adapted by authors, Georgia State Politics

The most important function of the General Assembly is to pass the state's operating budget each year. In fact, approximately half of the hours spent in session are related to the budget. This includes establishing spending priorities and setting tax rates. Additionally, lawmakers must enact other laws on a broad array of topics from education to roads and transportation. Another task of the General Assembly is to consider all proposed amendments to the Georgia Constitution. A two-thirds vote in both houses is the primary means for approving resolutions to place proposed constitutional changes on the ballot. Voters will then decide if the Constitution is to be amended.

The legislative process in Georgia has three components: first, it is a legal process governed by constitutional and statutory provisions (such as the requirement that appropriations and tax measures must originate in the House) as interpreted by state and federal court decisions. Second, it is also a parliamentary process governed by a host of special rules of procedure that specify how legislation will be considered in each house. Finally, and perhaps most importantly, it is a political process whereby both legislators and non-legislators (particularly the governor) compete for power and advantage.

The Historic 151st General Assembly

As observed by an article that appeared in the *Atlanta Journal and Constitution,* the 2010 election was particularly painful for the Democratic Party (Sheinin, *AJC,* 11/2/10). As the smoke cleared, the Democratic Party controlled only 85 of 236 seats in the Georgia House and Senate. For the first time since Reconstruction the state would have no statewide-elected Democrats. The pattern has not changed. Tables 4.1a and 4.1b bear proof of continuing Republican control both for Georgia State House and Senate and Georgia Congressional delegation as well.

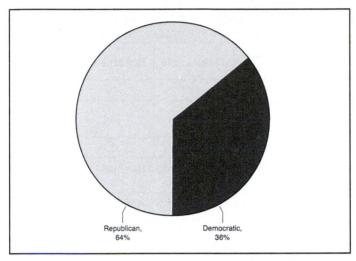

Figure 4.2   Republican Control of Assembly
Adapted by authors, Georgia State Politics

Democratic candidates lost all races above the county level, from Congress to the state's executive and legislative branches, Democrats unseated exactly one Republican (State Rep. Jill Chambers of DeKalb County). A glaring statistic is that the highest vote total for any Democrat (Ken Hodges in the attorney general's race) was the party's lowest since 1998, when the state had 1.9 million fewer voters. It was almost as if every new voter in Georgia over the past 12 years had decided to vote Republican. While Democrats had dominated Georgia politics through one-party rule, by 2010 a noticeable decline in split-ticket voting glaringly revealed the party's weakened state. Instead of the traditional re-instating election typical of most one-party systems, it was a re-aligning election.

And the Democrats' problems continued to pile on. On the day of its first meeting, the Republican caucus in the House grew to 109 members—its most ever—when Rep. Alan Powell of Hartwell switched sides. The very next day, two long-time South Georgia Democratic lawmakers made the switch. Less than two weeks later, two more Democrats moved to the Republican side. Then, joining this parade, Sen. Tim Golden of Valdosta moved over to the Republican side. Adding insult to injury, and in a move that was particularly embarrassing Representative Doug McKillip, who had just been elected by the Democratic members as Caucus Chair (the party's second highest position in the House) defected to the Republican Party. Two weeks later, Rep. Mike Cheokas of Americus joined the crowd. By the time the dust had settled, the Republican caucus had grown to 114.

Table: 4.1a	Georgia General Assembly: House & Senate Representatives in Numbers and Party Affiliations 2016			
	Total # Seats	Democrats	Republicans	Independents
US Senate	56	17	39	0
US House of Representatives	180	60	118	1
	246	77	157	1

Adapted by authors, Georgia State Politics

Table 4.1b	Georgia US Congressional Districts & Senate Representatives 2016			
	Total # Seats	Democrats	Republicans	Independents
Senate	2	0	2	0
House of Representatives	14	4	10	0
	16	4	12	0

Adapted by authors, Georgia State Politics

The ensuing problems weren't limited to Democrats, as newly reelected Republican Lieutenant Governor Casey Cagle quickly discovered. Even among Republicans, ideology trumped partisanship (JGalloway, *AJC*, 11/6/2010). In what was billed as a "power-sharing" agreement the Senate Republican Caucus voted to strip him of his power to appoint committee chairmen, the key to his influence. Others saw this move as more of a "palace coup" by Republican leaders in response to Cagle's support for a hospital tax during the prior session. Within days of the election, the caucus announced that they were going to significantly alter the power relationship between themselves and Cagle through three rules changes. These rules changes removed his power to appoint committee chairmen, the core component of the Lt. Governor's power; stripped him of his ability to determine the makeup of Senate committees; and stifled his ability to direct legislation to committees by forcing these decisions to be confirmed by the entire Senate. The real clout in the Senate devolved to an eight-member committee composed of President pro tem Tommie Williams, five GOP caucus officers, and two Senate appointees by Cagle. Cagle was expressly prohibited from membership on the committee. But by a few years later, various compromises allowed the system to return to the normal situation and the Lt. Governor resumed Senate leadership.

All of these election results, and institutional changes, continued to be painful in the following years. Apart from the general ways in which party control matters for legislative output, the 151st General Assembly was especially important due to its role in drawing new boundaries for national Representatives in the aftermath of the 2010 census. In a sign of the political nature of this task, Republican leaders in the House and Senate created a new joint office to handle the process of redrawing legislative district maps, ending an established pattern of using University of Georgia researchers for the work (Sheinin, *AJC*, 2/4/2011). If the process continues to move away from independent non-partisan sources, and into the hands of partisans, the Democrats are likely to suffer increasingly poor results in congressional elections throughout the following decade as well.

Constitutional Construction of the General Assembly

Basically, Article Three of the *Georgia Constitution* created a bicameral legislative branch, known as the General Assembly, composed of the Georgia House of Representatives and the Georgia Senate. Unlike the national legislative branch, however, members of both the House and Senate serve two-year terms and the entire General Assembly is up for reelection each term. The Senate is a smaller body, consisting of 56 Senators, each of whom is from a single member district. The House of Representatives has 180 Representatives, who are also elected from single-member districts. Some political observers have called for Georgia to adopt some multi-member districts, as is done in some counties and municipalities, but the idea has not gotten much traction.

At the beginning of each term, traditionally on the second Monday in January, the legislative session begins. Opening day is almost literally a circus because of the seeming pandemonium that ensues. Owing to the differences in the legislators' geographical districts, their religious, racial, and ethnic diversity, and their differences in occupations and their preoccupations, observers at the opening day ceremonies see a studied contrast in representation. There are farmers, ranchmen, stockbrokers, and businessmen who deal in commodities such as pork bellies. There are professional stockbrokers, bankers, and insurance salesmen, who as a group sometimes engage in tremendous efforts to prevent the boy scouts and good government representatives from controlling the varying ethics committees. Some see the spectacle as the chaos of the free enterprise system, some through the tragic lens of political science. The authors choose to represent the scene as an amusing image, as shown in Figure 4.3.

Figure 4.3   The Clowns Together
Courtesy of Lee M. Allen

As a part-time legislature, the General Assembly usually continues in session for a period of 40 working days; the 1992 session set a modern record by meeting from January 13th until March 31st. By concurrent resolution, the General Assembly may adjourn during any regular session to later dates at its own convenience, but neither house may adjourn during a regular session for more than three days or meet in any place other than the state capitol without the consent of the other house.

During special sessions, if they are called into being, neither house may adjourn more than twice, or for more than seven days at a time. If after thirty days of a session one house adjourns without similar action by the other house, the governor may adjourn both houses for up to ten days. However, if an impeachment trial is pending at the end of any session, the House can adjourn while the Senate remains in session until the trial is completed.

The Constitution Gives and Takes Powers

Among the specific powers granted to the legislature by the Constitution are: (1) to restrict land use in order to protect and preserve the state's natural resources and environment; (2) to maintain and regulate a state militia in cooperation with the Governor as commander-in-chief; (3) to tax, spend money, zone, and condemn property to comply with federal law and grant-in-aid requirements; (4) to ensure the continuity of state and local governments in periods of emergency resulting from disasters caused by enemy attack; (5) to act in concert with any county, municipality, nonprofit organization, or any combination thereof for promoting tourism; and (6) to tax, spend money, and regulate outdoor advertising near federal highways.

On the other hand, various specific limitations are placed on the law making power. Some of these are geared to economic activities. For example, the General Assembly does not have the power to grant incorporation to private persons except by formal enactment with standardized procedures, and modification of corporate charters and debts are specifically restricted. And it lacks the power to authorize any contract or agreement which may have the effect of defeating or lessening competition, or encouraging a monopoly. In addition, monopolies are declared to be unlawful and void in the State of Georgia. The General Assembly does not have the power to regulate the fees or charges of public utilities owned or operated by counties or municipalities except as authorized by the Constitution.

The drafters of the Georgia Constitution were careful to include checks and balances to ensure that state government officials would remain accountable to the people. So on occasion, the legislature may act to remove other officials from office via the impeachment process. The process starts in the House of Representatives, which has the sole power to vote impeachment charges against any executive or judicial officer of the state or any member of the General Assembly.

The Senate has the sole power to try impeachments. When sitting as a court during impeachments the Senate is presided over by the Chief Justice of the Supreme Court. But no official can be impeached, or removed from office, unless convicted by two thirds of the full membership. Upon such conviction, the defendant is removed from office and disqualified to hold and enjoy any office of honor, trust, or profit within the state or to receive a pension, but no other penalties are attached. However, impeachment does not relieve any party from any other criminal or civil liability.

The interesting case of the *Yazoo Land Grant Fraud* resulted in some specific prohibitions against corrupt practices. Prior to ceding its territorial claims to the lands reaching to the Mississippi River, successive Georgia legislatures made and then canceled millions of acres of land grants to the Yazoo Land Company (Current, 1983, p. 211). When the 1796 legislature attempted to void the land grant, the United States Supreme Court used the case of *Fletcher v. Peck* (1810) to void the state law, on grounds of "no impairment of contracts (Current, 1983, p. 271). Since then, except as specifically permitted, the General Assembly may not grant any donation or gratuity or forgive any debt or obligation owing to the public, and it cannot grant or authorize extra compensation to any public officer, agent, or contractor after the contract has been formalized or performed. Similarly, Article III of the Constitution specifically vests the power to issue insurance licenses to the Commissioner of Insurance instead of to the legislature *per se*.

Constitutional Requirements for Members of the General Assembly

At the time of their election, the members of the Senate must be citizens of the United States, at least 25 years of age, and citizens of Georgia for two years, and residents within their districts for at least one year. The members of the House of Representatives must meet similar requirements, except that they need to be only 21 years old when elected to office. Each Senator and Representative, before taking his or her legislative seat, must take an oath or affirmation as required by law. But some people who meet these qualifications are still not eligible for office, such as persons recently convicted of felonies; or persons holding civil offices under the United States, or who are on active duty with any branch of the armed forces of the United States. The latter provision is to avoid conflicts of interest and competing loyalties.

During their terms of office, legislators may not hold another state office. Except for a few leadership posts, they cannot be elected by the General Assembly or appointed by the Governor to any office or appointment having any "emolument annexed thereto" (salary or stipend), unless they resign their seat. And they may not be appointed to any civil office created during their term of office. Each house is the sole judge of the elections of their members. When a vacancy occurs, it is filled by the governor as provided by the Constitution and by statute.

Paying Members of the General Assembly

The pay of the members of the General Assembly is set by the legislature itself, but no increases in salary can take effect until the next session. At the time this book was written, legislators received a $17,342 annual salary and up to $6,900 for expenses during the annual legislative session. The expenses are known as per diem accounts and a mini-scandal arose in 2010 because of them.

One of the perks of being a member of the General Assembly is the per diem that pays some lawmakers more than $20,000 per year for travel and expenses while performing government duties (Sheinin, AJC, 4/13/10). This money is granted with little oversight, minimal auditing, and few questions or facts. A 2010 analysis found that lawmakers had billed the state for travel and expenses on more than one out of every four days while the General Assembly was out of session in 2008, 2009, and the first few months of 2010. Overall, their study found, members of the General Assembly billed the state for nearly $3.6 million in so-called per diem payments from January 1, 2008, through March 19, 2010.

The per diem payment system is justified in a state where the 180 members of the House and 56 members of the Senate are part-time legislators who meet for 40 days in an annual legislative session that can stretch for four months or more. But their obligations don't end when the gavel falls on sine die, marking the end of the session. And the demands are greater on top leadership and the heads of key committees. In the so-called offseason, many serve on special committees charged with studying a particular policy area or in regular committees, like Transportation, which often meets throughout the year in search of the elusive fix to the state's traffic woes. Constituent needs, too, don't end when the session ends. The per diem system is designed to compensate lawmakers when they must take time off from work and travel, in some cases, hundreds of miles to Atlanta for off-session work. Most legislators, too, have taken furlough days to help cut costs.

The system, however, is largely self-policed. Say it's July and a lawmaker needs to drive from his home district to the Capitol for a meeting. If the legislator is a rank-and-file member, he is supposed to first ask his committee chairman to approve the per diem payment. But every lawmaker can get per diem payments for up to seven days a year with no questions asked. Those days are known as a "committee of one days." If the lawmaker's committee chair signs off on the expense, the lawmaker comes to Atlanta and does his business. He then signs a voucher saying he worked that particular day and lists how many miles he drove. The voucher gets submitted to the Legislative Fiscal Office, and the lawmaker gets paid. Committee chairmen said the requests are largely on the "honor" system, although it is a crime to claim unearned expenses.

Lawmakers generally don't have to submit receipts to justify the $173 expense or keep a mileage log or even document the mileage driven. But once a month, the Fiscal Office produces a report detailing how much each lawmaker was paid in travel and expenses. In the House, the report goes to the chairman of the Committee on Information and Audits. In the Senate, it goes to the chairman of the Rules Committee.

Some members of the General Assembly who are not independently rich are in a difficult position. They are expected to be at the Capitol for 40 days of session, but even that is misleading. For example, the House and Senate may meet only on Monday, Tuesday, and Wednesday but there are also committee meetings on Thursday, even though Thursday doesn't count against the 40-day countdown. In the offseason, too, there are constituent concerns or occasions when local community groups make pilgrimages to the Capitol. They often expect their local lawmaker to show them around. As one member said, "Some people, they'll do it for nothing. They just won't get paid that day. I've got a job. I've got a business to run." This makes it difficult for ordinary citizen legislators to dominate the General Assembly.

Public Attitudes Toward the General Assembly

Students of legislative politics are fond of quoting Nelson Polsby's observation that for many Americans, "we hate Congress while we love our own congressmen." This is because our representative is a statesman; theirs is a politician. Ours is an astute fiscal manager; theirs is a spendthrift. Ours tends to the people's business; theirs plays around and threatens the underpinnings of American political culture. The legislative circus would be really sound and reasonable, except for the fact that this odd collection of other peoples' representatives controls the state's purse strings, the taxing, and spending policies.

However, quite apart from this national finding, Georgians tend to show the indifference that Georgians show toward the General Assembly rather than anger or contempt. A 2002 online questionnaire administered by the Marketing Workshop for the *Atlanta Journal-Constitution* revealed that respondents found the General Assembly to be largely irrelevant to their daily lives and that these respondents were paying little or no attention to what the legislature was doing (AJC, 1/14/02). Less than a third were paying a lot or some attention, and only 16% found the decisions made by the legislature to be very or somewhat relevant to their daily lives.

The General Assembly's Leadership

The General Assembly is composed of both party leaders and positions created by the Georgia Constitution which created three major legislative officials in each chamber. The Senate is governed by the President of the Senate (who is also the Lt. Governor); a President Pro Tempore, to preside when the Lt. Governor is absent and to act as President in case of the temporary or permanent disability of that official; and a Secretary of the Senate is also selected to maintain its official records. The primary officers of the House of Representatives are the Speaker of the House of Representatives; a Speaker Pro Tempore, elected to preside when the Speaker is absent; and a Clerk of the House who is chosen to oversee the maintenance of the records of that chamber.

General Assembly Responsibilities

The duties of the General Assembly include not only legislation but responsibility for the general welfare of the people of the state. Because of the obligation of each branch to maintain separation of powers, the Constitution requires the legislature to protect its prerogatives. The General Assembly cannot abridge its own powers, nor can any law enacted by the General Assembly be construed by the courts as acting to limit its powers.

Two major tasks of the General Assembly are to consider legislation and to enact law. Legislative proposals for new laws (bills) must go through a complex process before becoming law. Many bills never make it. The majority of bills are sponsored and introduced in the House, but the General Assembly may provide by law for the joint sponsorship of bills and resolutions.

First, in order to transact official business a quorum is necessary, which must consist of a majority of the members of each chamber. However, a smaller number may adjourn from day to day and compel the presence of its absent members. Each house determines its own rules of procedure and regulates its own employees.

General Assembly and Committees

Because legislation is so complex in modern society, the real work of the legislature is done in interim committees instead of on the floor of one or the other legislative chamber. Legislators can then specialize in areas which interest their constituents. By creating committees, each house in the General Assembly divides their membership into numerous small groups that specialize in one broad policy topic. This allows for members of the Assembly to position themselves within areas that are of special concern to their constituents and for the opportunity to more closely study bills than would be possible solely during a debate on the floor. Committees can be thought of as the legislative arenas in which the preliminary arena in which the committee will hear from the legislator who introduced the bill, other legislators who either favor or oppose the bill. Committees also go outside the General Assembly to learn the opinion of interests or persons concerned with a policy position. Committees are provided with very strong powers and can subpoena witnesses and records.

The General Assembly has four major types of committees. The first is the standing committee. Standing committees are established by the Senate and the House of Representatives for the management of their business. They are established by authority of rules separately adopted by the Senate and by the House. The appointment of committee members, chairs, and vice-chairs occurs at the beginning of each new term. The committee then has the responsibility of vetting the legislation. Each committee considers legislation within its field of expertise.

The second type of committee is study committees. These are committees that have been appointed or selected to perform a specific task or study a specific issue and meet year-round. As they examine these issues, reports are released which include any findings, recommendations, or legislative proposals a committee deems appropriate. Legislative study committees have become a forum for leaders concerned about public policy to stay active. While moving legislation to a study committee in the Georgia

General Assembly was often the political equivalent of being banished to Siberia, study committees are increasingly at work in public where they gather facts and provide forums for lively debate and public input.

The third type of committee is the conference committee. Conference committees are routine joint committees and are a response to the constitutional requirement that, for any bill or legislation to become an Act, it must be passed by both houses in precisely the same words and figures. In the case of significant bills, with substantial differences, the shortcut of a conference committee likely will be taken almost immediately. The use of conference committees reflects an ability to reconcile differences between the two chambers and suggests a give-and-take process because if the conference would be stalemated, the bill could fail. Each conference committee is composed of three members from the Senate and three members from the House of Representatives and chosen by the Standing Committee responsible for the bill. As a separate committee, they vote separately, not only on the final product but on any subsidiary questions put to a vote. A majority of the committee prevails.

Once a conference committee votes, it issues a "Conference Committee Report." These are presented to both the Senate and House and they must either accept or reject the Report in its entirety without amendments. While Reports will occasionally be rejected, causing it to be sent back to conference, they are generally submitted in the final hours of a session when the shortness of time might mean the bill would be lost or the General Assembly called into an extended or special session. Because of their strategic capability, conference committees can be used by party leaders to pressure their memberships.

The fourth type of committees are joint committees; these may be created at any time and are constituted of both House and Senate members for special issues and concerns. The conference committee is the most common joint committee.

The General Assembly and the *Art of the Possible*

Politics is often called the Art of the Possible. Very often well-intentioned but naive people ask the state legislature to pass a law that is realistically impossible, politically unfeasible, or simply stupid. Since legislators cannot tell their constituents that they are unwise or unintelligent, they have devised ways to *kill* a bill without triggering a confrontation with the voters. Two time-honored ways of doing this are to bury it in a committee, or to send it to some other group for study and evaluation. Each session of the Georgia legislature creates dozens of these so-called study commissions or task forces whose real job is to bury the new ideas. Sometimes they will issue reports, but often the proposed material simply vanishes without a trace, and the legislators are off the hook. Unfortunately this process also applies to proposals to support the general welfare instead of narrow special interest groups. The failure to be able to protect "The Commons" is perhaps the major reason why political science is called the Tragic Science.

Legislative bills can be enacted only if they are approved by a majority vote of all the members of both houses. In either house, when ordered by the presiding officer or at the desire of one fifth of the members present, a roll-call vote on any question must be taken and officially recorded in the journal. For appropriation bills, or on any issue requiring a two-thirds vote, each separate yea and nay vote is recorded. Ordinarily, after a general bill has cleared the committee process, and reached the floor for debate, its title must be read three times and on three separate days in each house before it can be voted on; and the third reading of such bill and resolution must be in the entirety when ordered by the presiding officer or by a majority of the members voting on the bill. Of course it may not be so ordered, and in fact each chamber's presiding officer can and sometimes do ignore the general rules of procedure. Sometimes this occurs with the specific approval of the house when time begins to run short, but sometimes shenanigans are pulled to give special favorable treatment to special interest bills that might not pass public scrutiny.

Once a bill has been passed by both houses it must be signed by both the President of the Senate and the Speaker of the House of Representatives before being sent to the Governor. No bill can become law unless the Governor signs it or fails to act upon it within six days from its transmission to the Governor, except where it is passed over the Governor's veto. Sometimes the General Assembly adjourns *sine die* or adjourns for more than 40 days prior to the expiration of the six-day period. In such cases, the bill becomes law if approved or not vetoed by the Governor within 40 days from the date of any such adjournment. Unlike the U.S. Constitution, the Georgia Constitution does not provide for an executive pocket veto.

If the Governor does veto a bill and if the legislature is still in session, the bill must be returned within three days, along with the reasons for the veto, to the presiding officer of the house where it originated. But if the General Assembly had adjourned *sine die*, or adjourned for more than 40 days, the Governor has 60 days to return it. However, in modern times the legislature has never lasted that long.

During legislative sessions, any vetoed bill or resolution may upon receipt be immediately considered by the originating house for the purpose of overriding the veto. If two thirds of the membership votes to override the veto, and the other house does the same, it becomes law despite the Governor's opposition. In the rare cases where bills and resolutions are vetoed during the last three days of the session and not reconsidered for overriding, the General Assembly can consider the issue at its next yearly session.

The General Assembly and Open Government

Because of occasional shenanigans, Georgia is especially sensitive to the desires of the citizens for open government. The State Constitution requires that sessions of the General Assembly and all standing committee meetings shall be open to the public, except where reasons of public policy justify. Each house has power to punish members for disorderly behavior or misconduct. This punishment can include censure or monetary fines, and in extreme cases even imprisonment or expulsion. However, no member can be expelled except by a vote of two thirds of their fellow members. For example, just prior to the opening of the 1998 session of the General Assembly State Senator Ralph David Abernathy III, the son of the civil rights leader whose name he shared, was arrested for attempting to smuggle a small amount of marijuana into the country through Hartsfield Airport in Atlanta.

The Customs Service confiscated the substance and imposed a small fine on the Senator, which reports indicated was a routine punishment for such a first and comparatively minor criminal infraction. However, the Senate moved to censure the Senator, and Republicans, particularly in the House, moved to impeach Abernathy, arguing that he had brought disrespect to the entire General Assembly. However, by the end of the session nothing had come of the impeachment attempt. In short, getting anything passed by the two chambers of the General Assembly is very challenging. Figure 4.4 illustrates this complex process.

The General Assembly and Home Rule

As might be expected according to the individualistic side of its complex political culture, Georgia has a strong commitment to home rule, which is defined as giving primary power to local authorities. While the General Assembly can enact laws overriding local legislation these bills not only require the usual reading requirements, the rules also stipulate that no such bill or resolution can be voted upon prior to the second day following the day of introduction, and the General Assembly must advertise a notice of intention to introduce specific local bills. This reflects Georgia's localistic traditions among the approximately (and ever-changing) 1,489 government entities in the state. Laws of a general nature always have uniform operation throughout the state, and preempt the enactment of local and special laws, except that the General Assembly may by general law authorize local governments to use their powers of local ordinance or resolution to exercise police powers, as long as they do not conflict with the general laws. This encourages flexibility.

Figure 4.4   How a Bill Becomes Law: The Process
SENATE

IDEA
Conceived by Legislator, Legislative Committees, citizens, groups of citizens, or copied from another state.

DRAFTING
Bills are drafted by Legislative Counsel and entered into legislative management system.

INTRODUCTION AND FIRST READING
Filed by a Senator with Secretary of the Senate who assigns it a number and prints.

On next legislative day, read first time and referred to Committee by President of the Senate. Bills are routinely assigned by subject matter; discretion lies with President.

COMMITTEE ACTION
Committee considers and studies Bill, receives expert testimony, and hears from all interested parties.

Committee alternatives are to: (1) Recommend Bill or Resolution Do Pass; (2) Recommend Do NOT Pass; (3) Recommend Do Pass with changes (amendments or substitutes); (4) Hold Bill. Final Committee action reported to the Senate in a written report.

SECOND READING
Bill read second time on legislative day following Committee report.

THIRD READING AND PASSAGE
The following legislative day, third reading and debate; amendments and substitutes adopted; final vote taken by roll call and recorded on passage of all General Bills.

TRANSMITTAL TO HOUSE
Bill then Engrossed signed by the Secretary of the Senate and transmitted to the House of Representatives.

Information taken from Georgia General Assembly website

HOUSE
FIRST READING Bill read first time and referred to Committee by Speaker of the House. **SECOND READING** On next legislative day, read second time. **COMMITTEE ACTION** Committee considers and studies Bill, receives expert testimony, and hears from all interested parties. Committee alternatives are: (1) Recommend Bill or Resolution Do Pass; (2) Recommend Do NOT Pass; (3) Recommend Do Pass with changes (amendments or substitutes); (4) Report without recommendation; (5) Hold Bill. Final Committee action reported to the House in a written report. **THIRD READING AND PASSAGE** The following legislative day, third reading and debate; amendments and substitutes adopted and final vote taken. **TRANSMITTAL BACK TO SENATE** Bill signed by the Clerk of the House of Representatives and transmitted back to the Senate. If House makes changes, Senate must agree or disagree to changes. If the two Houses fail to reach agreement on a measure, a Conference Committee may be established with three members from each House appointed by the Presiding Officer. To complete passage, both Houses must agree to report of Conference Committee.

Information taken from Georgia General Assembly website

No personal or population bills can be passed. Partly because of fears of rural versus city politics, and partly out of fears of favoritism, the state Constitution prohibits any bill using classification by size of population as a means of determining the applicability of any bill or law to any political subdivision, or as a means of using size to amend or repeal the general law. Similarly, no special law relating to the rights or status of particular private persons can be enacted. And when it comes to civil rights issues, the state lawmakers are not always given a free hand. Georgia is one of 15 states whose proposed election law changes are reviewed by the U.S. Justice Department.

In January of 1992, Georgia lawmakers were shocked when the U.S. Justice Department rejected the proposed redistricting maps for Georgia, which had been drawn up nearly seven months earlier. The rejection letter, signed by Assistant Attorney General John R. Dunne, said that the state's pattern of "racially polarized voting...appears to be exacerbated" by the proposed plans (Cook & Hendricks, 01-22-1992, p. A1). As a result of this federal bureaucratic decision, State House and Senate district maps, as well as U.S. Congressional district maps, were thrown back on the drawing board.

There were two reasons for the rejection: that they worked to benefit incumbents and that the proposed districts minimized Black voting strength. The problem areas involved southern rural Baldwin, Dougherty, Houston, and Peach Counties; and growing minority areas in suburban Atlanta Counties such as Clayton, Cobb, and Fayette. Overall, the Justice Department found fault with the legislative plans for almost all of Georgia south of Interstate 20. Since the Georgia Legislature was in session, the House and Senate reapportionment committees immediately scheduled action on the matter. One prominent politician agreed that some White incumbents had benefitted from the legislatively crafted districts (Cook & Hendricks, 01-22-1992, p. A1).

While State Rep. Tyrone Brooks (D-Atlanta), a critic of the proposed re-districting proposal, said voters should be angry with the legislators, not the Justice Department, another legislator took a different view. State Sen. Gene Walker (D-DeKalb), chairman of the Senate Reapportionment Committee, said "I'm disappointed in the kind of tone they used. I'm Black, and I'm not a racist." The Lt. Governor, Pierre Howard, also was disappointed at the federal bureaucratic ruling, saying that the legislature had tried to follow the federal Voting Rights Act (Walston & Cook, 01-22-1992, p. A8).

One state legislator took the high moral ground. State Sen. Don Johnson, announced candidate for the proposed new 10th Congressional District seat, said he would ask Lt. Governor Pierre Howard to take him off the map-drawing reapportionment committee to avoid potential conflicts of interest. He also chaired the Senate Appropriations Committee (Staff Report, 04-01-1992, p. A5). The authors are forced to conclude that charges of gerrymandering are perhaps an inescapable part of Georgia politics. The constitutionality of gerrymandering the new 11th Congressional District was challenged in 1994. The case was brought for a decision to a federal panel of three judges and alleged that this majority Black district, stretching from Stone Mountain to Savannah (approximately 260 miles), was neither compact nor contiguous as the high court had required.

In 1996, the U.S. Supreme Court in *Miller v. Johnson* held that the 11th District, which had been drawn with racial politics in mind, was unconstitutional, and its boundaries must be redrawn. With the *Miller v. Johnson* decision very much on their minds, the members of the Georgia General Assembly had to revisit the reapportionment "political thicket" following the 2000 Census. Since the U.S. Supreme Court had stated that race could not be the sole criterion for drawing or redrawing district boundaries, the question on the minds of the legislators was the degree to which race *could* count. Democrats, who controlled both houses, assumed that race would count for a whole lot less than it had previously, and that reapportionment maps that did not move large numbers of African Americans into a few districts, as they had after the 1990 Census, would pass constitutional muster. Republicans argued that districts that did not guarantee Black victories discriminated on the basis of race, meaning that fewer overwhelmingly Black districts meant fewer Republican districts. Besides, a new Bush Administration controlled the Department of Justice in Washington to which the maps, it was assumed, would have to go for "preclearance" (See Chapter 3) under the Voting Rights Act.

But the Democrats had an unanticipated ace up their sleeves. Rather than submitting their reapportionment maps to the Civil Rights Division of the Department of Justice, they bypassed the bureaucracy and took the new district plans to the Federal District Court for the District of Columbia, an option always available but seldom exercised. Republicans cried foul and asked that four Georgia voters, represented by Republican lawyers, be allowed to testify in the trial before the Federal District Court for D.C. That was permitted, but in the event had little bearing on the outcome. The maps for 13 new congressional districts—Georgia gained two additional districts in the 2000 Census—and all 180 State House districts were approved by the Court. An issue was raised regarding the map for the State Senate districts, contending that their construction diluted Black voting strength in Savannah, Albany, and Macon, and the Federal Court ordered the Georgia General Assembly to respond. It quickly did so, redrawing the lines in compliance with the Court's order, and the matter was resolved (http://www.ajc.com, 1/31/02). The upshot of this reapportionment fracas is that Democrats expected to win a majority of congressional seats in the 2002 election, and continue to control both houses of the General Assembly. Neither expectation came true. They lost control of the House, and while the number of seats they controlled did increase to five, the number of seats controlled by the Republicans stayed at eight.

The General Assembly and Appropriations and Budgets

Another issue raises almost as much smoke and fire—the appropriation and budgeting process. Funding for education, the biggest single expenditure of Georgia State Government, also engages the avid attention of dutiful legislators. The complex funding formulas are a ripe area for legislative debate. These issues are further discussed in Chapters 5 and 8 of this text.

However, the power of the purse is somewhat restricted in Georgia, which gives some strong budgetary powers to the Chief Executive. An important feature of the Georgia Constitution is that it requires the Governor to play a major legislative role. Within five days after the legislature convenes, the Governor must submit a budget message and a budget report, accompanied by a draft of a general appropriations bill. This bill must provide for the appropriation of the funds necessary to operate all the various state departments and agencies, and to meet the current expenses of the state for the next fiscal year.

In addition, the Constitution strictly prohibits riders on appropriation bills. Every bill must have a descriptive title, and no bill which refers to more than one subject matter can pass. Furthermore, no law or section of the State Code can be amended or repealed by mere reference to its title or to its number. The Constitution places precise restrictions on the way the legislature handles the finances of state government. The most important provision is that no money can be drawn from the treasury except by appropriation made by law.

Ultimately, the General Assembly is responsible for annual appropriation of state funds necessary to operate the state government. In addition, the state budget must include federal funds as well. To the extent that federal funds received by the state for various programs and projects exceed the amount appropriated in the general appropriations Act, these federal funds are appropriated by the state according to federal rules. The fiscal year of the state begins on the first day of July of each year and terminates on the thirtieth day of June in the following year. The total official revenue for the State of Georgia for Fiscal Year 2013, the last completely documented state budget, was $18,550,987,951.00. Not all of this was appropriated by the legislature, some came from fees, some from sales of property and services, and some from grants and loans from the federal government (Deal & Alford, 2015, p.13).

The scope of the general appropriations bill is strictly defined by Constitutional provision. Revenues appropriated by this bill can include only (1) materials fixed by previous laws; (2) the ordinary expenses of the executive, legislative, and judicial branches and bureaucratic departments; (3) payment of the public debt and interest thereon; and (4) support of the public institutions and educational interests of the state. All other appropriations must be made by separate bills, and each such bill can only embrace one subject.

Each annual general appropriations Act can continue in effect for only one fiscal year after adoption, after which it expires and a new one must be enacted. There is no perpetual funding in Georgia. In brief, the State of Georgia is required to balance its operational budget. The General Assembly cannot appropriate funds for any given fiscal year which exceed anticipated revenues and on-hand surpluses, as estimated in the Governor's budget report. Supplementary appropriations, if any, also cannot exceed these limits unless based on a tax base and collections, and these appropriations expire along with the annual appropriations. Neither House can pass a supplementary appropriation bill until the general appropriations Act has been finally adopted by both Houses and approved by the Governor.

All such appropriations must be made for specific sums, and no appropriation can allocate to any object the proceeds of any particular tax or fund unless the Constitution permits an exception. One major exception is money derived from gasoline and motor fuel taxes, which are set aside for providing and maintaining an adequate system of public roads and bridges in the state. Of course, in times of emergency, these rules are relaxed. In the event of invasion of the state by enemies, or in case of a major catastrophe, state funds may be utilized for defense or relief purposes according to the Governor's Executive Orders.

Other exceptions to the annual appropriations bill include the creation and administration of a trust fund for workers' compensation injuries and disabilities. And in any case in which any court imposes a fine or orders the forfeiture of any bond, the proceeds may be allocated for the specific purpose of providing training to law enforcement officers and to prosecuting officials. Another exception allows the General Assembly, by a three-fifths' vote of both houses, to designate any part or all of the proceeds of any state tax on alcoholic beverages to be used for prevention, education, and treatment relating to alcohol and drug abuse.

Public funds may be expended for the purpose of paying benefits and costs of retirement and pension systems for public officers and employees and their beneficiaries; and to establish or modify local retirement systems covering employees of county boards of education. The General Assembly may pass appropriations bills for the purpose of paying for a firemen's pension system. In these cases, the legislature must define funding standards which will assure the actuarial soundness of these retirement or pension systems.

In addition to the power of drafting the initial general appropriations bill, the Governor of Georgia has an item veto over appropriations bills passed by the General Assembly. The Governor may approve any appropriation and veto any other appropriation in the same bill, and any appropriation vetoed is eliminated unless the General Assembly overrides the item veto. Despite the powers of the Governor, the General Assembly remains very powerful.

Conclusion

At the beginning of every year, the old experienced hands and the newly elected freshmen converge on the Gold Dome in the sprawling city of Atlanta. They assemble with fire in their eyes, missions in their hearts, and IOU's in their pockets. As a group, they represent diverse economic and geographical interests. When one considers the vast differences in the legislator's occupational backgrounds, and their religious, racial, and ethnic diversity, it is a wonder that they can get together on anything. But when they do act, exercising the power of the purse, they are a potent force in Georgia's state politics.

Key Terms

Appropriations Process
Home Rule
Standing Committees
Joint Committee
Multi-member District
Single Member District
Miller v. Johnson
Sine Die

Essay Questions

1. Even in a one-party state like Georgia, there is still a lot of demographic diversity among elected officials. Discuss how this may impact on their perception of their role in the legislature.

2. In what ways does the committee structure facilitate or impede the passage of bills?

3. Describe the basic steps by which a bill becomes law in the General Assembly.

4. How has the federal government impacted on Georgia's redistricting efforts?

5. What role does the Lt. Governor have in the General Assembly?

Figure 5.1   The Governor's Mansion
Courtesy of Lee M. Allen

The Plural Executive of Georgia

In the United States, it is hard to find two State executive organizations that are identical. Because States reserve the right to organize themselves in any way they see fit, they often vary greatly with regard to their executive structure. In most states, the State of Georgia included all those who occupy the executive offices are directly elected by the people consistent with their Constitutional mandate. The executive branch in all 50 states is headed by a governor who is directly elected by the people. Other elective executive offices under the Governor's supervisory authority are the offices of the Lieutenant Governor, the Attorney General, the Secretary of State, the State School Superintendent of Education, Auditors, and offices of the various Commissioners. Implicitly, these designs of State executive offices carry with it the foundation of plural executives.

The Governor of Georgia

The Governor of the State of Georgia, Nathan Deal, is the heir to not only the last republican Governor, Sonny Perdue, but also to 37 Governors since the Civil War, five wartime Governors, and to the legacies of 25 pre-civil war Governors after the Revolutionary War. The modern Governor is the ultimate successor to James Oglethorpe, Proprietor and Trustee of the British Colony of Georgia, and after him to the three Proprietary Presidents, three Royal British Governors, and to 17 post-colonial and pre-federal state Governors. Because of the European Age of exploration, the territory that was to become Georgia came under the somewhat doubtful assertions of control and dominion of several royal Spanish Viceroys.

In fact, the modern Georgia Governor is the ultimate successor to untold generations of prehistoric native tribal chieftains. Creek and Cherokee peoples were living in the region prior to the European colonization of what is now the United States (World Almanac, 2010, p. 584). Although there are claims of Meso-American pyramid ruins in middle Georgia, no official excavations have been made. Some of our political traditions, like the names of many lakes and rivers, are rooted in the cultures of those pre-historic and colonial peoples and still influence our state in the modern era. There is no doubt that today immigrants from south of the border are coming to

Georgia. But while the earliest leaders in the area now known as Georgia might have based their power on physical strength or personal might of arms, modern Georgia chief executives owe their positions to intelligence, education, and the ability to win popular elections. These political processes are part of Georgia's inherent political culture and date back to King John's inability to use military force to persuade the British barons to give him a free hand over taxation. Still, it is said that the power of the executive is the Power of the Sword.

In short, the modern Georgia Governor is the latest of a very long and distinguished line of chief executives, and today presides over the most prosperous, largest population that the State of Georgia has ever had. Of course, this is not a history book, but a political science textbook, so it focuses on how political affairs function in the State of Georgia in the present day. Unlike many predecessors, and unlike the federal President, the Governor of the State of Georgia is not an all-powerful unitary Chief Executive. Instead of presiding over a responsive bureaucracy directed by their personal appointees, Georgia Governors must contend with a pluralistic structure directed by a variety of separately elected officials and a variety of appointed administrators.

Thus, instead of a simple pyramidal power structure, culminating in one person, the apex of the Georgia State Government structure resembles an oval crown with many points and no center of gravity. The other elected officials often contest the power of the Governor. Many of these other officials are topical experts who control their own separate administrative agencies. This complex structure is a main reason for declaring that the present Constitution of Georgia has created a bureaucratic governmental system where governors share powers. How can the Governor effectively initiate policy in this system?

These other elected executives include the Lieutenant Governor, who presides over the Senate; the Secretary of State, who has widely ranging administrative duties; the Attorney General who presides over the Department of Law; the State School Superintendent; and the Commissioners of Agriculture, Insurance, and Labor, each presiding over their own departments. These officials are separately elected by the people and do not have to belong to the same party or share the same political philosophy as the Governor. The result is often a lack of coordination, administrative headaches, and political conflict. Today, even though the Republican Party has in fact swept the polls to dominate the legislative and executive branches of government, much in-fighting and policy maneuvering still occur. How will any newly elected Governor cope with the challenges facing the state today?

Table 5.1   Georgia Gubernatorial Elections 1986–2014: Voter Turnout Candidates and Party Affiliation

Year	Voting Eligible Population*	Total Ballots Counted	Voter Turnout %	Winner	Vote %	Party Affiliation	Loser(s)	Vote %	Party Affiliation
1982	3,945,107	1,169,041	29.6	Joe Frank Davis	62.97	Dem	Robert H Bell	37.2	Rep
							n/a	n/a	n/a
1986	4,300,049	1,174,977	28.5	Joe Frank Harris	70.51	Dem	Guy Davis	29.49	Rep
							n/a	n/a	n/a
1990	4,588,953	1,449,654	31.6	Zell Miller	52.89	Dem	Jonny Isakson	44.54	Rep
							Carol Ann Rand	2.58	Liber
1994	4,498,431	1,545,297	31.0	Zell Miller	51.05	Dem	Guy Milner	48.95	Rep
							n/a	n/a	n/a
1998	5,326,337	1,792,808	33.7	Roy Barnes	52.49	Dem	Guy Milner	44.08	Rep
							Jack Cashin	3.45	Liber
2002	5,731,983	2,025,861	35.4	Sonny Perdue	51.39	Rep	Roy Barnes	46.23	Dem
							Garret M. Hayes	2.33	Liber
2006	6,115,331	2,122,185	34.7	Sonny Perdue	57.94	Rep	Mark Taylor	38.22	Dem
							Gary Hayes	3.84	Liber
2010	6,464,845	2,576,161	39.8	Nathan Deal	53.02	Rep	Roy Barnes	42.97	Dem
							John Monds	4.01	Liber
2014**	6,725,041	2,550,216	38.2	Nathan Deal	52.81	Rep	Jason Carter	44.83	Dem
							Andrew Hunt	2.36	Liber

* Voting Eligible Population (VEP) are usually those who are actually registered to vote and is therefore a superior count than Voting Age Population (VAP) which almost always include non-voting population such as convicts and non-citizens.
**2014 Write-ins as reported by the Georgia Secretary of State =.02
Source: Compiled and designed by authors: Georgia State Politics

To make things more complex, in addition to the individual elected officials, there are various constitutional boards and commissions which run their own specialized agencies. These include the state's Public Service Commission, the State Transportation Board, the State Board of Pardons and Paroles, The State Personnel Board, the Veterans Service Board, and the Board of Natural Resources. Generally, the boards function as committees with administrative powers defined in the constitution and therefore largely independent of the Governor's formal control. Each board has its own chairman, who presides over meetings and who has the power to break tying votes. Some of these boards are separately elected by the people of Georgia in general elections, some are elected by legislators, and some are appointed by the Governor with the advice and confirmation of the Senate. Governor Deal needs to try to coordinate these many different administrative actors if he hopes to address the economic problems that face the state today. How will he cope with our aging infrastructure, the growing water shortage problem, immigration pressures, and the many other issues confronting him?

The Powers of the Governor

With such a wide variety of executive officers sharing power, it may be surprising that the Governor of Georgia has been ranked among the more influential Governors in the United States. But although the formal powers are only moderate (Gray & Jacob, 1996, p. 202), the Governor of Georgia has informal power based on that fact that the office enjoys high prestige (Hepburn, 1987, p. 147). There are two reasons for this ranking. In one classical analysis of power, an Italian scholar suggested that when a ruler can rely on strong formal powers and resources to problems, those powers should be used vigorously. But when the formal powers of the ruler are insufficient, a wise ruler must use guile to achieve goals. In short, a prince must sometimes act like a lion, and sometimes like a fox (Machiavelli, 1952, p. 91). The key to the success of a Georgia Governor is how well he can balance these two sources of power.

In Georgia, with its history of suspicion of strong chief executives, its oppressive historical experiences, and many reform Constitutions restricting the Governor's formal powers, guile became a necessary qualification for the job. But there was an additional pillar of support for a wily Governor: Georgia's strong element of consensus politics in its long-time one-party system. The prestige of the Governor, both as titular head of government and as chief of the dominant political party, enabled the incumbent to influence events even when the formal powers might have been inadequate. This is as true today, with a newly resurgent Republican dominance, as it has been for the Democratic Party which recently lost the loyalty of voters.

The Constitution of the State of Georgia specifies that the chief executive powers shall be vested in the Governor. These formal powers enable the Governor to exploit several avenues of power and influence. The power and influence of Governors depends on their facility in playing various political roles. Perhaps most important of all these roles is his visibility as a mythical and symbolic leader, linked with the expectations of the general public. In this capacity, the Governor interacts with other state leaders and agencies, with cities and other states, and with the federal government and sometimes foreign powers. In fulfilling these roles, the Governor is acting as an intergovernmental middleman, a fulcrum of power and a center of political gravity.

In our federal system of government, the middleman role is complex. In the beginning, the system could be described as dual federalism, with separate spheres of responsibilities for state governments and the federal government, a sort of *layer cake* model. Until the Civil War, there was little overlap. But in time, as the states agreed to amend the Constitution of the United States, a more complex cooperative federalism developed, with commingling spheres, like a **marble cake** (Wilson, 1992 p. 67). This is especially true regarding economic powers, and with the exercise of our civil rights and liberties.

This cooperative federalism is characterized by a vertical bureaucratization of programs in the United States (Beer, 1978). In fact, every public policy with implementing programs is manifested at every level of government, and they are all functionally integrated, with costs shared by all three levels: federal, state, and local. One author suggested a picket fence model, in which the three "rails" of local, state, and federal government are crossed by a wide variety of policy arena "slats" (Nice, 1987, p. 10). However, this model does not help to explain how the "middleman" concept glues the components of the system together.

The authors suggest an **apple pie or perhaps peach cobbler** model of government, emphasizing the sticky unity of our federal system. In this model, we start with a heavy foundation of dough, filled with nuts and fruits and sweets, crisscrossed on top with more intersecting lines of doughy influence, some horizontal to reflect the various levels of government, and some vertical to reflect the varied organized interest groups and policy concerns seeking favorable acceptance by decision makers. This complex mixture is put under tremendous heat and pressure (see the melting pot), and the result is government like *apple pie*. In this cooperative model, the governor is the only state official with the power and visibility to influence the mixture, soften the impact of the nuts, and suggest the amount of dough to be used, to determine the consistency of the final product, and when to apply the heat to bring it to political completion.

The Chief Executive of a state has various roles to play. To be an effective governor, Nathan Deal will have to function as formal head of state (FHS),

Figure 5.2 Choosing Today's Role
Courtesy of Lee M. Allen

chief executive officer (CEO), chief financial officer (CFO), chief legislator, the commander of our state police and national guard forces, chief diplomat, and chief representative of the people. But he will not be the only legislator; he shares that role with the Lieutenant Governor, Casey Cagle. Nor is he the top lawyer, that elected position is the Attorney General, Samuel S. Olens. Similarly, the person who oversees educational functions in the state, which comprise the largest part of the state's overall operating budget, is yet another official, State School Superintendent, John d. Barge. The governor has to be a wily fox to get his way, because these other officials do not simply take orders from the Governor of Georgia.

As we have just discussed, there are many other popular and separately elected officials in the executive branch of government, many of which are discussed at length later in this chapter and other chapters. Nonetheless, the governor is the vital linchpin. In addition to the official powers granted by Article Four of the Constitution of Georgia, he has informal powers inherent in Georgia history and culture. The governor has prestige, status, and the loyalty and respect of the average citizen. But these are largely potential powers, and the degree to which they can be wielded depends upon the Governor's charisma and intelligence. The key is her/his ability to pick and choose roles to maximize effectiveness. Figure 5.2 depicts some of these choices.

The Chief Executive of a state has various roles to play, and one of the most important of these is **Head of State,** ceremonial and ritual leader, serving as the focus of identification of all the people of the state. To some, it came as a bit of a surprise when Governor Miller attacked the state flag during his State of the State speech to the 1993 legislative session. In Georgia, the flag issue has varying symbolic importance to different groups. Miller argued that the flag was adopted in 1956 to include the Confederate battle cross in opposition to court rulings for school desegregation (Winder, 1993, p. 5). This raised a storm of controversy: does the flag exist for internal purposes of uniting and representing people within the state, for representing the complex history and traditions of the state, or for the external purpose of representing the state to the outside world to maximize tourism, trade, and economic growth?

Miller's proposal to change the flag to reduce the prominence of the Confederate Stars and Bars was introduced into the Georgia State Senate, which wisely decided that so potent an issue should be referred directly to the voters, and passed Senate Bill 71 calling for a public referendum on the issue. But with an increasing level of anxiety, the House Speaker at the time, Thomas Murphy, and other leaders could not support the measure. Especially troubling to many powerful state politicians was the decision by various local government bodies, some controlled by African-American representatives, to refuse to fly the state flag, the first being the Atlanta-Fulton County Recreation Authority, which voted to remove the flag from the Atlanta-Fulton County Stadium, then the home of the Atlanta Braves baseball team (Salzer, 1994, p. D1). Finally Governor Miller requested that the House take no action on the matter, citing constitutional issues and costs. He summarized the issue by declaring: *"I made the fight and I lost the fight"* (Winder,1993 p. 8). Politically, it had become a "no-win" situation, and the Governor would never bring it up again.

But while Governor Miller would never touch the flag issue again, his successor, Governor Barnes, was not so reluctant. Early on in the 2001 legislative session, Barnes announced to a somewhat stunned General Assembly that he was bringing up the flag issue again and, just a week after it was introduced, Barnes called for a vote. Both Democrats and Republicans were caught off balance. Most Democrats followed the lead of the Governor. Most Republicans did not. On January 31, 2001,

Barnes signed H.B. 16, adopting a new compromise flag that reduced the stars and bars flag to a little banner, among other flags, at the bottom of a flag with the state seal in a blue field and with three broad stripes. Go to http:/ www.museumsouthernhistory.com/Flags.htm

Some Democrats who voted against the Governor and some who did not vote at all complained that the flag issue should have been decided in a referendum, which the Governor claimed was unconstitutional. Most Republicans, except for a number from the metro Atlanta area, agreed that a referendum was the proper way to go. Prompting the opposition to change the flag was the public opinion polls indicating an even split between Georgians over changing the state flag. However, on closer inspection, the evenness of the issue broke down. While only 37% of Georgia's majority White population approved of the change, 78% of African-American

Georgians supported it. Governor Barnes figured that if the issue was not resolved immediately, it would have poisoned the legislative well for the remainder of the session. Although his haste, and the heavy-handed manner in which he would exercise it, would further contribute to his reputation as "King Roy," Governor Barnes had managed to boost the reputation of the state externally as the progressive "Empire State of the South" without, he thought, doing great damage to his political career. In fact, it was argued that since the Republicans had to tone down their support for leaving the old flag alone, for fear of being labeled racist and mean-spirited, the Governor had really won a major victory on all fronts.

But the matter did not end there. Many would contend that the new Georgia flag was ugly and meaningless, with its inclusion of previous state flags and the U.S. flag so small as to be virtually unnoticeable at the bottom of a yellow banner in a blue background. But flags are not usually judged for their aesthetic appearance. It is their symbolism that makes them important to the people over whom they fly. And, while after the September 11, 2001, terrorist attacks on Washington, D.C., and New York City, Barnes could say: "There is only one flag, and it's the flag of the United States of America." "That's our flag." (ajc.com, 1/31/02) Not everyone was willing to disregard Georgia's traditional symbols. One might ask who would want to argue with that sentiment, but as Barnes assumed that no one would, he was quite wrong. The flag became one of the main sleeper issues in the 2002 campaign for governor.

Georgia's current official flag was adopted on May 8, 2003. It became official when the new Governor, Sonny Perdue, signed H.B. 380. The governor then took the added step of holding a referendum giving voters a choice between it and Barnes's compromise flag, based in part on the

Figure 5.3 The Georgia State Flag
Source: Flags that have flown over Georgia

Confederate flag, which was a painful reminder of slavery to many people. The new flag is more abstract, and more acceptable. So now the flag has a deep blue field with the state seal in the center, surrounded by 13 white stars (that symbolize the original 13 colonies). The state seal pictures three pillars (symbolizing the usual three branches of government in the United States: the Legislative, the Executive, and the Judicial) under an arch (symbolizing the Constitution).

Barnes defended his action; but many Republicans, outside the metro Atlanta area and in the business communities, condemned it. Sonny Perdue, who became the GOP nominee, made it a centerpiece of his campaign, promising that, when elected, he would submit the decision on what flag to have flying over Georgia to the voters in a referendum. The issue turned out to be a crucial one. Although Perdue stated on the day following his election that the flag issue was not a high priority with him, his supporters seem to feel differently. An analysis of the 2002 Georgia election reveals that heavy voter turnout was primarily responsible for the Republicans' gains statewide, the beginning of the end for Democratic Party rule. As a disappointed Roy Barnes quipped on leaving an Atlanta hotel ballroom following his concession to Perdue, "The flag brought out a White rural vote," and that voter sentiment was overwhelmingly Republican.

Perdue promised that he would resolve the flag issue once and for all by submitting it to the voters in a referendum, which he did in 2004. However, the choice confronting the voters did not include any flag with the confederate battle emblem, except the then current Barnes compromise flag. As a result, Perdue succeeded in using Barnes's idea to get the electorate to approve his suggestion. Of course, in our overheated peach cobbler form of democracy, there are still lingering controversies. Did the voters really approve a new flag, or really an old version of another flag? After all, the 13 stars could refer either to the early United States flag, or to the Confederate flag! So many of Perdue's new supporters, the ones known as the flaggers cried foul, claiming betrayal by Perdue. But the issue was practically resolved. Thanks to Sonny Perdue, Georgia now had its third flag in as many years, but this one is likely to hang around, ah, wave proudly for many years to come.

Besides Head of State, the Governor has several other important roles. Since the State of Georgia existed before it joined the United States, the Governor has some of the prerogatives of a nation-state leader. While these include the role of commander of the military and law enforcement arms of the state, the State Patrol and the National Guard, these are not a major concern of Governors today. More important are the political roles of the Governor as the chief legislator: setting the agenda, initiating the budget, and signing or vetoing legislative bills. There are two major parts to this latter role, the first with regard to legislation itself, especially the preparation of the annual budget proposal, and the second involving the convening of the legislature and the filling of vacancies in it.

A good state governor analyzes situations and figures out which roles would maximize his or her political influence and power.

As we observed in Chapter 4, the Governor's lawmaking role is significant. The Governor can convene special sessions, and his planning and budgeting staff always writes the annual appropriation bill as required by Georgia law. The Governor can set the agenda of each session by giving the opening speech especially during the State of the State Address. In the 1990s, Governor Zell Miller used this forum to give the General Assembly information on current problems of the state and to recommend legislative measures. Before becoming the Governor of the State of Georgia, Miller had a notable record of prior public service, as a citizen, a college professor, and finally as a Lieutenant Governor. In 1992, the *Georgia Rebound Program* demonstrated Miller's grasp of the legislative options. In addition, he used his appointment powers and political power over his party and over public opinion to influence the members of the General Assembly to support his policies. But as the flag controversy would reveal, he also knew when to back off from a controversial issue. More routinely, governors review each proposed bill or resolution and decide whether to approve and sign it, or to veto.

A governor can use the veto power as a tool to reward or punish members of the General Assembly for their support of or opposition to his legislative agenda. For example, in a 1997 legislative session, then Governor Miller used the line item veto powers to veto several legislators' pet projects (infamous pork barrel). What made this glaring is that appropriations had already been made for the vetoed projects. He did so in clear effort of "paying back" legislators who had opposed several of his favorite projects. While the legislators were not happy with the Governor's veto move, they realized even as a "lame duck" Governor, Mr. Miller was still in control. Commanding an approval rating of over 70%, he could make good on his threats. Having made his point, Governor Miller later relented, and the project monies initially vetoed were ultimately restored. A similar event happened during Governor Barnes governorship as well but in his case he overreached his powers. Here, his stance on the flag issue cost his re-election bid. His successor, Governor Perdue, not only adroitly handled the flag issue, but also the budget crisis that was caused by deregulating Wall Street and the *Great Recession* of 2008.

Perhaps the most important issue that Governor Perdue failed to resolve during his tenure was the water issue, as he called for prayers for rain instead of addressing the need for building an extensive system of water reservoirs. Unfortunately, water issues are not that exciting, even if they are controversial and expensive. Governor Nathan Deal must confront this issue since thus far the state of Georgia has lost court cases claiming rights to water from the Tennessee River and the reservoirs shared with other states. There have been whispers that the north Georgians and the Atlanta metropolis are planning to raid the water resources of the south Georgia

Table 5.2   Georgia State Constitutional Offices, Officers & Party Affiliation— 2016–2018

Governor	Nathan Deal	Republican
Lieutenant Governor	Casey Cagle	Republican
Secretary Of State	Brian Kemp	Republican
Attorney General	Sam Olens	Republican
State School Superintendent	Richard Woods	Republican
State Agriculture Commissioner	Gary Black	Republican
State Insurance Commissioner	Ralph Hudgens	Republican
State Labor Commissioner	Mark Butler	Republican

Source: Variable compiled by authors, Georgia State Politics

plains. The Governor must navigate carefully for an imminent answer on Georgia's water problem even if preoccupied current economic issues confronting the state (Great Recession) with an estimated mega 3.4–4.2 in revenue growth in 2015 and 2016.

The Plural Executive of Georgia

Parallel powers exist vis-à-vis the administrative apparatus of the state. The appointment of individuals to vacant positions is a significant tool in the administration of state government. When constitutional public offices such as the Attorney General become vacant, the Governor usually fills the vacancy. In most cases the appointment will be for the remainder of the unexpired term unless otherwise provided for by the Constitution. However, many appointments are conditional upon the confirmation of the State Senate.

The Governor is the top bureaucrat in the state system, and has the power to require information in writing from the other constitutional officers, as well as from all other officers and employees of the executive branch. The Governor may inquire into any subject relating to their duties. Along the same lines, the chief executive is charged with the responsibility to take care that the laws are faithfully executed, and he is the conservator of the peace throughout the state. The Governor must take an oath or affirmation to fulfill these duties as prescribed by law.

The terms of office, compensation, and allowances of Constitutional Officers are set by the current Georgia Constitution. Elections for Governor are held once every four years, beginning in 1986, on Tuesdays after the first Monday in November. The elections occur in the same way as for the state legislators, and by the same voters. The Governor-elect is installed in office at the next session of the General Assembly, and serves a four-year term with the possibility of one succession.

If Georgia Governors want a third term, they have to wait four years after their second term before they can run again. In order to qualify for the office of Governor, a person must have been a citizen of the United States for at least 15 years and a legal resident of the state for at least six years preceding the election, and must be at least 30 years old when assuming office. These requirements ensure that the Governor is familiar with the state, and can make informed decisions and appointments. But governors should be able to do more than make decisions; they should be able to provide their people with a vision of a better future.

Vision and Policy Initiative

Georgia has had lots of leaders with vision. Jimmy Carter's adroit ability to gauge the public mood led him all the way to the White House. Martin Luther King's "I Have a Dream" speech was an example of a leader's vision and ability to motivate followers. In the early 1990s the depressed state of the American economy cracked even Georgia's well-run economy. Beset by rising unemployment, reduced growth, and economic shortfalls, Governor Zell Miller, in 1992, created the *Georgia Rebound* proposal as the centerpiece of his budgetary and policy recommendations. The basic program goals were to anticipate and spur economic recovery and competitiveness in the state of Georgia. The plan balanced expenditures primarily with a slight increase in user fees, usually in areas where the fees were not sufficiently self-sustaining. The total estimated cost of his annual budget proposal was over 8.3 billion dollars.

In his first term, Miller's four-point expenditure program focused on economic development, educational improvements, environmental planning, and public safety. By increasing support for capital improvements and teacher salaries, the state workforce was better able to exploit economic opportunities such as new environmental technologies. At the conclusion of the 1992 legislative session, Governor Miller proclaimed the legislative session a success, with most of the *Georgia Rebound* approved and funded (LoMonte, 04-02-1992, p. B1). But, in politics, a Governor can only rarely afford to rest on his laurels, and stiff competition in his campaign for a second term in office led to his offering of a new vision, and a new message for the people and a new agenda for the legislature.

Whereas in his first term his plan had relied heavily on public construction projects, such as transportation facilities, waterways, and airways development; his new plan focused on education. Georgia had been a southern leader in educational progress, but had in recent years slipped back and lost ground. Governor Miller's new vision centered on building hope for better schools. Awakening to the financial problems of schools and students alike, the *Hope Scholarship Program* linked the idea of government scholarships and educational appropriations to a risky new revenue source: a state-sponsored lottery which promised to bring millions of new dollars into state coffers. The *Hope Scholarship* program basically pays the college tuition of any Georgia student who maintains a "B" or better grade point average. It all came together: a politician's vision, a legislative agenda, a constitutional amendment, and by 2007 the legislature was able to draw from state-sponsored lottery proceeds eight hundred forty-one million dollars ($841,000,000.00) for education.

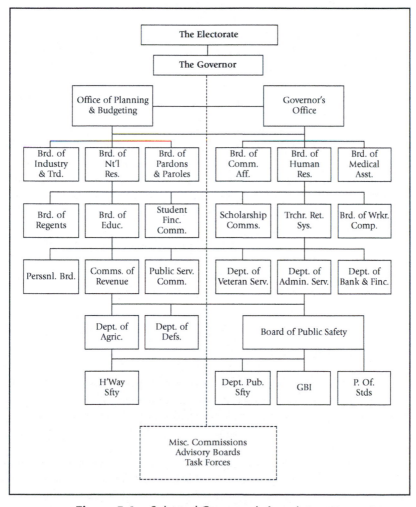

Figure 5.4   Selected Governor's Appointments
Compiled by Authors

Today, this program still supports several different educational grant and loan programs, all expected to expand as lottery revenues increase, designed to foster better pre-schools, grade schools, and ensure that every college student can pursue their educational dreams and help Georgia be better able to compete in the emerging global marketplace. Unfortunately, there have been some hiccups along the way, a confirmation that lottery proceeds alone cannot be the sole or reliable source to meet Georgia's projected educational funding needs. For example, due again to another recession and resulting Georgia economic woes, the current Governor Nathan Deal made known publicly his intent to cut back on Hope Scholarships, and therefore to restrict full funding grants only to students with a 3.7 GPA. This subject is discussed with more detail in Chapter 9 on education policy.

One would expect that a governor with vision, who proposes bold new programs and initiatives, would be rewarded with reelection by the Georgia people who appreciate that governor's energy and work ethic. But, according to a national syndicated columnist Bill Shipp, just the opposite is true. In a 2005 column that appears in *Valdosta Daily Times,* Shipp argues that activist governors in Georgia are likely either to just "squeak by" into a second term, or are defeated. Miller just squeaked by; Barnes was defeated. George Busbee and Joe Frank Harris were governors who did relatively little, and won reelection handily. Shipp believes that Sonny Perdue has modeled his administration after Busbee's and Harris's. The fact that Perdue won reelection overwhelmingly in 2006, despite a record of little accomplishment and some complaints of ethical violations, suggests that Shipp's thesis has some merit. And of course we need to remember that in the modern world no one person can do it all.

A good governor must have a good management team, and be able to appoint strong and active managers who share a common vision onto all of the boards and commissions over which a governor has appointive authority or political influence. However, in Georgia, the constitution provides for the direct election of several other major state officials.

The Lieutenant Governor

Like most states, Georgia elects a Lieutenant Governor. This is a relatively new position in Georgia, created for the first time in the 1945 Constitution (Pound & Saye, 1971, p. 60). Governor Perdue's first Lieutenant Governor, Mark Taylor, was elected at the same time, for the same term, and in the same manner as the Governor. However, they were unable to work together or share a governing philosophy. In fact, Perdue and Taylor came from different parties, and were known to dislike each other, owing to the fact that Taylor insulted then-Senator Perdue when he switched parties in 1998. While the Lieutenant Governor's job is basically to replace the Governor if necessary, he also serves as the President of the Senate. This can be a powerful position in its own right, almost as powerful as the Speaker of the House of Representatives. Custom and tradition gave the Lt. Governor power to appoint members to committees, and to assign bills to committees.

But when Republicans captured control of the Senate in 2002, they stripped the democratic Lieutenant Governor of much of his power as payback for payback. The new Lieutenant Governor, Casey Cagle, indicated a desire to have the traditional power returned to the Office of Lieutenant Governor. Given the fact that he was a Republican, close to Governor Perdue, and that Republicans control both houses of the General Assembly, no one was surprised when Republican Senators did just that on the first day of the 2007 session. After all, one reason for Republican success was that they had promised that they would be more efficient than the democratic controlled legislature. But when Cagle supported Perdue initiatives over those of ranking Republicans in the senate, they conducted a *palace coup* and stripped him of those legislative powers (Yarbrough, p. 6A). Still, Lieutenant Governors have various other executive duties as may be prescribed by the Governor or by law. Primarily, in case of the temporary disability of the Governor, the Lieutenant Governor exercises the powers and duties of the Governor, until such time as the disability ends. But in case of the death, resignation, or permanent disability of the Governor, the Lieutenant Governor becomes the new Governor until a successor is elected at the next general election.

But if such death, resignation, or permanent disability occurs within 30 days of the next general election, or if the term expires 90 days after the next general election, the Lieutenant Governor becomes Governor for the remainder of the unexpired term. When that happens, the office of Lieutenant Governor remains vacant, since the Georgia Constitution does not provide for a new Lieutenant Governor to be appointed. On those rare occasions where both the Governorship and the Lieutenant Governorship are vacant, the Speaker of the House of Representatives exercises the powers and duties of the Governor until a special election can be held within 90 days.

Attorney General

Another important Constitutional Official in Georgia is the Attorney General. Samual Olens was elected in 2010 in the historical republican sweep of state government. The Attorney General acts as the legal advisor of the Department of Law, and represents the state in the State Supreme Court for all capital felonies, and performs such other legal duties as may be required by the Governor or by law. One of the most important of these is authoring legal opinions on problems of interpretation of law for other state officials and agencies. No person can be Attorney General unless he or she

---

Figure 5.5a   Attorney General Olens' Statement on Supreme Court
Marriage Ruling

Obergefell v. Hodges

"Today the Supreme Court of the United States ruled the Constitution
requires a state to license a marriage between two people of the same sex
and to recognize a marriage between two people of the same sex when
their marriage was lawfully licensed and performed out of state. It does
not permit bans on same-sex marriage. In our system of government,
the Supreme Court bears the ultimate responsibility for determining
the constitutionality of our laws. Once the Supreme Court has ruled, its
Order is the law of the land. As such, Georgia will follow the law and
adhere to the ruling of the Court."

Source: Attorney General Olens' Statement on Supreme Court Marriage Ruling, June 26,
2015

Figure 5.5b   Attorney General Sam Olens' Statement on the
Supreme Court's Voting Rights Act Decision

Shelby County v. Holder

"When the Voting Rights Act was passed in the 1960s, several states and
local jurisdictions, including Georgia, discriminated against minority
voters. Discrimination is wrong, and Section 5 was an appropriate
response.

I am pleased, however, that the Supreme Court recognized today that,
"[n]early 50 years later, things have changed dramatically."

"The Voting Rights Act will continue to protect the rights of all voters
in all states, but will no longer treat some states differently based on
outdated formulas that thankfully no longer reflect current practices.
Section 2 of the Voting Rights Act makes clear that racial discrimination
in voting is illegal nationwide, and remains a strong and effective tool to
counter discrimination."

Source: Attorney Sam General Olens Statement:
law.ga.gov/press-releases/2013-06-25/statement-attorney-sam-general-olens-supreme-
court%E2%80%99s-voting-rights-ac, June 25, 2013

has been an active-status member of the State Bar of Georgia for seven years. The Attorney General is a vital link between the executive branch and the judicial branch of government.

Just as the Governor and the Lieutenant Governor may be at odds with each other, so, too, the Governor and the Attorney General may have difficulty getting along. Disputes over redistricting and other political matters pitted Governor Perdue against Attorney General Thurbert Baker, a Democrat. Perdue insisted that he was the legal voice of Georgia; Baker said that he was. The courts resolved the dispute in the Attorney General's favor, but the two did not resolve their differences. The arrival of Governor Nathan Deal and Samuel Olens in 2011, both Republican, signal a change. The interesting question is whether Attorney General, Samuel S. Olens will preserve the independence Baker (his predecessor) fought to preserve or side with the Governor on critical issues. Presented below are two excerpt reactions from that office on key controversial issue.

Educational Executives

There are two major education agencies serving in the State of Georgia and responsible for spending the bulk of taxpayer money. The first is the State Board of Education, dealing with primary and secondary education. The second is the Board of Regents. Richard Woods the State School Superintendent since 2014 is the elected chief executive officer of the State Board of Education, so unlike local school superintendents he is not appointed by the Board of Education.

The Georgia State Constitution provides that the Superintendent shall be elected at the same time and in the same manner and for the same terms as that of the Governor. Only 16 states elect their School Superintendent. In the other 34 states s/he is either appointed by the Governor or by the Board of Education itself. Some consideration has been given to having the Georgia Superintendent appointed and incumbent Superintendents have endorsed that suggestion. However, Georgia citizens like to elect as many of their public officials as possible, and once a position is elective it is hard to change; the General Assembly has not yet made the change to an appointive State Superintendent. And as long as the General Assembly and the Office of School Superintendent are controlled by Republicans, a move toward appointment is not likely to happen.

Unfortunately, the examples of Governors fighting with their Lieutenant Governors and Attorneys General have been repeated with School Superintendents. Both Miller and Barnes had issues with Republican Superintendent Linda Schrenko. In fact, Schrenko gave up the office in 2002 to run for the GOP nomination for Governor so that she could take on Barnes. But she was defeated by Perdue in the primary election. As a footnote, she was subsequently indicted and convicted for stealing over $600,000 in federal education funds, some of which went to defraying campaign expenses for her abortive gubernatorial race. As of the writing of this textbook, she was serving a prison sentence in a federal penitentiary in Florida.

Ms. Schrenko was succeeded in the Superintendent's Office by Kathy Cox, another Republican office holder. Her tenure was marred by a couple of controversial issues. One of those was her political surrender to the anti-science movement, the new luddites of our time. Specifically, she attempted to strike all references to the teaching of *evolution* in favor of the term *biological changes over time* as favored by some right wing conservatives. In fact, evolution is a term that has tremendous importance in science, applying to subjects in astronomy and physics as well as botany and biology. Georgia cannot expect new companies to move here if its educational environment is hostile to a good scientific education for company employees.

The global market is too competitive for the state to pander to modern luddites. She later said that she learned from the public outcry that accompanied her ill-advised effort, and learned that classroom standards represented something very important to the larger public, and to the larger entity of the nation; and that that was a great lesson for her (Galloway, 07-06-10). The other controversial issue was that after winning a multimillion dollar prize on a national game show, and announcing that she was going to give the money to three schools for the handicapped in Georgia, she declared bankruptcy instead. She then resigned from her position, moved to Washington, D.C., to work as the CEO of a new non-profit institute, and created a cloud of confusion about her motives and her values. When the voters elect someone to represent their interests, they expect the official to fulfill her obligations, and not cut and run after the fast bucks.

As stated, there are two separate educational entities in the State of Georgia. The entity responsible for colleges and universities is the Georgia State Board of Regents, whose regular members, like the Board of Education, are appointed by the Governor of Georgia and confirmed by the Senate. However, in addition to representatives chosen from the congressional districts, there are also five more Regents who are chosen at large; all Regents serve seven-year terms. Among state agencies, the Board of Regents is unique in the sense that its budget is not line-itemed. To insulate the University System from politics, the General Assembly appropriates monies to the Board of Regents in a lump sum, and the Constitution instructs the regents to allocate these monies as the Board sees fit. This seemingly peculiar insulation of the Board of Regents was initiated during the reform administration of Governor Arnall in the 1940s as part of a strategy to secure educational re-accreditation for the university system, whose professional accreditation had been lost.

The withdrawal of professional accreditation originally occurred when the previous Governor, Eugene Talmadge, had tried to manipulate and intimidate the Board and the entire university system for partisan purposes. This had been a typical problem in many states when corrupt party machines had used school systems to give jobs to party loyalists, regardless of any professional qualifications. In an attempt to prevent similar problems in the future, Governor Arnall and the legislature placed the system for micro-financing and micro-managing of higher education out of the budgetary reach of both the executive and the legislative branches. We will see more of the clash between reformist and partisan party organizations when discussing the "Three Governors Controversy" a little further in this chapter.

Other Elected Executives

The Secretary of State is another vitally important official but is dealt with primarily in another chapter. Some other major constitutionally elected officials include the Commissioner of Insurance, the Commissioner of Agriculture, and the Commissioner of Labor. These officials are elected in the same manner as the members of the General Assembly, and hold their offices for the same term as the Governor, although, unlike the Governor, they are indefinitely eligible for reelection. That is, they may serve as many terms as the voters will reelect them to serve. In 2010, the retirement of the long serving Tommy Irving, a Democrat, finally allowed the Republican candidate Gary Black a chance to be elected, and thus completing the historic Republican sweep of statewide offices for the first time since reconstruction.

Together with the other officials discussed above, these officials have another power in addition to their departmental duties. Any four of these elected constitutional officers can petition the Supreme Court of Georgia to declare that another elected constitutional executive officer (including the Governor) is unable to perform the duties of his or her office. When the grounds are properly based on physical or mental disability, the Supreme Court will provide a speedy and public hearing on the matter. This is a formal process that includes notice of the nature and cause of the accusation, process for obtaining witnesses, and assistance of counsel. Evidence at such hearings must include testimony from at least three qualified physicians in private practice, one of whom must be a psychiatrist. If, after hearing the evidence on disability, the Supreme Court determines that there is a disability and that it is permanent, the office will be declared vacant and a successor to that office will be chosen according to the Constitution and the laws of Georgia. But if the disability is not permanent, the Supreme Court must later determine when the disability has ended and when the officer can resume the exercise of powers of office. During the period of temporary disability, the powers of such office will be exercised according to law, usually by an assistant administrator, selected by the management team.

The figure below shows a spectrum of executive team management styles, ranging from unilateral one-person rule to an administrative pluralism where the nominal executive head is merely one of the management team players. As was stated earlier, modern government is too large and complex to be administered by any one person. The Chief Executive Officer may be called a Governor, or a President or a Director, but they can only function effectively if they have assistants with delegated power and authority. In Georgia, the Governor's departmental assistants are the other constitutional officers. But while there has to be a team, there are several different ways the Governor can interact with the other team members. For example, Thomas H. Ruger, the Military Governor of Georgia from January 13, 1868, to July 4, 1868, can be seen as a dictatorial manager imposing his will by fiat on other state leaders. He acted as a forceful lion in controlling people and events around him.

Governor Roy Barnes, on the other hand, Governor from 1999 to 2003, was more of a leader type of manager. As our review of the flag issue demonstrated, operating in the same general environment as his predecessor Miller, and with generally the same people in government, he was able to lead them in adopting a new flag for the state. When his popularity waned, and the Democrats were replaced by a new management team, the Republicans, the new team was able to reverse Barnes's policy. Perhaps the best example of a Governor who was really a team player was Joseph E. Brown, whose tenure ran from 1857 to 1865. Although not really a member of the elite plantation class, he helped put together a new secessionist management team, while acting the role of the star player, and captain of the team.

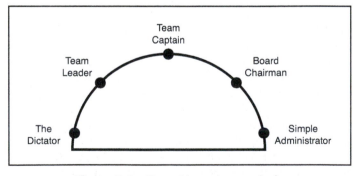

Figure 5.6   Team Management Style
Courtesy of Lee M. Allen and Marc G. Pufong

As a general rule, charismatic politicians are the most likely type of persons to win a governorship and shine in the office, their success due to their ability to exercise a dictatorial, leadership, or team captain style of management. But sometimes less political types get into the office, people who are more comfortable with just being members of the management team. In the year 1946 this happened when the popular Governor-elect, Eugene Talmadge, died before taking office. The new 1945 state Constitution did not specify who would assume the governorship in such a situation. At that point the incumbent Governor Arnall claimed a stewardship role, but the Lieutenant Governor-elect Thompson also claimed the post, as did the son of the deceased candidate, Herman Talmadge. In the period know as *the Three Governors Controversy* the Talmadge forces persuaded the legislature to *elect* him; but the Supreme Court ruled against Talmadge and designated Thompson as the true winner. But Melvin Thompson lacked the charisma for the job, and although he did preside over the state until the next general election (losing to Talmadge) he really functioned more as a simple administrator caretaker just part of the state's management team. Governor Thompson was never again elected to state office, and retired to Valdosta as a businessman and private citizen (Paulk, 02/27/11).

Governor James E. Carter

A generation or two ago, one Georgia Governor, James Earl Carter, succeeded in applying his understanding of the role of the chief executive to the Presidency of the United States. After serving in the United States Navy as a nuclear engineering officer, Jimmy Carter returned home to manage the family's peanut farm business, and to engage in public service. After serving in the State Senate, he became governor in 1971; and then established a reputation as an honest political reformer in the wake of the national Watergate scandal. He built a national political organization from scratch and became elected as President of the United States in January 1977.

He made his mark on the federal government by establishing two new cabinet departments, Energy and Education, and in passing the Civil Service Reform Act of 1978 (Allen, 1989). His training in science, engineering, and in the military had made him an administrator par excellence, presiding as the active chairman of the complex federal government. But even though he received the 2002 Nobel Prize for Peace due to his role brokering peace for a besieged Israel, he is perhaps best known for his failure to respond militarily to the Iranian Revolution, the hostage crisis, and the rise of the Shiite Theocracy. These issues, plus the intractable energy crisis, marred any chance of his being remembered as a great president.

Conclusion

How is a Governor to cope with such a complex and decentralized system of government and administration? How can a Governor be evaluated? Some researchers suggest that a good Governor can identify the needs of the people of the state, develop intergovernmental strategies to meet these needs, and persuade at least half the people (or their legislative representatives) to adopt his proposals. And then, of course, the implemented proposals must be acknowledged as having solved the problem. The Governor must be persuasive, that is, he must be foxy enough to understand the problems, aggressive enough to act on the information, and, sometimes, just be plain lucky.

Key Terms

Constitution of Georgia
Article One: Bill of Rights
Civil Rights
Civil Liberties
Freedom of Assembly
Freedom of Conscience to Worship
Freedom from Imprisonment for Debt
Right to Keep and Bear Arms
Right to Trial by Jury
Prohibition against Ex Post Facto Laws
Truth as a Defense Against Libel
Martin Luther King
Due Process Rights

Essay Questions

1. Why are constitutional rights so important?

2. Is there a difference between civil rights and civil liberties? What are they?

3. What is *eminent domain* and why is it important?

4. How has modern development affected perspectives on the right to bear arms?

5. Why is Martin Luther King such an important historical figure?

Figure 6.1   The Department of Transportation
Courtesy of Lee M. Allen

6
Administration and Agencies

The Georgia State Administration

What do a female tourist, a group of senior citizens, and a county commissioner have in common? They have all had negative experiences with modern bureaucracy. When the government machinery runs well, we call it an administration; when it runs badly, we call it a bureaucracy. In today's mass society, composed largely of alienated strangers, bureaucracy can be a nightmare. Administration can be defined as a complex rationally designed system of organization that relies on training, specialization, division of labor, record keeping, and hierarchical control to meet the needs of a technological mass society. Its evil twin brother, bureaucracy, can be defined simply as a nightmare of either personal but biased treatment, or an impersonal and perhaps even negligent government. This chapter describes some of the major administrative organizations and how they fit into the governmental system of the State of Georgia, and how they affect the lives of our citizens.

In what is becoming an increasingly common phenomenon among our corporate common carriers, who seem more concerned with maximizing their cash profits and less about simply providing a reasonable service for a reasonable fee, one tourist, a 300-pound woman returning from a bus trip to Ft. Lauderdale, was arrested in Macon, Georgia, for disturbing the peace when she objected to being kicked off the bus because the bus company driver was attempting to squeeze in a maximum number of passengers (Associated Press, 3-29-92). She had a right to complain, because once you have a ticket, the common carrier has traditionally had a duty to get you to your destination and not leave you stranded and alone in a strange place. In another case, a few resident senior citizens were playing their usual private game of bingo at McDonalds in Lavonia, Georgia, when the Georgia Bureau of Investigation closed the games down because they were not properly run by a non-profit, tax-exempt organization with a bingo license (Associated Press, 4-2-92).

In reaction, one elected official, Jimmy Helms, Chairman of the Paulding County Board of Commissioners, announced that he wanted to hire a professional manager to cope with the demands of modern population growth because amateurs such as he could not adequately run the county bureaucracy as efficiently as a professional public administrator (Associated Press, 2-23-92). Indeed, the existence of professional county managers, city managers, and school superintendents who are trained to moderate the conflicting demands of ordinary citizens, special interest groups, and corporations, and mindless bureaucrats running rampant is a major reason our complex government works as well as it does, most of the time.

Article IV of the Georgia Constitution establishes an administrative branch of government. Just as the principle of legislative primacy has yielded to executive dominance, so in turn the executive model is being replaced by an administrative model of government organization and policymaking. Most of the administrative machinery of the State of Georgia is run by various constitutional boards and elected and appointed officials whose names are largely unknown to the average citizen. Generally, these officials are not formally subordinate to the governor, except for reporting obligations, as we saw in the last chapter.

Public Administrators

Administrators are basically people. State government is one of the largest employers in Georgia. Including higher education personnel, over 114,000 people work for the State of Georgia (Fleischmann & Pierannunzi, 1997, p. 146). They are headquartered in buildings in Atlanta and their basic job is implementing the state's laws and policies. Together these administrative units' numbers, since the beginning of the state's history, have increased every time new programs and policies were created to cope with the increasing complexity of everyday life.

The growth of population has led to modern mass organization and an increasingly complex interdependent society. Few people really like the system, preferring the more individualistic lifestyles of the past, but rational organization is necessary today. When the invention of the railroad created jobs for conductors and engineers, it also required a Railroad Commission (the forerunner of the Public Service Commission); and the invention of the airplane created a need for both pilots and the employees of the Atlanta Airport. In fact, in every major policy area, such as education, law enforcement, health care, welfare, and economic regulation, a new bureaucracy has had to be created to ensure that the general public good will be protected. In addition, bureaucratic proliferation occurs in five technical areas of bureaucratic activity: information, service, regulation, licensing, and promoting. The result is an expanding administrative structure which in its size, complexity, and impersonality sometimes takes on a bureaucratic aspect in the minds of some citizens.

The stages by which modern societies have come to rely on mechanical bureaucracies can be traced. In the beginning, individuals and families took care of their own needs. But as society progressed, people learned that specialization and division of labor in a free market were more productive. Slowly, private organizations evolved which better satisfied peoples' needs. Except for taxation to support charities for the poor and disabled, monarchical governments encouraged these organizations with a minimum of interference, a laissez-faire approach. But as private organizations increased in power, adapting bureaucratic structures to profit-making enterprises, some became too self-serving and a few created destructive monopolies. Entering the industrial revolution, western democratic societies attempted to retain their sense of community by curbing monopolies and by creating welfare agencies.

As populations grew, the western societies created ever larger bureaucratic institutions to deal with large masses of people: armies, schools, social work agencies, and even prisons. But these facilities are very expensive to operate. Reforms and modification of the institutional society led to attempts to directly subsidize individuals. Poorhouses were closed, mental institutions were emptied, and individuals were given government pensions and welfare checks to take care of themselves, but bureaucracies continued to grow. Even recent suggestions to cut costs and bureaucracy by passing regulations requiring families to provide child support and for employers to provide family and health care, envision new enforcement bureaucracies. Truly, we live in a bureaucratic age.

In just one year the various agencies of the Georgia State Government made millions of phone calls, processed over a million driver's licenses,

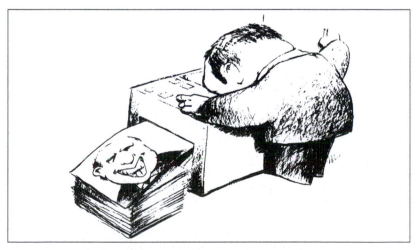

Figure 6.2   Bureaucratic Empire Building
Courtesy of Lee. M. Allen

almost two million vehicle titles, almost two and a half million income tax returns, close to six million vehicle registrations, and handled fifty million criminal justice inquiries (Christenberry, 1991, p. 19). Electronic media have added even more hundreds or thousands, if not millions, of more e-mails, faxes, and duplicative reporting requirements. Over 100,000 state employees carried on a bewildering array of activities. They administered the largest self-insurance program in the state, maintained real estate leases in almost 200 cities, provided services for many thousands of telephones, cell phones, and other new engineering marvels, and managed over 600,000 procurements transactions (Ibid). The state's personnel workforce is big business.

Constitutional Administration

Decades ago, Leonard White, a political scientist, predicted an eventual shift from legislative based government to bureaucratic based government (Nachmias & Rosenbloom, 1980, p. viii). In fact there is a long history of such predictions; most of the serious scholars who have contemplated the issue have agreed that a new locus of bureaucratic power is developing. This is reasonable, because bureaucratic government has several advantages over legislative and executive government. Some of the major ones are rational planning, specialization and division of labor, record keeping, and career orientation (Weber, 1958, pp. 196–199). Perhaps the major one is that it avoids what Max Weber called the "succession crisis." Weber identified a typology of historical change in government organization. According to that typology, new charismatic governments created by gifted individuals would experience a crisis when the leader died; much energy and effort would be diverted to solidify gains and create traditional governments based on the leader's ideas. But these governments too often hardened into rigid forms; and western political systems developed legalistic means of choosing new leaders and new policies. These legalistic procedures are the fundamental basis of bureaucratic organization (Weber, 1961, p. 112).

Of course, researchers have found some instances of this system of bureaucracy to be dysfunctional. It has been suggested that the Reagan Administration, which succeeded the Carter Administration, acted on assumptions that regulatory agencies and commissions were often harmful to society. In one well-known assertion, he said that government was not the solution to the problem, that government WAS the problem. These assumptions are that such organizations create contradictory policies with heavy compliance costs, perceive regulations as ends in themselves, and tend to devote resources to advance their own interests (Friedman, p. 24).

Perhaps the most influential of the anti-regulatory studies was the one conducted by Murray Weidenbaum, who calculated that the total economic impact of federal regulations was more than $100 billion (Cooper, 1988, p. 253). This report was cited in Congress, and charged regulatory agencies with being staffed by overly zealous and impractical officials. However, analysis of the Weidenbaum report by Mark Green showed that it was seriously flawed, that it was largely "puffing" for partisanship purposes, and that it exaggerated the costs of regulation and completely neglected the economic benefits of regulatory activity (Cooper, 1988, pp. 254–54). The reason that bureaucratic techniques and regulations are so pervasive is that they are superior to other forms of mass organization.

The old mold of traditionalistic monarchical government was broken in the new world. In America, new states and new governments were created by charismatic individuals with the vision and energy to implement their ideas. Colonial Georgia's Oglethorpe is a good example of a charismatic visionary. The creation of constitutional government, influenced by John Locke and Jean Rousseau, traditionalized many of Oglethorpe's principles for a new social order, and the American Revolution solidified them. Georgia's political evolution has largely been a continuation of the legalistic and bureaucratic transformations identified and articulated by Max Weber.

The student should note the similarities and differences between the structure of the federal government and the government of Georgia. The state of Georgia has a plural executive, not a unitary one. The powers of the chief executive must be shared with a number of other elected and appointed executive officers working in a number of agencies and departments.

In Georgia, the relationship between these officials is complex, requiring skill in intergovernmental relations. The governor must be a lion and a fox, able and willing to assume a variety of roles with facility. With such an able governor in charge, state government can be as sweet as an apple pie, or in this case, as sweet as a peach cobbler. In Georgia, under an effective leadership the various units of government can work together harmoniously, with joint policymaking and mutual accommodation.

While the Constitution of the State of Georgia specifies that the chief executive powers shall be vested in the governor, sometimes the administrative agencies function as a separate branch of government. This is especially true in Georgia, where the enactment of Article IV of the Constitution created an emphasis on independent administrative government. The primary thrust of this bureaucratic approach is due to a growing recognition of the need for expertise in governing and coordinating today's complex society. This tendency is reflected not only by the features of the plural executive described in the last chapter, but also by a wide variety of autonomous and independent departments, regulatory agencies, commissions, and authorities, described in Table 6.1.

Administrative Leaders

The Attorney General is probably, except for the Governor in the executive branch, and possibly the Lieutenant Governor and the Speaker in the

Table 6.1 Administrative Subdivisions
Executive Departments. 33
Executive Agencies 48
Statutory Advisory Boards 37
Decreed Advisory Boards. 20
Authorities & Corporations 30
Interstate Agencies. 8
Judicial Agencies 24
Legislative Agencies. 12
Inactive Agencies. 12
Total: **224**

Source: After Jackson and Stokes, *Handbook of Georgia State Agencies,* Univ. of Georgia. (Note: This is not an exhaustive list.)

legislative branch, the single most powerful individual official in Georgia's state government. As the state's chief lawyer, the Attorney General issues opinions on state law which serve to guide much of the state's and local governments' administrative apparatus. By exercising this power, the Attorney General can (1) interpret vaguely worded laws and regulations, (2) influence enforcement of laws and regulations, (3) advise legislators on probable constitutionality of pending bills, and (4) determine the scope of agency jurisdiction, and thus (5) can significantly determine public policy across the entire state. The Attorney General is also the state's chief administrative link with the courts and the legal profession.

The Secretary of State is another extremely important constitutionally elected official. The Secretary of State, along with the Board of Elections, oversees the elections process and tracks electoral changes in the State Constitution. Other duties include (1) recording financial statements from politicians, (2) granting charters to corporate entities, (3) issuing permits to do business, (4) maintaining registers of public officials, and (5) oversight of a myriad of occupational boards.

Workers in many trades and professions must be licensed before they can practice in the state of Georgia. Dozens of commissions and boards administer occupation admission standards and licensing procedures, regulate their particular areas of employment, and deal with complaints by consumers. Except for attorneys, oversight of these examining, certification and regulatory boards and commissions is usually the responsibility of the Secretary of State, acting through the Office of the Joint-Secretary of the State Examining Boards. Some of the Examining Boards are listed below. The first table shows the major health professional boards, the second depicts a variety of other occupational groups that are closely regulated.

Table 6.2 Examining and Licensing Boards Selected Health Professions
Composite State Board of Medical Examiners Georgia Board of Dentistry Georgia Board of Nursing Board of Examiners of Licensed Practical Nurses Georgia State Board of Nursing Home Administrators Georgia State Board of Pharmacy
State Board of Dispensing Opticians State Board of Examiners in Optometry Board of Examiners for Speech Pathology and Audiology Board of Hearing Aid Dealers and Dispenser
Georgia State Board of Physical Therapy State Board of Podiatry Examiners State Board of Examiners of Psychologists Georgia Board of Chiropractic Examiners Georgia Board of Occupational Therapy
State Board of Examiners for Certified Waters and Wastewater   Treatment Plant Operators and Laboratory Analysts Water Well Standards Advisory Council Board of Veterinary Medicine State Board of Examiners for Registered Professional Sanitarians
Source: Compiled by authors from materials in Jackson and Stakes (1988*), Handbook of Georgia State Agencies*, Univ. of Georgia.

Executive Commissions

Article IV of the Georgia Constitution creates several powerful executive Boards and Commissions. These boards and commissions include the Public Service Commission; the State Board of Pardons and Paroles; the State Personnel Board; the State Transportation Board; the Veterans Service Board; and the Board of Natural Resources. In each case, the qualifications, salaries, powers, and duties of their members are controlled by the constitution and not by the governor. The presiding chairmen of these boards are selected by a variety of complicated two-step processes, some of which are described in the paragraphs below.

The Public Service Commission

The Public Service Commission is created for the purpose of regulating utilities such as electrical power. It is composed of five members who are

Table 6.3   Other Examining Boards

Office of the Joint-Secretary of State
Examining Boards
Asbestos Licensing Board
State Board of Accountancy
State Board for Certification of Librarians

Georgia Real Estate Commission
State Board of Georgia Architects
Georgia State Board of Landscape Architects
State Board of Registration for Professional Engineers and Land

Surveyors
State Board of Registration for Professional Geologists
State Board of Registration for Foresters
Georgia Construction Industry Licensing Board
State Structural Pest Control Commission

State Board of Barbers
Georgia State Boards of Cosmetology
Board of Recreation Examiners
Georgia Board of Athletic Trainers

Board of Polygraph Examiners
Georgia Board of Private Detectives and Private Security Agencies
State Board of Registration of Used Car Dealers

Georgia Auctioneers Commission
Georgia Athletic Agent Regulatory Commission
Georgia State Board of Funeral Service

Source: Compiled by authors from materials in Jackson and Stakes (1988), *Handbook of Georgia State Agencies*, Univ. of Georgia.

Figure 6.3   Administrative Case Study

Former state Insurance Commissioner John Oxendine is an example of an administrative chieftain who served as a student assistant to a Georgia Governor (Joe F. Harris) who then appointed him as Chairman of the State Personnel Board and was then elected to four terms of office before relinquishing his political position in 2010. Lawyer, businessman, and right wing politician, he was a colorful individual who was fond of using his emergency lights to bypass traffic jams. But he turned more heads when, upon leaving office he awarded himself several insurance licenses without taking any of the usually required tests. In reaction, a bill has been introduced into the assembly to prevent a repetition of the stunt (WALB News, 03-06-11).

elected directly by the people for six-year terms. The chairman is selected by the members of the commission from among themselves. The exact jurisdiction, powers, and duties of the Commission are provided for by statutes enacted by the legislature and by regulations promulgated by the Commission.

The members of the Public Service Commission regulate the railroads, issue licenses, and set rates for power companies, telephone companies, and other public utilities. There is a great deal of controversy over the scope of powers of the Public Service Commission. As Georgia becomes increasingly urbanized and modernized, there are cries for an increase in regulatory efforts and for reform. Some of the areas of concern involve consumer complaints over the cost of electrical power, manufacturing interest in the adequacy of the transportation systems, general distress over the quality of water, and preservation of the state's unique environmental resources.

The State Transportation Board

In contrast, the members of the State Transportation Board, who serve five-year terms, are chosen by designated members of the General Assembly. There are as many members of this Board as there are congressional districts in the state. The member of the board from each congressional district is elected by a special caucus meeting of members of both Houses whose respective districts are embraced or partly embraced within each congressional district. A majority vote of these legislators chooses the members of the board, who in turn pick their chief executive officer from among their ranks. This commission is responsible for building and maintaining the roads and highways of the state of Georgia, and such other duties as provided by the legislature.

The patronage and politics involved in this area can be very considerable. For example, one businessman who had tried unsuccessfully for years to persuade the State Department of Transportation (DOT) to pave the road to his sod farm finally gave up and tried an alternative approach. He began donating money to political candidates. He was impartial, giving money to candidates of both parties. Soon, he was appointed to a special commission to ferret out waste in state government. As a result, the next time the businessman called DOT about his road he received prompt and friendly service (AJAC, 2-21-92). Not all citizens end up as happy as this individual.

Commissioner of Insurance

Insurance regulation is required by Article III, Section VIII of the State Constitution. That provision calls for the General Assembly to provide for statutory regulation of the insurance business, under the direction of a Commissioner of Insurance. The Commissioner of Insurance regulates the state's multi-million dollar insurance industry. The Commissioner sets criteria for licensing, sets standards for performance, and, within the framework of the law, sets rates for insurance policies for automobile drivers and homeowners and for fire, theft, and casualty losses. The present commissioner Ralph Hudgens replaced John Oxendine in 2010.

The State Board of Pardons and Paroles

Historically, The British King had power to intervene in criminal cases to provide justice or to settle political and military disputes by exercising the pardon power. Although presidents and governors usually have similar powers, in Georgia, the fear of abuse, corruption, and a desire to avoid hassle led to a delegation of that power to a five-person commission. The members of the State Board of Pardons and Paroles are appointed by the governor, subject to confirmation by the Senate. The Chairman of the Board of Pardons and Paroles, or any member designated by the board, may suspend the execution of a sentence of death; until the full board has an opportunity to hear the application of the convicted person for relief. The State Board of Pardons and Paroles also has the authority to pardon any person convicted of a crime who is later found to be innocent of that crime.

Thus the board, and not the governor, is vested with the power of executive clemency, including the powers to grant reprieves, pardons, and paroles; to commute penalties; to remove disabilities imposed by law; and to remit any part of a sentence for any offense against the state after conviction. However, the Constitution does not give the board a completely free hand. In a further division of power, the General Assembly of Georgia has a lot of direct control over pardons and paroles under the Constitution. Under some circumstances the legislature may prohibit the board from granting a pardon or parole to habitual felons or notorious criminals, and may even prescribe the terms and conditions for the board's granting of a pardon or parole to such persons. These conditions pertain to any person incarcerated for a second time for any offense for which he or she could have been sentenced to life imprisonment; and to any person who has received consecutive life sentences as the result of multiple offenses occurring during the same series of acts.

And the ever-popular anti-crime movement has resulted in some recent amendments to the Constitution which allows the General Assembly to set mandatory sentencing guidelines, and in addition a *two-strike* amendment means that a two-time loser is likely to face living in prison for a life term! When a sentence of death is commuted to life imprisonment, the board does not have the authority to grant a pardon to the convicted person until the person has served at least 25 years in the penitentiary. Georgia is not a good place for anyone to commit a crime and get caught.

The State Personnel Board

A strong governor usually has the power to directly hire and fire members of the administrative apparatus of the state, and thus to control the bureaucracy. With a weak executive, employees are more likely to respond to their immediate superiors instead of to the governor. In Georgia, power over state employees is given to a State Personnel Board, consisting of five members nominated by the governor and appointed after confirmation by the Senate. Their terms of office are five years, and they select their own chairman. This board sets policy for the State Merit System of Personnel Administration, and is further vested with such additional responsibilities and powers as provided by law. One critique may be in order here. While merit systems may indeed increase competency, it is sometimes at the cost of loyalty and adherence to executive policy. To further complicate matters, much of the sphere of authority of this board overlaps with another one: the Board of Veterans Service, which is described below.

The Veterans Service Board

Article IV of the State Constitution creates a State Department of Veterans Service and its oversight body, the Veterans Service Board which consists of seven members appointed by the governor, subject to confirmation by the Senate. The terms of its members are for seven years, and the members themselves appoint a commissioner who becomes the executive officer of the department. All members of the board and the department must be veterans of some war or armed conflict in which the United States has engaged. Exact duties and responsibilities of the board are described in statutes enacted by the General Assembly.

Any armed forces veteran who has been honorably discharged is given veterans preference in any civil service program established in state government. Wounded or disabled veterans are provided at least ten points if they have a 10% service connected disability, and all other veterans are entitled to at least five points. For, example if a passing grade on a test is required to get a job, the preference points are added to their scores. If tests are so easy that everyone gets high marks, veterans will get the jobs.

The Board of Natural Resources

The state of Georgia has traditionally relied heavily on its natural resources for trade and commerce. As environmental problems have developed, Georgia has acted to protect its fragile ecosystems by creating a Board of Natural Resources. Like the State Transportation Board, the size of the Board of Natural Resources is determined by according a member for each congressional district, with an additional five members to represent the state at large. And because of the geographical distribution of resources, at least one of the members must be from one of several counties specifically named in the constitution. And the members of the board are supposed to be representative of all areas and functions encompassed within the Department of Natural Resources. All members are appointed by the governor for seven years, subject to confirmation by the Senate. As usual, more powers and duties can be provided by legislative statute.

Intergovernmental Interactions

How do all of these agencies interact? The Legislature acts by committees. The executive branch per se operates by fiat and decree through the bureaucratic hierarchy. The judicial are trained in legal reasoning and hierarchy. How do the various agencies, representing a wide variety of perspectives and responsive to different interests, interact with each other to accomplish anything? Actually, there are four common patterns of agency interaction.

Usually, agencies are rational actors capable of identifying common interests and acting jointly to make and implement public policy. Sometimes one agency, perhaps enjoying sufficient funding levels, will take the initiative on a problem and other agencies will help out. This is called mutual accommodation. Sometimes, rival agencies will engage in friendly competition to see which can accomplish its goals first. This is called constructive rivalry. But unfortunately, there is yet another pattern. On rare occasions, two agencies will be controlled by opposing special interest groups, or will succumb to professional jealousy, and the result adversely affects the agencies and the public good. This pattern is called destructive conflict. Joint policymaking and mutual accommodation, formalized in contracts and memoranda of agreements, are the most routine patterns of bureaucratic interaction.

Federalism is a type of political system in which many disparate units and levels of government are coordinated by a central unit. In this apple pie mixture, the government of Georgia is part of the larger federal system. But that is not all, Georgia belongs to a variety of other coordinating units, such as the National Governor's Association. In addition, several interstate agencies exist, sometimes operating under binding compacts, such as the Southeastern Interstate Forest Fire Protection Compact Advisory Committee; other examples include the Southern States Energy Board and the Southern Growth Policies Board (Jackson & Stakes, 1988, p. 341). The Fisheries Commission, the Radioactive Waste Management Commission, and the Historic Chattahoochee Commission are other examples. Of course, most of the daily grind of bureaucratic activity is determined by functional problems, such as conservation.

Conservation of the Environment

The conservation of environmental standards and resources is a problem of increasing significance. Georgia's farmers have long understood the necessity to replenish the land to support their agricultural crops. Taking care of topsoil, planting the right crops, and fertilizing the *back forty* is second nature to good farmers. For many citizens of the state it is a simple step from soil conservation to environmental preservation. But for other Georgians, concerned perhaps with post-war modernization, or focused on short-term self-interest, or simply unmindful of the necessities of long-range planning, environmental preservation has been a low priority. However, with our water tables polluted by industrial and agricultural waste and pesticides, with the virgin timber almost gone, and many wildlife species already extinct, the consequences of reckless destruction today commands our attention.

Georgia ranks near the bottom of the list of states in terms of state-owned parks and wilderness land. The Board of Natural Resources is charged with increasing land holdings and protection of the environment. The duties of the department include maintenance and acquisition of land, regulation and conservation of fish and game, management of fisheries, and the enforcement of state hunting and fishing laws. Unfortunately, some of the goals of the board, as in the society at large, are often contradictory and irreconcilable.

Other Regulatory Areas

The promotion of economic development and trade and commerce is a major concern of Georgia State Government. As the traditional local forestry and agricultural economy of Georgia yields to manufacturing, commerce and recreation, several agencies have been created to coordinate the efforts of private companies and public agencies to foster economic and industrial growth. In today's global marketplace, the attraction, location, and encouragement of business enterprises and economic opportunities are legitimate, indeed essential, concerns of state government.

Special Authorities

There are some economic and functional policy areas that require narrow expertise, technical administrative competency, and unique management skills. Sometimes these policy areas involve geographical considerations that cannot be easily handled by local government, or dealt with in a cost-effective fashion by generic state laws or state agencies. Two obvious examples are the metropolitan airport in Atlanta, and the international seaport in Savannah, but there are many more. In fact, there are 391 different special districts in the state of Georgia, some of the 1,271 different governmental entities in the state.

Their interactions often depend upon the functional issues but may center on the resolution of intergovernmental conflicts; the need to facilitate development, or to provide flexibility for quasi-commercial enterprises. Often the driving force behind the creation of a special authority is the desire to finance an enterprise without exceeding the debt limitations of a parent governmental entity; or to quiet a taxpayer revolt by financing operations with specific user fees instead of with general revenues or property taxes.

However, the proliferation of special authorities has led to increasing concerns about waste and mismanagement. In 1972, the General Assembly enacted a reorganization plan designed to deal with the problem. This plan created a centralized State Financing and Investment Commission. The State Financing and Investment Commission might be called a super commission. It is composed of the major state political leadership: the Governor, the Lt. Governor, the Speaker of the House of Representatives, the Attorney General, the Commissioner of Agriculture, the State Auditor, and the Director of the Fiscal Division. Together, this collective body of political power can coordinate a powerful response to any problem. The goal is to ensure that Special Authorities contribute to efficient government.

In 1996, Article IX, Section IV was amended to allow the creation of "regional facilities." These regional facilities mean industrial parks, business parks, conference centers, convention centers, airports, athletic facilities, recreation facilities, jails or correctional facilities, or other similar or related economic development facilities. Counties and municipalities are authorized to enter into contracts with contiguous counties for the purpose of allocating the proceeds of ad valorem taxes assessed and collected on real property for development purposes, and unless otherwise provided by law, the regional facilities can qualify for any income tax credits, regardless of

Table 6.4 Types of Authorities
Agricultural Authorities
Building Authorities
Development Authorities
Educational Authorities
Foundations
Highway Authorities
Municipal Authorities
Park Authorities
Port Authorities
Power Authorities
Residential Finance Authorities
State Tollway Authority
Stone Mountain Memorial Association
World Congress Center Authority
Source: Compiled by authors.

where the business is located. Many people don't like bureaucracy. Although the pressures of modern society require the modification of government toward increasingly bureaucratic models, the creeping snails' pace and heartless impersonal nature of bureaucracy engenders hostility and anger. Nevertheless, the growth of bureaucracy is inevitable. One ironic effect is that the oversight powers of the legislature and the governor have dwindled as the size and scope of bureaucracy has grown.

Conclusion

The administrative machinery grinds slowly, but it usually grinds well. The charges against the lady tourist arrested on the bus were dropped and she initiated a lawsuit against the bus company. The senior citizens who couldn't play bingo have received a sympathetic ear from their state representative who initiated a provision to exempt their organization from criminal categorization. And now, of course, nonprofit organizations can run all sorts of raffles. And the county commission chairman who decided that a professionally-trained manager was necessary is simply falling in line with the trends, based on the requirements of the citizens of the state of Georgia.

The present Constitution of the State of Georgia, reflecting these pressures, has created the most administratively-oriented government in the history of the state. Unfortunately, once created, administrative organizations may turn into bureaucratic organizations, learning how to protect their funds, their resources and personnel staffing levels, and even their autonomy. It is the task of the other branches of government to ensure that the bureaucracy remains responsive to the general public, and not just to their particular clients and special interest group supporters.

Key Terms

Administration	Water Well Standards
Bureaucracy	Pardons and Paroles
Environmental Policy	Trade Licenses
Responsiveness to Citizens	Special Authorities

Essay Questions

1. Why does Article IV establish a fourth branch of government?
2. Georgia's governor has the power of appointment over many state boards. Discuss.
3. Who is the fourth most powerful official in the State of Georgia?
4. Why does increasing population result in more need for government agencies?
5. Describe some of the patterns of Intergovernmental Relations.

Figure 7.1 Local Courthouse
Courtesy of Lee M. Allen

The Georgia Judiciary

The Vested Judicial Power

Georgia's State Motto: "Wisdom, Justice and Moderation," not only reflects our traditional and individualistic cultural values, but also the rich heritage of the judiciary. The power of the courts is the power of the pen (reasonable explanations of decisions). Like the executive power, the judicial power is decentralized, but not as decentralized, because the judiciary is based on definite principles and has clear lines of authority running to a pinnacle of power, the state (and ultimately the national) Supreme Court. The judicial power of the state of Georgia is vested "exclusively" in seven classes of constitutional courts. Article VI, Paragraph II provides that all courts of the state shall comprise a unified judicial system.

Generally, the judicial branch of government enjoys a higher respect in the minds of the public than that of the other branches. As a result, the courts often resolve disputes between the other branches of government. For example, during the sorry political jockeying of the so-called three-Governor fiasco, arising from the premature death of Governor-elect Eugene Talmadge on December 21, 1946, the State Supreme Court had to resolve a bitter controversy. Three people claimed the Governorship: Ellis Arnall, the sitting Governor attempted to stay on; political boss Herman Talmadge was elected by the legislature; and the newly elected Lt. Governor, M. E. Thompson claimed to be acting Governor (Wolfe, 1991). The Supreme Court decided in favor of Thompson and the issue was resolved.

Authorized by the Georgia Constitution in 1835, it was not until 1845 that the Legislature formally established the Supreme Court of Georgia. Its first session was held at Talbotton, Georgia, on January 26, 1846, amidst uncertainty and skepticism. At issue was whether the Court's very existence would endure since it was assumed that "within ten years the Court would decide all questions of law and thus [other branches] would no longer be necessary" (www.gasupreme.us/history/#history). Today, the Georgia Supreme Court stands at the top of the legal ladder in the state judicial system. Starting at the bottom, in ascending hierarchal order, the seven constitutional courts provided under the 1983 Constitution are magistrate courts, probate courts, juvenile courts, state courts, superior courts, the Court of Appeals, and the Supreme Court. The Constitution provides that the judicial power of the State is vested in the listed classes of courts. The concept of judicial powers has to do with the power of the courts to interpret and apply the law's generalities to particular cases. This also applies to the Courts' review powers as well. Through judicial review, courts can determine whether or not state executive acts and state legislative acts, in the form of statutes, are valid (Gifis, 1973 p. 138).

In Georgia, the last three courts, namely, the superior courts, the Court of Appeals, and the Supreme Court, have high status because they have appellate powers and they are courts of unlimited (or general) jurisdiction, which can and do handle all types of legal cases, civil and criminal. By unlimited or general jurisdiction we mean that all three courts can and do handle all types of legal cases, civil and criminal. The general concept of jurisdiction speaks to "the range of legal authority (of the court) to hear and determine a case" or more specifically, the authority to enforce laws or pronounce legal judgments (Gifis, 2003). A descriptive overview of the various types of courts and their respective jurisdictions—unlimited and limited jurisdictions—is presented in the following pages. But first, how do Georgia judges get to Court?

Judicial Appointment in Georgia

For the most part, the Georgia State Constitution provides that almost all judges to Georgia Courts are elected by the people even if their initial appointment are done by the Governor. Georgia's first judicial nominating commission was established in 1972 by the executive order of Governor Jimmy Carter. Since then, each subsequent governor has followed Carter's example, maintaining what is called an "assisted appointment" method for filling court vacancies. As indicated below, under the current process in the State of Georgia, the commission recommends candidates for three courts only: the Court of Appeals, the Superior Court, and the Supreme Court. The judicial nominating commission consists of eighteen members, each appointed by the governor. For each listed court vacancy, the commission recommends five candidates (unless fewer than five are found to be qualified), but the governor is not bound to the commission's choices and may choose to appoint a judge not found on the list.

In the United States the methods of selecting state court judges vary widely among the states but can be placed into five broad categories—*legislative appointment, executive appointment, nonpartisan election, partisan election, and merit selection.* In many states, more than one method of selecting judges is used, with different selection methods for judges at different court levels or in different geographic areas. Even when the same selection method is used for all judges in a state, there are variations in how the process works in practice. The terms of office for judges and the procedures used to determine whether judges will retain their seats also differs from state to state. So, for example, Georgia uses varied methods of selection.

First, for judges of the Supreme Court, Court of Appeal and Superior Courts, the *assisted appointment* process is used for fill vacancies. When positions became vacant in these three courts occur these are known generally as interim vacancies. Under assisted appointment process (also known as the merit selection or the Missouri Plan) the governor chooses an appointee from a list of qualified candidates compiled by the judicial nominating commission. The interim judge selected must run in the next general election held at least six months after the appointment, and, if confirmed by voters, they may finish the rest of their predecessor's term. **Second**, for judges for the Juvenile Court, Magistrate Court, and State Courts varying selection methods are used that include mix of appointment, partisan elections, and nonpartisan elections. So, for example, in Georgia, judges of the probate courts compete in partisan elections, while other trial elections are nonpartisan (see Table 7.1 on the following page).

In the end, the *assisted appointment* method of judicial selection in Georgia only sets the stage for an electoral process of selecting judges by the people under either the nonpartisan or partisan election process. The motivation for either kind of judges is unclear and if known, is debatable. The fact is that the selection of judges through the ballot box on nonpartisan basis as initiated in the 1800s was intended to lessen political influence. Because many reformers in the early 1800s advocated for nonpartisan contested elections where voters select a candidate at the polls, the names of judicial candidates appeared on the ballot without party labels. Over the years things would change and different variations of the same emerge. Today there may be a primary election, followed by a general election but conducting judicial elections that are truly nonpartisan can be difficult.

A few "nonpartisan" election states (Michigan and Ohio are the notable examples) require a judicial candidate to win a party primary or are nominated at a party convention, before being placed on a nonpartisan ballot in the general election. In addition, recent federal court rulings (see *Weaver v. Bonner*, 309 F.3d 1312 [11th Cir. 2002]) have weakened States' ability to limit judicial candidates' participation in or affiliation with a political party, a trend that will likely undermine nonpartisan elections over time. In partisan elections as done in the state of Georgia, judicial candidates usually run initially in a party primary to win nomination before standing in the general election, in which party affiliation is indicated on the ballot.

In 2002, the U.S. Court of Appeals for the Eleventh Circuit held unconstitutional two provisions of Georgia Code prohibiting candidates from personally soliciting campaign contributions and a prohibition on

Table 7.1	Georgia Courts, Judicial Selection & Term of Office	
Georgia State Courts	**Mode of Judicial Selection**	**Term of Office**
Supreme Court	Nonpartisan election *	6 years
Court of Appeals	Nonpartisan election *	6 years
Superior Courts	Nonpartisan election *	4 years
Probate Courts	Partisan election**	4 years
Juvenile Courts	Appointed by the superior court judges of the circuit**	4 years
Magistrate Courts	Partisan contested elections or appointed for varying lengths**	4 years
State Courts	Nonpartisan election**	4 years

*Interim vacancies are filled by assisted appointment where the governor chooses an appointee from a list of qualified candidates compiled by the judicial nominating commission. If appointed, the interim judge must run in the next general election held at least six months after the appointment, and, if confirmed by voters, they may finish the rest of their predecessor's term.

**Employ varying selection methods, mix of appointment, partisan elections, and nonpartisan elections.

The assisted appointment method of judicial selection (also known as the merit selection or the Missouri Plan), is a process by which the governor appoints state judges with help from a commission or board nominating candidates instead of the Governor. Thirty-four states and the District of Columbia currently use some form of assisted appointment.

Source: Various source by author Georgia State Politics; see also discussion of selection methods by the *American Bar Association, A "How-to" Series to Help the Community, the Bench and the Bar Implement Change in the Justice System,* June 2008; *American Judicature Society, Judicial Merit Selection: Current Status,* 2011.

using or participating in the public communication of false, fraudulent, misleading, deceptive, or misrepresentative material. *Weaver v. Bonner*, 309 F.3d 1312 (11th Cir. 2002).

Unlimited and Limited Jurisdictions

Courts of Unlimited Jurisdiction

Moving up the hierarchical ladder, the first type of court with unlimited jurisdiction in the State of Georgia is the Superior Court. In practice Superior Courts are courts of both exclusive and unlimited (general) jurisdiction that are charged with the power to hear cases that involve state law. As provided by the 1983 Constitution, superior courts hear civil and criminal cases as well as felonies in the forty-eight superior court circuits in the State of Georgia. Unlike the Court of Appeals and the Supreme Court with appellate jurisdictional powers (charged with the authority to hear but not try cases), superior courts are primarily courts of first instance.

The Georgia Court of Appeals is the second court of unlimited jurisdiction which functions primarily as a court of first appellate review for many civil and criminal cases moving up from the Superior Courts in Georgia. For the most part the Court of Appeals hears cases that have already been tried by the state trial and superior courts, if the Supreme Court has no exclusive appellate jurisdiction over the subject matter. The purpose of such a review (whether performed by the Court of Appeals or the State Supreme Court) is to look for, and if found, correct any legal errors or errors of law made at the trial level; it is not supposed to alter jury verdicts or the outcome of bench trials. The Georgia Court of Appeals was established by a constitutional amendment of 1906. Under the 1983 Constitution it became a court of review which exercises appellate and certiorari jurisdictions in all cases not reserved to the Supreme Court.

The third court of unlimited jurisdiction is the Supreme Court, which also is the state's highest court and the court of last resort. It functions as an appellate court as well as a review court. More importantly, its jurisdictional authority is unlimited (see Table 7.4). The 1983 State Constitution provides that the Supreme Court shall be a court of review and shall exercise exclusive appellate jurisdiction specified cases. Thus, it exercises exclusive appellate jurisdiction in (a) all cases involving the construction of a treaty or of the Constitution of the State of Georgia or of the United States, and all cases in which the constitutionality of a law, ordinance or constitutional provision has been drawn in question; and also (b) all cases of election contest. And (c) the Supreme Court also has general appellate jurisdiction over decisions made in civil and criminal cases by a trial court or by the Court of Appeals.

The Supreme Court of Georgia also exercises general appellate jurisdiction on cases involving title to land, equity, involving wills, habeas corpus, extraordinary remedies, divorce and alimony cases, certifications to it by the Court of Appeals, and all cases in which a sentence of death has been imposed or could be imposed. Additionally, the Supreme Court may answer any question of law from any state or federal appellate court and may review by certiorari cases in the Court of Appeals which are of gravity or great public importance. Lastly, the Supreme Court has the power to make such orders as are necessary in the aid of its jurisdiction or to protect or effectuate its judgments. Ordinarily, trials are not held at the appellate level nor are parties to such cases invited to appear or testify before either the Court of Appeals or the Supreme Court. In the rare event that attorneys are invited to present oral arguments, such arguments are heard by a full court.

Courts of Limited Jurisdiction

In contrast to the courts of unlimited jurisdictions, the following four types of lower courts—the magistrate, probate, juvenile, and the state courts—are courts of limited jurisdiction. Their powers are prescribed by law for the kind of cases they are called upon to hear and render judgment. Some of the courts are created and their jurisdictional powers conferred by the State Constitution and others are said to be established by statutes (that is, laws made by the legislature or the General Assembly) and municipal and county ordinances. However, the lower courts are similar in the sense that their range of legal authority to hear and determine cases is limited to the very specialized types of cases they are called upon to determine. A descriptive overview of the scope and powers of the various courts of limited jurisdiction is presented below.

First, magistrate courts in the state of Georgia are created by county governments and therefore are primarily county courts. Under the 1983 Constitution, formerly justice of the peace courts, small claims courts, and county court were unified to a new name, namely, the magistrate courts. They are primarily courts of first resort quite distinct from Municipal Courts which are creations of city or municipal governments. These courts have uniform jurisdiction as provided by law. Both types of courts have uniform jurisdiction and for the most part are courts of limited jurisdiction with primary authority to handle county and municipal ordinances violations and preliminary hearings for certain kinds of criminal cases.

Specific to magistrate courts, their jurisdictions include minor civil and criminal offenses in violations of county ordinance where civil claims accepted for resolution within their civil jurisdictions must not exceed $15,000. For the most part, cases typically handled by county magistrate courts include the issuance of arrest warrants, preliminary hearings that often include sitting as court of inquiry (binding an accused over to a higher court or ordering a discharge), the administration of oaths, affidavits, performing marriages, or issuing bail for defendants. In civil cases, the jurisdiction of magistrate courts extend to contract cases, property damage, injury or conversion cases, landlord-tenant disputes, and deposit account fraud (bad checks). In Georgia, magistrate courts do not offer jury trials, and even where a proper request for a jury trial is made, the case will be transferred (not appealed) to a Superior or State court.

A second category of lower court is the Juvenile court. There are 159 juvenile courts in the 159 counties in the state of Georgia. As specialized courts, they have exclusive and original jurisdiction over minor juvenile matters. However, jurisdiction over those juveniles who commit very serious or otherwise violent capital offense jurisdiction resides instead in the superior courts. Additionally, while there is one juvenile court each per county, in some counties juvenile courts have concurrent jurisdiction with superior courts in child custody and child support matters arising from divorce cases, as well as in proceedings to terminate parental rights. In Georgia, juvenile courts handle cases involving deprived and neglected children under 18 years of age; delinquent and unruly offenses committed by children under 17 years of age; and traffic violations committed by juveniles. They also hear cases involving consent to marriage for minors, enlistment of minors in the military, and procedures for return of a runaway child resident who is taken into custody in another state.

The probate court, formerly courts of ordinary, is a third type of court of limited jurisdiction in the State of Georgia. Probate courts have both original and exclusive jurisdictions in the probate of wills and inheritance, the administration of decedents' estates, appointment of guardians, issuance of lunacy commissions, and the issuance of marriage licenses. Probate judges are also authorized to order involuntary hospitalization of an incapacitated adult or other individual and to appoint a legal guardian to handle the affairs of certain specified individuals. Probate courts also supervise the printing of election ballots and the counting of votes, and in some counties they have jurisdiction over traffic and issues of compulsory school attendance laws.

The fourth category of court of limited jurisdiction in Georgia is the state court. As a class of courts they exercise limited jurisdiction within a county. State courts are established by local legislation introduced in the Georgia General Assembly to handle minor criminal and civil cases in the larger urban counties and thus in that sense serve as a backup for the superior courts since they handle almost an identical type of cases. So for example, state courts would hear misdemeanors cases to include traffic violations, issue search and arrest warrants, hold preliminary hearings in criminal cases, and try civil matters so long as they are not committed exclusively to the jurisdiction of the superior courts. There are 70 state courts in the State of Georgia, with roughly 122 state court judges in the entire state. They are elected to four-year terms in county-wide nonpartisan elections. However, ordinal vacancies on State courts are filled by an appointment made by the Governor and when this happens, the appointed judges would then sit in competitive nonpartisan elections when the initial appointment lapses.

In summary, the judicial branch of the State of Georgia consists of seven constitutional courts of limited and unlimited jurisdictions. Their jurisdictional powers range and vary from exclusive to general powers. Among these powers are the appellate and exclusive powers conferred to these constitutional courts especially to the Courts of Appeal and the Supreme Court of Georgia.

Other Quasi-Judicial Institutions

In addition to the courts noted previously, the general assembly may authorize the establishment of municipal courts and allow some administrative agencies to exercise quasi-judicial powers. When municipal courts are created, they are courts of limited jurisdiction in that they have jurisdiction only over violations of city laws, or ordinances, and such other jurisdiction as provided by law. For example, the City Court of Atlanta has unique status in the Georgia Judicial System in that it blends municipal court powers, magistrate court powers, and civil court powers. Whenever such courts are created, they are said to be endowed with "original jurisdiction." This means that a person can begin the resolution of their legal issue by first going to that court for resolution of the problem. Often the scope of powers of these minor courts overlap with existing constitutional courts which often have the same original jurisdiction, thus allowing parties to go to convenient forums with their litigation. However, if a party is unhappy with the decision of the lower court, that person may appeal to a higher court, which will have the power of "appellate jurisdiction" and the authority to reverse the lower court's decision. Lower courts cannot reverse the decision of appellate courts.

Also, there are special units within some agencies that look like courts and function like courts, but are not really judicial courts at all. These are "quasi-judicial" units or administrative courts created by legislature and the authority to hold hearings into alleged violations of administrative laws (rules and regulations made by bureaucracies) These units usually have an officer called an administrative law judge (ALJ) who specializes in

Figure 7.2 We Have the Final Decision
Courtesy of Lee. M. Allen

administrative law; functioning independently of the unified legal system, except of course for appellate courts' judicial review. As the trend toward an administrative state continues, such functional quasi-judicial units will become more common.

It should be noted that the powers of juries, judges, and courts are likely to be diminished when legislators push to establish a system of mandatory sentencing guidelines, because it takes sentencing discretion away from these institutions. For example, under a constitutional amendment enacted in 1996, the General Assembly may now enact legislation, which if approved by two-thirds of the members in each house would provide for the imposition of sentences of life without parole both for persons convicted of murder, and for those convicted for a second offense involving murder, armed robbery, kidnapping, rape, aggravated child molestation, aggravated sodomy, or aggravated sexual battery.

Another recent constitutional amendment provides authorization for the creation of special pilot projects for courts. These may serve as venues for experiments in social policy. In some jurisdictions, they might for example be used to minimalize incarceration for non-violent drug offenses, which can clog up the prisons while violent criminals may avoid prison terms or be let out early because of budget constraints. The General Assembly may enact legislation providing for, as pilot programs of limited duration, courts which are not uniform within their classes in jurisdiction, powers, rules of practice and procedure. Similarly the standards for selection, qualifications, terms, and discipline of judges for such pilot courts and other matters can now be enacted by the General Assembly. Although the constitutional amendment specifies that the new pilot courts created by the Georgia General Assembly shall not deny equal protection of the laws to any person, any kind of special treatment of particular kinds of accused persons should always be subjected to careful scrutiny.

Historically, a wide variety of other courts have existed under Georgia's prior constitutions. These include *Justice of the Peace Courts, Small Claims Courts, county recorder's courts,* and *civil courts.* However, these varied courts generally ceased to exist on June 30, 1983, (the date the new Constitution went into effect) unless they were incorporated into the present system. While the presiding officers of these courts had a variety of titles, the old and honorable title of "judge" is used to include magistrates, judges, senior judges, and even Justices of the Supreme Court. It is usually a good idea to address them as "Your Honor," and to address Supreme Court members as "Justice."

The power of judges is strictly limited by the Constitution. Judges can only react to existing cases and controversies properly brought before them. However, judges are mobile within the court system, and often substitute in other courts, if they are requested to do so, and if they have permission from the judges of their own court. In general, each court in the system may exercise only those powers necessary for it to perform its constitutional or statutory duty. However, in Georgia excluding the lower courts (i.e., the magistrate, probate, juvenile, and state courts), only the superior and appellate courts have the power to issue any of the following historical writs; notably, *mandamus, prohibition, specific performance, quo warranto,* habeas corpus *and injunction.*

As a relic of early English common law, a writ as a formal written order issued by an administrative or judicial body (a court) enjoining the person to whom it is issued to do or refrain from some specified act. Some writs are positive and some are negative. For example, the writ of mandamus is a positive order directed to state officials to do their duty; when duly issued, specific performance enforces private contracts; and prohibitions and injunctions prevent specified actions from being committed or performed. In the end, each superior court, state court, and other courts of record in the State of Georgia may grant a new trial on any legal ground they may deem proper and necessary.

The Unified Judicial System

All courts of the state comprise a unified judicial system, according to Article VI, Paragraph II of Georgia Constitution which provides that all courts of the state shall comprise a unified judicial system. Georgia's courts can be roughly divided into three different categories (see Table 7.4). As discussed above the *courts of limited jurisdiction* are the first category of courts most Georgians encounter. They only hear certain specific types of cases and are local to their city or county. Courts in this category include magistrate courts, juvenile courts, probate courts, state courts, and municipal courts.

The second category of courts is the *Superior Courts* which hear serious crimes and larger civil cases in dollar amount. The superior courts are the state's trial courts of general jurisdiction. The courts are divided into 10 judicial districts, with 49 circuits and 205 judges (see Table 7.3). Each county has its own superior court. In Georgia therefore, certain types of cases must go to superior courts; and others may go to superior courts.

The third category of courts is the *Courts of Appeal* which review, and sometimes change, the rulings of the lower courts if an appeal is filed. An appeal would go first to the Court of Appeals of Georgia and from there, either party can ask for further review from the Supreme Court of Georgia, which is the highest court in Georgia.

The jurisdiction of the Georgia *Municipal Courts* varies throughout the state. Whatever the jurisdictions of municipal courts may be, they are established by the cities' and towns' ordinances in Georgia that establish them. For the most part, these classes of courts handle traffic offenses, local ordinance violations, conduct preliminary hearings, issue warrants, and in some instances hear misdemeanor shoplifting and possession of marijuana cases. Unlike their counterpart constitutional courts in Georgia, municipal court judges are often appointed by local mayors while some are elected. As already noted there are more than 370 municipal courts operating in Georgia. However, all judges of municipal courts are members of the Council of Municipal Court Judges. The Council was created by Georgia Law 36-32-40 (2010) to further the improvement of the municipal courts and the administration of justice. The Council assists municipal court judges throughout the state in the execution of their duties and promotes and assists in their training of Municipal Court Judges (see Ga. Code Ann. § 36-32-40 [2010]).

As observed above there are two appellate-level courts: the *Supreme Court* and *Court of Appeals*. Except otherwise provided in any recently amended constitution, the courts of each class must have uniform jurisdiction, powers, rules of practice and procedure, and selection, qualifications, terms, and discipline of judges. However, probate courts are exempt from adhering to the uniform organizational or procedural standards.

The counties in Georgia are geographically divided into 49 *judicial circuits*, each of which has at least one judge. That is, each county has at least one superior court, magistrate court, a probate court, and where needed, a state court and a juvenile court. Some circuits are single county circuits and others are comprised of two or more counties. Sessions of court must be held in each county at least twice a year. The total number of superior court judges is 205. The number of judges per circuit ranges from one to 15. In rural areas with small case loads, the General Assembly may allow the judge of the probate court to serve as the judge of the magistrate court, but in the absence of a state court or a juvenile court, the superior court would exercise all of these jurisdictions. Superior courts have jurisdiction over title to land (see Table 7.3).

The Lower Courts

Centuries of experience have shown that cases should be handled locally where the issues and persons are well known. Forum shopping for judges who favor a particular point of view is generally prohibited. On some occasions however, when a case is brought to the wrong court, that court will transfer it to the appropriate court in the state having proper jurisdiction or venue.

Divorce cases are usually tried in the county where the defendant resides, but if the defendant is not a resident of the state, then it will usually be tried in the county in which the plaintiff resides. Special rules apply to military personnel or their dependents residing on any United States army post or military station. The specific exemption in the rules allows military personnel to file for divorce in any adjacent county to their current resident.

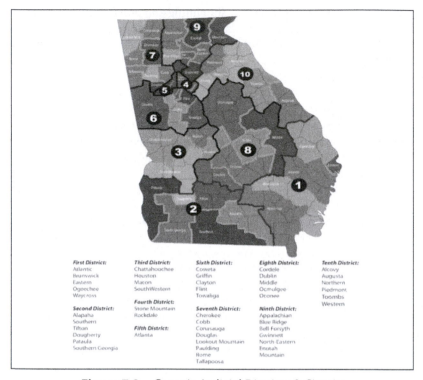

First District:	Third District:	Sixth District:	Eighth District:	Tenth District:
Atlantic	Chattahoochee	Coweta	Cordele	Alcovy
Brunswick	Houston	Griffin	Dublin	Augusta
Eastern	Macon	Clayton	Middle	Northern
Ogeechee	SouthWestern	Flint	Ocmulgee	Piedmont
Waycross		Towaliga	Oconee	Toombs
	Fourth District:			Western
Second District:	Stone Mountain	**Seventh District:**	**Ninth District:**	
Alapaha	Rockdale	Cherokee	Appalachian	
Southern		Cobb	Blue Ridge	
Tifton	**Fifth District:**	Conasauga	Bell-Forsyth	
Dougherty	Atlanta	Douglas	Gwinnett	
Pataula		Lookout Mountain	North-Eastern	
Southern Georgia		Paulding	Enotah	
		Rome	Mountain	
		Tallapoosa		

Figure 7.3   Georgia Judicial Districts & Circuits

See The Judicial Council of Georgia, the Administrative Office of the Courts,
http://www.eighthdistrict.org/images/Georgia-Circuits.jpg
http://www.georgiacourts.org/find-your-court?menu=main
http://www.eighthdistrict.org/images/Georgia-Circuits.jpg

Have you ever signed a loan for a car, or cashed a check written by a bank? If you have, and a legal problem develops, where can you be sued? Suits against the makers and endorsers of promissory notes, or the drawers and acceptors of bills of exchange or like instruments, will be tried in the county where the maker or acceptor resides. Special problems develop when there are multiple parties on one side of a lawsuit. Determining the proper venue (court with jurisdiction) is often a problem in multiple party cases.

Multiple parties may be joint obligors (owing child support), joint tort-feasors (two fraternity brothers hazing freshmen), joint cosigners or co-partners of a loan. Multiple party defendants may be tried either in their county of residence or in the county where the alleged offense occurred. All other civil cases, except juvenile court cases, are tried in the county where the defendant resides. Equity cases, such as injunctions in domestic disputes, are tried in the county where the defendant resides.

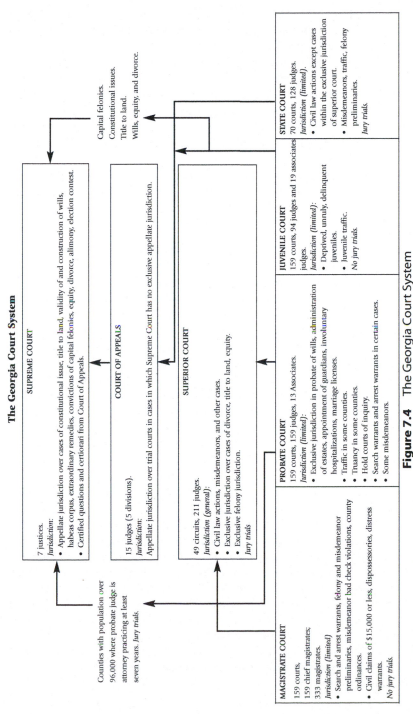

Figure 7.4   The Georgia Court System

Profile Supreme Court of Georgia reformulated with layout from *Administrative Office of the Courts*, *www.georgiacourts.org*, by authors, 2016

All criminal cases are tried where the crime was committed, except cases filed in the superior court where the judge is satisfied that an impartial jury cannot be obtained in that county. Superior courts have very broad jurisdictional powers. For example, except certain juvenile cases which are not within its jurisdiction, superior courts have exclusive jurisdiction over trials in all felony cases and in all cases with respect to titles to land; in divorce cases; and in equity cases. In addition, superior courts have appellate jurisdiction from municipal, magistrate, and probate courts—that is, a reviewing power to correct any legal mistakes that might have been made by the lower courts of limited jurisdiction.

Every week in Georgia, many hundreds of people are sent to prison. They are convicted of serious felonies such as murder, kidnapping, assault, robbery, and auto theft.

Justice Administration and Reforms

A popular approach throughout the nation to address any perception of an out-of-control criminal activity is to increase the size of its jails. As in most states, Georgia has followed that trend as well. In Georgia, the Department of Corrections is given the administrative responsibility to create a safer Georgia by effectively managing offenders and providing opportunities for positive change. To that end, an 18-member Board of Corrections is appointed by the Governor. One member each is drawn from the 14 congressional districts with four at-large members, all of whom must go through the consent of the Georgia State Senate. Collectively, their tenure is staggered for five-year terms of office. Functionally, the Board of Corrections is charged with the administrative duty to act as a policy-making statutory board. It also has the legal capacity of a board.

Administratively, the Board of Corrections is charged with developing the rules governing the conduct and welfare of employees under its authority. It administrates the assignment, housing, the feeding, clothing, treatment, discipline, rehabilitation, training, and hospitalization of all Georgia inmates under its custody; as well as all probationers sentenced to its supervision. Tied to their duties, board members also serve on the following committees: the Budget, Correctional Industries, Education/Programs, Facilities/Probation, Food & Farm, Health Services, Nominating, Operations, Recidivism, and Utilities. The actual daily operations and management of the Board of Corrections institutions, facilities, and probation systems are the responsibility of a Commissioner. This apparent painstaking setup process ensures accountability in the executive functions of corrections task in the State of Georgia which in turn instill confidence on those who pay the bill, the taxpayers.

With much talk about *criminal justice reform* on his arrival to office, Governor-elect Nathan Deal set into motion several initiatives drawn from his earlier campaign promises on reform. **First**, by signing of HB 1176, the criminal justice reform act in 2012 Deal laid what was termed "a foundation of cost-saving energy within Georgia prison facilities." An aspect of that bill was aimed at restoring judicial discretion that allowed judges to depart from the previously mandatory minimum sentences in "very limited circumstances." For example, a judge would have the option to decide a drug-related case where the defendant was not the ringleader of the criminal enterprise or in other situation where the prosecution, defense attorney, and judges agree. **Second**, in 2014, Governor Nathan Deal signed HB 349 into law, the so-called "second edition of criminal justice reforms" to implement "smart on crime" policies to "save tax dollars and promote public safety."

Interestingly, Governor Deal included into HB 349, a provision suggested by his Special Council on Criminal Justice Reform which recommended that the Department of Corrections put in place a new automated assessment instrument [the Next Generation Assessment (NGA)]. The NGA is a law enforcement tool designed to identify the risks of re-arrest, non-compliance, and criminogenic needs of offenders which was intended to give the Department of Corrections the ability to instantly retrieve pertinent security-related background information on each offender as well as assign offenders to specific programming based upon their specific needs. In a press release from the Governor's office, Mr. Deal maintained that "HB 349 was another step in the right direction in making Georgia smarter on crime...." and further that "... Public safety will be improved by giving prosecutors leverage in certain cases and by ensuring that our prison resources are reserved for the 'kingpins' while the 'mules' are given a chance at reform" [http://gov.georgia.gov/press-releases/2013-04-25/deal; Swift, 2013]

Third, advancements in criminal justice reform were also initiated with the signing of Senate Bill 365 into law. The purpose of the bill was intended to help rehabilitate offenders to successfully reenter society by removing barriers to employment, housing, and education. For example, it provided for creation and therefore for the Department of Corrections to create additional educational opportunities for offenders by establishing GED Testing Centers in all state prisons, thus making basic education more readily available to intimates. The FY2015 (House Bill 744) Appropriation was $1,162,580,006 in total funds and $40,554,658 in State funds with an additional FY2015 authorization of $12,675 to fill new positions. The overall fate of Governor Deal reform initiatives in all three phase is still in the air in 2016 although the Governor is already making victory laps for the success in all the phases.

Georgia's Jails and Their Occupants

According to a *HuffPost* article of September 2015, the United States has less than 5% of the World's population yet it incarcerates about a quarter of its citizen in prison—some 2.2 million people and according to a 2011 *Bureau of Justice Statistics*, one adult out of 34 is in some form of correctional control. Georgia is no exception to that trend. As one of the largest prison systems in the United States, in 2016 the *Georgia Department of Corrections* boast some 55,000 state prisoners, some 160,000 probationers and one of every 13 Georgian is in some form of correctional supervision.

To no surprise, Georgia's jails house about two thirds as many inmates as Georgia's state facilities. There are 146 jails serving Georgia's 159 counties, ranging from Schley and Evans (less than 10 inmates each) up to Cobb, Fulton and Gwinnett (over 2,000 inmates each) and the biggest—DeKalb (over 3,000 inmates). *Jailers Issue Monthly* reports that the Department of Defense break the populations of jailers into four groups: (1) inmates awaiting trial, (2) inmates serving state sentences, (3) inmates serving county sentences, and (4) "other" inmates, including municipal cases, private probationers, illegal immigrants, inmates are bound for the Federal system,.

First, inmates awaiting trial are the largest group—about 60% of the total. Growth in this group soared in the mid-1990s, when mandatory sentencing laws and severe parole policies came into effect, motivating ever-larger numbers of jail inmates to risk going to trial rather than plea-bargain to the certainty of a long prison term. The other three groups—state, county, and "other"—are roughly the same size.

Historically, about one in six Georgia prison inmates had been a first-time convict with a non-violent crime. In 2012 Georgia legislature passed HB1176, a Governor Nathan Deal initiative, with the aim to curb the growth of prison population by steering the least dangerous, least hardened offenders away from prison through pre-trial intervention, diversion, drug courts and treatment programs, and raising the dollar thresholds that define property felonies. The expectation was that over time, these measures will reduce the percentage of first-time non-violent convicts in Georgia's prison. In 2015 the result was mixed.

With approximately 12,000 staff, the Georgia Department of Corrections currently operates 40 state prisons, 24 county work camps, transitional centers, prisoner boot camps, or pre-transitional centers, 17 diversion centers, 13 detention centers, and two probation boot camps. Throughout Georgia's 159 counties there are 146 jail facilities with a combined rated capacity of 54,704 inmates. In the past 10 years, the inmate population in Georgia has doubled, giving the state the dubious distinction of having the country's fifth largest number of adults residing in prison. According to *U.S. Dept. of Justice Bureau of Justice Statistics*, in 2013, the crime rate in Georgia was about 16% higher than the national average of incarcerated adults per

100,000. According to the Georgia Department of Corrections, Georgia has released an average of 20,000 offenders per year over the last five years. Similarly in Georgia, the *Pew Center on the State* in 2011 reported that 21% of those who have max-outs are released with no supervision at all.

Property Crime and Crime Rate

Property crimes alone account for roughly 89.3% of the crime rate in Georgia which was number 8 with a 3281.2 per thousand in 2014, or a 20% higher than the national rate. The remaining 13.1% therefore, were violent crimes and was about 5% higher than other states. In 2014, Georgia had a probationers' rate 66% higher than the national average number of per 100,000 people. While taxpayers paid 39% lower than the other states per inmate in 2014, Georgia still came ahead of most states in case ration rate (Bureau of Justice Statistics, U.S. Dept. of Justice 2008–2010). The median property tax in Georgia is $1,346.00 per year for a home worth the median value of $162,800.00. Counties in Georgia collect an average of 0.83% of a property's assessed fair market value as property tax per year. Georgia is ranked number 33 out of the 50 states, in order of the average amount of property taxes collected. Georgia's median income is $60,114 per year, so the median yearly property tax paid by Georgia residents amounts to approximately 2.24% of their yearly income. Georgia is ranked 31st of the 50 states for property taxes as a percentage of median income. The exact property tax levied depends on the county in Georgia the property is located in. Fulton County collects the highest property tax in Georgia, levying an average of $2,733.00 *(1.08% of median home value)* yearly in property taxes, while Warren County has the lowest property tax in the state, collecting an average tax of $314.00 *(0.51% of median home value)* per year.

Overcrowding Jail

The Georgia State law provides that if you have a felony conviction anywhere in the United States and if you are then convicted of another felony in Georgia that does not require the death penalty, you must do the maximum sentence the judge gives you without the possibility of parole (i.e., early release in Georgia).

In 1994, Georgia imposed one of the toughest criminal penalty laws in the nation. The *two strikes* measure proposed by then-Governor Zell Miller in a run-up to his 1994 re-election campaign required judges to impose at least a 10-year sentence on anyone convicted a first time of any of the following seven crimes: *murder, armed robbery, kidnapping, rape, aggravated child molestation, aggravated sodomy,* and *aggravated battery.* Those convicted a second time must spend the rest of their lives in prison with no opportunity for parole and thus thousands have been sentenced under the two strikes law since the measure took effect in 1995.

Ten years later in 2005, critics were pointing to two important defects of the two strikes law; notably, *prison overcrowd* and *inflexibility*. Put differently, critics argued that the law was responsible for jamming state prisons and forcing judges to impose sentences that did not always fit the crime. In an *Associated Press* interview, Sunny Perdue, then Governor of Georgia at the time declined to seek legislative review of the harsh punishment or the two-strike law. While conceding that the effect of the two-strike are problems that may not have been foreseen when the laws were passed years ago, Perdue maintained that the situation was one that must be continually assessed (Pettys, *Associated Press*, January 04, 2005).

Thus far, the "three strikes and you're out" has been muted or has not found further discussion in the new reform initiatives carefully orchestrated by Governor Deal since 2011. This policy is a popular approach that addresses the perception of out-of-control criminal activities. Under this plan, an offender sentenced for a third felony, regardless of the gravity of the crime, automatically receives a life sentence.

In Georgia, this policy is known as "two strikes and you're out." It has been the chief culprit to much overcrowding and larger populations within jails/prisons. Sentencing more people require more beds, which leads to more prison construction to make it larger to fit more prisoners. Although there seems now to be a decrease in the crime rate, Georgia keeps sending more and more people to prison. Critics of this approach continue to argue that "locking up" more people (when the rate of crime is actually declining) is certainly punitive but has little or no effect on the overall rate of crime. It continues to be quite costly for the following reasons: (1) prison beds are expensive and must come at the expense of something else, probably higher education, if the experience of California is instructive; (2) prisoners who are not released early grow old in prison, and while in their middle and late age they pose little threat to society, they are likely to be in poor health and in need of expensive medical treatment, and; (3) prisoners with no hope for parole require much more scrutiny and control by prison personnel and tend to be more violent than prisoners who know that "good behavior" may get them released.

The measures Mr. Deal has pushed include giving judges more leeway in sentencing for low-level offenders and allowing charter schools into prison to help inmates get a high school diploma. Mr. Deal appreciates that most prisoners will be released eventually, so society has a big stake in ensuring they have help to find a job and avoid falling into a life that will send them back to prison.

The prison population has reduced while keeping crime low, and Georgia is not alone. According to Pew Charitable Trust study, from 2008 to 2013 the 10 states that instituted prison reforms and cut their incarceration rates saw a greater drop in crime rates than the 10 states that increased their prison populations most.

Discretionary Venue

People are not the only civil and criminal defendants. Legally, corporations can also be classified as persons, and can be regulated, sued, and punished for violations. Where for example, should a case involving a large company be tried? Is it where the company has its multi-million dollar headquarters or where its truck, for example, ran over a pedestrian on a rural road? In Georgia, the Constitution provides that questions of venue will be determined by the state legislature by statute. Nevertheless, the power to change the venue in civil and criminal cases is vested in superior courts. That is, such a power is reserved by law to the expert discretion of the presiding judge in a case.

The Higher Courts

The Court of Appeals consists of twelve judges who, like many of the administrative commissions discussed in the previous chapter, elect from among themselves a presiding officer, here called the Chief Judge. Members of the Court of Appeals may sit in panels of not less than three judges as prescribed by law or and by its rules.

Students should be mindful that the Court of Appeals is a court of review, it exercises appellate and certiorari jurisdiction. Unlike appeals that are styled as a matter of right of the petitioner, the writ certiorari is a discretionary review. Georgia Courts of Appeals therefore exercise appellate and certiorari review in all cases not committed to the Supreme Court or conferred on other courts by law. The decisions of the Court of Appeals set precedents that bind all courts except the Supreme Court. In Georgia, the Court of Appeals may also certify a question to the Supreme Court for clarification of a point of law, to which it will then be bound. Lastly, in the event of an equal division of the judges when sitting as a body, the case will be immediately transmitted to the Georgia Supreme Court.

The Supreme Court is composed of seven justices, who elect their own Chief Justice. That however had not always been the case. The first three judges to the Georgia Supreme Court were chosen by the General Assembly in 1846. The Constitution was amended in 1896 to provide for the addition of three justices to the Court and to provide that justices and the chief justice would be elected by the people. In 1945, 100 years after the creation of the Court, a seventh justice was added as required by the Constitution of 1945 and since that time the composition of the Court has remained the same. The Chief Justice of the Supreme Court acts as the chief presiding and administrative officer of the court. In other words, the Chief Justice has approximately the same role with regard to the court system that the Governor has with the bureaucracy.

The Justices also elect a Presiding Justice to serve if the Chief Justice is absent, disqualified, or otherwise is recused from a case. A majority vote is necessary to hear and decide cases. If a Justice is disqualified or recused from any case, a substitute judge from the superior court may be designated by the remaining Justices to serve. The Georgia Supreme Court is primarily a court of review, but relative to other state courts, it exercises exclusive jurisdiction in the following cases:

Table 7.2   Supreme Court's Exclusive Jurisdiction
1. In the construction of a state treaty,
2. the construction of the State Constitution,
3. in construction of the United States Constitution,
4. determining the constitutionality of a law,
5. the constitutionality of an ordinance,
6. interpretation of a constitutional provision,
7. all cases of election contest, and
8. answer questions of law from other jurisdictions.
Source: Compiled by authors

Unless otherwise provided by law, the Georgia Supreme Court also has appellate jurisdiction in the following classes of cases:

Table 7.3   Appellate Jurisdiction
1. Cases involving title to land;
2. in all equity cases;
3. all cases involving wills;
4. any habeas corpus cases;
5. cases involving extraordinary remedies;
6. all divorce and alimony cases;
7. cases certified by the Court of Appeals; and
8. cases in which a sentence of death was imposed or could be imposed.
Source: Compiled by authors

In addition to the classes of cases described above, the Supreme Court of Georgia may review by certiorari cases from the Court of Appeals which are of gravity or great public importance. The decisions of the Supreme Court bind all other courts as precedents. The Supreme Court is required, with the advice and consent of the council of the affected class or classes of trial courts, to issue orders adopting and publishing uniform court rules and record-keeping rules which shall provide for the speedy, efficient, and inexpensive resolution of disputes and prosecutions. Each council shall be comprised of all of the judges of the courts of that class. The Supreme Court and the Court of Appeals must dispose of every case at the term for which it is entered on the court's docket for hearing or at the next term.

There are also many judicial bureaucratic agencies, most of which operate under the oversight of the Supreme Court's administrative function. They supervise the state's practicing attorneys, create

Administrative District Councils, issue rules of court, and set standards in a wide variety of contexts. Twenty-four agencies are listed in *The Handbook of Georgia State Agencies*. Excluding the court entities already discussed above, these are listed on Table 7.3.

Controlling Judicial Personnel

Because of the neutral non-partisan orientation of the courts, and the special training of judicial personnel, the selection, terms of office, compensation, and discipline of Judges creates special problems. Superior court and state court judges are elected on a nonpartisan basis for a term of four years. The Judges of the Court of Appeals and the Justices of the Supreme Court are elected on a nonpartisan basis for a term of six years. In addition to age and residency requirements set by the state legislature, appellate, superior, and state court judges must have been admitted to practice law for seven years. Lesser experience is required for juvenile court judges who only need to have practiced law for five years. The level of experience for Probate and Magistrate judges is not set in the constitution, but rather by the General Assembly. Probate and Magistrate Judges are not required to have formal legal training. In fact, it is not uncommon in rural areas for these judges to lack any formal education beyond high school.

In the higher courts, legal training, a license to practice law, and extensive experience in the courts is expected. When Justice George T. Smith lost his legal challenge to the mandatory retirement age, Governor Miller appointed an experienced replacement. The newest Georgia Supreme Court Justice was a 36-year-old African American woman whose appointment was deemed "a dream comes true" (*Associated Press*, 1-18-92, p. A3). Judge Leah Sears-Collins (later Leah Ward Sears), was at the time of her appointment in 1992 a trial court judge in Atlanta who became the first woman and the youngest justice to sit on the Supreme Court of Georgia.

Her appointment was followed by the appointment by Governor Miller of yet a second woman, Carol W. Hunstein that year. These two women, along with Justices Benham and Melton, both African American males, gave the Georgia Supreme Court a truly representative composition in 1992: two women, one an African American and another white woman, two African American males, and three white males. Thirteen years later, in 2005, Justice Sears was elected by her fellow justices to be Chief Justice of the Supreme

Court of Georgia thus becoming the first African American woman to serve as Chief Justice of any State Supreme Court in the United States.

During her tenure, Chief Justice Sears earned a reputation as a justice committed to upholding both an independent judiciary and the rule of law. Chief Justice Sears served in that capacity until her retirement in 2009. She was succeeded by Carol W. Hunstein, the second female Justice who also became the Chief Justice to the Supreme Court of Georgia in 2009.

The unique training required to qualify as a judge sometimes makes it difficult to select candidates who are ideally representative of all of the various identity and interest groups in the State of Georgia.

The 202 Superior Court and appellate court judges receive compensation and allowances as provided by law, and may also receive county supplements. County governing authorities have authority to supplement salaries under the current Constitution. Over 800 judges who serve in the lower courts are paid by their respective entities. An incumbent's salary, allowance, or supplement cannot be decreased during the incumbent's term of office. Additionally, all judges must reside in the geographical area in which they are selected to serve. The age of 75 years is the mandatory retirement for

Table 7.4   Georgia Judicial Agencies
State Bar of Georgia Board of Bar Examiners District Attorney's Offices Judicial Administrative District Councils Judicial Council and Administrative Office of the Courts
Judicial Qualifications Commission Judicial Nominating Commission for the State of Georgia Council of Juvenile Court Judges Council of Magistrate Court Judges The Council of Probate Court Judges of Georgia Executive Probate Judges Council of Georgia Advisory Council for Probation Prosecuting Attorneys' Council of the State of Georgia The Council of State Court Judges of Georgia Superior Court Clerks Training Council The Council of Superior Court Judges of Georgia Superior Courts Sentence Review Panel
The Institute of Continuing Judicial Education of Georgia Board of Court Reporting of the Judicial Council
Georgia Indigent Defense Council
Source: After Jackson, E. L., *The Handbook of Georgia State Agencies.* (Athens, Georgia: Institute of Government, Univ. of Georgia, 1975).

Figure 7.5   Beneath the Robes
Courtesy of Lee. M. Allen

all judges. The Georgia judicial structure is depicted on Figure 7.1. In a nutshell, the Georgia court system consists of courts of limited, general, and appellate jurisdictions. It has five classes of trial-level courts: the magistrate, probate, juvenile, state, and superior courts. All of these also include the approximately 350 municipal courts operating locally within the state of Georgia.

Judicial Vacancies and Removals

Article Six, Section VII, Paragraph III of the Georgia Constitution specifies that routine judicial vacancies will be filled by appointment by the Governor (except as otherwise provided by law). Generally, an appointee to an elective office serves until a successor is duly selected and qualified, following the next general election which is more than six months after such person's appointment. In Georgia, the Governor does not have the power to suspend or remove a judge for misconduct. Instead, the power to discipline, remove, and cause involuntary retirement of judges is vested in the Judicial Qualifications Commission.

The Judicial Qualifications Commission consists of seven members. Two are judges selected by the Supreme Court; three are members of the State Bar elected by the Board of Governors of the State Bar; and two are non-lawyer citizens appointed by the Governor. Any judge may be removed, suspended, or otherwise disciplined for willful misconduct in office, or for willful and persistent failure to perform the duties of office, or for habitual intemperance, or for conviction of a crime involving moral turpitude, or for conduct prejudicial to the administration of justice which brings the judicial office into disrepute.

In the unusual circumstance that a judge is indicted for a felony by a grand jury of the state or of the United States, the Attorney General or district attorney will inform the Judicial Qualifications Commission. The commission then reviews the indictment, and determines whether the indictment adversely affects the administration of the office or the rights and interests of the public. If so, the commission will suspend the judge immediately, pending the final disposition of the case or until the expiration of the judge's term of office, whichever occurs first.

It should be noted that indictments are not convictions, and sometimes are motivated by political considerations. If an indicted judge who is suspended from office is not immediately tried at the next regular or special court term, the suspension will be terminated and the judge will be reinstated to office. If the indictment is not prosecuted, or if the judge is acquitted, or if the conviction is later directly overturned, the judge shall be immediately reinstated to the office.

When a judge is suspended, he or she will continue to receive a salary. Furthermore, the commission does not review the indictment for a period of 14 days from the day the indictment is received. During this period of time, the indictment may be quashed, or the judge may resign or authorize the commission to suspend him from office. Any such voluntary suspension is subject to the same conditions for reinstatement, or declaration of vacancy as for a non-voluntary suspension. After any suspension is imposed, the suspended judge may petition the commission for a review. If then the commission determines that the judge should no longer be suspended, it may reinstate the office.

Of course, immediately upon initial conviction for any felony, the Constitution requires that the judicial official must be immediately suspended from office, and may not receive any more salary, allowance, or compensation. But if the conviction is later overturned and the judge is reinstated to the office, then he is entitled to receive any back pay. For the duration of any suspension, the governor will appoint a replacement judge. And upon a final conviction with no appeal or review pending, the office shall be declared vacant and a successor to that office will be appointed by the governor as described above.

It is interesting to note that the sunshine law does not apply to the Judicial Qualifications Commission. The findings and records of the commission, and even whether the judge has or has not been suspended, is not open to the public; nor is it admissible in evidence in any court for any purpose. Accordingly, no action shall be taken against a judge except after hearing and in accordance with due process of law. Also, no removal or involuntary retirement shall occur except upon order of the Supreme Court after review. However, any judge may be retired for disability which constitutes a serious and likely permanent interference with the performance of the duties of office. Because there is no perfect political or judicial system, and yet our society needs to inculcate a general trust in these systems, problems are downplayed and an internal peer review method is used to prevent widespread abuse of judicial misconduct.

The State Attorney General

According to the National Association of Attorneys General, the attorney general is elected in 43 states, as well as in Guam, and is appointed by the governor in only five states (Alaska, Hawaii, New Hampshire, New Jersey, and Wyoming). Georgia's Constitution Article V Section III provides for the office of the Attorney General who also heads the Department of Law in Georgia. As mentioned in Chapter 5 under plural executive, the Attorney General (AG) is *popularly elected* at-large as one of the six executive officers who serve as part of Georgia's plural executive as provided in the Constitution of the State of Georgia. Thus, unlike the federal Constitution, the Constitution of the State of Georgia does not vest most of the executive power in one office.

As the Attorney General or Georgia's chief legal officer the occupant of that office, while serving a distinct role (see Table 7.5), also serves as a vital link between the executive, the legislative, and the judicial branches of government in the State of Georgia. Just as states existed before the federal government came to existence, in the State of Georgia there was an office of the Attorney General long before there was a formal State Constitution and the State Supreme Court. In one way, the history and reputation of that office suggest that there was in the State of Georgia a need that precedes the necessity for a Supreme Court. Ironically, the turbulent political history and debate that led to creation of the Georgia Supreme Court on own stead provide further evidence to understand the importance of the office of the Attorney General.

Officially, the office of Attorney General dates back to 1754 when King George II appointed William Clifton, an English lawyer, as the first Attorney General of the State of Georgia. *But was Clifton the first to serve in that capacity in the nascent territory?* It depends how one set up the details of recoded history and here is why. Preceding Clifton was Williams Stephens, though a non-lawyer, who was selected in 1737 to serve as an *unofficial* counselor to Colonial officials under Georgia's first form of government adopted by the Trustees of the Colony. The Colonial Charter of 1732 had no provision for the office of an Attorney General. With the expiration of the Royal Charter in 1753, the institution of a more conventional form of government ushered the appointment of a Governor who was provided with the powers to constitute the Courts and define its powers.

It is a reasonable argument that when William Clifton was appointed by King George II as the Attorney General of the State of Georgia in 1753, he was indeed the first *formal* AG but not necessarily the first person to occupy or serve as counselor to Georgia's Colonial officials. As noted above, William Stephen had served in that capacity in 1737. Carol Ebel in her 2015 *New Georgia Encyclopedia* article on William Stephens provides a pointed overview of Stephens's role in the colonies from his nomination in 1837 and 1838. A view which correlates more with the conclusion that he was functionally Georgia's first Attorney General. For example, in Ebel's own assessment of William Stephens' work with the Colonial Government from his nomination on November 1, 1737, she surmised that while Stephens possessed no authority to make executive decisions, "he acted as an impartial observer who used his legal knowledge to provide sound advice."

Charged with the task of designing Georgia's court system, the new Attorney General William Clifton's plan presented to the Governor on December 12, 1754, constituted what by most account is the origin of the Georgia Judicial system. Many years after and almost 10 Attorney Generals later (between 1753 and 1798), the Georgia Constitution of 1798 and 1868 would grant the Governor with the powers to appoint the AG and made explicit the qualifications and duties of the occupier of that office. For example, while the Judiciary Act of 1797 made the duty of AG to be primarily the prosecution of criminals, the post-Civil War Constitution of 1868 made the Attorney General a constitutional officer, and for the first time the legal advisor to the Governor and other executive departments of the State of Georgia. The entry to the office remains by gubernatorial appointments as first appeared in the Constitution of 1798 as well the requirements for residency, citizenship, age, and bar membership in the 1868 Constitution.

Today, the Department of Law is headed by the Attorney General and organized into five legal divisions and one division of operations. There is an "Attorney General Division" which includes the front office, a Special Prosecutions Unit, the Counsel to the Attorney General, and the Communications Office. The Attorney General is the chief law enforcement officer of the state, but the duties of the Department of Law is carefully circumscribed by law. So for example, the law prohibits the Attorney General from providing legal advice or assistance to the private citizens. However, the Georgia Constitution and the Official Code of Georgia gives the Attorney General the authority to offer opinions regarding various legal issues on behalf of the State of Georgia or its agencies. The Attorney General also has the authority to represent the State of Georgia in capital felony appeals before the Supreme Court of Georgia and in civil cases before any court within the state, in the United States Supreme Court, or any state in the United States. According to the National Association of Attorneys General, the Attorney General is elected in 43 states, as well as in Guam, and is appointed by the governor in five states (Alaska, Hawaii, New Hampshire, New Jersey, and Wyoming).

Similarly that office is also charged with the powers to prosecute public corruption cases. That office therefore may bring criminal charges against any person, persons, business, or businesses involved in illegal activity with the State of Georgia. The Department of Law may also conduct investigations regarding questionable activity concerning any state agency, department, person, or business that has engaged in business with the State of Georgia. Finally, among its other duties is the power to initiate (or not) any civil or criminal action in accordance with the expressed request of the Governor of the State of Georgia, prepare all contracts and agreements for matters that involve the State of Georgia, and lastly, serve as a legal advisor for state agencies, departments, authorities, and the Governor of the State of Georgia (see Figure 7.4).

The complexity of the multi-headed executive branch in Georgia, and the role of the Supreme Court as a political actor, is illustrated by a dispute that arose in 2003 between the Republican Governor Sonny Perdue and the then occupier of the office of the Attorney General of the State of Georgia, Democrat Thurbert Baker. In the unsettled conditions prevailing as conservative Republican partisans began to rise to prominence, Mr. Baker was perhaps the most powerful of the old guard Democratic officeholders. He was initially appointed to office in 1997, and then was elected and re-elected in statewide elections in 1998, 2002, and 2006. Mr. Baker received

---

Table 7.5   The Duties of the Attorney General of Georgia

- To serve as the attorney and legal advisor for all state agencies, departments, authorities, and the Governor.
- To provide opinions on legal questions concerning the State of Georgia or its agencies, which are binding on all state agencies and departments.
- To represent the State of Georgia in all capital felony appeals before the Supreme Court of Georgia.
- To represent the State of Georgia in all civil cases before any court.
- To represent the State of Georgia in all cases appearing before the Supreme Court of the United States.
- To prosecute public corruption cases where criminal charges are filed against any person or business for illegal activity when dealing with the State of Georgia.
- To initiate civil or criminal actions on behalf of the State of Georgia when requested to do so by the Governor.
- To prepare all contracts and agreements regarding any matter in which the State of Georgia is involved.

Source: Georgia State Constitution Article 5, Section 3, Paragraph 4.

a Bachelor of Arts degree from the University of North Carolina at Chapel Hill in 1975 and a law degree from Emory University's School of Law in 1979.

In addition to being an active member of his community, Mr. Baker also served as a lawyer for the U.S. Environmental Protection Agency and had managed his own firm prior to his appointment and subsequent election as the Attorney General of the State of Georgia. But when Sonny Perdue was elected governor and tried to order Mr. Baker to drop a legal appeal involving a democratically drawn legislative redistricting map, the Attorney General dug in his heels and refused to do so, citing his constitutional independence from the governor. The Georgia Supreme Court sided with Baker in *Perdue v. Baker*, affirming the separation between the two offices (see post decision below). At the very limit, the issue the Georgia Supreme Court was called to answer in that case was whether *the Governor of the State of Georgia had the legal authority to direct the attorney general not to proceed with litigation involving state government.* Put differently, who has the ultimate power over litigation on behalf of the State of Georgia—the Governor or the Attorney General?

In April of 2004, a Fulton County Superior Court judge had sided with Baker, but Perdue appealed to the Georgia Supreme. According to the Superior Court Judge Constance Russell "The current Governor's honest belief that a different course might be better cannot override the duty of the executive branch of government to enforce and uphold the laws of the State of Georgia." At the time of Governor Perdue's request for withdrawal of the case to the AG, even if the Superior Court agreed with Perdue, it could have been impossible for the U.S. Supreme Court to agree to withdraw a case it has already heard. Because lawyers can't be ordered to do just anything a client wants, such as file a frivolous lawsuit, the governor could very well direct the Attorney General to go forward with a case, but cannot direct the Attorney General *to not go* forward.

Because of the imminent consequence of the outcome of the Governor Perdue case for structure of power throughout Georgia State government, the decision of Georgia Supreme Court could (a) maintain status quo or (b) give the Governor control over the other statewide elected executive-branch officials (the commissioners of insurance, agriculture and labor, the secretary of state and the superintendent of schools). The outcome as the case did not look good for the Governor as he perhaps expected. The table offers statements from each about how they felt about the decision of the Supreme Court of Georgia.

In 2010, Mr. Baker mounted a campaign for the governorship, but was defeated in the primary by the former Governor Roy Barnes, who unfortunately was also defeated in the general elections in the November 2010 election by Nathan Deal.

Table 7.6   *Perdue v. Baker* 2004
Does the Governor of the State of Georgia have the legal authority to direct the Attorney General <u>not to proceed</u> with litigation involving state government? NO, but the answer could be yea if what the Governor requests is not illegal. The Attorney General cannot carry out illegal orders. It is that simple.
Statement of Attorney General Thurbert Baker After Georgia Supreme Court's Decision in *Perdue v. Baker,* September 5, 2003
"Today's ruling by the Georgia Supreme Court is a clear victory for the people of Georgia and a win for good government. I am extremely gratified by the decision, which affirms the Attorney General's independent authority to pursue legal actions which are in the best interests of the people of Georgia. I am also heartened that the Court's decision upholds the important checks and balances drawn into the Georgia Constitution and statutes, and enables me to continue to independently discharge my duties as the duly-elected Attorney General and chief legal officer of this State." "I cannot thank enough our legal team who worked many long days and late nights on this landmark case. In particular, I would like to recognize. . . . ". . . undertook this representation on a strictly pro bono basis at no cost to the taxpayers of Georgia. Their willingness to put their beliefs in good government and the independence of the Office of the Attorney General above financial considerations speaks volumes as to their integrity and professionalism, and I am extremely proud to have had them represent my office in this case."
Statement of Governor Sonny Perdue regarding the Georgia Supreme Court decision in *Perdue v. Baker,* Thursday, September 4, 2003
"I am deeply troubled by this decision. The Georgia Supreme Court was presented with an historic opportunity to make a crucial decision concerning who legitimately serves as the client on behalf of the State of Georgia and who serves as the legal counsel. Today, the Court missed that opportunity to decide this serious constitutional issue and left us with more questions than answers. The people of Georgia would all do well to study this decision and others to determine their impact on our state. "I am comforted by the fact that two Justices of the Georgia Supreme Court saw clearly the constitutional issue at stake. They followed the common-sense, plain wording of the constitution and statutes in deciding the Governor's role as the client, stating that 'only one official of the executive branch can control the course of litigation and, according to the Constitution of this state, that official is the Governor.'"

The successor to Mr. Baker is Mr. Sam Olens, who upon election became the 53rd person to hold that title in the State of Georgia. Sworn since January 10, 2011, Sam Olens not only became Georgia's Attorney General but the head of the Department of Law. As his predecessors, as the Attorney General, he serves with fidelity the people of the State of Georgia by defending and upholding the U.S. and Georgia Constitutions and the rule of law. Mr. Olens is a 1983 graduate of Emory University School of Law. Prior to being elected to Attorney General, Mr. Olens was Chairman of the Cobb County Board of Commissioners where he served as Commissioner from August 2002 through March 2010. A registered mediator/arbitrator with the Georgia Office of Dispute Resolution, Olsen is admitted to practice law in Georgia and the District of Columbia.

How one understands the role of the Attorney General depends on how they understand the formally stated powers of the Attorney General presented in (Figure 7.5). So for example, is the occupant of that office limited to the listed powers as they appear there? Put differently, is the Attorney General's duties more expansive than provided by law? Is the Attorney General a law maker or a law enforcer; a legislator or executive? Must he carry out all orders from the governor or only those have legal and moral soundness? These questions are worth keeping in mind as you are invited to read the actual Court case that led to the case as was presented in Court. It is also important to understand the principle at stake and the importance of separation of powers and checks and balances. An important consequence of the case *Perdue v. Baker* 2004 is that it help established independence in the department of law.

Olens' key initiatives since becoming the Attorney General in 2011 has been on issues supporting government transparency for which he worked closely with the Georgia State Legislature for the passage of open government legislation HB 397, for which Governor Nathan Deal signed into law on April 17, 2012. There is also the Open Government Mediation Program, an initiative offered by the Attorney General's office designed to assist members of the public in general in filing a complaint if they establish that their local governments may not be complying with requirements of the Open Meetings Act or the Open Records Act. Specifically, it allows citizens who have complaints with their local government, who may not be complying with the requirements of the Open Meetings Act or the Open Records Act. Mr. Olens also took liking with securing water rights for Georgians and curbing incidence of human trafficking, particularly child sex trafficking, across the state. For example, in 2011, he worked with state legislators to strengthen penalties for sex trafficking, making Georgia's law one of the toughest in the nation.

In 2012, he spearheaded the first comprehensive revision of Georgia's sunshine laws in more than a decade. In 2013, he led the effort to stem the epidemic of prescription drug abuse with a law that requires pain management clinics to be licensed and regulated. In 2014, Olens spearheaded a video contest among Georgia's high school students to increase awareness of prescription drug abuse. Olens has also worked to protect Georgia's rights and natural resources. He is defending Georgia from federal regulatory overreach and has represented the State in crucial litigation to preserve our water rights, while removing legal barriers that were delaying the critical deepening of the Savannah Harbor. In addition to co-chairing the Federalism/Preemption Committee, he serves on the following committees: Energy and Environment, Substance Abuse, Human Trafficking, Law Enforcement and Prosecutorial Relations, Internet Safety/Cyber Privacy and Security.

Mr. Olens' first five years in office presents an opportune time to ask whether his tenure has been predicated on upholding the laws as he finds them and therefore uphold the independence of his office, or has he yielded instead to the political branches of leadership or guidance and if so, how?

District Attorneys

Another significant official in the state's legal system is the district attorney. The Constitution mandates a district attorney for each judicial circuit, who is elected circuit-wide for a term of four years. More specifically, the Constitution required that all successors of present and subsequent incumbents are elected by the electors of their respective circuits at the general election held immediately preceding the expiration of their respective terms. It also requires that vacancies are filled by appointment of the governor. The qualifications include having been an active-status member of the State Bar of Georgia for three years immediately preceding such person's election. The district attorneys receive such compensation and allowances as provided by law and like some judges may also receive local supplements to their compensation and allowances.

It is the duty of the district attorney to represent the state in all criminal cases in their superior court and in all cases appealed from the superior court or the juvenile courts and to perform such other duties as shall be required by law. District attorneys enjoy immunity from private suit for actions arising from the performance of their duties. Any district attorney may be disciplined, removed, or involuntarily retired as provided by general law (see Article VI, Section VIII).

Transitional Notes

The City Court system of Atlanta survived the constitutional revisions of 1983. In addition, the municipal courts, county recorders' courts, and Civil Courts of Richmond and Bibb counties, and several of the administrative agencies having quasi-judicial powers, also continued with the same jurisdiction as these courts and agencies had when the 1983 Constitution went into effect. On the other hand, justice of the peace courts, small claims courts, and magistrate courts operating on the effective date of the new Constitution and the County Court of Echols County became magistrate courts. The County Court of Baldwin County and the County Court of Putnam County became state courts, with the same jurisdiction and powers as other state courts. Reshaping of court systems and jurisdictions, along with the redistricting of legislative seats, and the redefinition and existence of municipalities and special purpose authorities, is part and parcel of the ferociously and ever-changing face of American federalism.

Conclusion

The structure and functioning of the state judiciary in Georgia is unique. It is perhaps the most traditionalistic of the branches of government. The power of the judiciary, and indeed the courts are seemingly dispersed among many agencies and jurisdictions. And judges, as members of the legal profession, are immersed in centuries of legal lore and tradition pre-dating democratic government itself. To a great extent, the profession attempts to embody what Daniel Elazar calls the basic traditionalistic ethic: a political actor attempting to carry out a positive role in the community, but limited to securing the continued maintenance of the existing order. However, unlike the historical monarchies and aristocracies that created judicial function, the members of the modern American judiciary are not expected to benefit personally from their activities.

Similarly, over time, the professional members of the regular public services, the career administrators, and bureaucrats, may be expected to develop a similar high level of status and acceptance. However, the British judiciary existed for hundreds of years in a dependent relation with the British crown, before judges achieved constitutional independence in the Americas. If a similar amount of time is necessary for the various public administrators to achieve equal status in their own fields, it is no wonder that bureaucrats have a long way to go to match the esteem currently given to the judicial branch of government in the State of Georgia.

Key Terms

Administrative Law Judge
Appeal
Appellate Jurisdiction
Certiorari

Court of Appeal
Department of Law
Discretionary Venue
Exclusive Jurisdiction
Immunity
Judicial Circuit
Jurisdiction
Judicial Qualification Commission
Limited Jurisdiction
Magistrate Court
Original Jurisdiction
Sunshine Law
Superior Court
Supreme Court
Unlimited Jurisdiction
Vested Powers

Essay Questions

1. Discuss the hierarchical order of the seven constitutional courts in Georgia.

2. In what way does the City Court of Atlanta have a unique status in the Georgia legal system?

3. Explain the state of Georgia's "two strikes and you're out" policy. How is it related to prison overcrowding?

4. Explain the structure of the Georgia Supreme Court and address each court's jurisdiction. You should also detail each court and their respective numbers.

5. Compare and contrast the appointment of judges/justices and the nonpartisan election of judges/justices.

6. Who are the members of the Judicial Qualifications Commission in Georgia? How does the Judicial Qualifications Commission impact the removal of judges/justices in the state?

7. What is the role of the Department of Law and the Attorney General within the Georgia State Government? What is the relationship, if any, between the Department of Law and the Supreme Court of the State of Georgia

Figure 8.1 Georgia Department of Revenue
Courtesy of Lee M. Allen

Budgeting and Finance

What does budgeting and general economics have to do with state government? Isn't it true that government doesn't have to budget because it has unlimited income mainly from tax dollars? Actually, this myth about government could not be more wrong. Every state government, including Georgia's, has a constitutional requirement to carefully budget its money. In fact, arguments over how to obtain budget money and how to spend it constitute the bulk of all political conflict. Politics can be defined as the struggle over who gets what, when, and how (Lasswell, 1936), but most political battles take place over who pays what, where, how, why, and when. The state's fiscal (budget) year runs from July 1 to June 30, and every day sees conflict over finances. This section begins with taxes.

As the chief executive official in the State of Georgia, the governor oversees the state budget and therefore possesses great power over all state finances. Additionally, the governor is responsible for the nomination of over a thousand officials to a variety of positions in state government, one of the largest rosters of any U.S. state. Those nominated however, must be approved by the state legislature. Georgia statutes that control these processes are codified as *Rules and Regulations of the State of Georgia*. The budget of a government is a summary or plan of the intended revenues and expenditures. There are three types of government budget: the operating or current budget, the capital or investment budget, and the cash or cash flow budget.

State Taxes and Revenues

Like all the rest of us, states have to pay their bills. Unlike the United States Government, which does not separate operational budgets and capital budgets, all states, except for Vermont, have to balance their operational budgets. An operational budget includes the expenses for ongoing routine operations. In contrast, a capital budget is used for expensive long-term building projects such as highway and bridge construction. While it is recognized that building projects may have to be funded by bonds and other debt-creating instruments, most Constitutions usually require that operational budgets must be paid for on an ongoing basis. That is,

Figure 8.2   Georgia 2016 Fiscal Statistics
Source: U.S. Debt Clock, at March 6, 8:18 pm.
http://www.usdebtclock.org/state-debt-clocks

states cannot spend more than they take in as revenue. Thus, they must have revenue sources that provide enough income for them to meet their needs and responsibilities each year.

Because Georgia sells bonds to borrow money for capital projects, the state is in debt, like the other states, like the federal government, like most home owners; indeed, like most people. The total indebtedness of the State of Georgia as of March 2016 was about 6.5 billion dollars (U.S. Debt Clock, Georgia). In fact, every Georgian owed about 5.5 thousand dollars when per capita debt is calculated into account. Why corporations are not included in this figure is unknown to the authors.

It should be noted that the entire debt is only about one tenth of state GDP and less than half of annual revenues. The average household should be so lucky! The residents of Georgia have less than half of the debt burden of the average state, and only half of the per capita debt burden. The State of Georgia has low taxes and a sound fiscal structure.

The tax powers of the state are too valuable to be left only to the fads and fancies that buffet our politicians. Article VII of the Georgia Constitution deals with taxation and finance. It places the power to tax with the General Assembly, although that power may be delegated in part to local governments. Currently, the bulk of Georgia's revenue comes from three sources: ad valorem taxes, income taxes, and sales taxes.

Ad valorem is a Latin term meaning "according to the worth." An ad valorem tax is a tax determined by the value of that which is taxed. Those of you who own cars know that you have to buy license tags for your car each year. In addition to a small license tag fee, which varies from county to county in Georgia, you used to have to pay an ad valorem tax on the value of the automobile. But if your car was an old *junker*, there might not be an ad valorem tax assessed. Under new laws when you buy a car, especially a new or relatively new car, you may have to pay hundreds of dollars according to the value of your vehicle. Because of variations in local government tax levels, the amount that you pay can vary markedly from county to county.

Ad valorem taxes on automobiles are reported to be among the most popularly detested levies in the nation. When the Republican candidate for Governor of Virginia came up with the idea of eliminating the ad valorem tax on automobiles in the Commonwealth, his candidacy took off, and he won the 1997 race going away. In 1998, a number of gubernatorial candidates in several states, including Guy Milner, the GOP nominee in Georgia, followed Virginia Governor Gilmore's lead in running against this tax. Milner, however, lost the election.

The county, acting as a subdivision of the state, also collects ad valorem taxes on tangible personal property and tangible real property. Tangible personal property includes all manner of possessions—jewelry, furs, boats, and even money itself. Tangible real property is real estate—land. Since land cannot be moved or hidden, it is a stable source of revenue for the government. Over time, states have allowed local governments to assess the property tax and to keep the proceeds to defray their own expenses. Because land is used for a variety of purposes, and the purposes often determine its value, differently used property is taxed differently. For example, agricultural land is taxed at 75% of the value of other land, and the land on which you live is entitled to a homestead exemption, a reduction of the taxes you would otherwise pay.

Only nine states lack a state individual income tax. Georgia is not, certainly not, one of them. In Georgia the personal income tax is a very important source of revenue for the state. Based, at least in theory, on the ability to pay, the income tax is progressive, meaning that the more income you earn, the more tax you pay. If a tax is designed so that people with small incomes pay a smaller percentage, it is called a regressive tax. However, the progressive scale is somewhat flat, so that for example in 2011 income exceeding $7,000 was taxed at a maximum rate of only 6.0%. Thus, a person earning over one million dollars a year would pay at the same rate as a person earning only $7,001.

Like the ad valorem tax, the income tax is also unpopular. Republicans in the 1998 Session of the General Assembly promised to try to repeal the income tax over a period of several years. However, they could not muster the necessary votes, partly because they couldn't figure out how to replace all that lost revenue. They were no more successful in the next two sessions, where they barely mentioned what was clearly a scheme whose time had not yet come. In addition to the individual income tax, Georgia, like 46 other states, levies an additional income tax on corporate profits. Similarly, like 45 other states, Georgia has a sales tax. Although it is officially set at 4%, counties may add an extra 1% local option sales tax and an additional 1% special local option sales tax providing the latter is approved by the local citizens in a voting referendum.

In 1996, voters approved an amendment to the Georgia Constitution permitting school districts to add another Special Local Option Sales Tax (SPLOST) if they could get a majority of the voters to agree to it. Agreement would allow one more penny to be added to the overall sales tax. Usage of the basic 4% sales tax and the 1% optional tax is fairly standard throughout the state; but the additional special 1% tax is earmarked for use only for special capital building projects—such as a new courthouse, a new jail, road construction—and has an automatic "sunset" provision which acts to terminate the tax within five years or less of its approval. The same provisions apply to the school district SPLOST. With all these *piggyback* sales taxes, many people in Georgia pay sales tax of 7%.

It is common for progressive states to try to exempt from sales taxes certain necessities such as food, medicine, and clothing so that sales taxes will be less burdensome on poor people. Although Governor Zell Miller recommended in 1990 that certain food items be exempted from the tax, and the Georgia legislature then passed laws to that effect, the wording of the law was subsequently challenged in court and the State Supreme Court invalidated the food exemption because the language was unclear and confusing. When the Governor and the General Assembly pass a tax or a revenue bill, the Supreme Court gets a shot at it, and of course eventually it can go full circle back to the legislature.

In 1996, the General Assembly again passed a law which exempted food from the sales tax and which would be fully effective by 1998. Thus,

Figure 8.3   Juggling the Budget
Courtesy of Lee. M. Allen

food joins some 60 other sales tax exemptions in Georgia, including Bibles and the fuel used to heat chicken houses. In the 1998 Session of the General Assembly, bills were introduced to exempt from sales taxes Boy Scout popcorn, wheelchairs, children's caskets, crop dusting planes, grass sod, and about a dozen other things (*VD Times,* February 12, 1998, p. 3-A). Although its sponsor argued that the Boy Scout popcorn provision would only result in a loss of about $11,000 a year in revenue, and besides it was only fair since Girl Scout cookies are exempt, all of these tax exemptions add up to a sizable amount. The exemption on food alone is estimated to cost the state treasury about half a billion dollars every year.

In addition to the major forms of taxes described above, Georgia also collects revenue from a variety of other types of taxes. These include the so-called *sin* taxes on alcohol and tobacco products; severance taxes on lumber products taken from state-owned lands; and motor fuels taxes on every gallon of gasoline sold in the state. The motor fuels tax revenues are then earmarked for building and maintaining the state's fine system of roads and highways.

In the 1980s, many states joined a growing movement to derive some revenue from legalized gambling, but Georgia lawmakers at first resisted the temptation to establish a lottery or pari-mutuel betting on horse racing. The success of the lotteries in other states, however, put great pressure on Georgia legislators and in 1991 the General Assembly passed a bill placing a constitutional amendment for a state lottery on the November 1992 ballot, to allow the citizens to make their voices known on the issue. The voters spoke, and approved the budget amendment. In the first state budgetary period of operation, the proceeds from the lottery were over $879 million, including a surplus of income over expenditures of approximately $28 million in additional revenue for the state (see O.C.G.A. §§50-27-1–50-27-34, 1992).

This was a substantial vindication of the governor's plan. However, financial experts caution us not to rely too heavily on these funds, because as the novelty of the new lottery wears off, sales might decline, so that future income from this source may be less than hoped for. In fact, by 1998 there were signs that interest in the Georgia Lottery was indeed tapering off. However, by that time over $550 million a year was going to education in Georgia. Moreover, the anticipated decline in lottery interest was apparently premature. In FY 2006, the Georgia lottery had its best year ever.

Are Georgians overtaxed or undertaxed? That may sound like a silly question, for whoever feels that he or she is undertaxed? Objectively, however, when Georgia is compared to other states, how does Georgia fare? In a recent year, per capita state and local tax revenue in Georgia was around $1,800, which placed Georgia 32nd among the states. And, when this per capita state and local revenue is examined as a percentage of personal income, Georgia ranked 37th. In other words, Georgia ranks below the median both in terms of the amount of taxes collected from the average person and according to the amount that each person could afford to pay (Dye, 1997, p. 508). Tax-paying Georgia citizens can be thankful that, comparatively, Georgia ranks as a rather low-tax state. By signing into law the $100 million tax cut in 1994 and a $205 million reduction in 1998, Governor Miller reduced the tax burden even further.

How about the distribution of the tax burden? Are Georgians fairly taxed according to income levels? Again, that might sound like a silly question, because no one ever thinks his or her own tax burden is fair. And the fact is that Georgia ranks 27th in the nation in terms of tax progressivity (Gray and Herbert, 1996, pp. 314–315). That means that Georgia is slightly less fair than the average in assessing taxes in proportion to ability to pay.

Does Georgia need tax reform? Many economists and political scientists argue that it does. Although a study of state tax systems in 1990 showed that Georgia's system was particularly elastic and therefore likely to be able to withstand fiscal crises, by the time the study was published, Georgia, like the rest of the nation, was in fact beginning to experience growing fiscal crisis (Gold, 1990, pp. 31–33). Owing to the increasing severity of the Great Recession of 2008, personal income in Georgia was down, while personal misery was on the rise. With a decline in federal grants in aid to the states, a decline in state revenue collections, and an increase in necessary operating expenditures, Georgia, like the rest of the states, was in serious fiscal trouble. To be sure, other states were suffering worse, but the knowledge of that did not ease our pain very much. Editorials in major newspapers like the *Atlanta Journal/Constitution* and other influential voices around the Peach State raised the cry for meaningful fiscal and tax reform.

Another suggestion for reforming Georgia's tax system is to tax services along with the sale of commodities. In an economy more and more dependent on services, it makes sense to tax car washing, dry cleaning, haircuts, lawyer's fees, dentist's fees, etc. Moreover, since those with higher incomes tend to spend more of their money on services than those with lower incomes, a tax on services would be more progressive than sales taxes on commodities. Whether the General Assembly will seriously consider tax revision, especially if it entails new taxes, depends largely on whether the state experiences another fiscal crisis.

But surpluses are rare. One *solution* that the state has to fall back on when confronted with budgetary shortfalls is raising user fees or by borrowing. The instrument by which debt is incurred is called a bond. When the state sells bonds, with a promise to buy them back with interest, it borrows money. Bonds may be either general obligation bonds or revenue bonds. A general obligation bond, in a sense, creates a lien on all the taxpayers of the state, since the guarantee of repayment to the buyers is placed on the *full faith and credit* of the state. This means that future tax revenues will be used to retire the bonds when they come due. A revenue bond, on the other hand, is retired with the revenues from particular money-making enterprises (e.g., tolls from bridges, fees from water and sewer systems, profits from education loans). Should those revenues fall short, however, the investors would be in danger of diminished or no returns, or even losing their investment entirely. For that reason, revenue bonds are riskier than general obligation bonds and must offer higher interest rates to capture investment capital. Allowable reasons for state debt are depicted on Table 8.1.

Article VII, Section IV of the Georgia Constitution addresses the matter of state debt. Paragraph I of that section contains a list of six purposes for which the state may incur debt. The purposes include crisis events, like debt to repel invasion, for suppression of insurrection; and more routine problems such as temporary cash flow shortages or problems financing local governments or special projects.

The ability of a state to sell bonds to investors depends largely on a state's bond rating. The higher a state's rating, the more attractive its bonds are on the bond market. The two principal bond rating agencies are Moody's and Standard and Poor's. Moody's gives Georgia its highest rating (AAA), while Standard and Poor's put Georgia in its second highest rating category (AA+) (AJ/AC, Jan. 13, 1994).

Table 8.1   Allowable State Indebtedness
1. Public debt without limit to repel invasion, suppress insurrection, and defend the state in times of war.
2. Public debt to cover for a temporary deficit in the state treasury in any fiscal year created by a delay in collecting the taxes of that year.
3. General obligation debt for: a. capital budgets to acquire and develop land, waters, highways, buildings, or facilities of the state and its agencies and authorities. b. educational facilities for school systems and public libraries. c. loans to political subdivisions and local authorities, for water or sewerage facilities.
4. Guaranteed revenue debt obligations issued by instrumentality of the state for: a. Toll bridges or toll roads, b. land public transportation facilities, c. water facilities or systems, d. sewage facilities or systems, e. loan programs for citizens for education.
Source: Compiled by authors.

Georgia State Budget

State budgets are determined by economic conditions and the aspirations of its people and leaders. In 2002, the General Assembly responded to Governor Barnes's continuing state development plans and passed a $16.1 billion budget for FY 2003. This budget included $625 million in revenue from the lottery, dedicated to education, and this level of lottery income will, one hopes, be a constant revenue source for the foreseeable future. In 2006, well into Georgia's *Republican Revolution*, Governor Perdue recommended a $17.4 billion budget, including $811 million in revenue from the lottery. The state's political parties may talk like they are worlds apart, but in fact they basically react similarly in meeting the needs and desires of the general population.

By far the largest single expenditure goes to school districts for primary and secondary education, over six billion dollars. Over three billion dollars is also spent for basic human resources and for health care which is becoming more expensive each year. Nearly 1.8 billion dollars was appropriated for higher education: universities, colleges, technical training, and adult education. And despite a slight reduction in crime levels, public safety and protection costs over a billion and a half dollars also.

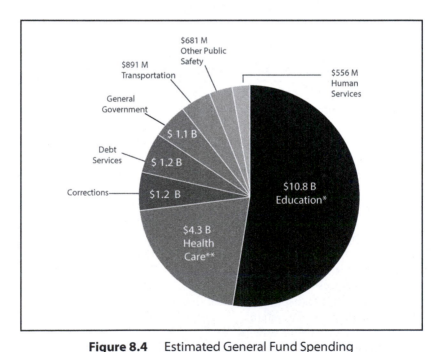

Figure 8.4   Estimated General Fund Spending
Source: Georgia Budget & Policy Institute. 2015. *Georgia Budget Primer 2016,* page 15.
Internet at: http://gbpi.org/georgia

Table 8.2   Compare Georgia State Appropriations and Expenditures

Departments/Agencies	FY 2004	FY 2005
General Assembly	—	33,304,450
Audits and Acc'ts	28,419,231	28,443,466
Judicial Branch	—	151,569,708
Admin. Serv. Dept	37,517,312	28,629,573
Agri/Forest/Soil	77,617,148	74,236,576
Banking & Fin.	10,217,590	9,850,558
Comm. Affr. Dept	92,731,539	73,887,133
Comm. Health Dept	2,011,823,963	2,147,704,748
Defense Dept	8,098,333	7,407,075
Early Care & Learn	260,696,996	274,081,522
Econ. Devel. Dept	36,523,339	25,812,690
Educ. St. Bd.	5,917,260,821	5,933,991,990
E'ee. Ret. Sys.	617,000	617,000
Gov. Office	32,287,900	36,085,865
Human Res, Dept	1,369,004,995	1,372,493,288
Insurance Office	15,954,891	15,573,172
Juv. Justice	269,525,852	265,188,338
Labor Dept	52,681,121	48,925,839
Law Dept	14,284,933	13,229,060
Law Enforce/Prisons	1,118,709,725	1,069,405,642
Merit System	—-	—
Motor Vehicle	78,678,802	77,218,681
Natural Res. Dept	91,995,916	90,744,022
Pub. Sch. Eee. Ret. Sys.	1,420,898	1,420,896
Public Serv. Comm.	8,525,022	8,073,708
Regents, Bd. of	1,632,486,526	1,658,443,732
Revenue Dept	486,853,675	460,305,370
Sec. of State	34,138,096	35,407,299
Student Fin. Comm.	470,454,458	538,248,636
Teacher Ret. Sys.	2,173,044	2,138,000
Tech. Adult Educ.	300,344,227	288,122,395
Transportation Dept.	674,016,210	646,858,968
Veterans Service	22,630,531	21,017,073
Worker's Comp.	16,646,671	14,503,707
Gen. Oligat. Debt	675,479,942	923,167,993
TOTAL FUNDS	**15,829,696,526**	**16,376,087,996**

Source: Georgia Office of Planning and Budget, The Governor's Budget Report Amended FY 2005 & 2006 (Feb. 2007), p. 114.

Roughly half a billion dollars is spent for capital construction projects, and for transportation construction and repairs. The remaining monies are spent for a wide variety of miscellaneous activities, like economic development, agricultural programs, and for purchasing land to preserve environmental resources. The following tables display a breakdown of the state budget that was prepared by Governor Deal for 2016. Arguing over the distribution of government revenues in Georgia is as American as apple pie. Public school education gets the biggest slice of the pie in Georgia, well over one third. Large pieces go to health care, human resources, and to higher education. Smaller pieces go to prisons and to roadway and other heavy construction projects. A large portion of the budget goes to miscellaneous projects within departmental agencies. The Pei chart in Figure 8.4 provides a fair representation of Georgia s budget.

Educational Expenditures

Although local school boards administer school district policies, the funding is largely controlled by state authorities. One of the principal responsibilities of most state governments is public education, and Georgia is no exception. In fact, Georgia devotes more than half of its entire budget each year to primary, secondary, and higher education. This educational turf is divided between two major bureaucracies: the State Board of Education and the State Board of Regents. The great bulk of the state appropriations is allotted to the secondary and grade school institutions, over ten billion dollars most of which is supervised primarily by the State Board of Education.

Overall responsibility for administering Georgia's system of primary and secondary education rests with the State Board of Education. It makes policy for the state education systems, sets standards for teacher education programs, certifies teachers, establishes minimal salary levels, imposes graduation requirements, etc. Its members represent each of the congressional districts and are appointed by the governor and confirmed by the state senate. Members of the State Board of Education serve for seven-year terms. As discussed in Chapter 3, the State School Superintendent is the chief executive officer of the State Board of Education, but local school district superintendents actually control the schools' operations and budgets.

State Income Sources

Investigation of any subject, issue, or concern in government almost always leads discussants to the subject of money; how much is needed against how much is available. The State of Georgia is certainly not any exception to this generalization. It should not be forgotten that there are over 1,400 local governments in Georgia. As explained in the next chapter, each of these local government operatives in Georgia is a taxing entity, funding and serving the variety of needs of the state's socio-economically diversified citizenry. Some of their money is locally raised and spent, but much of it comes from Georgia State Revenues.

State Income Sources and Budget

Income in the State of Georgia, known as revenue, is derived from a variety of sources. Included in income sources are the two largest: income taxes and sales taxes. Others include such taxes as motor vehicle licenses, the so-called sin taxes on alcoholic beverages and tobacco, and property taxes entire budget each year to primary, secondary, and higher education. This educational turf is divided between two major bureaucracies: the State Board of Education and the State Board of Regents. The great bulk of the state appropriations is allotted to the secondary and grade school institutions, over six billion dollars ($6,084,626,829), most of which is supervised by the State Board of Education. The lottery, passed by the voters as a constitutional amendment, has proven to be a rather phenomenal success. It will be generating revenues from the Georgia Lottery Corporation of over a billion dollars in years to come (OPB, 2007). Now, in 2016, there is talk about permitting gambling casinos to open in Georgia.

Faced with such figures, even the most die-hard opponents of the lottery plan threw in the towel. One writer said: *"accept it for what it is . . . a voluntary, flat rate tax of 37% on every dollar spent on the lottery"* (Wooten, 1993, p. F7). That is pretty good for a sin tax, in fact it is a heavier tax than state governments impose on any other *bad habit*. This is also a big economic boom for the state treasury, and is likely to remain so, at least until all the other states adopt a similar lottery. While Georgia commits the money to educational purposes, some experts believe it would be wiser to shift the money into the general fund, or for special one-time projects (Wooten, 1993, p. F7). But however you cut the pie, it looks as though it is here to stay.

When the sales tax was enacted in Georgia, a very small tax was applied to most purchased goods, initially excluding services. Today, the early low sales tax has risen to more than 4%, and as a result the state's lowest and middle income citizens pay higher percents of their income into the state's coffers. This "regressive tax" (harder on poor people) has, however, become so critical to Georgia's budget that it is not anticipated that any substantial change will take place in the near future. More critical is federal government largess.

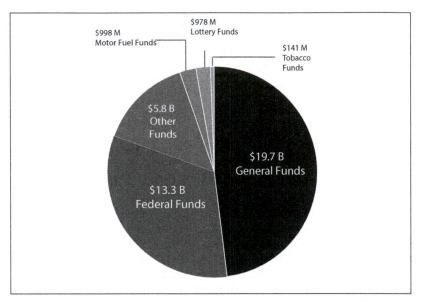

Figure 8.5   Estimated Total 2016 Revenues: 40 Billion Dollars
Source: Georgia Budget & Policy Institute. 2015. *Georgia Budget Primer 2016,* page 13.
Internet at: http://gbpi.org/georgia

Income to the state from federal sources is substantial in Georgia, estimated to be over 13 billion dollars in 2016. Because of the traditional reluctance of our citizens to accept the strings attached to federal money (and the penalty of increased federal control of state interests), the income from such sources is not as much as it might be. In fact, the State of Georgia receives among the lowest per capita for federal funding from grants in the entire United States.

The means of management of the State's budget is established in the State's Constitution which prohibits borrowing money for each year's current operating budget. All state operations are, therefore, on a pay-as-you-go system. Unfortunately, often revenues dribble in years behind times, because of structured payment schedules or because of delinquent taxpayers. The figure below shows the proportion of these major revenue sources in a pie chart form. Although the State does meet its constitutional limits in spending, by generally limiting itself to anticipated revenues it collects, each biennial session of the legislature, as well as the increasingly frequent special sessions, must engage in constant juggling of funds to balance the budget. The State Reserve fund is used to fill in occasional gaps.

One reform often suggested to control over-inflated budgets is the exercise of the governor's line item veto power. Former Governor Miller used this power on several celebrated occasions, against the secret legislative educational slush fund (Lauth & Reese, 1993, pp. 15–16) and as well as an indigent legal services fund and a provision involving excess federal funds (Ibid, p. 16). But a recent study has shown that this may be an over-rated power. As the researchers indicated:

> The line-item veto is used in Georgia as an instrument for resolving inter-branch difference on appropriations bills, but it is not a[n] instrument of partisanship, and it is not primarily an instrument of fiscal restraint (Lauth & Reese, p. 21).

Local Government Expenditures

Sometimes opportunity knocks, and government must meet the demands of the increasingly competitive global economy. In 1996 the City of Atlanta played host to the International Olympic Games. The construction projects involved, but more importantly the increased global image of Atlanta (and Georgia) as an international economic player, were worth billions of dollars in trade and tourism in the future. To help the economy, the State of Georgia granted a charter to a special purpose entity named the Metropolitan Atlanta Olympic Games Authority, (MAOGA). Following the lead of Los Angeles, MAOGA was determined to support the Games by private financing and donations, without direct substantial governmental subsidies. The bulk of revenues came from selling television rights, corporate sponsorships, ticket sales, and merchandise proceeds; but, of course, some governmental support was necessary, even if it was only utility hook-ups and public safety protection.

Such governmental support was offered by a wide variety of county and city entities. For example, the Atlantic City Council elects a number of its members as board members of special purpose government authorities, and MAOGA is no exception to the rule. The city also worked closely with the Atlanta Committee for the Olympic Games (ACOG), a private sponsor. One measure of city participation in the Olympic effort was its support of negotiations between ACOG and the Atlanta Braves organization. The ACOG proposed to build a new stadium in downtown Atlanta, and then to lease it to the Braves for 20 years; but the Braves demanded that the city agree to maintain the facility for the duration of the contract. Faced with a threat to move the team from the downtown area if the new stadium deal was not approved, the city agreed, but only after the Braves' organization agreed to sweeten the pot with annual maintenance payments totaling about four million dollars during the course of the contract (Blackmon, 1993, p. H4). After this effort, similar talks began with the Fulton County Commission, another player in this complex issue. In short, budgets tend to grow from year to year, even when big projects are not underway.

Although city governments are mere creatures of the state, and are almost certain to lose in any power contests with the state or federal

Table 8.3 Program Revenues and Expenses Compared

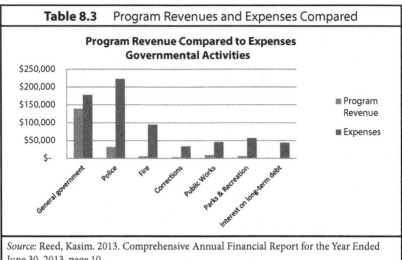

Source: Reed, Kasim. 2013. Comprehensive Annual Financial Report for the Year Ended June 30, 2013, page 10.

governments, they can at least take symbolic actions against what they perceive to be unfair laws or practices. For example, in 1994, Atlanta's city council passed a resolution declaring October 27th to be *Unfunded Mandates Day* (Banks, 1994, p. 7) as part of a highly visible effort to complain about the state and federal governments' tendency to enact laws requiring cities to provide services without providing financial resources to compensate the city for the new strains on its budget. Local government budgets, like their policy areas, are closely intertwined and interdependent. The City of Atlanta keeps close track of how much major programs cost, as well as the money they bring in from fees and fines.

All local governments have budgets, and even relatively small cities receive revenues and make expenditures that make it apparent that even small municipal government is really big business. Georgia is a state that takes pride in its local communities. For example, the City of Valdosta, with a population of just over 50,000, had a budget for fiscal year 2003 of nearly 48 million dollars. Today the budget for the City of Atlanta is over half a billion dollars, in the billions of dollars. Table 8.4 shows the services provided by those funds and the amount that each receives. In 2014, the Atlanta City Council voted to approve a $567 million budget, up from $539 million the year before. (Blau, 2014). If past patterns are any guide, the bulk of the city's own revenues will come from its general fund source, especially property taxes. But it will also obtain substantial revenues from state and federal grants and loans.

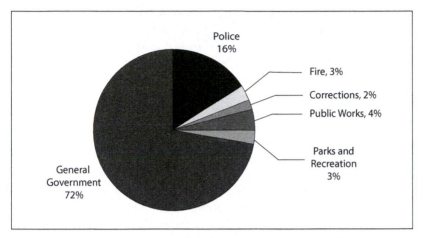

Figure 8.6   Program vs. General Funds Revenues
Source: Reed, Kasim. 2013. Comprehensive Annual Financial Report for the Year
Ended June 30, 2013, page 10.

The Police and Fire Departments fall under the Public Safety Function. The Public Works Function includes a multitude of services, including sanitation, sewer and storm sewer, water, and the city's motor pool. Parks and Recreation Function includes all the cultural and recreational activities that citizens demand and expect, but also the services provided by the municipal cemetery and the city arborist.

Table 8.4 Valdosta General Fund Budget: 2003		
Department	**Amount**	**Percent**
Police	$8,338,909	17.0%
Fire	5,576,605	12.0
Public Works	16,761,938	35.0
Parks and Recreation	4,073,171	9.0
General Government	10,638,678	22.0
Judicial Function	246,022	0.005
Housing and Development	2,258,578	5.0
Totals:	**$47,893,901**	**100.0**
Source: City of Valdosta: Fiscal Year 2003 *Annual Budget.*		

General Government Function covers Administration, including Mayor and Council, City Manager, City Attorney, and Elections responsibilities, as well as Human Resources, Finance, and Engineering.

If Valdosta city finance is big business, a city such as Atlanta which is eight times larger, is *really* big business. In the early 1990s, as described in the first edition of this textbook, Atlanta's General Fund Budget was listed at $375,760,947. But it's growing fast. That was the basic operational cost of running the city services and government, not counting such things as capitol building costs and special purpose fund expenses such as the great International Airport, an expensive proprietary enterprise. As of FY 2005, the routine general fund budget was much larger, almost three times as large: $946,986,220. When other fiduciary and proprietary funds are added, the total 2005 budget is almost seven billion dollars, a drop of about two billion dollars after the initial start-up costs of the city's airport expansion program. And of course the city's revenues are not as extensive as the city fathers would like them to be, and nowhere near as large as the state government's revenues.

The reader may notice that local budgets do not list judicial expenses. The Judicial Function does not include the Courts discussed in Chapter 7. They are maintained by the State Government. The local judicial function applies only to the administration of the Municipal Court, which hears and decides all cases brought by the Valdosta Police Department and the City Marshals and which concern a violation of a local ordinance or misdemeanors under state law. Housing and Development Function encompasses Community Development (Grants, Substandard Housing,

Table 8.5 Atlanta Appropriations—2005				
Acc't. Group	Gov't. Funds	Propri. Funds	Fiduciary Funds	Total
Personnel	359,218,537	225,969,814	3,424,201	588,612,552
Other Op. Exp.	134,609,129	763,792,683	34,241,101	932,642,913
Loans/Invest.	—	691,710	10,289	702,000
Internal Exp.	28,723,064	37,375,016	155,168	66,253,249
IGR/ITF Exp.	47,575,608	36,055,448	14,369,244	98,000,299
Capital Exp.	117,327,586	2,745,162,691	16,569,127	2,879,059,401
Debt Serv.	57,829,398	719,457,471	427,587	777,714,466
Reserve for App.	201,702,902	1,332,771,385	6,809,495	1,541,283,781
GRAND TOTAL:	**946,986,220**	**5,861,276,218**	**76,006,222**	**6,884,268,660**
Source: City of Atlanta 2005 Budget, Office of Budget and Fiscal Policy. pp. 2–7.				

Table 8.6 Percentage Summary of Atlanta Appropriations: 2005		
Acc't. Group	**Total**	**Percent**
Personnel	588,612,552	8.6 %
Other Op. Exp.	932,642,913	13.5
Loans/Invest.	702,000	0.00
Internal Exp.	66,253,249	0.03
IGR/ITF Exp.	98,000,299	0.05
Capital Exp.	2,879,059,401	42.5
Debt Serv.	777,714,466	12.8
Reserve/App.	1,541,283,781	22.4
TOTAL:	**6,884,268,662**	**99.9**
Source: City of Atlanta 2005 Budget, Office of Budget and Fiscal Policy. pp. 2–9.		

Main Street Program, Code Enforcement), Urban Redevelopment (Weed and Seed, Community Empowerment, Urban Development Action Grants, Community Development Block Grants), and Protective Inspection (Building, Plumbing, Electrical, as well as Planning and Zoning). An examination of the budget, therefore, not only tells us what a government spends; it tells us what a government does. It is not always easy to accurately identify categories of expenditures. As priorities change, and as new political figures attempt to initiate new policies, the reporting categories of our budget documents are often revised, making comparisons from year to year difficult. For example, it should be noted that the personnel costs of government are kept down in part by the contracting out of services to private businesses.

Local Income Sources

Most cities in Georgia rely on the same kinds of revenue sources to provide them with the funds they need to allocate services. As we pointed out earlier on in this chapter, taxes are the principal sources of revenue for all governments, although there are several kinds of taxes. Valdosta derives its revenue mainly from eight different taxes, supplemented by fees, fines, interest income, and intergovernmental revenue. The table above identifies each of these revenue sources and the total amounts and percentages that they produce.

Conclusion

Each year, billions of dollars are spent by the Georgia State Government and its agencies for general secondary education, and additional billions are spent for human resources, health care programs, and for higher education. Law enforcement, corrections, capital construction projects, and transportation programs cost hundreds of thousands of dollars, and more money is spent for a wide variety of miscellaneous activities like purchasing land and for preserving environmental resources.

Budgetary politics is often a fierce struggle over who gets what, and who pays. But, in general, the people of Georgia have enacted a Constitution that creates a complex array of checks and balances to ensure that the powers of the state are used effectively to benefit the health and well-being of all the citizens.

Key Terms

Ad Valorem Taxes
Debt-creating Instruments
Georgia Lottery
Individual Income Tax
Power to Tax
Sin Taxes
Special Local Option Sales Tax
Tangible Real Property
Unfunded Mandates Day

Essay Questions

1. In your opinion is Georgia really a low-tax state?

2. Does Georgia need tax reform?

3. What are some of the purposes for which the state may incur debt?

4. Are Georgians overtaxed or undertaxed?

5. Should the State's Constitution prohibit borrowing money?

Figure 9.1   Children at Play
Courtesy of Lee M. Allen

State Education Policy

Local government has a lot in common with educational institutions in the State of Georgia as described in this chapter. Local primary and secondary school districts as well as college institutions have the power to tax and levy fees for services, to hire personnel, to make regulations and rules, to maintain public safety, and they all have the power to compel obedience. But it is common to think that they also have a higher mission, an idealistic duty to educate our children and to help society to continue to improve over time. And of course education and local government have something else in common: both are arenas of political conflict. In this chapter we will review the major educational institutions, their structures, their goals and policies, and their finances.

State Educational Structure

Public education is a principal responsibility of most state governments, and Georgia is no exception to the rule. Article VIII of the Georgia Constitution speaks to the view that education is the most important function of the state government. This article provides for the governance, administrative structure, and for the financial support of public education at the elementary and secondary and college levels. Thus, it no surprise, therefore, that Georgia routinely devotes more than half of its entire budget each year to primary, secondary, and higher education. In 2010, the Georgia General Assembly took this responsibility seriously enough to allocate more than 58% of the state budget to funding all levels of education in the state. Between 2010 and 2015 with the recession in full gear, education took a hit suffering a drop of 3.5% from 2010.

Traditionally, a distinction is made between the public schools offering of kindergarten through twelfth grade and post-secondary institutions. This division is reflected in three major bureaucracies: the State Board of Education, the State Board of Regents, and since 2007 the restructured Georgia Technical School Systems. The high levels of budget appropriations to these three types of institutions reflect a commitment by the citizens of this state to provide a sound educational foundation to future generations of citizens and leaders of Georgia. We discuss these institutions and the overall policy and politics.

First, the overall responsibility for administering Georgia's system of primary and secondary education rests with the State Board of Education. The public school system (prekindergarten through grade 12) operates within districts governed by locally elected school boards and superintendents. The State Board of Education makes policy for the state education systems, sets standards for teacher education programs, certifies teachers, establishes minimal salary levels, imposes graduation requirements, etc. Its members represent each of the 14 congressional districts and are appointed by the governor and confirmed by the state senate. Members of the State Board of Education serve seven-year terms. As discussed in Chapter 5 on Plural Executives, the State School Superintendent is the chief executive officer of the State Board of Education, but local school district superintendents actually control the schools' operations.

In 2013, Georgia had 1,703,332 students enrolled in a total of 2,387 schools in 218 school districts up from 1.6 million in 2008 when the last serious accounting was made. There were 109,365 teachers in the public schools, or roughly one teacher for every 16 students, which was equal to the national average. There was roughly one administrator for every 280 students, compared to the national average of one administrator for every 295 students. On average Georgia spent $9,099 per pupil in 2013, which ranked it 37th highest in the nation. The state's graduation rate was 71.7% in 2013.

Second, in addition to the basic primary and secondary educational system, Georgia has an extensive college and university system encompassing over 100 campuses. There are 35 public institutions of higher learning in the state, divided into five tiers: research universities, regional universities, state universities, four-year state colleges, and two-year colleges. And as discussed below Georgia also has a Technical college system. The governance of the University System of Georgia (USG) is the responsibility of the State's Board of Regents. It sets goals and dictates general policy to educational institutions as well as administering Public Library Service of the state which includes 58 public library systems. The University System of Georgia is also charged with dispensing public funds allocated by the state's legislature to the various USG institutions *but* not the lottery-funded HOPE Scholarship.

Remarkably, the University System of Georgia is the *fifth* largest university system in the United States with student enrollment of about 318,027 students in the 29 USG public institutions. This ranking is current, placing USG one rank below the fourth place it occupied up until 2013. Also with 29 institutions, the system is about 6 below the 35 institutions previously posted thanks to a 2013 merger of 8 institutions into 4 which drastically reduced what previously was a fairly large number of institutions that made up the USG system. In 2015–16, system enrolment figures saw an

---

When the Going Gets Tough:
Education and Massive Budget Cuts in Georgia

In a *Georgia Trend* article published in December 2009 titled "Georgia Schools Grapple with Massive State Budget Cuts," the Peach County School Superintendent Susan Clark bemoans Georgia's Education budget cuts of the 2009–2010 school year, a trend that continues. In late July 2009, when the budget news came down from Atlanta, the Superintendent recalled that it was a week before teachers in the Peach County school system would report to work for the school year. School systems were told "to cut almost $800,000 from the budget. This cut however, did not include furloughing teachers for three days, nor did it include the $2 million cut the Peach County School System had already made from their budget for that year, nor did it include the $8 million cut that was already slated over the previous six years.

To the Peach County School Superintendent, the budget cut news presented a dilemma as it did for 179 other school superintendents in the state of Georgia. Her immediate reaction was to call to meeting all school principals in Peach County as well as all of the central leadership. The intent of the meeting was to figure out how to manage the sudden 3% budget cut in state funding on Education as it continued from the initial spring 2009 massive cuts made during the legislative session.

According to Ms. Clark, "we brainstormed every possibility until we felt there were only two options which required either (a) to cut personnel, roughly 39 positions. What this meant also was that we had to cut kindergarten paraprofessionals and (b) cut elementary school music and physical education teachers. Since this option could not be seriously considered, we moved to the next option. The second option was no plan "B." It consisted moving to a four-day school week in order to save roughly $400,000 in transportation and energy costs. In the bigger picture, the 2009–2010 budget cuts were not in isolation. It was part of a seven consecutive year cut in the Georgia state funding for education initiated by Gov. Sonny Perdue and the Georgia state legislature.

Source: Compiled by authors from various sources and mostly from "How Low Can They Go?" *Georgia Trend,* http://www.georgiatrend.com/cover-story/12_09_education.shtml, December 2009

---

increase of 5,093 students more than the previous academic years (2014–2015) which stood at 312,936 students. Table 9.1 provides a comprehensive enrollment in Georgia, the surrounding states, and nationally.

The USG employs over 47,000 faculty and staff to provide teaching and related services to students and communities across the State of Georgia.

Table 9.1   Georgia Higher Education Enrollment vs. Surrounding States: By Sex, 2012

State	Total students	Male students	Percentage	Female students	Percentage
Georgia	545,358	219,797	40.30%	325,561	59.70%
Alabama	310,311	131,513	42.38%	178,798	57.62%
Florida	1,154,929	481,483	41.69%	673,446	58.31%
South Carolina	259,617	104,944	40.42%	154,673	59.58%
U.S. total	20,642,819	8,919,087	43.21%	11,723,732	56.79%

Source: Drawn from the *"National Center for Education Statistics,"* Total fall Enrollment in degree-granting institutions, by attendance status, sex, and state or jurisdiction: 2011 and 2012" (Table 304.30).
Please Note: The figures here exceeds USG system figure since it covers the state of *higher education* in Georgia as a whole. In 2012, 59.7 % of all postsecondary students in Georgia were female, which was higher than the national rate of 56.8%. The table lists postsecondary student enrollment by sex in Georgia, those of surrounding states, and National as well.

The system also oversees an independent research unit that employs faculty and host visiting students and interns but does not grant degrees. The Board of Regents has estimated that all USG institutions has a combined $14.1 billion economic impact on the state of Georgia making the system's overall effect a net positive return on the state taxpayer investment.

Governor Nathan Deal's fiscal year 2016 budget proposal (and later HB 76) called for total spending of $44.61 billion, up from $43.24 billion in fiscal year 2015. State fund spending was proposed to total $21.78 billion, with the majority of that spending (about 54.8%) going toward education. In his budget presentation speech to Georgia legislators, the governor identified education as a major factor in the state's overall improving economic health and declared that a strong education system was essential for the state. Specifically, 24.61 billion was allocated to the K-12 and to Higher Education. Governor Deal signed the official budget (HB 78) on May 11, 2015. The final budget had many of the same features as the governor's proposed budget, including education improvements and prison reform.

Ultimately, the educational system in Georgia is comparable to those of other southern states in terms of structure and design. However, the Georgia educational system stands out by the large percentage (54.8% in 2015) of the state budget devoted to education. For example, Tennessee devoted approximately 32.5% in 2015 of the state budget to education, while the State of Florida allocated 26.2% of its 2016 annual budget to the combined K-12 and higher education (down from 28.2% in 2010). Table 9.2 shows and invites readers to see and judge for themselves Georgia State

Table 9.2 Georgia State Spending in Education and Other Functions as a Percent of Total Expenditures vs. Surrounding States for FY 2014

State	K-12 Education	Higher Education	Public Assistance	Medicaid	Corrections	Transportation	Other
Georgia	24.3%	18.8%	0.1%	21.6%	3.6%	5.9%	25.7%
Alabama	20.5%	20.6%	0.2%	23.3%	2.4%	6.4%	26.6%
Florida	19.2%	7.0%	0.3%	32.0%	3.8%	12.1%	25.6%
South Carolina	18.4%	23.6%	0.4%	24.6%	2.8%	6.5%	23.7%
Tennessee	18.3%	14.2%	0.3%	30.6%	3.1%	5.7%	27.8%

Source: By Authors drawn from the National Association of State Budget Officers

Note**: "Other" expenditures here include "Children's Health Insurance Program (CHIP), institutional and community care for the mentally ill and developmentally disabled, public health programs, employer contributions to pensions and health benefits, economic development, environmental projects, state police, parks and recreation, housing and general aid to local governments."

Please Note: Georgia State spending for FY 2014 is shown here for Education (K–12 and Higher Education and broken down by function compared to surrounding states expenditures in the same functional areas to provide for additional context). Figures are rendered in percentages to indicate the share of spending relative to the total budget spent per category.

So for example, in the fiscal year 2014, **K–12 education** and **Higher Education** each accounted for **24.3% and 18.8%** respectively or cumulative for both **43.3%** of Georgia's total expenditures. Georgia's overall funding and expenditure for **K–12 education** and **Higher Education** (tallying **43.1%**) does not include GA Technical Colleges and other educational efforts funded by the State which averages yearly 54–58%. Georgia's total funding for Education.

spending in education policy and other policy areas as a percent of its total expenditures versus those of the surrounding states listed for FY 2014 for which information was readily available.

Third, the Technical College System of Georgia (TCSG), so named since 1988, was formerly the Department of Technical and Adult Education (DTAE). It the third pillar of educational system post-12th grade charged with the mission of providing technical training to your people in this state. It oversees the Georgia's 22 technical colleges, its economic and workforce development programs, and its adult education programs. Administered by a Commissioner charged with daily administrative responsibilities for 22 satellite campuses, it has a State Board which is composed of members from the state's fourteen congressional districts, and nine members at large, with the duty to establish standards, regulations, and policies for the operation of the Technical College System. The office of the Commissioner is in Atlanta.

In December 2014, the State Board of the Technical College System of Georgia gave their approval to Governor Nathan Deal to nominate Gretchen Corbin as the system's next commissioner. Ms. Corbin replaced Commissioner Ron Jackson, who served as the system's Commissioner since 2006. Ms. Corbin is the fourth person to head the Technical College System in Georgia since its inception in 1988. She was preceded by Dr. Kenneth Breeden (1988 to 2004), Mike Vollmer (2004 to 2006), and of course, Ron Jackson (2006 to 2015).

Georgia State legislature has given as primary task to the Technical College System of Georgia the powers to create a well-educated, technically trained, and highly competitive workforce, thus ensuring economic success for both the state and its citizens. The TCSG commissioner, along with the State Board of the TCSG, which is composed of members from the state's 14 congressional districts, and nine members at large set standards and establishes regulations, and policies for the smooth operation of the system and its swelling student enrollments of well over 170,860 as of 2012.

There are two technical divisions in University System of Georgia (USG) institutions that are also under the supervisory authority of TCSG. Furthermore, TCSG also supervises the adult literacy program and economic and workforce development programs. The system operates the Georgia Virtual Technical Connection, a clearinghouse for online technical courses. The Technical College System of Georgia serves the people and the state by creating a system of technical education whose purpose is to use the latest technology and easy access for adult Georgians and corporate citizens. Some of the core courses are now made transferable for students between the TCSG and USG to facilitate movement of students to four-year USG institutions.

An important aspect of the legislative mission of the TCSG is to provide technical education to boost the economic development of the state by providing quality technical training through its network of technical colleges. To accomplish that mission the TCSG assigns to each of the technical colleges "a service delivery area," which covers a certain number of counties. These service delivery areas delineate the jurisdiction for which each college is responsible for the delivery of training services based on the business and industry represented.

Admission to Georgia's technical colleges therefore relies on eligibility and academic criteria: candidates must be at least 16 years old and possess a high school transcript. Some programs require students to be older and have either a General Education Development (GED) diploma or high school diploma. The occupational programs offered by the technical colleges all require credentials below the baccalaureate degree. Accordingly, students can earn an associate degree, an expanded program of study that facilitates career mobility and continuing education at the baccalaureate level. That could well be a traditional diploma or a technical certificate of credit, a short-term targeted program that prepares them for specific jobs. Students are not restricted to only attend college located in the service delivery area where they reside, they can elect to attend anywhere. Those entering degree programs are eligible for Georgia's HOPE Scholarship.

Georgia's technical colleges therefore offer a wide variety of career-oriented programs that involve high-tech training and specialized skills—including accounting and banking, early childhood care and nursing, and machine tool technology. These programs are often tailored to the state's specific needs.

Local School Districts

As noted above, members of the Georgia Board of Education represent 14 congressional districts. These districts are largely (but not entirely) defined by county lines. Each of Georgia's 159 counties maintains a separate school system, and 21 of the larger cities have independent school systems. The Georgia Constitution provides for separate Boards of Education to manage and control each of these many school systems and allows them to be either elected or appointed, as a local option. Most of the Boards of Education in Georgia are elected.

The administration of school policy in each district is the responsibility of the state's Department of Education, the local school boards, and their local school superintendent, who is appointed by the local Board. Primary education is big business in Georgia, absorbing almost five billion dollars in state funds and perhaps as much or more in local funds. Where there is public money to spend there is politics, it is that simple.

In the early 1980s, the national government's publication of *A Nation at Risk—The Imperative for Educational Reform,* brought to light problems with proliferation of school districts, the amount and quality of their control and direction of the educational process. This resulted in extensive reform of States' educational systems. By the late 1980s, challenges to funding reforms became the focus, particularly when it became apparent that the almost decade-old reforms of educational quality associated with teachers and students had produced little success—testing of students revealed that many students were still performing well below the national average.

Governance of School Districts

School districts are the single most common type of special purpose district government in Georgia. School districts are either county-based or independent, and can be a combinations of the two. They are relatively autonomous even if they have no independent sovereignty. School districts *do not* have to seek special permission from the State for every little thing they do, however, they are constrained by their *mission requirements* and *responsibilities, the state Constitution, state statutes* and the state's Department of Education. Table 9.3 below outlines some of the responsibilities of school districts.

Funding, Accountability, and Efficacy

The source for funding basic elementary services at each school district is primarily derived from state formula funds, local option property taxes on residents' habitations, and other privately-owned lands, taxes on businesses,

Table 9.3　School Responsibilities
1.　Prepare children to join society.
2.　Teach them the basic skills, the three r's.
3.　Acquaint them with their historical heritage.
4.　Strengthen their sense of morality.
5.　Strengthen their interpersonal skills.
6.　Ensure that they have a sense of self worth.
7.　Promote a sense of national patriotism.
8.　Prepare them for a job or a career.
9.　Give them guidance and counseling.
10.　Strengthen their bodies as well as their minds.
11.　Libraries and arts and sciences facilities.
12.　Provide trained and dedicated teachers.
13.　Train them to meet the new global challenges.
14.　Prepare them for a changing future.
Source: Compiled by authors.

sales taxes, and bond revenues. Generally, it is the locally-elected school boards and their professional staffs who are responsible for overseeing daily operations of local school budgets, and the Boards set appropriate tax rates for property in the district (within state constitutional limits).

Though parents and voters may not be familiar with every specialized aspect of the children's education, they are always aware of the level of taxation in the community, quick to fault any doubtful expenditures, and generally familiar with where responsibility rests; in the hands of the Board of Education. And at the local school district level, both blame and credit is quickly assessed and acted upon in the voting booth. Community satisfaction with budgetary and teaching policy is reflected in re-election; while failure in either area is usually reflected in community unrest and by voter election of a new school board at the first opportunity.

Of course, in Georgia, school districts are also closely accountable to state agencies. Like other local governments and special districts, school districts have no independent sovereignty, no right to exist independent of the authority and approval of the state government. In Georgia, the state Department of Education reviews local school districts to make sure that they comply with the requirements of the State Constitution.

A century ago, many school districts in the United States were run directly by city officials, but sometimes politics got in the way of education. Take the City of Chicago, Illinois, as an example. With a strong mayoral system of government, the mayor directly appointed the school teachers. As could be expected, political supporters of the mayor usually got their jobs because of their loyalty to political parties, and not because of their skills. The consequence was that patronage, and not merit or ability, determined who was hired as teachers. And so with Chicago, with a large ethnic immigrant population, this often meant that the credentials of the teachers were often doubtful. What this means is that some teachers either could not readily read or write English; and if they could barely speak English language, they could not effectively teach the students they were hired to teach.

The average local school board meets once or twice a month. Citizens and parents are invited to attend the sessions and to bring complaints and issues to the board meetings. Board members often work on committees, such as textbooks, curriculum, facilities, personnel, and budgeting. They review proposals and recommend policy to the board. But always the local citizens, and particularly the parents of the school children, are keenly sensitive to the costs of education and are anxious to make sure that they retain control over their schools, the teachers that are hired, and the skills, lessons, and attitudes that are inculcated. And since every community has differences of opinion over what should be taught, and how it should be taught and by whom, it is not uncommon to find people filing lawsuits to get their way if they find themselves outvoted at the local level. With billions of dollars at stake, and their children's future at risk, it is little wonder that passions over educational policies sometimes boil over into the political arena.

Much of the state funding for the primary and secondary levels of education is appropriated in the form of *Quality Basic Education* (QBE) funding standards which started in the mid-1980s. Established by law, the purpose of the QBE is to foster equity, merit, and standardization of the curriculum and reward for good performance. The QBE grant program sets a number of requirements that include a statewide basic curriculum, incentives, and rewards for teachers, and improved statewide performance standards. In 2010, Governor Sonny Perdue signed a state budget plan that included $393 million for all levels of education in the state. This was viewed as a clear signal for a continued commitment to education in spite of economic downturn that threaten the state's fiscal well-being (Office of Communications, June 8, 2010).

In the end, it is the duty of the local community to raise more money to supplement state funding, which may require taxation for operational costs and bond issues for capital expenditures (new classrooms). To the public at large, and certainly for parents of school age children, a system of public funded education is a good deal; but there are many who also feel conflicted. They feel they are being taxed too heavily, and would welcome the opportunity to challenge these tax policies.

In Georgia, downplaying political conflict at the school district level and a focus on providing quality education is usually the best move. Usually this is done by hiring a highly-trained professional education manager,

Figure 9.2 Educational Burden
Courtesy of Lee. M. Allen

the superintendent. In this type of system, the organization chart is very similar to the council/manager form of local government, but the influence of the professional manager, the Superintendent of Schools, is very closely related to the strength of their educational credentials. So for the most part a superintendent must have a terminal degree, usually a doctorate in educational administration. While an outstanding superintendent might seek to influence the board with their personal charisma, it is more likely to be their efficacy, brief, their expertise in education, personnel management, and budgeting that determines their degree of success on the job. It is important to understand that the superintendent does not make basic educational policy but only implements policies adopted by the local board members.

Georgia Department of Education (GaDOE)

Lastly, a little known effect is how the organization structure of the administration of school district affects the operations of schools. In many ways structure matters. Educational systems, like all administrative systems, have a hierarchical structure. All hierarchies are identifiable from top to bottom, with decreasing control evident at the bottom of the chart. For instance, if one were to review the organization chart (power chart) of the school system in the graph provided below, it is apparent that assigned power exists at the top of the hierarchy, while the least power in the system is associated with those at the bottom, the teaching faculty and the students.

The hierarchical "flow chart" of the educational bureaucracy also reveals that there are many levels of bureaucracies, but the main ones are the state level officials, particularly the *Georgia Department of Education* (GaDOE), the 11-member State Board of Education, the independently elected State School Superintendent, and the almost 200 locally elected school boards. Each of these has thousands of career specialists who function as administrative, technical, or line level bureaucrats with complex duties.

The Georgia Department of Education (GaDOE) is charged with the mission of overseeing public education throughout the State of Georgia. It ensures that laws and regulations pertaining to education are followed and that state and federal money appropriated for education is properly allocated to local school systems. That department also provides education-related information to students, parents, teachers, educational staff, government officials, and the media. The Georgia Department of Education is comprised of five offices under the State School Superintendent that include the Office of External Affairs and Policy; the Office of Standards, Instruction and Assessment; the Office of Education Support and Improvement; the Office of Finance and Business Operations; and the Office of Technology Services.

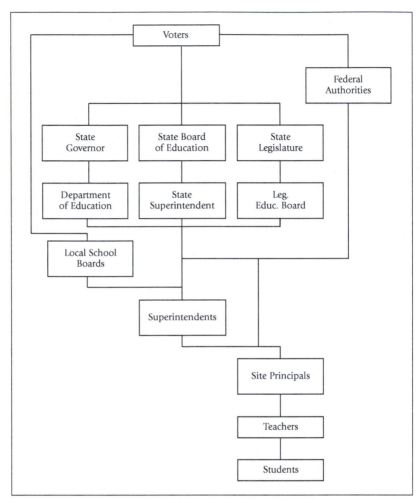

Figure 9.3 Educational Bureaucracies
Courtesy of Lee. M. Allen

Candidates for local school district boards are presumed to have appropriate abilities, skills, and interests, to convince the voters that they will represent their interests. Of course, professionally trained superintendents often have major impact on who will run for the positions on school boards. In theory, the voters constitute the clientele of the educational bureaucracy. Although displayed on the chart as a unitary entity, the *voters* are of course really a disparate collection of pressure groups, all with independent and often contradictory goals.

Sources of Funds for School Districts

The vast majority of educational funds in Georgia are received from taxes, local property and sales taxes, local bonds, and state general revenue taxes. The State of Georgia limits the amount of property taxes the cities can adopt. Sometimes, parents may support increased requests for federal funding in the form of "grants." However, other participants in the school's governance may be reluctant to do so, because the federal money may have strings attached to it that do not fit the goals and values of the local community, reflecting other national regions instead.

Federal grants for such things as demonstration projects in sex education are a prime example. School districts are less likely to object to state grants, however, because there is usually more compatibility of values at the local and state levels. For example, Georgia state law requires public schools to teach abstinence education in addition to providing information regarding sexually transmitted diseases and HIV as part of the health curriculum in middle and high schools. Unfortunately, there are often funding disparities between and within school districts, so that some schools have more money than others. When this happens it is because when parents donate money to their children's schools comparatively little attention is paid; but when public sector funds are not fairly distributed you can be sure that it will become a major political dispute.

Inner-city schools, especially in the Atlanta metropolitan area, are often the subject of discussion, research, and special funding requests. Though often receiving special attention and funds, these inner-city schools tend to deteriorate rapidly, because of the large numbers of pupils they try to serve. And since sometimes poverty-stricken families reside there, and as more and wealthier people move to the suburbs, this weakens the revenue bases of the schools. In 2007, the state attempted to balance out the differences with additional funds, such as $278 million under the basic Equalization Formula and $245 million for pre-kindergarten programs.

Higher Education in Georgia

As noted above, the Georgia public school system (prekindergarten–grade 12) operates within districts governed by locally elected school boards members and superintendents. The Georgia State Constitution requires that the state general assembly provide a "free public education prior to college or postsecondary level." The State Constitution also notes that the required education shall be supported through taxation. Thus, the State of Georgia devotes more than half of its entire state budget each year to educational programs, including primary, secondary, and higher educational efforts (see Figure 9.4).

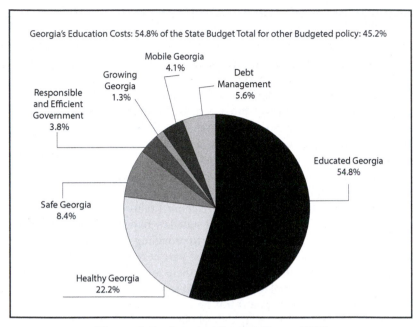

Georgia's Education Costs: 54.8% of the State Budget Total for other Budgeted policy: 45.2%

Mobile Georgia 4.1%

Growing Georgia 1.3%

Responsible and Efficient Government 3.8%

Debt Management 5.6%

Educated Georgia 54.8%

Safe Georgia 8.4%

Healthy Georgia 22.2%

Figure 9.4   Selected Budget Year—2013
Compiled by Authors

Governor Nathan Deal's proposed FY2015 budget totals $18.16 billion or an increase of $273 million over FY2011. However, state university programs would see their funding cut about $300 million, down to a total of $1.74 billion for FY2012, over the next 18 months under Deal's amended 2011 and 2012 budgets. The total FY 2010 budget was approximately $18.57 billion. Education accounted for approximately $10.79 billion of the total budget of 58.10%. This included the state department of education, early care, teacher retirement system, the technical college system of Georgia, and the university system (The Governor's Budget Report 2015). The trend data (Table 9.4) presented does only reveal Georgia's progressivity in the area of education but says very little how various constituents to the overall funding pool are impacted. The variable cuts suffered by state universities since 2010 while the overall trend held steady is one example.

In the last legislative session, the Georgia General Assembly voted to appropriate nearly $1.8 billion for post-secondary education, or higher education, in the state. Traditionally, a distinction is made between the colleges and universities, and the two-year colleges, technical colleges, and adult education training facilities. The higher levels of education are administered by the State Board of Regents, and there is little formal local community control, or local funding from the area. Instead of a local board, there is usually an institutional college president, often assisted by

Table 9.4	Trends in Georgia Spending in Education (K–12 and Higher Education) as a Function of its Overall Budget: 2009 to 2017
FY Years	**Combined K–12 & Higher Education**
2017	53.1%
2016	54.1%
2015	53.1%
2014	53.3%
2013	54.5%
2012	42.7%
2011	46.6%
2010	46.3.%
2009	46.1%

Source: By authors from variable sources and mostly National Association of State Budget Officers and the U.S. Census Bureau, 2011 Annual Survey of State Government Finances.

a faculty senate on campus. Political administration of Georgia's system of higher education rests with the State Board of Regents, and by the system Chancellor, hired by the Regents. The Regents make policy for the state's academic institutions, set standards for faculty, establish salary levels, impose graduation requirements, etc. Its members are appointed by the governor and confirmed by the state senate.

The Regents, in turn, select the Chancellor of the System, usually conducting a nationwide search to find a good professional educator. An effective administrator is needed, because Georgia has over 100 college and university campuses. Hundreds of thousands of students attend the extensive system of public colleges and universities, studying a wide variety of subjects and academic disciplines. There are 35 public institutions of higher learning in the state, divided into four basic tiers: research universities, regional universities, four-year institutions, and two-year colleges. Georgia has a unified system of higher education, with a common core curriculum, with specialized programs on each campus.

Colleges and universities are vital to healthy economic growth, particularly in these times of global competition. Georgia has been putting large sums of money into higher education in the last decade. Under the guidance of former Chancellors Stephen R. Portch, Thomas C. Meredith, and currently Hank M. Huckaby with funding made available from the Georgia lottery, the Georgia legislature has provided operational funding but supported downsizing the number of USG institutions. In addition, the Hope Scholarship Program continues to play a role in supporting college-bound Georgians in paying the college tuition of those who maintain a "B" or better grade point average in high school. This program, linked to Miller's original Georgia Rebound initiative, contained a number of economic initiatives outside of education, has allowed the state to also create a solid educational grant and loan program, which ensures that every student can pursue their educational dreams and be able to compete in the emerging global marketplace.

Insulated from political pressures and partisan bickering, the Board of Regents acts as trustee of Georgia's 29 public colleges and universities, with a nearly $1.5 billion budget and a student population of about 318,000 students. The system Chancellor is continuing to exhibit the kind of strong leadership Georgia enjoyed in the past, while working with a close-knit Board of Regents mostly appointed by Governor Barnes. Under this group, the number of institutions designated as universities has until as recently as 2013, increased. However, the sitting governor comes under criticism for appointing business and political elites of their liking to the board, quite often those who have been contributors to his campaigns, and the Board of Regent is predominantly white males (Vickers, 1994, p. C11). These appointments can be tricky business, for although political pressures led the legislature to pass laws to insulate the board and its activities for the university system against political tampering, politics in other forms of course continues to play a role in educational policy and administration in Georgia.

Among Georgia state agencies, the Board of Regents is unique because its budget is not presented as a line-item budget. As discussed in an earlier chapter, after the Talmadge Administration tried to manipulate the university system for partisan advantages, the Constitution was rewritten to require the General Assembly to appropriate monies to the Board of Regents in a lump sum, to be used as the Board of Regents deems proper. The subtle disciplinary characteristics and features of higher education require special insulation from partisan politics. Thus, once money is appropriated, the system of higher education is generally placed out of the budgetary reach of both the executive and the legislative branches.

Table 9.5 casts the net wide as it illustrate the composition of Georgia higher education enrollment versus surrounding states with race and ethnicity demographic for 2012.

Educational Policy

Educational policy in Georgia continues to evolve, while searching for a way to improve the skills and score levels of the state's students. The *Quality Basic Education* grant noted above is rooted in the *Georgia Quality and Basic Education Act of 1986*. This educational reform was intended to enhance student and teacher performance but was challenged in 1995 on the grounds that it failed to significantly improve student achievement levels (Zanardi,

Table 9.5   Georgia Higher Education Enrollment vs. Surrounding States: By Race/Ethnicity, 2012

State	Population category	White	Black	Hispanic	Asian	Pacific Islander	American Indian/ Alaska Native	Two or more races	Non-resident alien
Georgia	Postsecondary students	51.00%	34.12%	5.27%	4.20%	0.15%	0.32%	1.95%	3.00%
	General population	52.6%	35.2%	5.4%	4.3%	0.2%	0.3%	2%	N/A
Alabama	Postsecondary students	61.76%	29.84%	2.65%	1.65%	0.09%	0.75%	1.16%	2.09%
	General population	63.1%	30.5%	2.7%	1.7%	0.1%	0.8%	1.2%	N/A
Florida	Postsecondary students	48.03%	20.01%	23.14%	3.12%	0.21%	0.41%	2.29%	2.80%
	General population	49.4%	20.6%	23.8%	3.2%	0.2%	0.4%	2.4%	N/A
South Carolina	Postsecondary students	62.64%	28.47%	3.21%	1.53%	0.13%	0.41%	1.82%	1.79%
	General population	63.8%	29%	3.3%	1.6%	0.1%	0.4%	1.9%	N/A
U.S. total	Postsecondary students	58.04%	14.35%	14.43%	5.79%	0.31%	0.84%	2.45%	3.79%
	General population	60.3%	14.9%	15%	6%	0.3%	0.9%	2.5%	N/A

Source: By authors selected from *National Center for Education Statistics*, "Fall enrollment in degree-granting postsecondary institutions, by race/ethnicity of student and state or jurisdiction: 2012" (Table 306.60.).

Please Note: In the Fall semester of 2012, a total of 545,358 students were enrollment in all higher education institutions public and private. Of these an approximately 51% were White and approximately 34.1% were Black students. During that time, 52.6% of the state's general population was White and 35.2% was Black, with other ethnic groups comprising the remainder. The table here provides demographic information for both postsecondary students and the general population in Georgia and surrounding states.

1994). In 2003, a revision of the Quality Core Curriculum (QCC) was prompted by the results of an external audit conducted by Phi Delta Kappa International which revealed crucial gaps in the curriculum and a general lack of rigor. As a result of these findings, state teachers and other education experts developed a new curriculum, known as the *Georgia Performance Standards*. The implementation of the new standard began in 2005, focusing on English, math, science, and social studies (Mewborn, 2009).

Today, *Quality Basic Education* monies are still available to local school districts for various initiatives to improve education services. Additionally, the Georgia Board of Education has also decided to phase out the high school *general diploma* in favor of more rigorous programs in vocational education and college preparatory tracks. Until Georgia students' educational indicators improve, such as competency ratings and higher SAT scores (in 2009, a comparison of state SAT scores ranked Georgia 47 of 50 states and the District of Columbia.), educational policy will continue in flux.

Funding Education in Georgia

Georgia public school systems are funded primarily through state and local dollars with the majority provided based on the Quality Basic Education (QBE) formula. Based on the number of full-time equivalent (FTE) students in a program, and the expense to educate students—it costs more to educate a severely disabled student in special education than it does to teach a ninth-grader taking a regular course load. The average total expenditure per student for FY 2008 (the latest year available from the Georgia Department of Education) was about $9,000.

However, this figure varies wildly from county to county. For example, the figure is just over $8,340 in Peach County, Georgia, but nearly $13,500 for the Atlanta Public Schools system. While there may be justifications for cost differences across the system due perhaps to "teacher and principal salaries, electric bills, insurance, text books etc., there is no inflationary factor built into the formula (Grillo, 2009).

Few ideas about how to improve American education have generated as much controversy and struggle as public financial aid to private and religious education. America was founded in large part by refugees from religious wars, who determined to defuse the potential for strife by separating the powers and finances of church and state. But today, as the average quality of public education falls below acceptable levels, particularly with regard to the technical skills so vital in an era of global competition, attacks on the public school system are mounting. The poor showing of students' test scores is probably attributable to several factors, such as open enrollment, grade inflation, poor discipline, and the decline of the traditional family in the post-industrial era. Among the reformers, some persons would like to create a private educational marketplace, in which both private and religious schools would be eligible to receive public funds in the form of certificates or *portable vouchers* for students (Delk, 1993, p. F2). Traditionally, this policy has had very strong opposition.

However, since the founding of the public school system, erosion of the so-called *wall of separation* between church and state has been slow and steady. While there are no public calls as yet for mandatory religious taxes, many supporters of *school choice* see a window of opportunity to gain publicly financed support of private and religious institutions. Some supporters claim that test scores in private institutions are higher; but critics attribute some of that to *creaming*, because the public schools have to admit all who apply, while private institutions can deny admission and services to persons at their discretion.

The cost of supporting private institutions through vouchers would require a tax boost of between 3–7% according to former House Speaker Tom Murphy (*Associated Press,* 11-15-93, p. 1); a cost of perhaps two billion dollars. A bill to do just this was introduced in the 1994 legislative session, in the form of a proposed constitutional amendment, but it failed to gain support and was not acted upon. In 2002, the U.S. Supreme Court addressed the constitutionality of a voucher plan in Cleveland, Ohio, and held that, despite the fact that most of the children attending private schools in that city would be attending church-related schools supported by the Roman Catholic Church, that fact alone did not violate the First Amendment requirement of separation of church and state (*Zelman v. Simmons-Harris, Hannah Perkins School v. Simmons-Harris, Taylor v. Simmons-Harris* [2000]). That ruling opens the door for voucher systems everywhere.

School boards serve to set policies such as property tax rates for their districts (under state limits); and to choose textbooks; to make capital improvement proposals; and a host of other decisions—but perhaps the most important work of the boards is the hiring of a professionally trained superintendent who will implement the board's educational policies. Skilled professionals, focused on the technical and educational aspects of their jobs, are less likely to be imbued with outlandish ideas and political partisanship.

No Child Left Behind Act

The No Child Left Behind Act, enacted by Congress in 2001 and reauthorized in 2008, sets nationwide standards for improving public education by the end of the 2013–14 school year. When George Bush became the President of the United States in 2001, he announced this new initiative to improve the quality of education across the nation. While generally regarded as a state prerogative, education has also been regarded as a federal problem for at least the last 50 years. The President's initiative was known as the *No Child Left Behind Act* (NCLB). The NCLB requires states including Georgia to test students frequently to assess their progress. If schools repeatedly underperformed, their students may transfer to schools that do perform, and the underperforming school may be closed.

Teachers and schools administrators in Georgia and elsewhere have complained bitterly that the NCLB is really a "no child left untested" program that require teachers to "teach to the test," instead of concentrating on knowledge acquisition and analytical and creative thinking. Moreover critics charge that the NCLB is an "undefined mandate," in that it requires states to make expenditures that are not compensated by the federal government. Despite the criticism, the Bush Administration insisted that NCLB is working and there is some scant evidence that some provisions have been successful in improving the quality of public education.

In 2009, the Georgia General Assembly enacted HB 251, which provides additional choice options to parents. This law states that local school systems must offer parents the option to enroll their child in any school in the local school system, if space is available. School systems are not required to provide transportation for families opting to exercise the choice option. If there are more students requesting a school by choice than there are slots available, students are assigned by lottery.

Common Core

Common Core, or the Common Core State Standards Initiative, is an American education initiative that outlines quantifiable benchmarks in English and mathematics at each grade level from kindergarten through high school. The Georgia State Board of Education adopted these standards on July 8, 2010, with an endorsement by 2010 Georgia Governor Sonny Perdue and planned to implement them during the 2014–2015 school year.

In 2014, Georgia Governor Nathan Deal issued an executive order prohibiting the federal government from implementing any education standards within the state. The order also asserted that all decisions on curriculum would be made at the local level. However, many schools still chose to employ at least some elements of the Common Core standards. Later in 2014 and again in 2015, the Georgia Department of Education released revised versions of the Common Core standards for public comment, as the standards were still being met with criticism. These versions were still used in Georgia schools as of July 2015.

Race to the Top

In 2010, Georgia and nine other states as well as the District of Columbia were selected as "Race to the Top" winners. Like No Child Left Behind, *Race to the Top* is a federal attempt to improve the quality of schools. This Obama administration initiative is rooted in the Reinvestment Act of 2009 and awards winning states a portion of $3.4 billion to improve education by, among other things, turning around low performing schools and implementing college standards. Georgia was awarded $400 million (over four years) of the Race to the Top funds in order to meet state goals such as increasing the high school graduation rate, improving college entrance exam and achievement scores, strengthening teacher quality, and improving workforce readiness. The State Board of Education adopted these standards in July of 2010. (See The Georgia Department of Education [GaDOE], "Georgia Wins Race to the Top" GaDOE Communications Office, August 24, 2010.)

In spite of all these measures, in the 2012–2013 school year, Georgia had the fifth lowest graduation rate in the country. According to the 2015 *Building a Grad Nation* report, the national high school graduation rate hit a record high of 81.4%, and for the third year in a row, the nation remained on pace to meet the goal of 90% on-time graduation by 2020. The state of Georgia however ranks low. The overall adjusted ranking for Georgia for 2013, the year for which data is available, is at 71.7%. This sixth annual update on America's high school dropout challenge published in 2015 shows that these gains have been made possible by raising graduation rates for groups of students that have traditionally struggled to earn a high school diploma. Low-income as an opportunity gap is real. According to 2015 *Building a Grad Nation Report*, low-income students are graduating at a rate 15 percentage points behind their more affluent peers. The growth and spread of concentrated poverty in our schools and neighborhoods has enormous consequences for the nation's most disadvantaged students.

Educational Morality

Plato said that those in charge of a city must see that education is not corrupted without their noticing it. If a school graduates many people with high school diplomas who cannot read or write, then those in charge are not doing their jobs. Who is in charge of our educational policy? State level participants include the legislators who are members of educational oversight committees in the General Assembly, members of the Board of Regents and its staff, members of the Department of Education and its staff, the governor's appointed officials in the Department of Education, and occasionally members of the judiciary, who hear policy disputes in their courtrooms. The Legislative Education Board and many individual committees are responsible for reviewing all aspects of educational policies and finances, including reactions to policy initiatives introduced by other participants.

At the local secondary level, influential persons associated with policy formation and implementation in the education system are primarily the various locally elected Boards of Education, the administrators hired by them, and the professional faculty of the technical schools and colleges and the universities. These experts serve with the explicit responsibility for carrying out policies established by these boards and implicitly with the policy mandates of more distant representatives of the public's wishes, such as state agency personnel, the state school superintendent, and the members of the General Assembly. The superintendents of the school districts, school principals, and finally the professional faculty members of the schools implement the lowest level of policy, line level interaction with the students. The professional administrative and bureaucratic levels, which are not elected, may actually hold major power over the public bodies nominally responsible for making policy, because they inform their respective elected bodies of the direction local policies should take. In addition, the faculty and teachers themselves, sometimes individually, and sometimes through their representatives, such as the Georgia Association of Educators, often affect educational policy as well.

The educational establishment is the largest bureaucracy in the state, as it is in many states, and examining the successes and failures inherent to the system may clarify general understanding of bureaucracies throughout the state. Candidates for local independent school districts are also presumed to have such abilities, skills, and interests as are needed for them to be selected by the voters to represent their interests. An English philosopher and legislative leader, Edmund Burke, described two fundamental types of representatives, the delegate, faithfully executing the desires of constituents; and the trustee, who uses personal wisdom on behalf of constituents if for some reason they are unaware of their own best interests. Thus, the primary factor in the success in this hierarchical model is the voters, and one hopes their responsible selection of those who will make policy for the educational bureaucracy. When the voters are informed of the facts and sensitive to their own best interests, and act responsibly on that knowledge, this is an ideal system. All we need to do then is to allow voters to select good delegates as their representatives on local school boards, and they will provide the professional educators with local community input on value preferences. But whenever these professionals raise questions of expertise and superior judgment that runs counter to local culture, the political hackles of the school board and the general public is certain to rise.

Conclusion

Amidst the complexity of the system of public education in the State of Georgia is the obvious fact that it functions inter-dependently. Yet, while one may be tempted to draw hasty conclusions about the state of education in the State, we cannot just look at the secondary and higher education systems themselves for any conclusive understanding of how they function. The responsibility to ensure that the state's younger generations are adequately prepared for the challenges of the future and that current institutions are well equipped to trained rests on a wide variety of people: the general citizenry, elected officials, professional educators, the students themselves, and the parent especially. In our emerging climate of global economic competition, the need for strong educational institutions has never been greater.

Key Terms

Creaming
Chancellor
Grant
Georgia Rebound Initiative
No Child Left Behind Act
Portable Voucher
Quality Basic Education Funds
Race to the Top
School Choice
State Board of Education
State Board of Regent
Voucher System
Wall of Separation

Essay Questions

1. Explain the hierarchical structure of the basic educational system in Georgia.
2. Explain the structure of the University System of Georgia. How has higher education in Georgia been impacted by the use of a lottery?
3. Georgia contributes more than half of its budget to education. Can this devotion to education be seen in the performance of Georgia students compared to those from other states?
4. How might incompatibility between national and state values impact funding for education in Georgia?
5. Among Georgia state agencies, the Board of Regent is unique because its budget is not presented as a line item budget. Discuss how this historical arrangement came about and the measure that was taken.

Figure 10.1   Savannah City Hall
Courtesy of Lee M. Allen

10
Local Government

Local governments in the United States are understood as government with jurisdiction and powers below the level of the State governments. Most states therefore have at least two tiers of local government: counties and municipalities. In some states, counties are divided into townships. There are several different types of jurisdictions at the municipal level, including the *city, town, borough*, and *village*. The types and nature of these municipal entities varies from state to state. Many rural areas and even some suburban areas of many states have no municipal government below the county level.

In other areas consolidated city–county authority exist, where a city and county functions are managed by a single municipal government. For example, in some New England states, *towns* are the primary unit of local government and *counties* have no governmental function but exist in purely perfunctory capacity such as for census data gathering. In addition to general purpose local governments, there may be local or regional special-purpose local governments, such as school districts and districts for fire protection, sanitary sewer service, public transportation, public libraries, or water resource management. Such special purpose districts often encompass areas in multiple municipalities.

According to U.S. Census Bureau on Government (2012) there were roughly **89,055** local government units in the United States (see Table 10.1). Information compiled is in three areas: government organizations, public employment, and government finances. The categories compiled in the end provide a convenient basis for categories suitable for understanding local government in the United States. These categories are (1) County Governments; (2) Town or Township Governments; (3) Municipal Governments; and (4) Special-Purpose Local Governments. The data collected from these areas allows for (1) identifying the scope and nature of the state and local governments' powers in the United State; (2) classifying local government organizations, powers, and activities; (3) providing authoritative benchmark data on public finance and public employment; and (4) measuring state and local governments' fiscal relationships.

Types of Authority Assigned to Local Government

Political power in a state can be divided into *three* spheres. They are the powers exclusive to the local government, the powers assigned exclusively to state government, and lastly, the powers that are shared between two levels of government (local and state government). Within the local government sphere of powers, there are *four* categories within which the State governments can exercise its discretionary authority.

These categories are: (1) Structural powers—the power to choose the form of government, charter, and enact charter revisions; (2) Functional powers—the power to exercise local self-government in a broad or limited manner; (3) Fiscal authority—the powers to determine revenue sources, set tax rates, borrow funds, and other related financial activities; and (4) personnel—the powers to set employment rules, remuneration rates, employment conditions, and collective bargaining.

Typically, the broadest discretionary powers are applicable to local government structure, and the narrowest are given to finance. Also, local governments endowed with discretionary authority may not always exercise it. For example, the adoption or amendment of a local government's municipal charter is infrequent. Structurally, States as units in the United States have the obligation to handle the majority of issues that are the most relevant to individuals within their jurisdiction. Under this arrangement because state governments are left little or no authority to engage in revenue

Table 10.1 Governments in the United States	
Type of Government	**Number**
Federal	1
State	50
County	3,144
Municipal (city, town, village...) *	19,429
Township (in some states called Town) **	16,504
School district (utility, fire, police, library, etc.)	14,000
Special purpose	39,000
Total	**87,576**

* Municipalities are any incorporated places, such as cities, towns, villages, boroughs, etc.
** New England towns and towns in New York and Wisconsin are classified as civil townships for census purposes.
Sources: Authors from various sources
United States Census Bureau, 13 USC 161.
O'Connor, Robert and Nick Swift, "U.S. Local Government and Mayors of largest Cities"

raising activities to pay for goods and services, they generally will raise revenue through either taxes or bonds.

This certainly explains why, for example, state governments tend to impose severe budget cuts or raise taxes any time the economy is faltering. Each state has its own written Constitution, government, and code of laws. The U.S. Constitution stipulates only that each state must have "a Republican Government" and nothing more. This explains why there are often great differences in law and procedure between individual states, concerning issues such as property, crime, health, education, and many more.

Georgia in My Mind

The state of Georgia is divided into 159 counties (the largest number of any state other than Texas), each of which has had home rule since at least 1980. This means that Georgia's counties not only act as units of state government, but also in much the same way as municipalities.

In Georgia, all municipalities are classified as a *city*, regardless of population size. According to the *New Georgia Encyclopedia* article (last update, November 2015) there are 535 incorporated cities and towns in Georgia. Unlike the laws of other states, there is no legal difference in Georgia between cities and townships. In many states there are significant legal differences among the designations *city, town, village,* and *hamlet.* Georgia law, however, makes no distinction among cities, towns, and municipalities.

For an area to be incorporated as a city, special legislation has to be passed by the General Assembly (state legislature); typically the legislation requires a referendum amongst local voters to approve incorporation, to be passed by a simple majority. This most recently happened when citizens in two municipalities, Peachtree Corners (population 31,704) in Gwinnett County, and Brookhaven (population 49,000) in DeKalb County, through local referendum elected to become independent incorporated municipalities. Brookhaven became the seventh city to incorporate since Sandy Springs was created in 2005. Certainly, it became second largest in DeKalb County following the creation of Dunwoody in 2009.

Before that, in 2005 and 2006, several communities near Atlanta had done the same. Sandy Springs, a city of 85,000 bordering Atlanta to the north, incorporated in December 2005. One year later, Johns Creek (62,000) and Milton (20,000) incorporated, which meant that the entirety of north Fulton County was now municipalized. The General Assembly also approved a plan that would potentially establish two new cities in the remaining unincorporated portions of Fulton County south of Atlanta: South Fulton and Chattahoochee Hills. Chattahoochee Hills voted to incorporate in December 2007; South Fulton voted against incorporation, and is the only remaining unincorporated portion of Fulton County.

A municipal charter is a written document, is a city's fundamental law so to speak, which provides a municipality with the authority to exist and function. In this respect it is similar to a state or national constitution. In Georgia, each municipality has a charter that establishes its basic governmental structure, form of government, corporate boundaries, and municipal powers. A city's municipal powers may include, but are not limited to, appropriations and expenditures, contracts, emergencies, environmental protection, nuisance abatement, planning and zoning, police and fire protection, public transportation, sanitation collection and disposal, streets and roads, taxes, and water and sewer services. Because city charters are legal fiction, charters may be revoked either by the legislature or by a simple majority referendum of the city's residents.

The latter last happened in 2004, in Lithia Springs. Revocation by the legislature last occurred in 1995, when dozens of cities were eliminated *en masse* for not having active governments, or even for not offering at least three municipal services required of all cities. New cities may not incorporate land less than 3 miles (4.8 km) from an existing city without approval from the General Assembly. The body approved all of the recent and upcoming creations of new cities in Fulton County. Four areas have a *consolidated city-county* government: Columbus, since 1971; Athens, since 1991; Augusta, since 1996; and Macon, which was approved by voters in 2012.

Local Government

In the State of Georgia and in several states in the United States, the primary local level of government is the county, which often functions as a subdivision of the state, and is subject to the actions of the state legislature and the limitations of the State Constitution. Only the states of Connecticut and Rhode Island lack county government, although in Louisiana and Alaska similar local structures exist, called, respectively, parishes and boroughs. In addition, all states have municipal corporations, although they may be variously called cities, towns, or villages.

Many states classify cities according to first class status, second class, or third class status, specifying the types of municipal structure and degree of local autonomy they enjoy. In addition, all states have created various single purpose special districts to provide specific services to local communities. School districts are the single most common type of special purpose district, and public utilities are the second most numerous, like water and health districts.

Counties and municipalities, or permitted combinations of the two, are given home rule, meaning that they don't have to seek special permission from the state for every little thing they do. General local government entities are given supplementary powers by Article IX, Section II of the Georgia Constitution. These powers are listed in Table 10.2.

Table 10.2   Municipal Responsibilities
1. Authority for police and fire protection.
2. Garbage and solid waste collection and disposal.
3. Public health facilities and services, including hospitals, emergency services, animal control.
4. Street and road construction and maintenance.
5. Parks and recreational programs and facilities.
6. Storm water and sewage and disposal systems.
7. Water storage, treatment, and distribution.
8. Create and maintain public housing.
9. Provide public transportation.
10. Libraries and arts and sciences facilities.
11. Terminal and dock and parking facilities.
12. Codes for building, plumbing, and electricity.
13. Air quality control.
Source: Compiled by authors.

The General Assembly may (and often does) expand these powers, and in addition may regulate, restrict, or limit them. In other words, local government in Georgia is very much state government applied locally. Currently, a lot of activity centers on special single purpose districting. Special districts have proliferated all over the country, and Georgia is no exception. While the school district is still the most common type of special district, it is also the one kind of special district that is actually declining in terms of real numbers, because of consolidation. Also called authorities, special districts have been created to provide transportation, soil conservation, libraries, water, sewage disposal, etc. In short, because they can be empowered to collect taxes and to make expenditures, these special purpose governments are in fact just as much governments as are the more common and traditional general purpose governments, such as counties and municipalities.

County Government

Georgia has 159 counties, more than that of any other state except Texas. The Georgia Constitution in Article IX states that there shall not be more than 159, but within that framework counties may merge or consolidate, providing that a majority of the voters in each of the counties approve. This is an unlikely event given the attachment that Georgians have to their counties. The Constitution requires a degree of uniformity in county government. Each county must elect a clerk of the superior court, a judge of the probate court, a sheriff, and tax officials. Traditionally, the tax officials have been a tax collector and a tax receiver, but in some counties these offices have been replaced by a single tax commissioner. Of course, each county elects a set of county commissioners, and may elect a variety of other county officials. Generally, Georgia's political sub-divisions enjoy home rule jurisdiction. The county commissioners, and any other elected officials, are subject to the home rule provisions of Article IX. The idea of home rule is that a municipal government is allowed to conduct its own affairs with a minimum amount of interference from state authorities, as long as the local options are consistent with the Georgia State.

In general, the powers of local government in cities and counties are defined in their official state charters. The form or structure is the primary determining factor in how power is distributed and in how both personnel and budgets will be managed. If the form allows primary power with one individual (a strong mayor) the individual will be held accountable for conditions and issues associated with personnel and budget matters; the reverse is true when the form provides for responsibility divided among an entire city council or on the county commission.

Georgia County Government

In Georgia, the 159 separate counties are run by county commissioners who function as a legislative body, although they may have executive responsibilities as well. Actually, Georgia county government can take a variety of forms (Ammons & Campbell, 1993). The most common type of county government is the traditional form which is found in 93 of Georgia's counties. In the traditional form, commissioners serve as both legislators and executives, although they may entrust more of the executive authority to the chairperson, who may serve either in a part-time or a full-time capacity.

The second most frequently used form of county government in Georgia is the commission-administrator form. In the 34 counties that employ this system, the commissioners appoints a full-time administrator to administer the day-to-day activities of the county. While t h e administrator may have some power over budgetary matters and may hire and fire some county employees, those powers are somewhat limited.

Limited, that is, by comparison to the powers of a county manager. The commission-manager form is the third most popular form of county government in Georgia. Employed in 20 counties, the commission appoints the manager (just as it does in a county-administrator system), but the managers' duties are somewhat more substantial than they are in the county-administrator system. The manager has the power to hire and fire all department heads, prepare and submit the budget to the commission, and generally administer the county's affairs in the same manner that a city manager manages the city government.

Georgia is unique among the states in having single commissioner county governments. As of 1995, 13 Georgia counties utilized the single commissioner system (ACCG, Survey of County Governments, 1995). In such a system, found only in small rural counties, the commissioner is both the legislator and the executive. Challenged in 1994 as a violation of the 1965 Voting Rights Act, the single commissioner system in Bleckley County was upheld by the U.S. Supreme Court (*Holder v. Hall*, no. 91-2012, 1994). The court held that Bleckley County, which was 22% African American, did not dilute minority voting strength by having only one county commissioner.

DeKalb County is the sole example of the final form of county government in Georgia. In 2010, it had an elected executive, much like a president or a governor or a strong mayor, who has the power to appoint and remove department heads, prepare and submit the budget, and who can also veto ordinances passed by the commission. The rest of the commissioners serve as the legislative branch of county government. Five of the seven are elected in county districts, the other two commissioners are elected at-large within the county. With the obvious exception of single commissioner county government, county commissions in Georgia range in size from 2 to 11 commissioners (see Table 10.2). With the exception of counties that have only one commissioner, 97 counties' commissioners serve staggered terms, while 49 serve concurrent terms.

The County Commission creates a budget to manage the services necessary to respond to citizen demands, such as road and bridge building, health services, law enforcement, and legal services. Funding for these elementary services is primarily derived from property taxes on residents' habitations and owned lands. The Commissioners are responsible for setting the tax rate for property in the county, within state constitutional limits. They are also responsible for contracting to build roads, bridges, county facilities—including jails, libraries, hospitals, and other health facilities, as well as provision for fire protection, sanitation, and emergency and disaster relief.

Many other individuals charged with responsibility for implementation of the many functions of the county level of government are publicly elected, including the Clerk of the Superior Court, the Tax Commissioner, the Sheriff, and the Judge of the Probate court. And of course the County Commissioners also hire a wide array of professionals to staff the bureaucracies and offices to meet the citizens' needs. Though voters may not specifically be familiar with the broad allocation of powers given in the commission's charter, they are familiar, almost intuitively, with where responsibility rests; and at the county level blame and credit are quickly assessed in the voting booth. Success in budget and personnel power is reflected by repeated reelections; while failure in either area is often reflected by rejection of a county commissioner or a county sheriff. For example, in the author's home county, Lowndes, the

| Table 10.3   County Commission Size ||
No. of Commissioners	No. of Counties
1	13
3	18
4	2
5	98
6	12
7	10
8	3
9	1
11	2
Source: ACCG Survey on County Governments, 1995	

entire county commission was defeated for reelection in 1996 in either the primary or the general election.

Disgruntlement within the electorate over the manner in which the incumbent commissioners handled the financial and infrastructure arrangements for a new chemical plant to locate in Lowndes County resulted in this clean sweep. Four years later, all but one of them were out of office, either deciding not to run for reelection, or having been defeated. And, in 2010, community discontent over the decision to build a new wood biomass incineration plant, with probable pollution, threatens to result in similar political turmoil (Bergstrom, 9-29-10).

City Government

Unlike some states, Georgia does not differentiate among its municipalities by labeling them as first, second, or third class according to population size. In general, all municipal corporations are treated equally, but occasionally the General Assembly may make laws that are applicable only to cities of a certain population size. Officially, all urban areas are simply called *municipalities* without the distinctions found in other states which designate municipal government as, for examples, towns, townships, boroughs, etc. Of course, many local officials like to call their home towns *cities*, but that is a matter of local concern, and not a reflection of any state policy.

Local Government in Georgia

In ancient times, cities were often free and independent states, city-states exercising sovereign power. But in the modern world and certainly in Georgia, cities are mere creatures of the state. That is, local governments have no independent sovereignty, no right to exist independent of the authority and approval of the state government. The mechanism by which this authority is granted, and the precise powers and geographical scope of the city is the city charter. The city charters can be granted, and a new local government will come into existence.

An old standing joke in Georgia says that every town (remember that *town* is not a legal designation) is a county seat. Certainly most towns want to be known as viable and important centers of population and commerce. But if a town starts off well, but then declines in population, or fails to provide enough services to justify its continued existence, it may actually lose its charter. In Georgia, the state reviews local governments to make sure that municipal entities continue to be worthy of their charters.

The City Charter in Georgia

In the early 1990s, the town of Good Hope in Walton County had a population of 181 persons; the town of Newborn in Newton County had a population of 404 people; and Deepstep in Washington County had a population of 120 inhabitants. All three of these communities were among the hundreds of small cities examined to determine if they should have their municipal charters revoked. This review was conducted by a special government commission established by former governor Joe Frank Harris.

A recent law passed by the state General Assembly authorized the Local Government Commission to survey small cities in rural Georgia to determine whether they remain viable. The criteria enacted require providing, or contracting for, a minimum of three municipal services: such as water, sewers, or zoning (Osinski, 1994). If cities are losing too much population to be viable, and lapse on such services, they might be culled from the ranks of Georgia municipalities. Update in 2010: according to a recent Google search of their modern websites, Good Hope has grown to 210 persons and Newborn has increased up to 520 persons. As for Deepstep, students may conduct their own research to determine its status.

State officials say that problems that might lead to revocation of a city charter include not only declining population and dwindling services, but also cities which are inefficient, or providing duplicate services that could be provided by an alternative local government (Osinski, 1994). However, no one predicts the wholesale revocation of hundreds of city charters in Georgia. Where the commission does detect a problem, the city is formally notified and given at least a year to mend its ways or justify its existence. Given the loyalties many Georgians feel toward their hometowns, few observers expect that the commission will, in fact, recommend the demise of many cities. In fact, some of these cities, like Good Hope, have weathered the storm, and because they lie close to growing metropolitan areas, are beginning to grow again.

If there is any doubt that Georgians are loyal to their home place, the reaction to a decision by the State Department of Transportation to remove hundreds of place names from the official roadmap of Georgia in 2006, because those places were not incorporated and added *clutter* to the map, should remove that doubt. The clatter over the clutter was heard from one end of the state to the other. Even Governor Perdue then Governor of the State of Georgia weighed and sent a letter to the State Transportation Board and the Transportation Commissioner, protesting the deletion of these tiny dots on the map. The DOT responded by promising to restore the dots.

City Government Forms

Throughout the United States there are four fundamental forms of city government. Georgia has examples of each of the major forms. The most basic form is some kind of a combination of a Mayor and Council Government. This form of government is the oldest in the United States, dating to its heritage from the British system more than 400 years ago. This form has had many modifications over the centuries, but basically there are two versions, depending on whether the formal powers of the mayor are strong or weak.

Strong Mayor/(Weak) Council

In the strong mayor/council form of city government the mayor has major powers particularly associated with personnel and budget. The mayor can *hire or fire* city personnel without approval by the city's council—regardless of the number of the council or the employee's position in the city. However, rarely does this occur even in settings in which mayors are identified as *strong*. Political havoc can occur; the mayor needs council support both publicly and politically. Thus, even with strong personnel powers granted by a city's charter, few mayors would consistently circumvent the powers delegated a city's council and risk losing wide-ranging public support over repeated elections. Atlanta is often depicted as a clearly identifiable strong mayor/council city, which like both Chicago and New York have a city charter giving both personnel and budgeting power to their mayors.

Effectively, the publics' voices are limited to what the mayor perceives as essential to the city's needs. Council members in such cities must rely on either advocating or rejecting the mayor's position, and suffer the

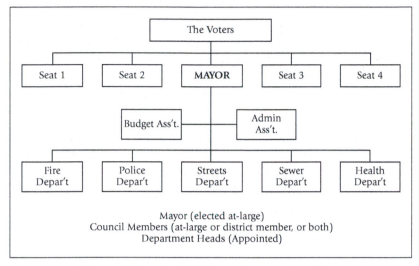

Figure 10.2   Strong Mayor Organization Chart
Courtesy of Lee. M. Allen

consequences of the public's interpretation of the mayor's impact on each area's residents' life. The standard type of organization chart for a strong mayor system is shown in Figure 10.2 on the next page.

The flow of power, the vertical and horizontal lines, indicates the form of the city's government, whether it is strong or weak mayor or council, or modifications where other elected positions intersect either budget, personnel, or both.

The City of Atlanta

Atlanta is the largest city in the State of Georgia, and in fact serves as a transportation, communication, and cultural hub of the southeastern United States. The City of Atlanta serves as the state capitol, and with a total population of 416,474, ranks 39th in size among the nation's great cities.

During the political and constitutional reform movements in Georgia of the mid-1970s, the Atlanta city charter was redrafted, and various changes and improvements reforms took effect in 1974. The old Board of Aldermen was reorganized as a City Council, and a mayor/council form of government was instituted. Instead of electing all of the members at-large, two thirds of the 18 new city council members were elected (four-year terms) from 12 districts to foster better urban representation; among the remaining six at-large posts was the position of President of the Council, the former vice mayor position, which today serves as the council's presiding legislative leader.

As a political rule of thumb, the bigger the city, the stronger the mayor, and Atlanta is no exception to the rule. The mayoralty of Atlanta is a qualified strong mayor/city council system. The mayor operates as the city's chief executive officer, enjoys a veto power over council actions, and prepares the annual city budgets for the council's review and approval. Although in the past, council members have not succeeded to the mayoralty position, that was changed when District Two Councilman Bill Campbell ran on a platform of "make the system work" and was inaugurated as mayor on January 3, 1994 (Campbell was reelected in 1997). In 2001 Campbell was replaced with Shirley Franklin, who has been designated as one of the nation's best mayors. In 2006, Campbell was convicted on corruption charges.

Some of the complexity of local government functioning and intergovernmental relations is seen by the linkages between the city government and special purpose governments in the area. At the sub-local level, dozens of neighborhood planning units are incorporated in the council districts, influencing the elections to the council and serving as a focus for the council's legislative focus and planning efforts. Expanding its geographical focus, the City Council also elects a number of its members to be directors and board members of various special purpose government authorities. These include such entities as the Atlanta Regional Commission (ARC) and the Solid Waste Management Authority (SWMA).

The Atlanta City Council meets twice a month. Citizens are invited to attend the sessions and to bring complaints, issues, and sometimes even *thank-you's* to the council meetings. Here is local government in the raw: vital, emotional, and sometimes characterized by hot-tempered exchanges of opinion and viewpoint. Council members are assigned to various functional committees, which meet twice a month, and whose function is to review proposals, recommend legislation to the council, and oversee daily departmental operations. These committees are concerned with such areas as public utilities, finance, human resources, zoning, and transportation. Members may serve on three or four such committees, including the Committee on Council, the executive committee of the city council. Of course, the exact powers of the mayor and the council will vary with the personalities of the people involved. A mayor with a strong personality and a canny political style may be able to gain power even when the city council is designed to be dominant.

For their part-time, but politically intensive jobs, the city council members in 2009 received salaries of close to forty thousand dollars a year, and were responsible for the operation of the city and its annual budget of nearly one billion dollars, including bonds and the capital construction projects of water and sewer connections under the streets and also the Airport Authority budget allotments. As is routine in Georgia, the mayor receives a higher salary. But when a five-member citizen commission appointed by

Mayor Franklin recommended that the Mayor's salary be raised by more than 50%, from $147,500 to $225,000, with concomitant raises of 17% for council members, from $39,473 to $46,183, there was opposition. Because of the *Great Recession* of 2008, money was getting very tight, so the council opposed the plan (AJC, 01-06-09).

The city government exercises two types of legislative enactments: ordinances and resolutions. Ordinances are the ordinary laws of a city, binding on the citizens and business of daily life. In contrast, resolutions are non-binding, used to project a sense of the local government's feelings on various issues.

Weak Mayor/(Strong) Council

Mayor/council relationships are similar to the strong mayor/council systems, but effectively the power of the government as identified in the city's charter is held in the hands of the city's council as a group instead of concentrated in the mayor's hands. Like any governor, the mayors of such cities must *rule* by political skill, charisma, or both. Cities with a weak mayor system have both personnel and funding power chartered to the city's council members. The mayor can only seek public support politically, and seek to acquire support of the city's council members through use of political manipulation and personal charisma.

In this type of system, the organization chart is very similar to the strong mayor system, but the power of the mayor is considerably reduced. The mayor generally is little more than a typical council member, and all decisions must be by majority vote. The mayor must either submit to the council's decision, or seek to influence the council with personal charisma and political influence. In particular, the personnel and budgeting powers of the mayor are greatly reduced, and usually the mayor will not control the agenda of the meetings. Organizational depictions of this form of government will not reveal a general structural difference, but the flow of power will be significantly modified to the benefit of the council. Essentially, the weak mayor system results in a legislatively-dominated political system.

There is little information from various municipalities in Georgia as to whether they have a strong mayor/council or a weak mayor/council form of government. We do know, however, that regardless of the strength of the mayor, some form of mayor-council government is considerably more popular than any other type of municipal government in Georgia. In one study, 85% of the cities responding indicated that they had a mayor-council form (see Weeks & Hardy, 1993). By contrast, fewer than 13% of Georgia's cities employed the next most popular of the municipal government types, the council-manager form, although half of all responding larger cities (with more than 10,000 population) did.

Council-Manager Form of City Government

Moving to become one of the most popular forms of government after World War II, with expansion of expectations for professionalism by the public, the council-manager form of government rapidly increased.

This form is also referred to as the *corporate* form of government, in that it splits the responsibility for directing policy-making and implementation of policy. Elected city leaders are charged with responsibility for making policy, while an individual they collectively hire, the city manager, is charged with implementing the mayor and council's policies. The operation of this form of government is similar to the form of special district governments, especially school districts, which are discussed below; and it reflects the business management style of many major corporations. For instance, the council and mayor are comparable to the corporation's Board of Directors, as policymakers, while the city manager is comparable to the chief executive officer (CEO) of a corporation.

According to this model, the city manager does not make policy but only implements policies adopted by elected leaders. However, in reality, the city manager may acquire a substantial amount of power and be requested to provide major input to council members and the mayor in decisions associated with both personnel and budgets. Unfortunately, because the council and mayor must stand for election periodically, the city manager's position is subject to the stability of the council. When the council and/or mayor are changed in the majority that hired the manager, a high probability occurs that the manager will be terminated from his or her position; another hired, and the process continues.

The Council-Manager system may be popular today, but there was a time when it had to compete for popularity with a form of municipal government that is now all but extinct. That is the commission form of city government.

Commission

It is said that "necessity is the mother of invention," and that is no less true in government than elsewhere. A devastating flood destroyed Galveston, Texas, in 1900. This disaster provided the opportunity for Galveston to experiment with a brand new form of local government, the commission. In the commission form of municipal government, executive and legislative functions are entrusted to the same persons, who, in effect, wear two hats. When they're wearing their legislative hats, commissioners are policy-makers. But when they switch to their executive hats, they are department heads. Thus, one commissioner will head the Department of Public Safety, another the Public Works Department, a third will be mayor, and so on.

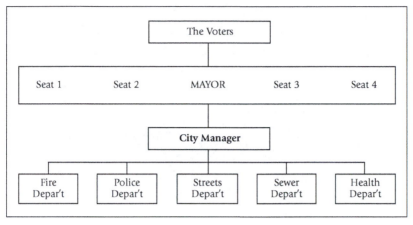

Figure 10.3   Council Manager Organization Chart
Courtesy of Lee. M. Allen

The problem with this system is that there is relatively weak executive control. Today most former commission cities have abandoned that form. Georgia is no exception; in the study cited above, only three responding cities retained the commission form of government (less than 1%).

Americans in general and many Georgians treat politics and government with a wry sense of humor; they are a necessary evil and we can't live with them and we can't live without them. About the best thing we can do is to remember Winston Churchill's quip to the effect that democracies are the worst form of government, except that the alternatives are even worse! Politicians will always make more promises than they can keep, and we just have to grin and bear it.

Special District Governments

The State of Georgia has over 600 governments identified as special districts. Special district governments are governments associated with singular interests. Thus, special district governments may be seen throughout the state, both statewide and at regional levels, served by both appointed and elected boards. The forms of the boards vary as much as do the geographical areas and specialized topics they manage. Included in the varieties of special government districts are school districts, airports, sanitation, housing, and soil conservation districts. Some, such as an airport authority, require a big investment for construction and operation. As a general rule, the board or commission that is elected or appointed to manage the concern of the single purpose government is accorded a major degree of autonomy, but is usually cross-linked to adjoining city and county governments by appointed board memberships.

Figure 10.4 Local Government Promises Revealed
Courtesy of Lee. M. Allen

Organizational Structure

The special purpose form of government, focusing on a particular type of service, usually relies heavily on a professional ethic and organizational style. It is most similar to the council-manager form of government, and was first used in the nineteenth century to reform the Chicago school district by removing it from the corrupt political practices of the big city *party machine*. In this form, the responsibility for directing policy-making is placed in an elected board, which then appoints an expert administrator for implementation of policy. Often the administrative director will dominate the board because of his or her expertise as well as the administrator's operational control. Figure 10.5, shows this type of organization.

Special District Funding

Each district also has independent local taxing power, judicial power, and executive power, in addition to its primary allocated lawmaking powers in its special purpose area or function. A high degree of growth in special districts has proliferated across the nation, as well as in Georgia. Much of the reason for the growth is linked to the so-called taxpayer revolt; citizens won't vote for general tax increases, but they understand and tolerate tax burdens for identifiable and needed services.

Today, there is a *fad* to create local special districts; it almost seems as if such fads come along periodically, with new types of special districts being established whenever opportunity to do so arises. (It is noted by the authors

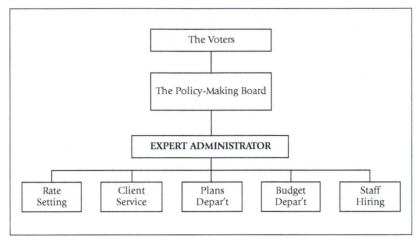

Figure 10.5   Special Purpose Government Chart
Courtesy of Lee. M. Allen

that rarely do the special districts *go out of business* even when the fad passes). The multiplicity of special districts throughout the state comprises another tier of taxing and governing entities. Each special entity carries responsibility to the people of Georgia both for service and for efficient use of public monies.

Educational Districts

It should be mentioned that school districts are a particular example of local special purpose governments. Traditionally, a distinction is made between the public schools offering of kindergarten through twelfth grade, and the higher educational, or college institutions. This division is reflected in two major bureaucracies: the State Board of Education and the State Board of Regents. These agencies and local governments are discussed in more detail in Chapter 9.

Too Many Governments?

One frequently heard criticism of local government in Georgia and everywhere is that there are simply too many governments. Why do we need 159 counties, 531 municipalities, 180 school districts, and hundreds of other special districts? The simple answer is that we probably don't, but how do we get rid of governments that may no longer be necessary?

It is probably safe to say that no plan to eliminate or merge counties will succeed in Georgia. The attachment to county is just too strong. But annexation and consolidation are still possible approaches to the problem of too many governments. Georgia law provides for four methods of annexation, where one government absorbs people and property in immediate proximity to it. A municipal corporation can annex if its local legislative delegation can get the General Assembly to pass a local act, or if it passes a resolution to annex and holds a referendum in the to-be-annexed area or areas, or by one of two petition procedures. The first procedure allows the municipality to annex if all the owners of all of the land in the area to be annexed petition for annexation. The second procedure allows the municipality to annex land where 60% of the landowners and 60% of the others petition for annexation. In either case, there must be a public hearing and the passage of an ordinance for the annexation to be completed. In cases where a municipality completely surrounds an unincorporated area of fewer than fifty acres, the municipality may annex the *island*.

Consolidation is a process by which a county, its municipalities, and perhaps its special districts become one government. Successful consolidation of school districts has taken place all over the country, with the number of independent school districts declining quite dramatically. Consolidation of counties, cities, and special districts, however, has been quite rare. Although there have been 27 proposals for city-county consolidation in Georgia between 1933 and 1997, only three have succeeded: Columbus-Muscogee County, Athens-Clarke County, and Augusta-Richmond County. Probably the principal obstacle to successful consolidation in Georgia is the requirement that there must be a majority vote in support of consolidation in each of the governmental entities to be consolidated, even if the overall vote is in favor of a merger. In 1987, for example, a proposed consolidation of Brunswick and Glynn County failed because the residents of Brunswick opposed it, even though a majority of the residents on the Islands (St Simons, Sea Island, and Jekyll Island) supported it along with the residents of rural Glynn County. In fact, this was a *textbook case* of the failure of consolidation proposals. African Americans, who had established a power base in Brunswick were reluctant to have that power diluted by merging with majority White unincorporated communities in the County. Arguments that consolidation would eliminate duplication of services and reduce expenses, and ultimately taxes, largely fell on deaf ears in the city.

Conclusion

Under America's *apple pie* system of federalism, there is no easy way to separate one government's functioning from another, as none functions independently. Yet, ultimately, each entity must also be viewed in isolation if we are to understand it. The complexity of viewing all levels of our state's government is properly the enterprise of a substantial number of books, and a substantial number of researchers; far more than the scope appropriate to this small volume on Georgia state government. In our hectic day and age, the need for strong local governments has been met by continued growth and evolution of local government forms, meeting the modern challenges.

Key Terms

Corporate
Commission
Council-Manager or Corporate form of Government
Consolidation
County Government
Home Rule
Municipalities
Party Machine
Single Commissioner System
Single Commission Commissioner
School District
Special Purpose District
Strong Mayor/Weak Council
Weak Mayor/Strong Council

Essay Questions

1. Identify responsibilities of local governments in Georgia.
2. In what ways are municipal governments *creatures of the state*?
3. Explain why a city might lose its municipal status.
4. Compare and contrast the Strong Mayor/(Weak) Council model, the Weak Mayor/(Strong) Council model, and the Council Manager form of city government.
5. What are the arguments for and against consolidation?
6. One of the frequently heard criticisms of local government in Georgia and everywhere is that there are too many governments. Why do we need 159 counties, 531 municipalities, 180 school districts, and hundreds of other special districts?
7. List and discuss in detail the four forms of city governments in Georgia.

Figure 11.1   Statue of Herman Eugene Talmadge
Courtesy of Lee M. Allen

The State Constitution

"To perpetuate the principles of free government, insure justice to all, preserve peace, *promote the interest and happiness of the citizen and of the family,* and transmit to posterity the *enjoyment of liberty,* we the people of Georgia, relying upon the protection and guidance of Almighty God, do ordain and establish this Constitution"

The Preamble to the GA State Constitution.

Constitutions are higher laws and therefore set out the basis rules under which the government will operate. They are notoriously foundational, leaving most of the detail to be made effective in due course while giving due considerations and by appropriate secondary legislation. They take precedence over statutes and are more difficult to change even if changing is not impossible as the history of constitutional change in Georgia aptly demonstrates. However, rarely do preambles that accompany them, command such importance as to be given legal effect. The preamble to the Georgia State Constitution is one of those. It is a brief introductory statement describing in broad terms the principles which the Constitution is meant to serve. For the most, preambles express in glorying but general terms the intentions of those (the people) who framed the document.

Rarely does constitutional preamble grants or prohibits rights or authority. The Supreme Court of Georgia has seemingly given judicial notice to the preamble of the Georgia State Constitution in several cases. For instance, the preamble was cited in a 1982 case *Roberts v. Ravenwood, Church of Wicca,* and later another part of it such as "...*promote the interest and happiness of the citizen and of the family*" cited *family issue* court cases (for example, *Clabough v. Rachwal, Dixon v. Dixon,* and *Arnold v. Arnold*). All these makes reasonable argument to abide both to the rule of law and to the spirit of the law that enable those laws to exit and accepted.

Reflecting State Diversity

It is well-known in academic circles that much of Georgia's Constitution reflects the political theories of an Englishman, John Locke, as adapted by the American experience after the British monarchy was rejected by the colonies. It is less well-known and understood that Georgia's Constitution is also indebted to the French theorist Jean J. Rousseau, for his theory of the general will. Rousseau argued that in a democracy the structure of government, and its functioning and policies, should reflect the general will of all the people. This is the essential basis of democratic theory, that the government should represent the people and their desires. And if we had a simple society, and a simple undifferentiated economy, and if we had ethnic and cultural unity, then our Constitution could be simple, too. However, those are a lot of ifs, and unfortunately, none of them are true.

Georgia is, in fact, a large and complex state, the biggest east of the Mississippi River and with a correspondingly rich and complicated economy and multifaceted culture. Therefore, we should expect lots of diversity, and that as a result our Constitution would be complex also, as in fact it is. But underlying that political complexity is an orderly and rational system of government that reflects Georgia's civilization and culture, and the general will of its citizens. This chapter focuses on explaining how our system of government does reflect the will of the people of Georgia, but that it does so by reflecting the varied desires and policy preferences of many different groups of people, as they were described in Chapter 3. How can the wills and desires of different people, with different ideas, be incorporated into one government and one constitution? One definition of politics is that it is the process that determines who gets what, when, and how (Lasswell, 1936); it should be expanded to include who is and who is not taxed.

James Q. Wilson describes how a complicated federal government can have several different types of public policies. His typology is based on an analysis of winners and losers in political conflict, who benefits from a policy and who has to pay for it. Generally his model can be used to describe not only financial cost/benefit situations, but regulatory cost/benefit situations as well. He derives four scenarios: majority benefits and it incurs the cost; the majority benefits and a minority incurs the cost; the minority benefits and the majority incurs the costs; and finally isolated policies. Wilson names these four types of policies: majoritarian, interest-group policies, client centered policies, and entrepreneurial policies. These are depicted in Table 11.1.

Within Wilson's typology, Rousseau's concept of the general will is best expressed in majoritarian policies, ones that benefit all of the people, and are paid for all of the people. An example of majoritarian policy is when the state capitol building's construction and maintenance is paid for out of general revenues. In contrast, interest-group policies benefit one smaller group of people and are paid for only by that group of people, who thus incur both the costs and the benefits of that program. A good example can be found in the hunting and fishing laws of the state. Hunters and fishermen pay fees for their hunting and fishing licenses, and the money collected from

Table 11.1 Wilson's Typology			
		BENEFIT	
		Majority	Minority
COST	Majority	Majoritarian	Client Politics
	Minority	Entrepreneurial	Interest Group

them is used to regulate wildlife and to stock the forests and rivers with game. Few people seriously contest the equity of either the majoritarian or special-interest policies as described by Wilson.

However, the other two types of policies—client centered policies and entrepreneurial policies—generate a great deal of controversy and constitutional activity. That is because both of them involve taking money or resources from one group of people and redistributing money or benefits to other groups of people. When government collects money from the majority of the people and gives to a small group of people, Professor Wilson calls it client politics. An example might be welfare programs, or food distribution programs; the larger part of society pays the cost of helping out a smaller part. On the other hand, when government collects money from a small group of people and uses it to give benefits to a larger group or to the majority, Professor Wilson calls that entrepreneurial politics. An example might be taxes levied on businessmen who own manufacturing facilities which pollute our air and water, and then uses the money to protect the environment. Society wants strong industry, of course, but we need good air and water, too, so we tax the small number of big polluters and use the revenues to benefit society as a whole. Every element of our State Constitution reflects one or more of these four types of policies.

All of the different provisions of the Constitution of the State of Georgia can also be looked at as policies which are so important that they have been lodged within the Constitution to protect them from routine political maneuvering. And each policy generally falls into one of the four categories of policies described by Professor Wilson, depending on who benefits from the policy, and who bears the cost of the policy. So while it is true that in a democratic society the will of the people usually determines the substantive policies and procedures of the state, it is also true that the politics of state government reflects all of the different interest groups, and so can sometimes be controversial, benefiting only a few of our citizens, and result in complex laws and constitutional provisions. The more the variation in regions, industries, peoples, and activities that a state encompasses, the more and varied the representatives of the interest groups will be. In Georgia, they may be called lobbyists, interest groups, special interest groups, or pressure groups, but they are all concerned with pursuing their own agendas and policy preferences. These interest groups have two major ways of pursuing their political goals: financing the political campaigns of their representatives and supporters, and lobbying for regulations, laws, and constitutional amendments that institutionalize their policy preferences. Groups which are not effective in lobbying for their preferred policies are unlikely to be well-served by the policies which are enacted.

This chapter is not concerned with the variety of techniques interest groups use to influence policy-making, but rather in describing the end results: the extent to which the Constitution is fundamentally majoritarian or not. Are the people of Georgia generally receiving their fair share of the state's budget? Have they succeeded in maintaining their democratic political influence, and changing the law and the state's Constitution to reflect their changing needs? As we discussed in Chapter 4, Georgia's General Assembly is quite sensitive to the needs of interest groups; but constitutional provisions require popular ratification, and an analysis of the policy types within the Constitution will enable us to determine the extent to which the people of the state favor majoritarian policies. The relative power of all of the contending interest groups in Georgia is reflected in the Constitution and its recent amendments.

The Constitution of 1983

The present Constitution of the State of Georgia, as ratified in 1983 and amended over the last 20 years, is short, just over 40,000 words as measured on a word processor. In structure, it consists of a preamble and 11 articles. Cursory overview of the Constitution shows that most of its provisions are intended to be majoritarian in conception and function. However, there are sections which seem to indicate that interest-group policies, client-centered policies, and even some entrepreneurial policies exert significant influence in the Constitution.

The preamble is a short positive invocation expressing the hope of all Georgians that the Constitution will serve our overall needs and desires for freedom and justice. Article One of the Constitution of the State of Georgia begins basically as a Bill of Rights emphasizing the powers of the people and their rights and privileges *vis-a-vis* the government; it also has a second section on the origin and structure of government and a third section focusing on property rights. The basic organization of this article is clearly majoritarian oriented, as is Article II, which continues the theme of popular sovereignty, detailing the requirements of popular voting, elections for the most important state offices, and procedures for removal of public officials. Both of these articles are designed to benefit the majority of the population.

Articles III through VI, discussing the four branches of state government, also clearly convey the general intent that the government is designed to be under general popular control, and can thus be categorized as majoritarian as well. All of these articles illustrate the importance of the representatives of the people in framing the laws of the state, and reflecting the wills and desires of the people as a whole.

In contrast, Article VII is a very different story altogether. Article VII is the taxation article, granting the power to tax, the power to exempt from taxation, and it describes the purposes for which debt may be incurred. Let us look at the various sections of that article. Section One describes the general power of taxation, including taxes on tangible and intangible property (including the income tax). It should be noted that most of the language of this section is extremely detailed as to what types of tangible property are to be taxed, such as trailers, motor vehicles, real property, and agricultural products. The specifications here, and the fact that the section allows the General Assembly to modify the tax rates and methods for these categories, indicates that interest group competition over policy is probably intense, and probably not simply majoritarian in operation.

This is even more noticeable in Section Two, which lists specific exemptions from the state's ad valorem taxation. There are primarily four categories of exemption: homesteads, locally granted exemptions, holdover exemptions from the prior Constitution and laws, and an exemption for disabled veterans. These exemptions are clearly designed to benefit their respective groups, and are thus not majoritarian. The toleration for locally granted exemptions, when multiplied by the hundreds of governmental taxing entities in Georgia, makes it certain that interest-group policies, client-centered policies, and entrepreneurial policies could each be identified with a minimum of additional research.

Similarly, Sections Three and Four of Article VII provide explicit exceptions to the majoritarian principle. Section III creates the basic practice of putting all revenues in the state's general fund. However, it allows agricultural revenues to be treated differently and used for the promotion of agricultural produce, a clear example of interest-group policy. Of course, most people will agree that the special conditions and hazards of agricultural productivity and perishability justify this exception to the majoritarian principle. Section III also allows general revenue funds to be dispensed as grants to counties and municipalities, a clear example of client-centered policy embedded in the Constitution.

These are usually justified in terms of disaster relief programs and in promoting economic growth. Section IV, detailing the purposes and guarantees for public debt in Georgia, both at the state and local levels, by underwriting special programs and capital building projects, also creates a wide variety of client-centered policies and expenditures. This section basically allows counties and other local entities to borrow money for large construction projects and public improvement programs. Although Article VII is obviously not simply majoritarian in its operation, it allows local flexibility in responding to the needs of the people of the State of Georgia, and so allows our Georgia government to respond to needs on a priority basis.

Article VIII, concerning public education is, in monetary terms, the largest and most important function of state government. This article provides for the governance, administrative structure, and for the financial support of public education at the elementary, secondary, and college levels. Since it takes general revenue funds and allocates them to specific educational entities, school districts and colleges, it is clearly an example of client-centered policy. And since some paragraphs allow the use of lottery money to support education, this article also provides an example of entrepreneurial policy, by taxing one group, the lottery gamblers, for the benefit of another group, students in the State of Georgia. Gambling, although occasionally leading to excess, is in essence *malum prohibitum,* that is not bad in and of itself, usually a victimless crime except as it might damage the economic security of an addict's children. Dedicating the proceeds of a lottery to the children and students of the state displays a sophisticated understanding of the problems in forging public policy.

As discussed in Chapter 1, Georgia's political culture is a blend of traditionalistic and individualistic elements, with a moralistic tinge, that would generally be hostile to state-approved gambling activities. However, in this case the need to secure adequate levels of funding for education overrides minor moral considerations, and having gamblers pay a x marks this entrepreneurial tax policy as an understandable exception to the tendency of moralistic cultures to outlaw everything that does not conform to their particular perception and interpretation of the world around them.

Article IX deals with counties and municipal corporations. Lacking sovereignty, these local governments are creatures of the state, and subject to the State Constitution and to state laws. The article describes the allowable structures, powers, and governance of county, city, and special purpose governments; and relations among these and between them and the state as a whole. In Wilson's typology, perhaps the essential significance of a multiplicity of little governments is that it allows small regional populations to control themselves, enjoying their own unique political and cultural lifestyles. In this view, the entire article is an example of interest group politics, centered not so much on financial policies, but upon other political values, primarily freedom and diversity. Home rule is a very comforting policy to many of the citizens of the State of Georgia. In short, the Constitution clearly reflects our respect for individuals and local traditions.

The Amending Process

Article X is the amending article. It allows amendments to the Constitution to be proposed either by the General Assembly or by a constitutional convention. It is based on the Madisonian idea that frequent elections to facilitate change are superior to suppressing dissent, and thus risking subsequent violent change. It provides for amendments to be submitted to the voters, with a majority of those voting necessary for ratification. In Wilson's typology, this article is clearly majoritarian in conception. It underscores Georgia's commitment to democratic governance, so that if it is the general will of the people to change their Constitution, then they may do so through the ballot box.

Article X establishes identical procedures for either amending the existing Constitution or for replacing it with a totally new one. An amendment or an entirely new Constitution may be proposed either by a two-thirds vote on a resolution by both houses of the General Assembly or by a convention called by a two-thirds vote of the General Assembly. Under the 1983 Constitution, however, all amendments have been proposed

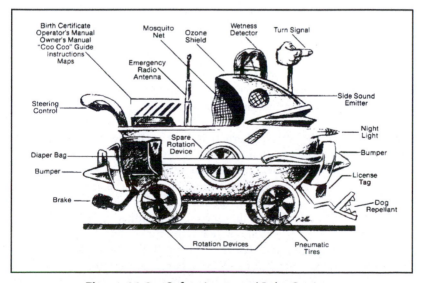

Figure 11.2   Safety Improved Baby Carriage

by a two-thirds vote on a resolution in the General Assembly, not by a convention process.

Should a convention route be taken, the General Assembly determines the procedures by which it would be called and the procedures by which it would operate. Whichever process is used, once proposed, an amendment or a new Constitution must be submitted to the electorate for ratification. A simple majority (50% + 1) of those actually voting in the first general election in an even-numbered year following the proposal is all that is required for ratification. The governor has no official veto power over amendments or new Constitutions, so the decision of the people is final. Hopefully, only necessary amendments should be ratified, otherwise the Constitution may become cluttered up with frills that may look ridiculous or unfair, but that *lock in* some special benefit to an interest group enjoying temporary political power.

Finally, Article XI provide for the date of the effective implementation of articles for the effectuation of the 1983 Constitution. It concludes in Paragraph VI that: "this Constitution shall become effective on July 1, 1983; and except as otherwise provided in this Constitution, all previous Constitutions and all amendments thereto shall thereupon stand repealed." Now that the 1983 Constitution has in fact been adopted, this section is inoperative, except as perhaps a model for the next time a similar process occurs.

Constitutional Changes

What changes have been made in the Constitution of the State of Georgia since it was ratified in 1983? The reader can tell by comparing the original version and then by looking at the most up-to-date version of the Constitution. There are several ways to do so. The state has a contractor who services the updating and printing of the document, but attempts to get copies can be cumbersome. The Georgia Secretary of State website provides a downloadable version that may or may not be textually the same (i.e., amended) after every election where there has been amendments submitted and approved by the voters. Alternatively, the unabridged and instructor's editions of this textbook often include the text of the Constitution in the appendix. If the reader has a copy of one of the unabridged editions, and reads it, it should also be noted that original contents remaining from the 1983 wording are in normal font, but other sections are in an italic font; to represent any new additions to the Constitution ratified after 1983 (deleted and omitted portions may be annotated in the appendix).

What are the significant changes since 1983? This is not always easy to determine, because several of its sections have been amended as many as five times, so the individual provisions may vary from year to year, and sometimes even our elected officials have trouble keeping track. This is not surprising, because as researchers know, one of the many problems of identifying the law at any level is its lack of coherency (Elza, 1991, p. 162). However, every constitutional amendment is noted in the Official Code of Georgia, annotated, affectionately known as the *mickey code* as a mnemonic for its publisher, the Michie company.

A perusal of the Code showed that in the last 30 or so years there have been many proposed amendments. As of 2012, a total of ninety-four (94) proposed amendments have been sent to the citizens for consideration. Of those, seventy-two (72) have been ratified, and the remaining twenty-two (22) rejected by the voters. In percentage terms, the substance of the Constitution has been changed by about 35%.

Summary Analysis

A casual inspection of Table 11.2 shows that the pace of amendment is slowing down, and that when the General Assembly has offered proposed amendments to the people the likelihood is that they will be ratified. Further

Table 11.2 Table of Constitutional Changes Proposed			
Year	Proposed	Rejected	Rejected
1984	11	1	10
1986	9	1	8
1988	15	9	6
1990	9	1	8
1992	8	1	7
1994	6	1	5
1996	5	1	4
1998	5	1	4
2000	7	1	6
2002	6	2	4
2004	2	0	2
2006	3	0	3
2008	3	0	3
2010	5	0	5
2012	2	0	2
Total	96	19	77
GA total number of amendments ratified through 2014. Compiled by authors, 2016			

analysis led the authors to conclude that many of the amendments are the sort of technical trivia that scholars love to criticize as being too minor to deserve to be elevated to constitutional status.

Minor changes in the tax code, restrictions on offenders as voters and office-holders, procedures for suspending indicted officials, punishments for accepting gratuities, and perhaps instructions on how to appoint replacements for vacant offices could be handled by statute. Many others, such as the creation of re-development zones and community improvement districts do represent progress in creating new governmental entities and probably do belong in the Constitution.

Table 11.3 shows some of the major structural (page) changes in the Constitution since it was adopted in 1983. Of the 11 Articles, the ones most significantly amended have been the voting Article II (84.0% ±) reflecting restricting the right to vote and serve in office of public offenders; the tax and finance Article VII (45% ±) detailing tax classifications and debt provisions; and Article III (45% ±) increasing the powers of the legislative

Table 11.3 Changes Listed by Sections			
Portion	**Topic**	**# New Pages**	**% Change**
ARTICLE I	Lottery Allowed	2 of 6	+ 30%
ARTICLE II	Ineligible Voters	4 of 5	+ 80%
ARTICLE III	Powers of Leg.	7 of 18	+ 40%
ARTICLE IV	Powers of Lids.	0.5 of 4	+ 12%
ARTICLE V	no change	—	0%
ARTICLE VI	Court Organization & Jud. Discipline	3 of 10	+ 28%
ARTICLE VII	Classif. of Prop. & Local Options & Public Debt	6 of 13	+ 45%
ARTICLE	Bds of Educat. & Tax Options	3 of 8	+ 36%
ARTICLE IX	Re-devel. Zones Inter-gov't Relat. Regional Facil. Comm. Imp. Dist.	5.5 of 17	+ 32%
ARTICLE X	—	—	0%
ARTICLE XI	Indust. Parks	.5 of 3	+ 15%
Totals:	all changes	27.5 of 97	+ 28%

Source: Compiled by authors, 2010.

branch of government. Similar expansion of taxing and operational changes for boards of education (Article VIII); local government (Article IX); and the judicial branch (Article VI) were ratified. One outstanding trend of the last decade or so toward improved funding of education in Georgia was reflected in Hope grants and substantial increases in the powers of boards of education to levy taxes and issue bonds, subject of course to voter approval.

Significant changes were also made in the area of special purpose districts and operations. Article IX was amended to allow the creation of local community improvement districts with local revenue sources; this built on other amendments that approved the creation of regional facilities such as industrial parks and re-development zones. In comparison, Articles V (Executive) and X (Amending) were not changed. A summary depiction of the number of proposed amendments and the years for their consideration by the voters and subsequent ratification is depicted in Table 11.3.

Other significant changes are the amendments establishing, in great detail, procedures for dealing with judges who have earned official actions and changing the structure of the courts by allowing the creation of special court projects. There were technical changes in the replacement appointive duties of the governor to fill vacancies. On a more positive note, one amendment gives increased power to local governments to contract with each other to provide services. By using memorandums of understanding (MoU's) and memoranda of agreement (MoA's) or simple contracts for services, the field of intergovernmental cooperation was much strengthened.

In terms of intergovernmental relations, perhaps the single most interesting amendment to be ratified involved the amendment that established The Georgia State Finance and Investment Commission, the *super commission* responsible for approving general obligation bonds. The Constitutional Commission's members include the Governor, the Lt. Governor, The Speaker, The Attorney General, the Commissioner of Agriculture, and the State Auditor. See Article VII, Section IV, Paragraph VII, which passed on November 4, 1986. An attempt by Governor Perdue to establish a similar commission to evaluate the entire revenue and expenditure picture and make recommendations has not met with similar success.

In terms of policy politics, some of the most interesting amendments are changes in the tax and appropriations provisions, intended for a variety of purposes. In main they allow for more flexible legislative appropriations for children, injured workers, and indigent persons. They also allow more latitude for allotments to entrepreneurial efforts in technology, manufacturing, and agriculture. Investment *seed capital* is offered for new small business ventures, as are provisions for a new agricultural crop fund. One hopes that the majority of these amendments will help to alleviate misery and to spur economic development. To enable readers to more easily identify these amendments, the sections of the Constitution which have been amended recently are italicized in the Appendix containing the Constitution of the State of Georgia.

Annotations on Selected Amendments

Ratification of an amendment to Article I, Section II, Paragraph VII (d), which took effect on and after January 1, 1995, now allows the holding of raffles by nonprofit organizations and repeals contrary laws enacted prior to January 1, 1995. Since the state government is allowed to hold a lottery, this gives other local governments and organizations the power to hold revenue raising raffles. This provision maintains the power of the state to regulate such activities by saying that laws which may be enacted by the General Assembly may restrict, regulate, or prohibit the operation of such raffles. Article III, Section VI was amended by adding Paragraph VII, on the regulation of alcoholic beverages, particularly in the counties and municipalities of the state for the purpose of regulating, restricting, or prohibiting the exhibition of nudity, partial nudity, or depictions of nudity in connection with the sale or consumption of alcoholic beverages. It provides delegated regulatory authority for the adoption and enforcement of regulatory ordinances by the counties and municipalities of this state. It helps to control the spread of *red light* districts. Although some would argue that these types of activities are mere *malum prohibitum*, there is little doubt that every culture needs to have some control over such activity, and keep its visibility at a low profile.

Despite the fact that overall crime rates have been declining for years, the *tough-on-crime* mentality continues to be a popular choice for many Georgia political elements. Article IV, Section II was amended restricting the powers of the courts and of the Board of Pardons and Paroles. The new Paragraph II (b) (2) provides that the General Assembly may by general law provide for minimum mandatory sentences and for sentences which are required to be served in their entirety for persons convicted of armed robbery, kidnapping, rape, aggravated child molestation, aggravated sodomy, or aggravated sexual battery. And sub-section (3) provides that the General Assembly may similarly provide for the imposition of sentences of life without parole for persons convicted of murder, and for anyone who is twice convicted of murder, armed robbery, kidnapping, rape, aggravated child molestation, aggravated sodomy, or aggravated sexual battery, the so-called *two-strikes law.* These types of offenses are universally recognized as *malum in se,* bad and evil in and of themselves, with clearly identifiable victims. When and if the General Assembly specifies, the board of pardons and parole shall not have the authority to consider categories of such persons for pardon, parole, or commutation from any portion of such sentence.

One result of this policy has been a great increase in the size of the prison population, one of the highest in the world. In contrast, the next article was amended by a new paragraph, Paragraph X of Article VI, Section I, which authorizes pilot projects in the courts. This substantially modifies the court structure of the state, by allowing the General Assembly to enact legislation providing for, as pilot programs of limited duration, courts which are not uniform within their classes in jurisdiction, powers, rules of practice and procedure, and also the selections, qualifications, terms, and discipline of judges for such pilot courts. Some of these were intended to deflect persons accused of minor offenses to community treatment facilities instead of hard core penitentiaries. This can have particular application to status offenses, *malum prohibitum*. These can be young persons experimenting with controlled substances. The hope is that treatment is more likely to salvage them as useful citizens, instead of placing them among hardened criminals after which they may become unsalvageable.

Article VIII, Section VI was modified so that boards of education may impose new sales and use taxes for educational purposes, as long as they are approved by a majority of the local voters. The voters have to be given information about which capital outlay projects the money is for, the maximum cost of such projects, with the maximum period of time not to exceed five years. Nothing in this amendment prohibits counties and municipalities from imposing additional local sales and use taxes authorized by general law.

In these days of continued taxpayer revolt, ways to finance public improvement without new taxes has led to a variety of budget cutting and privatization initiatives. One amendment, altering Article IX, Section II, Paragraph VII authorized the General Assembly to provide for the creation of enterprise zones by counties or municipalities, or both. This allows for exemptions, credits, or reductions of any tax or taxes levied within such zones by the state, a county, or any municipality, or any combination thereof, if persons, firms, or corporations create job opportunities within the enterprise zone for unemployed, low, and moderate income persons.

Similarly Article IX, Section IV was amended to allow the creation of *regional facilities*. These regional facilities mean industrial parks, business parks, conference centers, convention centers, airports, athletic facilities, recreation facilities, jails or correctional facilities, or other similar or related economic development facilities. Counties and municipalities are authorized to enter into contracts with contiguous counties for the purpose of allocating the proceeds of ad valorem taxes assessed and collected on real property for development purposes. Unless otherwise provided by law, the regional facilities can qualify for any income tax credits, regardless of where the business is located.

Finally, in one amendment that looked as if it were very narrowly drawn, Article XI, Section I was amended so that any person owning property in an industrial area may voluntarily remove the property from that industrial area, by filing a certificate to that effect with the clerk of the superior court in that county. Once the certificate is filed, the property described in the certificate, together with all public streets and public rights of way within the property, abutting the property, or connecting the property to property outside the industrial area may be annexed by an adjacent city.

Recent Constitutional Amendments

In 2006, three proposed constitutional amendments were on the general ballot, and all three were ratified by the voters. Probably the most important one was to restrict the use of the power of eminent domain; it passed by an overwhelming vote. The other two also passed easily; one was to protect the traditional rights of fishing and hunting by managing natural resources for the public good; the other to authorize the General Assembly to dedicate revenue from special motor vehicle license plates. These new amendments have been finally incorporated into the official copy of the Constitution posted on the website maintained by the Secretary of State's Office, and are highlighted in the instructor's edition of the textbook.

In 2008, Georgia voters had an opportunity to vote to ratify three more possible amendments. As usual, they covered a multitude of issues, but two of them involved taxes, which was passed by the voters, and the third on new special purpose districts, which did not pass muster. The first of the tax measures was an amendment on encouraging the preservation of Georgia's forests through a conservation use property tax reduction program. It was ratified and the formal language will eventually be found in Article VII, Section I, Paragraph III. The second offered amendment to authorize local school districts to use tax funds for community redevelopment purposes was also ratified and will eventually be found in Article IX, Section II, Paragraph VIII. However, the third offered amendment to authorize the creation of special Infrastructure Development Districts, to oversee the provision of new infrastructure to underserved areas was defeated.

And in 2010, Georgia voters had an opportunity to vote to ratify five more possible amendments. As usual, they covered a multitude of issues, but as we might expect, five of them had a link to taxes. The first proposed amendment was to allow competitive contracts to be enforced in Georgia Courts. With 100% of precincts reporting on election night, it was ratified and should soon be formally written up to be placed in Article III, Section VI, Paragraph V; and in particular sub-paragraph C will be substantially re-written. It had a plurality of 1,633,066 non-partisan votes (67.6%) of the total of 2,416,456 votes cast (Hinton, 2011).

However, the proposed amendment listed as second on the ballot, to add an extra $10 tag fee on private passenger vehicles for the benefit of statewide trauma care expansion, was defeated. With 100% of precincts reporting, the No votes were 1,342,555 (52.6%) out of the 2,550,391 total votes cast on the issue. The third amendment, to allow the state to execute multi-year contracts for projects to improve energy efficiency and conservation, appeared to be doing well on election night. But despite this early lead, later events indicated that it was not to be ratified and incorporated within the Constitution (Ibid).

In contrast, amendment number four was *barely ratified*. Its purpose was to allow state agencies to execute multi-year contracts for long-term transportation projects. This would remove it from the normal budgeting cycle, thus limiting legislative oversight. With 100% of precincts reporting, the original votes were trending toward No, at 1,216,780 (50.1%); as against the Yes votes, which numbered 1,212,863 (49.9%). As sometimes happens with such close tallies, the final count reversed the outcome, as it was determined to be in favor of the amendment passing. The exact wording will be placed in Article VII, Section IV, Paragraph XII.

Finally, in 2010, the Fifth Amendment, intended to allow owners of industrial-zoned property to choose to remove the industrial designation from their property, was overwhelmingly passed by the voters. With 100% of the precincts reporting, the yes votes numbered 1,520,636 (63.5%) out of the total of 2,394,526 votes cast. It will be placed in Article XI, Section 1, Paragraph IV.

Also in 2010, a special statewide referendum was placed on the ballot, designed to get voter approval for the legislature to provide for inventory of businesses to be exempt from state property tax. With 100% of precincts reporting it attained a healthy majority of yes votes, 1,310,116 (54.0%) out of 2,425,702 votes cast (Ibid).

Conclusions

By applying Wilson's classification of policy model, it can be confidently asserted that Georgia's State Constitution with its amendments is fundamentally majoritarian, except as tax and local options are structured to allow narrower interest-group policies to flourish, hopefully for general economic improvement. While there are examples of client policies (taxing the many to benefit the few) and even entrepreneurial policies (taxing the few to benefit the many) these are generally justified in promoting the public good. Generally, the Constitution of the State of Georgia is an accurate reflection of the fundamental structure of the state's economics and politics. Unlike some states, with antiquated and outmoded government systems, the Georgia State Government, responding to the voice of the people in their varied interest groups, has attempted to create a modern flexible system of functional branches and specialized agencies to meet the growing needs of an increasingly sophisticated urban society.

It is certain that the traditionalistic elements of our people are yielding to the disruptive demands of an increasingly individualistic economic and social setting. It is the genius of the State of Georgia that a regional leader can move into the age of mass bureaucracy, and yet retain the traditional style that has always made the Peach State a symbol of well-managed change. Having already had 10 Constitutions in its history, it is unlikely that the 1983 Constitution will be the last.

It is the contention of the authors that the political culture of the state is evolving from traditionalistic to individualistic, and with the approval of gambling venues, perhaps a decreasing element of moral responsibility. This can be attributed to three main factors: (1) in part to the large numbers of northern professionals and managers migrating southward to the Peach State; (2) increasing numbers of foreign derived workers (mostly Hispanic); and (3) in part to the undeniable modernization of the state's economy. Whatever the proportion, Georgia is in a state of transition. As a result, it can be expected that the current Constitution will continue to gradually reflect the changing demographics of the state and will undergo such dichotomous amendment that within another two decades, or even sooner, it may need another complete revision.

It is important enough to repeat: the state is undergoing economic changes and new people are moving into Georgia, bringing their new ideas with them. The new emphasis on enterprise zones and redevelopment districts exemplifies the dramatic professionalization of our emerging administrative government; and until recently merit systems had all but completely replaced the earlier system of political patronage. Now the pendulum is swinging back. The merit system has been weakened, and the current attack on public sector workers across the United States, particularly in the Great Lakes region, is sure to be reflected in new proposed amendments in 2012.

While the 1998 session of the General Assembly hinted at the declining power of the *good old boy* legislative network and the emphatic participation by new, more professional legislators oriented to the Republican Party, the recently re-achieved one-party dominance by Republicans may yet disappoint reformers. Good old boy Republicans are not going to be very different. One thing is sure: the times are changing in Georgia. And if history provides any one lesson, it is this: when the times change in Georgia, so does the Constitution.

Key Terms

Amendment
Client Policies
Client-Centered Policies
Entrepreneurial Policies
General Will
Interest Group-Type
Majoritarian
Policies Special
Interest Policies
The Amending Process
Rousseau Theory of General Will

Essay Questions

1. Explain James Q. Wilson's policy typology. How does it relate to the will of the people impacting policies?

2. How might the Georgia Constitution be amended?

3. Compare and contrast the U.S. Constitution and the Constitution of the State of Georgia. What are the similarities and dissimilarities?

4. State and discuss the most amended Article of the Georgia Constitution and please comment on the various (historical) reasons stated or inferred for this frequent revision.

5. What changes have been made by the Constitution of the State of Georgia since it was ratified in 1933?

6. List and discuss the procedure provided by Article X of the Georgia Constitution for amending the Constitution. Further explain why your authors believe that the process is based on Madisonian idea and Wilson's typology.

One

Georgia State Questions

Chapter 1: Introduction to Georgia Politics

1. Which of the following is not a state power?
   a. Education
   b. Transportation
   c. Police protection
   d. Mail delivery

2. State laws must be compatible with all of the following, except:
   a. State constitutions
   b. The U.S. Constitution
   c. Federal laws
   d. The U.N. Charter

3. The U.S. Constitution:
   a. Is longer than Georgia's
   b. Is shorter than Georgia's
   c. Has fewer amendments than Georgia's
   d. Has more amendments than Georgia's
   e. Both b and c are correct

4. Only one state has had more constitutions in its history than Georgia. That state is:
   a. Alabama
   b. New York
   c. Louisiana
   d. Massachusetts

5. The current Georgia Constitution can best be described as the:
   a. Restoration Constitution
   b. Bureaucratic Constitution
   c. Secession Constitution
   d. Reconstruction Constitution

6. As of 2013 revision, the number of amendments to Georgia's Constitution stood at _____ with _____ rejection:
   a. 86 with 66
   b. 77 with 19
   c. 432 with 188
   d. 11 with 10

7. The body of the Georgia Constitution contains:
   a. A preamble and 11 articles
   b. A preamble and 7 articles
   c. A preamble and 32 articles
   d. 16 articles

8. Amendments to the Georgia Constitution are ratified by:
   a. The county commissions in a referendum of simple majority
   b. County commissions and city councils in a referendum by extraordinary majority
   c. A "simple majority" of the people in a referendum
   d. The governor of Georgia in a referendum

9. Georgia has a plural executive, which means:
   a. Georgia has two governors, one for domestic affairs, one for foreign affairs
   b. Georgia has a constitutional relationship between the governor and the CEOs of major businesses like Coca-Cola
   c. Georgia has many independently elected executives
   d. The Georgia governor appoints all the other executive officers to his cabinet

10. Under Georgia plural executive, which of the following is not an executive officer in Georgia?
    a. Lieutenant Governor
    b. Attorney General
    c. Commissioner of Agriculture
    d. State Auditor

11. The authors of this text argue that the dominant political culture in Georgia is closest to which of Daniel Elazar's type of political culture?
    a. Traditionalistic
    b. Individualistic
    c. Moralistic
    d. Capitalistic and Socialistic

12. Where would one find Georgia's Bill of Rights?
    a. Georgia Declaration of the Rights of Man
    b. Article I of the Georgia Constitution
    c. Amendments I through XI of the Georgia Constitution
    d. Georgia has no written Bill of Rights

13. As used in the text, "Devolution" means:
    a. Transferring power from the national government to the state governments
    b. Transferring power from the state governments to the national government
    c. Devil worship
    d. Transferring power from local governments to the national government

14. Your text argues that States are free:
    a. To exceed federal constitutional protections
    b. To supersede federal constitutional protections
    c. To deny, disparage, or abuse peoples' rights
    d. To ignore the federal government whenever it suits them

15. According to the authors of your text, an understanding of Georgia's political culture helps us understand:
    a. That the political culture is evolving from traditional to libertarianism
    b. Why the State of Georgia for so long was a one party system
    c. That the Georgia State Constitution is fundamentally more principle than other state constitutions
    d. The U.S. Constitution is more pluralistic than it is majoritarian

Chapter 2: Civil Rights and Civil Liberties

1. The original purpose of the new British colony in Georgia was to provide a haven for:
   a. The poor
   b. Army veterans
   c. Religious minorities
   d. Convicts and criminals

2. Which of the following is not a major section in Article I of the Georgia Constitution?
   a. Civil liberties
   b. Origin and structure
   c. Limiting taxation
   d. General provisions

3. A majority of the paragraphs in Article I, Section I involve:
   a. Civil rights
   b. Civil liberties
   c. Popular government
   d. Intergovernmental relations

4. Which of the following is not described in the first paragraph of Article I of GA Constitution?
   a. Life
   b. Liberty
   c. Happiness
   d. Property

5. Which of the following are elements of due process?
   a. Notification of action
   b. An open and public hearing
   c. Benefit of legal counsel
   d. All of the above

6. Which of these liberties are usually non-controversial?
   a. Right to assemble in groups
   b. Right to circulate petitions
   c. Right to send petitions to officials
   d. All of the above

7. In Georgia, the right to a jury trial includes all but which ONE of the following:
   a. A jury of peers
   b. A jury of officials
   c. An impartial jury
   d. A speedy trial

8. The government's use of which of the following is limited:
   a. Searches
   b. Seizures
   c. Warrants
   d. All of the above

9. Which of the following are protected against a government's use of unreasonable searches?
   a. Persons
   b. Houses
   c. Papers
   d. All of the above

10. Accused persons must be given all of the following except:
   a. An opportunity to leave the state
   b. A copy of the accusation
   c. A list of witnesses
   d. A right to confront witnesses

11. Which of the following became a major civil rights figure?
   a. James Oglethorpe
   b. Martin Luther King
   c. Neither of the above
   d. Both a and b

12. As provided by Article I of the Georgia Constitution, the State of Georgia may:
   a. Declare someone to be a noble if they are a citizen of the US and resident of this state
   b. Declare someone to be a peasant if they are a citizen of the US and resident of this state
   c. Declare someone to be a citizen only if they are a citizen of the US and resident of this state
   d. Declare someone to be an aristocrat if they are a citizen of the US and resident of this state

13. Article I, Section II, Paragraph III of the Georgia Bill of Rights name all but one of the following branches of government:
   a. Legislative
   b. Judicial
   c. Bureaucratic
   d. Executive

14. Which of the following statement is TRUE under the Constitution of the State of Georgia?
   a. No money may be taken from the treasury for any local or foreign church
   b. The state may establish for each person the right to worship
   c. The state may freely make laws that support the right to religious beliefs
   d. The state may grant title of nobility, peasantry, and aristocracy

15. A comprehensive Bill of Rights was finally included in which of the following Georgia Constitutions:
   a. The Legislative Constitution of 1777
   b. The Reform Constitution of 1798
   c. The Confederate Constitution of 1861
   d. The Executive Reform Constitution of 1945
   e. The Restoration Constitution of 1877

Chapter 3: Political Participation in Georgia

1. According to a 1998 legislation passed by Georgia General Assembly, candidates are required only _____ _____to win a general election in Georgia:
   a. 33 1/3% of the votes
   b. 45% plurality
   c. 50% + 1 majority
   d. 66 2/3% extraordinary majority

2. Georgia's voter registration system is:
   a. Permanent
   b. Periodic
   c. Episodic
   d. Idiotic

3. The reading in Chapter 3 on Georgia's political parties suggests that in spite of gains made by the Republican Party since the mid-90s, the Democratic Party in Georgia still control which of the following:
   a. The State House of Representatives
   b. The Governorship
   c. The Congressional Delegation
   d. The State Senate
   e. None of the above

4. According to your text, the turnout in the Georgia gubernatorial election of 2008 was:
   a. Less than 30%
   b. About 40%
   c. Less than 50%
   d. About 61%

5. The no match, no vote legislation passed by the Georgia Assembly in 2005 required:
   a. That convicted felons produce photo identification to vote in Georgia
   b. That mental incompetents refrain from voting
   c. That legal residents produce identification cards and proof of citizenship in order to vote
   d. That names of voters are periodically purged from the State's voter registration

6. All of the following were true prior to the passage of the Georgia Ethics Act of 1992 except:
   a. Lobbying was akin to bribery and therefore was illegal in Georgia
   b. Lobbying was a misdemeanor and those who paid a fee of $5.00 were called registered agents
   c. Lobbyist did not have to declare which bill they were working to pass or defeat
   d. Lobbyists were required to pay an annual registration fee of $200.00 to the State Ethics Commission and to carry a tag

7. The political party systems in Georgia can best be described as:
   a. Hierarchical
   b. Stratarchical
   c. Monarachical
   d. Polyarchical

8. Which of the following would not be considered a federal encroachment on states' prerogatives in the area of voting:
   a. The 15th Amendment
   b. The 26th Amendment
   c. The 1st Amendment
   d. The Voting Rights Act

9. Your textbook argues that Georgia has a system of interest groups that is:
   a. Strong
   b. Weak
   c. Responsive
   d. Pro-labor

10. All of the following are factors that affect the ability of powerful interest groups to influence public policy discussed in Chapter 3, except:
    a. Medical Association of Georgia
    b. Queer Nation Atlanta
    c. Coca-Cola
    d. Georgia Association of Educators

11. By the term access, the text means political interest groups seek:
    a. To be influenced by political decision-makers
    b. To influence the outcome of public policy
    c. To present a slate of candidates to run for public office under the group's name
    d. To capture control of government

12. Several factors that are positively associated with political participation include all of the following, except:
    a. A high degree of urbanization
    b. A politically active youth core
    c. A high median family income
    d. A small percentages of disadvantaged minority

13. Political interest groups in Georgia may:
    a. Not contribute money to candidates running for public office
    b. Contribute as much money as they wish to candidates for public office
    c. Contribute a maximum of $1,000 to candidates for local office and $16,000 to candidates for statewide office
    d. Contribute no more than $10,000 to any candidate for public office

14. Voter turnout in Georgia:
    a. Is high compared to national turnout
    b. Is low compared to national turnout
    c. Is on a par with national turnout
    d. Affects turnout in Alabama and South Carolina

15. According to Article 2 of the Georgia Constitution, which of the following can't vote in Georgia?
    a. A citizen of the United States
    b. A legal resident of Georgia and of the county in which you wish to vote
    c. Someone 18 years of age by election day
    d. Convicted felons and mental incompetents

Chapter 4: The Legislative Branch

1. Georgia's bicameral legislature consists of:
   a. A Senate and a House of Delegates
   b. A Senate and a House of Burgesses
   c. A Senate and a House of Commons
   d. A Senate and a House of Representatives

2. Members of the General Assembly (consisting of both houses) serve terms of office of:
   a. Two years
   b. Four years
   c. Six years
   d. Two years for the lower house and six years for the upper house

3. The lower house of the General Assembly consists of:
   a. 30 members
   b. 56 members
   c. 150 members
   d. 180 members

4. The upper house of the General Assembly consists of:
   a. 36 members
   b. 56 members
   c. 76 members
   d. 96 members

5. According to your text, it is a safe conclusion that since about the 2010 elections in Georgia:
   a. The Republican Party controlled less seats in the House and Senate of the Georgia Assembly
   b. The Democratic Party controlled more seats in the House and Senate of the Georgia Assembly
   c. The Republican Party has indeed had a rough and painful election cycle
   d. The Democratic Party controlled less than 86 of the 236 seats in the House and Senate of the Georgia Assembly

6. The Georgia State Senate's presiding officers are:
   a. The Lt. Governor and the President Pro Tempore
   b. The Speaker of the House and the President Pro Tempore
   c. The Governor and the Lt. Governor
   d. The Governor and the Majority Leader

7. The General Assembly's lower house officials are:
   a. The Speaker of the House and the Speaker Pro Tempore
   b. The Lt. Governor and the Speaker of the House
   c. The Governor and the Lt. Governor
   d. The Speaker of the House and the Secretary of State

8. The General Assembly usually meets:
   a. All year long
   b. Every other year
   c. 40 working days a year
   d. Only in August

9. Which of these is not a type of committee in the Georgia General Assembly?
   a. Sitting
   b. Standing
   c. Special
   d. Joint

10. If the Governor vetoes a bill, both Houses of the General Assembly can override that veto by a vote of a:
    a. Simple majority
    b. Two-thirds majority
    c. A three-fifths majority
    d. A three-fourths majority

11. The State of Georgia:
    a. Must balance its operational budget
    b. Can spend as much money as the governor requests
    c. Can print more money if it runs out
    d. Has perpetual funding

12. Who presides over Georgia's State Senate?
    a. Governor
    b. Lieutenant Governor
    c. Senate Majority Leader
    d. Senate Majority Whip

13. For a public official to be impeached in Georgia all of the following would happen, *except*:
    a. The Georgia House of Representatives must vote on charges
    b. The Georgia Senate must convict by a two-thirds majority of its full membership
    c. The courts must find the public official guilty of a serious crime
    d. The public official must be an executive officer, a judicial officer, or a member of the state General Assembly

14. In Miller v. Johnson, a case concerning "affirmative gerrymandering/racial gerrymandering" the U.S. Supreme Court:
    a. Abolished the "county unit system" in Georgia
    b. Invalidated Georgia's Eleventh Congressional District on equal protection grounds
    c. Made Georgia create the 5th Congressional District
    d. Decided against Zell Miller's impeachment trial

15. In Georgia, the scope of revenue appropriated by the "general appropriation bill" includes all of the following, *except:*
    a. Material fixed by previous laws
    b. The ordinary expense of the executive, legislative, and judicial branches and bureaucratic departments
    c. Payment for public debt and interest thereon
    d. Support of the public institutions and educational interests of the state
    e. Payment of taxes and interests to the Federal Government

Chapter 5: The Plural Executive of Georgia

1. The authors of your text argue that the current Georgia Constitution has created a "bureaucratic system of government" where the governor:
   a. Has absolute control over the state's executive branch
   b. Does not share power with other elected executive officials
   c. Is not an all-powerful unitary chief executive or ranked as an influential governor in the use of its formal powers
   d. Appoints a large pool of members of state boards, commissions, and offices

2. When it comes to making laws, the governor:
   a. Is a significant player
   b. Has no role to play at all
   c. Is confined to signing or vetoing bills
   d. Has the sole legislative power

3. Georgia governors can serve:
   a. One 4-year term
   b. One 2-year term
   c. Two 4-year terms
   d. As many terms as they are elected to in succession

4. To be elected governor of Georgia:
   a. A person must be a citizen of the U.S. and be at least 35 years old
   b. A person must be male
   c. A person must own property in Georgia and have been a resident for at least 15 years
   d. A person must be a citizen of the U.S. for at least 15 years, and a legal resident of Georgia

5. The Georgia Attorney General heads:
   a. The Department of Law
   b. The Justice Department
   c. The State Supreme Court
   d. The State National Guard

6. Which of the following is not an elected public office in Georgia?
   a. State Commissioner of Agriculture
   b. State Commissioner of Revenue
   c. State Commissioner of Insurance
   d. State Commissioner of Labor

7. The Governor of Georgia serves in all but one of the following positions:
   a. The top state administrator in the state system
   b. The filler of constitutional vacancies or public offices
   c. Conservator of the peace throughout the state
   d. The top state judge

8. The Georgia Hope Scholarship Program is funded:
   a. By the General Assembly from the general fund
   b. By the governor from license tag fees
   c. By proceeds from the lottery
   d. By the county governments in Georgia

9. If the governor dies, resigns, or is permanently disabled:
    a. The lieutenant governor becomes the new governor
    b. The governor's wife becomes the new governor
    c. A new election is called in thirty days
    d. The Speaker of the House becomes the new governor

10. The Governor acts as Chief Legislator by performing all but which of the following functions:
    a. Convening special sessions
    b. Writing the annual appropriations bill
    c. Delivering the annual State of the State Address
    d. Serving as President of the Senate

11. Who is the chief of state of Georgia?
    a. Governor
    b. Lieutenant Governor
    c. Secretary of State
    d. Attorney General
    e. Speaker of the House

12. According to your text, to include Georgia, an elected State School Superintendent:
    a. Is found in all 50 states
    b. Is unique to Georgia
    c. Is found in a majority of the states in the United States
    d. Is found in only 16 states in the United States

13. The Georgia Board of Regents:
    a. Has a non-line-itemed budget in order to insulate the University System from politics
    b. Consists of 18 members appointed by the governor
    c. Oversees the Georgia Board of Education and University System of Georgia
    d. Serves a 10-year term of office

14. Which among the following former governors benefited the most politically from the flag issue in Georgia?
    a. Zell Miller
    b. Roy Barnes
    c. Sonny Perdue
    d. Jimmy Carter

15. To cope with such a complex and decentralized system of government such as the State of Georgia:
    a. The governor can identify the needs of the people through a state-wide survey
    b. The governor can seek assistance from the Congress
    c. The governor must be foxy enough to understand the problems and aggressive enough to act on the information
    d. The governor must form alliances with other members of the pluralist executive to better respond to the people's needs

Chapter 6: Administration and Agencies

1. Max Weber's *succession crisis* is:
    a. A typology of historical change in government organizations
    b. What happens when a newly appointed bureaucrat replaces one who is stepping down
    c. A model of bureaucratic inertia
    d. Probably the major problem with bureaucracies today

2. The Article of the Georgia Constitution that establishes the Bureaucracy is:
    a. Article I
    b. Article II
    c. Article III
    d. Article IV

3. The Georgia Public Service Commission regulates:
    a. The Insurance Industry
    b. Electric Power Companies and Railroad Companies
    c. Certification for Insurance Practice
    d. The Cable and Satellite Companies

4. Members of the State Transportation Board:
    a. Are appointed by the governor
    b. Are chosen by the General Assembly
    c. Are elected by the people
    d. Are appointed by their U.S. Congressmen

5. The State Board of Pardons and Paroles:
    a. Has the power to grant reprieves, pardons, and paroles
    b. Has no power to commute sentences
    c. Has the power to impose sentences
    d. Has the power to build prisons

6. The State Personnel Board includes most of the following, except:
    a. Consists of five members nominated by the governor
    b. Sets policy for the State Merit System
    c. Selects its own chairman
    d. Tracks employment offers made by the state of Georgia

7. Veterans preference means that veterans:
    a. Don't have to take state merit exams
    b. Automatically get the state jobs for which they apply
    c. Get bonus points on merit exams
    d. Prefer public sector jobs to private sector jobs

8. The Georgia Board of Natural Resources:
    a. Has a complicated task of policing Georgia's rivers and lakes
    b. Is charged with environmental protection
    c. Primarily engages in oil exploration
    d. Operates all the state's zoos and lakes

9. Special Authorities are created in Georgia with the purpose:
    a. To finance an enterprise to get around debt limitations
    b. To avoid raising taxes
    c. To serve the needs that cut across traditional governmental boundaries
    d. All of the above

10. The number of state bureaucrats in Georgia:
    a. Is approximately 114,000
    b. Is approximately 184,000
    c. Is approximately 344,000
    d. Is in the millions

11. The Commissioner of Insurance does all of the following, except:
    a. Sets criteria for licensing insurance companies
    b. Sets standards for performance of insurance companies
    c. Sets rates for insurance policies
    d. Mandates that all pre-school through 8th grade are properly insured

12. Who selects Georgia's State Superintendent of Schools?
    a. State Board of Education
    b. Governor
    c. General Assembly
    d. Voters

13. The Georgia Secretary of State does all of the following, *except*:
    a. Oversees the elections process
    b. Carries out Georgia's foreign policy with other countries
    c. Records financial statements from candidates for public office
    d. Grants charters to corporations

14. All of the following applies to the *State Financing and Investment Commission except:*
    a. Is an example of a Super Commission
    b. Includes among its members the Governor, Speaker of the House, Agriculture Commissioner
    c. Tries to ensure that Special Authorities contribute to efficient government
    d. Includes among its members the Speaker of the House and the Attorney General of the United States

15. It is the contention of the authors of the text that:
    a. The political culture is evolving from individualistic to libertarianism
    b. Georgia is in the state of transformation
    c. The Georgia State Constitution is fundamentally more majoritarian than it is pluralistic
    d. The U.S. Constitution is more pluralistic than it is majoritarian

Chapter 7: The Georgia State Judiciary

1. Courts of limited jurisdiction in Georgia include all of the following except which court:
   a. Magistrate
   b. Probate
   c. Juvenile
   d. Superior

2. A judge in Georgia may be removed from office by:
   a. The governor
   b. The General Assembly
   c. The Judicial Qualifications Commission
   d. All of the above

3. ALJ is an abbreviation for:
   a. Alter Legis Judicium
   b. A legal joke
   c. Administrative Law Judge
   d. Another Lenient Judge

4. While the state's Constitution provides that each county in Georgia shall have at least one superior court, the state of Georgia has only one _____.
   a. Supreme Court
   b. Superior Court
   c. Magistrate Court
   d. Probate Court

5. Two fraternity brothers hazing freshmen would be called:
   a. Joint obligators
   b. Joint tort-feasors
   c. Joint co-signers
   d. Joint custodians

6. Judges may be removed for:
   a. Willful misconduct
   b. Habitual intemperance
   c. Conviction of a crime involving moral turpitude
   d. All of the above

7. The number or approximate number of inmates currently serving time in Georgia's prisons is approximately:
   a. 4,400
   b. 53,123
   c. 463,000
   d. 5,400,000

8. The Georgia Court of Appeals consists of:
   a. 5 judges
   b. 9 judges
   c. 12 judges
   d. 27 judges sitting three in a panel

9. The current Georgia Supreme Court consists of:
   a. 7 justices
   b. 9 justices
   c. 12 justices
   d. 159 justices

10. The Chief Justice of the Georgia Supreme Court is:
    a. Appointed by the governor to be Chief Justice
    b. Elected by the people as Chief Justice
    c. Elected by the Supreme Court
    d. Appointed by the General Assembly

11. Georgia's highest state court is:
    a. Supreme Court
    b. Court of Appeals
    c. Superior Court
    d. Probate Court

12. Members of Georgia's Supreme Court serve for how many years?
    a. 2 years
    b. 6 years
    c. 8 years
    d. Tenure for life

13. All other judges in Georgia must retire:
    a. At age 55
    b. At age 65
    c. At age 75
    d. Never

14. Members of the Judicial Qualifications Commission:
    a. Are all judges
    b. Are all state legislators
    c. Are judges, lawyers, and non-lawyer citizens
    d. Are not allowed to be lawyers

15. Compared to other institutions of the Georgia Government:
    a. The Supreme Court of Georgia is a relatively new institution
    b. The Supreme Court of Georgia is one of the oldest institutions
    c. The Department of Law is a nineteenth-century creation of pluralist governance
    d. The Supreme Court of Georgia is older than the U.S. Supreme Court

Chapter 8: Budgeting and Finance

1. A quick examination of the debt of the state of Georgia suggest that since the fiscal years since 2009 through 2016, the total indebtedness of the State has been hovering around:
   a. Over $14 billion
   b. Nothing, because the state is required to pay as it goes
   c. Nearly $3 trillion
   d. Approximately $10 million

2. The bulk of Georgia's revenue comes from all of the following sources, *except:*
   a. Ad valorem taxes
   b. Income taxes
   c. Sales taxes
   d. The lottery

3. Comparatively, Georgia ranks as:
   a. A high-tax state
   b. A low-tax state
   c. A fair-tax state
   d. An unfair-tax state

4. A revenue bond:
   a. Is retired with the revenues from money-making enterprises and is usually a risky undertaking
   b. Is based on the full faith and credit of the state
   c. Is a tie that links a taxpayer to his state government
   d. Affects the retired and older and affluent population

5. The largest single expenditure in the Georgia State Budget is:
   a. Transportation
   b. Education
   c. Welfare
   d. Corrections

6. In 2002, the Georgia General Assembly gave back about _____ in tax relief to the people of Georgia.
   a. Less than $100 million
   b. Less than $200 million
   c. More than $300 million
   d. More than $400 million

7. Georgia's bond ratings are:
   a. Very high
   b. Very low
   c. Set by the General Assembly
   d. Dictated by the governor

8. Income of over $7,000 a year is taxed in Georgia at a rate of:
   a. 6%
   b. 28%
   c. 35%
   d. 62%

9. Exempted from Georgia's sales tax are all of the following, *except:*
   a. Bibles
   b. Food
   c. Fuel used to heat chicken houses
   d. Girl Scout cookies
   e. Raincoats for pre-school kids

10. Georgia's sales tax rate varies from:
    a. 3–6%
    b. 4–7%
    c. 8–10%
    d. 11–15%

11. The authors of your text argue that, *budgetary politics*:
    a. Is a vital tool to analyze patterns and cycles so that trends can be extrapolated and the future predicted and prepared for
    b. January to December
    c. Runs concurrently with the so-called budget cycle from July to June of each year
    d. Is a fierce struggle over who gets what and who pays

12. A capital budget is:
    a. Used for maintenance of the capitol building
    b. Used to fund routine operations
    c. Used for expensive long-term building projects
    d. Used to fund capital death penalty appeals

13. By 2009, the Georgia lottery was producing $_____ in revenue for education.
    a. Under $100 million
    b. Over $800 million
    c. Over $1 billion
    d. Over $5 billion

14. Elementary, secondary, and higher education together consume approximately what percent of the Georgia State annual budget?
    a. Nearly 40–45%
    b. Nearly 53–58%
    c. Nearly 60–75%
    d. Nearly 19–25%

15. According to Article VII, Section IV, which of the following is not the purpose for which the state of Georgia may incur debt:
    a. Crisis event
    b. Debt to repel invasion
    c. Debt for the suppression of insurrection
    d. Debt for temporal cash flow shortages
    e. Debt for state of transformation

Chapter 9: State Education Policy

1. The State Board of Education:
    a. Makes policy for state education systems
    b. Sets standards for teacher education programs
    c. Certifies teachers
    d. All of the above

2. The number of public school systems in Georgia is:
    a. 127
    b. 159
    c. 181
    d. 203

3. The Board of Regents of the University System of Georgia is:
    a. Appointed by the governor
    b. Appointed by the General Assembly
    c. Elected by the people
    d. Selected by the State Board of Education

4. The number of public institutions of higher learning in Georgia is:
    a. 25
    b. 35
    c. 63
    d. 159

5. State School Board members:
    a. Are all teachers
    b. Are appointed by the governor and confirmed by the Senate
    c. Represent state legislative as well as congressional districts
    d. Must have doctorates in education

6. The State School Superintendent is:
    a. Appointed by the governor
    b. Appointed by the governor and confirmed by the Senate
    c. Elected by the people
    d. Appointed by the General Assembly

7. In the state budget passed between 2010 and 2016, education received:
    a. Not quite $10,000,000
    b. Nearly $1,000,000,000
    c. Nearly $3,500,000,000
    d. Nearly $10,000,000,000

8. Local School District Superintendents:
    a. Are elected by the people
    b. Are appointed by the governor
    c. Are appointed by the County Commission
    d. Are appointed by the local Board of Education

9. Georgia's University System:
    a. Includes all public and private colleges and universities in Georgia
    b. Includes 29 public research universities, regional universities, four-year universities, and two-year colleges
    c. Includes all colleges and the technical college system of Georgia
    d. Includes only UGA, Georgia Tech, Georgia State University, and the Medical College of Georgia

10. The head of the University System of Georgia is called a:
    a. President
    b. Chancellor
    c. Provost
    d. Commissioner

11. A voucher system to fund private education:
    a. Exists in Georgia
    b. Does not exist in Georgia
    c. Has never been proposed in the General Assembly
    d. Has never been considered by the General Assembly

12. The Hope Scholarship Program requires that a recipient:
    a. Maintain a B average in college
    b. Make all A's
    c. Attend only a public institution in Georgia
    d. Is personally selected by Zell Miller

13. The state appropriation for education in Georgia:
    a. Is all the money that local school districts can spend
    b. Is a small percentage of the money that local school districts spend
    c. May be supplemented by local school districts
    d. Does not exist

14. Church-related schools in Georgia:
    a. Are fully funded by the state's taxpayers
    b. Are illegal under Georgia Constitution
    c. May only be operated by the Southern Baptist Convention
    d. None of the above

15. It is the contention of the authors of the text that:
    a. Educational establishment is the largest bureaucracy in the state
    b. Georgia educational system is in the state of pluralist transfiguration
    c. The Georgia State Constitution is fundamentally more egalitarian than it is pluralistic
    d. The U.S. Constitution is more pluralistic than it is majoritarian

Chapter 10: Local Government

1. In Georgia, this county has a single member county commission:
    a. Fulton
    b. Cobb
    c. Bleckley
    d. Lowndes

2. According to your text, the City of Atlanta is closest to this form of municipal government:
    a. Strong mayor/weak council
    b. Weak mayor/strong council
    c. Council-Manager
    d. Commission

3. Once granted by law, a municipal charter may:
    a. Never be revoked
    b. Be revoked only if population declines
    c. Be revoked if population declines and services stop
    d. Be revoked without cause

4. The current number of special districts in Georgia is about:
    a. 34
    b. 125
    c. 436
    d. 627

5. According to your text, local governments in Georgia are known as:
    a. Counties
    b. Municipalities
    c. Special districts
    d. Townships

6. The number of counties in Georgia is:
    a. 46
    b. 93
    c. 159
    d. 227

7. Each county in Georgia must elect the following *except:*
    a. A clerk of the superior court
    b. A sheriff
    c. A judge of the probate court
    d. A dogcatcher

8. Which of the following services is a special district most likely to carry out?
    a. Provision of water utility service to a group of contiguous local communities
    b. Regulation of interstate commerce
    c. Administration of prison facilities for the state government
    d. Election of state legislators

9. What is the purpose of a special district?
    a. To provide services to several neighboring communities
    b. To decide disputes between city department heads
    c. To elect a delegate to a convention
    d. To serve as a state capital or county seat

10. The most common type of county government in Georgia is:
    a. The commission-administrator format
    b. The traditional format
    c. The commission-manager format
    d. The single commissioner format

11. Consolidation of cities and counties in Georgia:
    a. Is a very popular process
    b. Is never used
    c. Has been used three times in over 60 years
    d. Has been used 60 times in three years

12. What is home rule?
    a. The principle that police need a warrant to search one's residence
    b. The principle that any state should be able to secede
    c. The principle that justifies geographic representation
    d. The principle that local governments should be given substantial governing authority

13. The system of municipal government most like a Business Corporation is:
    a. Council-Manager
    b. Weak mayor-Council
    c. Strong mayor-Council
    d. Commission

14. According to your text, the City of Atlanta is_____?
    a. A Class A City
    b. A Class I City
    c. A Class B City
    d. A municipality as is every other municipal corporation in Georgia

15. It is the contention of the authors of the text that in this chapter:
    a. The political culture of the state is evolving from traditional to individualistic
    b. The state of Georgia is in the state of transformation
    c. Georgia's educational system fails to meet Edmond Burke's test of delegate and trustee
    d. Georgia's Constitution guarantees each of its citizen the right to be educated in an institution of their choice

Chapter 11: The State Constitution

1. How many articles are there in the Georgia Constitution?
    a. 7
    b. 11
    c. 17
    d. 25

2. The current version of the Constitution of the State of Georgia was written in:
    a. 1777
    b. 1860
    c. 1945
    d. 1983

3. Which of the following statements about the Constitution is mostly true?
    a. John Locke is the exclusive source for basic theory
    b. Constitutional theory is extremely complex
    c. Jean Rousseau is the exclusive source for basic theory
    d. Georgia is a simple state and needs a simple Constitution

4. Which of the following is not one of James Q. Wilson's types?
    a. Capitalistic policies
    b. Majoritarian policies
    c. Interest-group policies
    d. Entrepreneurial policies

5. Which of the following is a good example of Wilson's majoritarian policy?
    a. Welfare policy
    b. Hunting and fishing
    c. The Capitol Building
    d. Pollution taxes

6. Which is a good example of Wilson's client-centered type?
    a. Welfare policy
    b. Hunting and fishing
    c. The Capitol Building
    d. Pollution taxes

7. Which is a good example of Wilson's interest group-type?
    a. Welfare policy
    b. Hunting and fishing
    c. The Capitol Building
    d. Pollution taxes

8. Which is a good example of Wilson's entrepreneurial type?
    a. Welfare policy
    b. Hunting and fishing
    c. The Capitol Building
    d. Pollution taxes

9. Accordingly, the authors of this text assert that in the Georgia State Constitution, true majoritarian policies:
    a. Are the prevailing type except in the area of tax and local options
    b. Exist only in the civil rights articles
    c. Exist only in the taxation articles
    d. Hardly exist at all

10. The belief that government should serve the general public is in:
    a. Client-Group policies
    b. Majoritarian policies
    c. Interest Group policies
    d. Entrepreneurial policies

11. Generally, the Georgia State Constitution rejects all of the following ideas, except:
    a. Right of governing comes from conquest
    b. Right of governing comes from divine will
    c. Right of governing comes from ethnic superiority
    d. Allows for the amendment of the Constitution to be proposed either by the General Assembly or by a constitutional convention

12. Which of the following is NOT specifically authorized in the Georgia State Constitution?
    a. The rights of the people
    b. Limits on government power
    c. Limits on government officials
    d. A blend of traditional and individualistic culture with a moralistic tinge

13. Since the adoption of the current Georgia Constitution in the 1980s:
    a. Over 80 amendments have been proposed
    b. Over 60 amendments have been ratified
    c. Over 19 amendments have been rejected
    d. All of its 11 articles have been amended by the state legislature

14. Among the 11 Articles of the Georgia Constitution, the most amended article is
    _____?
    a. The Second
    b. The Fourth
    c. The Eighth
    d. The Last

15. It is the contention of the authors of the text that:
    a. The political culture is evolving from individualistic to pre-traditional
    b. Georgia is in the state of transformation
    c. The Georgia State Constitution is fundamentally more majoritarian than it is pluralistic
    d. The U.S. Constitution is more pluralistic than it majoritarian

Appendix

Two
The Georgia State Constitution

Georgia State Politics:
The Constitutional Foundation
(From 1983 as Revised through January 2013)

Georgia has had twelve ruling documents, from the colonial charter issued in 1732, to the current state constitution, adopted in 1983. The Council of Safety, Georgia's Patriot rulers during the American Revolution, adopted a set of Rules and Regulations in 1776. Then came Georgia's first constitution in 1777, followed by updated versions in 1789 and 1798. A new constitution was adopted at the beginning of the Civil War in 1861, and at the end of the war in 1865. Another new constitution was adopted soon after the beginning of Reconstruction in 1868, and at its end in 1877. There have been three constitutions in the modern era—in 1945, 1976, and the current constitution of 1983. This page presents the full text of each of these documents, plus a link to the most recently amended version of the current constitution.

Table of Contents

Sources

Compiled by authors from various sources but mostly from Office of Georgia Secretary of State's web resources, most recently revised and update 2003 Georgia Constitution based on the 1983 Constitutions and subsequent amendments. Does not include recent amendments or changes to Georgia Constitution since 2013. Format, presentation, and comments, intended for academic purposes and use only.

Georgia Department of State Web Link:
http://sos.ga.gov/admin/files/Constitution_2013_Final_Printed.pdf

The Georgia State Constitution

Preamble

To perpetuate the principles of free government, insure justice to all, preserve peace, promote the interest and happiness of the citizen and of the family, and transmit to posterity the enjoyment of liberty, we the people of Georgia, relying upon the protection and guidance of Almighty God, do ordain and establish this Constitution.

Article I.
Bill of Rights

Section I.
Rights of Persons

To perpetuate the principles of free government, insure justice to all, preserve peace, promote the interest and happiness of the citizen and of the family, and transmit to posterity the enjoyment of liberty, we the people of Georgia, relying upon the protection and guidance of Almighty God, do ordain and establish this Constitution.

Paragraph I. *Life, liberty, and property.* No person shall be deprived of life, liberty, or property except by due process of law.

Paragraph II. *Protection to person and property; equal protection.* Protection to person and property is the paramount duty of government and shall be impartial and complete. No person shall be denied the equal protection of the laws.

Paragraph III. *Freedom of conscience.* Each person has the natural and inalienable right to worship God, each according to the dictates of that person's own conscience; and no human authority should, in any case, control or interfere with such right of conscience.

Paragraph IV. *Religious opinions; freedom of religion.* No inhabitant of this state shall be molested in person or property or be prohibited from holding any public office or trust on account of religious opinions; but the right of freedom of religion shall not be so construed as to excuse acts of licentiousness or justify practices inconsistent with the peace and safety of the state.

Paragraph V. *Freedom of speech and of the press guaranteed.* No law shall be passed to curtail or restrain the freedom of speech or of the press. Every person may speak, write, and publish sentiments on all subjects but shall be responsible for the abuse of that liberty.

Paragraph VI. *Libel.* In all civil or criminal actions for libel, the truth may be given in evidence; and, if it shall appear to the trier of fact that the matter charged as libelous is true, the party shall be discharged.

Paragraph VII. *Citizens, protection of.* All citizens of the United States, resident in this state, are hereby declared citizens of this state; and it shall be the duty of the General Assembly to enact such laws as will protect them in the full enjoyment of the rights, privileges, and immunities due to such citizenship.

Paragraph VIII. *Arms, right to keep and bear.* The right of the people to keep and bear arms shall not be infringed, but the General Assembly shall have power to prescribe the manner in which arms may be borne.

Paragraph IX. *Right to assemble and petition.* The people have the right to assemble peaceably for their common good and to apply by petition or remonstrance to those vested with the powers of government for redress of grievances.

Paragraph X. *Bill of attainder; ex post facto laws; and retroactive laws.* No bill of attainder, ex post facto law, retroactive law, or laws impairing the obligation of contract or making irrevocable grant of special privileges or immunities shall be passed.

Paragraph XI. *Right to trial by jury; number of jurors; selection & compensation of jurors.*

(a)   The right to trial by jury shall remain inviolate, except that the court shall render judgment without the verdict of a jury in all civil cases where no issuable defense is filed and where a jury is not demanded in writing by either party. In criminal cases, the defendant shall have a public and speedy trial by an impartial jury; and the jury shall be the judges of the law and the facts.

(b)   A trial jury shall consist of 12 persons; but the General Assembly may prescribe any number, not less than six, to constitute a trial jury in courts of limited jurisdiction and in superior courts in misdemeanor cases.

(c)   The General Assembly shall provide by law for the selection and compensation of persons to serve as grand jurors and trial jurors.

Paragraph XII. *Right to the courts.* No person shall be deprived of the right to prosecute or defend, either in person or by an attorney, that person's own cause in any of the courts of this state.

Paragraph XIII. *Searches, seizures, and warrants.* The right of the people to be secure in their persons, houses, papers, and effects against unreasonable searches and seizures shall not be violated; and no warrant shall issue except upon probable cause supported by oath or affirmation particularly describing the place or places to be searched and the persons or things to be seized.

Paragraph XIV. *Benefit of counsel; accusation; list of witnesses; compulsory process.* Every person charged with an offense against the laws of this state shall have the privilege and benefit of counsel; shall be furnished with a copy of the accusation or indictment and, on demand, with a list of the witnesses on whose testimony such charge is founded; shall have compulsory process to obtain the testimony of that person's own witnesses; and shall be confronted with the witnesses testifying against such person.

Paragraph XV. *Habeas corpus.* The writ of habeas corpus shall not be suspended unless, in case of rebellion or invasion, the public safety may require it.

Paragraph XVI. *Self-incrimination.* No person shall be compelled to give testimony tending in any manner to be self-incriminating.

Paragraph XVII. *Bail; fines; punishment; arrest, abuse of prisoners.* Excessive bail shall not be required, nor excessive fines imposed, nor cruel and unusual punishments inflicted; nor shall any person be abused in being arrested, while under arrest, or in prison.

Paragraph XVIII. *Jeopardy of life or liberty more than once forbidden.* No person shall be put in jeopardy of life or liberty more than once for the same offense except when a new trial has been granted after conviction or in case of mistrial.

Paragraph XIX. *Treason.* Treason against the State of Georgia shall consist of insurrection against the state, adhering to the state's enemies, or giving them aid and comfort. No person shall be convicted of treason except on the testimony of two witnesses to the same overt act or confession in open court.

Paragraph XX. *Conviction, effect of.* No conviction shall work corruption of blood or forfeiture of estate.

Paragraph XXI. *Banishment and whipping as punishment for crime.* Neither banishment beyond the limits of the state nor whipping shall be allowed as a punishment for crime.

Paragraph XXII. *Involuntary servitude.* There shall be no involuntary servitude within the State of Georgia except as a punishment for crime after legal conviction thereof or for contempt of court.

Paragraph XXIII. *Imprisonment for debt.* There shall be no imprisonment for Debt.

Paragraph XXIV. *Costs.* No person shall be compelled to pay costs in any criminal case except after conviction on final trial.

Paragraph XXV. *Status of the citizen.* The social status of a citizen shall never be the subject of legislation.

Paragraph XXVI. *Exemptions from levy and sale.* The General Assembly shall protect by law from levy and sale by virtue of any process under the laws of this state a portion of the property of each person in an amount of not less than $1,600.00 and shall have authority to define to whom any such additional exemptions shall be allowed; to specify the amount of such exemptions; to provide for the manner of exempting such property and for the sale, alienation, and encumbrance thereof; and to provide for the waiver of said exemptions by the debtor.

Paragraph XXVII. *Spouse's separate property.* The separate property of each spouse shall remain the separate property of that spouse except as otherwise provided by law.

Paragraph XXVIII. *Fishing and hunting.* The tradition of fishing and hunting and the taking of fish and wildlife shall be preserved for the people and shall be managed by law and regulation for the public good.

Paragraph XXIX. *Enumeration of rights not denial of others.* The enumeration of rights herein contained as a part of this Constitution shall not be construed to deny to the people any inherent rights which they may have hitherto enjoyed.

Section II.
Origin and Structure of Government

Paragraph I. *Origin and foundation of government.* All government, of right, originates with the people, is founded upon their will only, and is instituted solely for the good of the whole. Public officers are the trustees and servants of the people and are at all times amenable to them.

Paragraph II. *Object of government.* The people of this state have the inherent right of regulating their internal government. Government is instituted for the protection, security, and benefit of the people; and at all times they have the right to alter or reform the same whenever the public good may require it.

Paragraph III. *Separation of legislative, judicial, and executive powers.* The legislative, judicial, and executive powers shall forever remain separate and distinct; and no person discharging the duties of one shall at the same time exercise the functions of either of the others except as herein provided.

Paragraph IV. *Contempt's.* The power of the courts to punish for contempt shall be limited by legislative acts.

Paragraph V. *What acts void?* Legislative acts in violation of this Constitution or the Constitution of the United States are void, and the judiciary shall so declare them.

Paragraph VI. *Superiority of civil authority.* The civil authority shall be superior to the military.

Paragraph VII. *Separation of church and state.* No money shall ever be taken from the public treasury, directly or indirectly, in aid of any church, sect, cult, or religious denomination or of any sectarian institution.

Paragraph VIII. *Lotteries and nonprofit bingo games.*

(a) *Except as herein specifically provided in this Paragraph VIII, all lotteries, and the sale of lottery tickets. And all forms of pari-mutuel betting and casino gambling are hereby prohibited; and this prohibition shall be enforced by penal laws.*

(b) *The General Assembly may by law provide that the operation of a nonprofit bingo game shall not be a lottery and shall be legal in this state. The General Assembly may by law define a nonprofit bingo game and provide for the regulation of nonprofit bingo games.*

(c) *The General Assembly may by law provide for the operation and regulation of a lottery or lotteries by or on behalf of the state and for any matters relating to the purposes or provisions of this subparagraph.*

Proceeds derived from the lottery or lotteries operated by or on behalf of the state shall be used to pay the operating expenses of the lottery or lotteries, including all prizes, without any appropriation required by law, and for educational programs and purposes as hereinafter provided.

Lottery proceeds shall not be subject to Article VII, Section III, Paragraph II; Article III, Section IX, Paragraph VI (a); or Article III, Section IX, Paragraph IV(c), except that the net proceeds after payment of such operating expenses shall be subject to Article VII, Section III, Paragraph II. Net proceeds after payment of such operating expenses shall be separately accounted for and shall be specifically identified by the Governor in his annual budget presented to the General Assembly as a separate budget category entitled "Lottery Proceeds" and the Governor shall make specific recommendations as to educational programs and educational purposes to which said net proceeds shall be appropriated.

In the General Appropriations Act adopted by the General Assembly, the General Assembly shall appropriate all net proceeds of the lottery or lotteries by such separate budget category to educational programs and educational purposes. Such net proceeds shall be used to support improvements and enhancements for educational programs and purposes and such net proceeds shall be used to supplement, not supplant, non-lottery educational resources for educational programs and purposes.

The educational programs and educational purposes for which proceeds may be so appropriated shall include only the following:

(1) Tuition grants, scholarships, or loans to citizens of this state to enable such citizens to attend colleges and universities located within this state, regardless of whether such colleges or universities are operated by the board of regents, or to attend institutions operated under the authority of the Department of Technical and Adult Education;

(2) Voluntary prekindergarten;

(3) One or more educational shortfall reserves in a total amount of not less than 10 percent of the net proceeds of the lottery for the preceding fiscal year;

(4) Costs of providing to teachers at accredited public institutions who teach levels K-12, personnel at public postsecondary technical institutes under the authority of the Department of Technical and Adult Education, and professors and instructors within the University System of Georgia the necessary training in the use and application of computers and advanced electronic instructional technology to implement interactive learning environments in the classroom and to access the state-wide distance learning network; and

(5) Capital outlay projects for educational facilities; Provided, however, that no funds shall be appropriated for the items listed in paragraphs (4) and (5) of this subsection until all persons eligible for and applying

for assistance as provided in paragraph (1) of this subsection have received such assistance, all approved pre-kindergarten programs provided for in paragraph (2) of this subsection have been fully funded, and the education shortfall reserve or reserves provided for in paragraph (3) of this subsection have been fully funded.

(d) *On and after January 1, 1995, the holding of raffles by nonprofit organizations shall be lawful and shall not be prohibited by any law enacted prior to January 1, 1994. Laws enacted on or after January 1, 1994, however, may restrict, regulate, or prohibit the operation of such raffles.*

Paragraph IX. *Sovereign immunity and waiver thereof; claims against the state and its departments, agencies, officers, and employees.*

(a) *The General Assembly may waive the state's sovereign immunity from suit by enacting a State Tort Claims Act, in which the General Assembly may provide by law for procedures for the making, handling, and disposition of actions or claims against the state and its departments, agencies, officers, and employees, upon such terms and subject to such conditions and limitations as the General Assembly may provide.*

(b) *The General Assembly may also provide by law for the processing and disposition of claims against the state which do not exceed such maximum amount as provided therein.*

(c) *The state's defense of sovereign immunity is hereby waived as to any action ex contract for the breach of any written contract now existing or hereafter entered into by the state or its departments and agencies.*

(d) *Except as specifically provided by the General Assembly in a State Tort Claims Act, all officers and employees of the state or its departments and agencies may be subject to suit and may be liable for injuries and damages caused by the negligent performance of, or negligent failure to perform, their ministerial functions and may be liable for injuries and damages if they act with actual malice or with actual intent to cause injury in the performance of their official functions. Except as provided in this subparagraph, officers and employees of the state or its departments and agencies shall not be subject to suit or liability, and no judgment shall be entered against them, for the performance or nonperformance of their official functions. The provisions of this subparagraph shall not be waived.*

(e) *Except as specifically provided in this Paragraph, sovereign immunity extends to the state and all of its departments and agencies. The sovereign immunity of the state and its departments and agencies can only be waived by an Act of the General Assembly which specifically provides that sovereign immunity is thereby waived and the extent of such waiver.*

(f) *No waiver of sovereign immunity under this Paragraph shall be construed as a waiver of any immunity provided to the state or its departments, agencies, officers, or employees by the United States Constitution.*

Section III
General Provisions

Paragraph I. *Eminent domain.*

(a) Except as otherwise provided in this Paragraph, private property shall not be taken or damaged for public purposes without just and adequate compensation being first paid.

(b) When private property is taken or damaged by the state or the counties or municipalities of the state for public road or street purposes, or for public transportation purposes, or for any other public purposes as determined by the General Assembly, just and adequate compensation therefor need not be paid until the same has been finally fixed and determined as provided by law; but such just and adequate compensation shall then be paid in preference to all other obligations except bonded indebtedness.

(c) The General Assembly may by law require the condemnor to make prepayment against adequate compensation as a condition precedent to the exercise of the right of eminent domain and provide for the disbursement of the same to the end that the rights and equities of the property owner, lien holders, and the state and its subdivisions may be protected.

(d) The General Assembly may provide by law for the payment by the condemnor of reasonable expenses, including attorney's fees, incurred by the condemnee in determining just and adequate compensation.

(e) Notwithstanding any other provision of the Constitution, the General Assembly may provide by law for relocation assistance and payments to persons displaced through the exercise of the power of eminent domain or because of public projects or programs; and the powers of taxation may be exercised and public funds expended in furtherance thereof.

Paragraph II. *Private ways.* In case of necessity, private ways may be granted upon just and adequate compensation being first paid by the applicant.

Paragraph III. *Tidewater titles confirmed.* The Act of the General Assembly approved December 16, 1902, which extends the title of ownership of lands abutting on tidal water to low water mark, is hereby ratified and confirmed.

Section IV
Marriage

Paragraph I. *Recognition of marriage.*

(a) *This state shall recognize as marriage only the union of man and woman. Marriages between persons of the same sex are prohibited in this state.*

(b) *No union between persons of the same sex shall be recognized by this state as entitled to the benefits of marriage.*

This state shall not give effect to any public act, record, or judicial proceeding of any other state or jurisdiction respecting a relationship between persons of the same sex that is treated as a marriage under the laws of such other state or jurisdiction.

The courts of this state shall have no jurisdiction to grant a divorce or separate maintenance with respect to any such relationship or otherwise to consider or rule on any of the parties' respective rights arising as a result of or in connection with such relationship.

Article II
Voting and Elections

Section I
Method of Voting; Right to Register & Vote

Paragraph I. *Method of voting.* Elections by the people shall be by secret ballot and shall be conducted in accordance with procedures provided by law.

Paragraph II. *Right to register and vote.* Every person who is a citizen of the United States and a resident of Georgia as defined by law, who is at least 18 years of age and not disenfranchised by this article, and who meets minimum residency requirements as provided by law shall be entitled to vote at any election by the people. The General Assembly shall provide by law for the registration of electors.

Paragraph III. *Exceptions to right to register and vote.*

(a) No person who has been convicted of a felony involving moral turpitude may register, remain registered, or vote except upon completion of the sentence.

(b No person who has been judicially determined to be mentally incompetent may register, remain registered, or vote unless the disability has been removed.

Sections II
General Provisions

Paragraph I. *Procedures to be provided by law.* The General Assembly shall provide by law for a method of appeal from the decision to allow or refuse to allow any person to register or vote and shall provide by law for a procedure whereby returns of all elections by the people shall be made to the Secretary of State.

Paragraph II. *Run-off election.* A run-off election shall be a continuation of the general election and only persons who were entitled to vote in the general election shall be entitled to vote therein; and only those votes cast for the persons designated for the runoff shall be counted in the tabulation and canvass of the votes cast.

Paragraph III. *Persons not eligible to hold office.* No person who is not a registered voter; who has been convicted of a felony involving moral turpitude, unless that person's civil rights have been restored *and at least ten years have elapsed from the date of the completion of the sentence without a subsequent conviction of another felony involving moral turpitude; who is a defaulter for any federal, state, county, municipal, or school system taxes required of such officeholder or candidate if such person has been finally adjudicated by a court of competent jurisdiction to owe those taxes, but such ineligibility may be removed at any time by full payment thereof, or by making payments to the tax authority pursuant to a payment plan, or under such other conditions as the* General Assembly may provide by general law; or who is the holder of public funds illegally shall be eligible to hold any office or appointment of honor or trust in this state. Additional conditions of eligibility to hold office for persons elected on a write-in vote and for persons holding offices or appointments of honor or trust other than elected offices created by this Constitution may be provided by law.

Paragraph IV. *Recall of public officials holding elective office.* The General Assembly is hereby authorized to provide by general law for the recall of public officials who hold elective office. The procedures, grounds, and all other matters relative to such recall shall be provided for in such law.

Paragraph V. *Vacancies created by elected officials qualifying for other office. The office of any state, county, or municipal elected official shall be declared vacant upon such elected official qualifying, in a general primary or general election, or special primary or special election, for another state, county, or municipal elective office or qualifying for the House of Representatives or the Senate of the United States if the term of the office for which such official is qualifying for begins more than 30 days prior to the expiration of such official's present term of office. The vacancy created in any such office shall be filled as provided by this Constitution or any general or local law. This provision shall not apply to any elected official seeking or holding more than one elective office when the holding of such offices simultaneously is specifically authorized by law.*

Sections III
Suspension and Removal of Public Officials

Paragraph I. *Procedures for and effect of suspending or removing public officials upon felony indictment.*

(a) As used in this Paragraph, the term "public official" means the Governor, the Lieutenant Governor, the Secretary of State, the Attorney General, the State School Superintendent, the Commissioner of Insurance, the Commissioner of Agriculture, the Commissioner of Labor, and any member of the General Assembly.

(b) Upon indictment for a felony by a grand jury of this state or by the United States, which felony indictment relates to the performance or activities of the office of any public official, the Attorney General or district attorney shall transmit a certified copy of the indictment to the Governor or, if the indicted public official is the Governor, to the Lieutenant Governor who shall, subject to subparagraph (d) of this Paragraph, appoint a review commission.

If the indicted public official is the Governor, the commission shall be composed of the Attorney General, the Secretary of State, the State School Superintendent, the Commissioner of Insurance, the Commissioner of Agriculture, and the Commissioner of Labor.

If the indicted public official is the Attorney General, the commission shall be composed of three other public officials who are not members of the General Assembly.

If the indicted public official is not the Governor, the Attorney General, or a member of the General Assembly, the commission shall be composed of the Attorney General and two other public officials who are not members of the General Assembly.

If the indicted public official is a member of the General Assembly, the commission shall be composed of the Attorney General and one member of the Senate and one member of the House of Representatives.

If the Attorney General brings the indictment against the public official, the Attorney General shall not serve on the commission. In place of the Attorney General, the Governor shall appoint a retired Supreme Court Justice or a retired Court of Appeals Judge.

The commission shall provide for a speedy hearing, including notice of the nature and cause of the hearing, process for obtaining witnesses, and the assistance of counsel. Unless a longer period of time is granted by the appointing authority, the commission shall make a written report within 14 days.

If the commission determines that the indictment relates to and adversely affects the administration of the office of the indicted public official and that the rights and interests of the public are adversely affected thereby, the Governor or, if the Governor is the indicted public official, the Lieutenant Governor shall suspend the public official immediately and without further action pending the final disposition of the case or until the expiration of the officer's term of office, whichever occurs first.

During the term of office to which such officer was elected and in which the indictment occurred, if a *nolle prosequi* is entered, if the public official is acquitted, or if after conviction the conviction is later overturned as a result of any direct appeal or application for a writ of certiorari, the officer shall be immediately reinstated to the office from which he was suspended.

While a public official is suspended under this Paragraph and until initial conviction by the trial court, the officer shall continue to receive the compensation from his office.

After initial conviction by the trial court, the officer shall not be entitled to receive the compensation from his office. If the officer is reinstated to office, he shall be entitled to receive any compensation withheld under the provisions of this Paragraph.

(c) Unless the Governor is the public officer under suspension, for the duration of any suspension under this Paragraph, the Governor shall appoint a replacement officer except in the case of a member of the General Assembly. If the Governor is the public officer under suspension, the provisions of Article V, Section I, Paragraph V of this Constitution shall apply as if the Governor were temporarily disabled. Upon a final conviction with no appeal or review pending, the office shall be declared vacant and a successor to that office shall be chosen as provided in this Constitution or the laws enacted in pursuance thereof.

(d) No commission shall be appointed for a period of 14 days from the day the indictment is received. This period of time may be extended by the Governor. During this period of time, the indicted public official may, in writing, authorize the Governor or, if the Governor is the indicted public official, the Lieutenant Governor to suspend him from office. Any such voluntary suspension shall be subject to the same conditions for review, reinstatement, or declaration of vacancy as are provided in this Paragraph for a nonvoluntary suspension.

(e) After any suspension is imposed under this Paragraph, the suspended public official may petition the appointing authority for a review. The Governor or, if the indicted public official is the Governor, the Lieutenant Governor may reappoint the commission to review the suspension. The commission shall make a written report within 14 days.

If the commission recommends that the public official be reinstated, he shall immediately be reinstated to office.

(f) The report and records of the commission and the fact that the public official has or has not been suspended shall not be admissible in evidence in any court for any purpose. The report and record of the commission shall not be open to the public.

(g) The provisions of this Paragraph shall not apply to any indictment handed down prior to January 1, 1985.

(h) If a public official who is suspended from office under the provisions of this Paragraph is not first tried at the next regular or special term following the indictment, the suspension shall be terminated and the public official shall be reinstated to office. The public official shall not be reinstated under this subparagraph if he is not so tried based on a continuance granted upon a motion made only by the defendant.

Paragraph II. *Suspension upon felony conviction.* Upon initial conviction of any public official designated in Paragraph I of this section for any felony in a trial court of this state or the United States, regardless of whether the officer has been suspended previously under Paragraph I of this section, such public official shall be immediately and without further action suspended from office. While a public official is suspended from office under this Paragraph, he or she shall not be entitled to receive the compensation from his or her office.

If, during the remainder of the elected official's term of office, the conviction is later overturned as a result of any direct appeal or application for a writ of certiorari, the public official shall be immediately reinstated to the office from which he or she was suspended and shall be entitled to receive any compensation withheld under the provisions of this Paragraph. Unless the Governor is the public official under suspension, for the duration of any suspension under this Paragraph, the Governor shall appoint a replacement official except in the case of a member of the General Assembly.

If the public officer under suspension is a member of the Senate or House of Representatives, then a replacement member for the duration of the suspension shall be elected as now or hereafter provided by law, in a manner the same as or similar to the election of a member to fill a vacancy in the General Assembly but to serve only for the duration of the suspension.

If the Governor is the public officer under suspension, the provisions of Article V, Section I, Paragraph V of this Constitution shall apply as if the Governor were temporarily disabled. Upon a final conviction with no appeal or review pending, the office shall be declared vacant and a successor to that office shall be chosen as provided in this Constitution or the laws enacted in pursuance thereof. The provisions of this Paragraph shall not apply to any conviction rendered prior to January 1, 1987.

Article III
Legislative Branch

Section I
Legislative Power

Paragraph I. *Power vested in General Assembly.* The legislative power of the State shall be vested in a General Assembly which shall consist of a Senate and a House of Representatives.

Section II
Composition of General Assembly

Paragraph I. *Senate and House of Representatives.*

(a) The Senate shall consist of not more than 56 Senators, each of whom shall be elected from single-member districts.

(b) The House of Representatives shall consist of not fewer than 180Representatives apportioned among representative districts of the state.

Paragraph II. *Apportionment of General Assembly.* The General Assembly shall apportion the Senate and House districts. Such districts shall be composed of contiguous territory. The apportionment of the Senate and of the House of Representatives shall be changed by the General Assembly as necessary after each United States decennial census.

Paragraph III. *Qualifications of members of General Assembly.*

(a) At the time of their election, the members of the Senate shall be citizens of the United States, shall be at least 25 years of age, shall have been citizens of this state for at least two years, and shall have been legal residents of the territory embraced within the district from which elected for at least one year.

(b) At the time of their election, the members of the House of Representatives shall be citizens of the United States, shall be at least 21 years of age, shall have been citizens of this state for at least two years, and shall have been legal residents of the territory embraced within the district from which elected for at least one year.

Paragraph IV. *Disqualifications.*

(a) No person on active duty with any branch of the armed forces of the United States shall have a seat in either house unless otherwise provided by law.

(b) No person holding any civil appointment or office having any emolument annexed thereto under the United States, this state, or any other state shall have a seat in either house.

(c) No Senator or Representative shall be elected by the General Assembly or appointed by the Governor to any office or appointment having any emolument annexed thereto during the time for which such person shall have been elected unless the Senator or Representative shall first resign the seat to which elected; provided, however, that, during the term for which elected, no Senator or Representative shall be appointed to any civil office which has been created during such term.

Paragraph V. *Election and term of members.*

(a) The members of the General Assembly shall be elected by the qualified electors of their respective districts for a term of two years and shall serve until the time fixed for the convening of the next General Assembly.

(b) The members of the General Assembly in office on June 30, 1983, shall serve out the remainder of the terms to which elected.

(c) The first election for members of the General Assembly under this Constitution shall take place on Tuesday after the first Monday in November, 1984, and subsequent elections biennially on that day until the day of election is changed by law.

Section III
Officer of the General Assembly

Paragraph I. *President and President Pro Tempore of the Senate.*

(a) The presiding officer of the Senate shall be styled the President of the Senate.

(b) A President Pro Tempore shall be elected by the Senate from among its members. The President Pro Tempore shall act as President in case of the temporary disability of the President. In case of the death, resignation, or permanent disability of the President or in the event of the succession of the President to the executive power, the President Pro Tempore shall become President and shall receive the same compensation and allowances as the Speaker of the House of Representatives. The General Assembly shall provide by law for the method of determining disability as provided in this Paragraph.

Paragraph II.   *Speaker and Speaker Pro Tempore of the House of Representatives.*

(a) The presiding officer of the House of Representatives shall be styled the Speaker of the House of Representatives and shall be elected by the House of Representatives from among its members.

(b) A Speaker Pro Tempore shall be elected by the House of Representatives from among its members. The Speaker Pro Tempore shall become Speaker in case of the death, resignation, or permanent disability of the Speaker and shall serve until a Speaker is elected. Such election shall be held as provided in the rules of the House. The General Assembly shall provide by law for the method of determining disability as provided in this Paragraph.

Paragraph III. *Other officers of the two houses.* The other officers of the two houses shall be a Secretary of the Senate and a Clerk of the House of Representatives.

Section IV
Organization and Procedure of the General Assembly

Paragraph I. *Meeting, time limit, and adjournment.*

(a) The Senate and House of Representatives shall organize each odd-numbered year and shall be a different General Assembly for each two-year period. The General Assembly shall meet in regular session on the second Monday in January of each year, or otherwise as provided by law, and may continue in session for a period of no longer than 40 days in the aggregate each year. By concurrent resolution, the General Assembly may adjourn any regular session to such later date as it may fix for reconvening. Separate periods of adjournment may be fixed by one or more such concurrent resolutions.

(b) Neither house shall adjourn during a regular session for more than three days or meet in any place other than the state capitol without the consent of the other. Following the fifth day of a special session, either house may adjourn not more than twice for a period not to exceed seven days for each such adjournment. In the event either house, after the thirtieth day of any session, adopts a resolution to adjourn for a specified period of time and such resolution and any amendments thereto are not adopted by both houses by the end of the legislative day on which adjournment was called for in such resolution, the Governor may adjourn both houses for a period of time not to exceed ten days.

(c) If an impeachment trial is pending at the end of any session, the House shall adjourn and the Senate shall remain in session until such trial is completed.

Paragraph II. *Oath of members.* Each Senator and Representative, before taking the seat to which elected, shall take the oath or affirmation prescribed by law.

Paragraph III. *Quorum.* A majority of the members to which each house is entitled shall constitute a quorum to transact business. A smaller number may adjourn from day to day and compel the presence of its absent members.

Paragraph IV. *Rules of procedure; employees; interim committees.* Each house shall determine its rules of procedure and may provide for its employees. Interim committees may be created by or pursuant to the authority of the General Assembly or of either house.

Paragraph V. *Vacancies.* When a vacancy occurs in the General Assembly, it shall be filled as provided by this Constitution and by law. The seat of a member of either house shall be vacant upon the removal of such member's legal residence from the district from which elected.

Paragraph VI. *Salaries.* The members of the General Assembly shall receive such salary as shall be provided for by law, provided that no increase in salary shall become effective prior to the end of the term during which such change is made.

Paragraph VII. *Election and returns; disorderly conduct.* Each house shall be the judge of the election, returns, and qualifications of its members and shall have power to punish them for disorderly behavior or misconduct by censure, fine, imprisonment, or expulsion; but no member shall be expelled except by a vote of two-thirds of the members of the house to which such member belongs.

Paragraph VIII. *Contempts, how punished.* Each house may punish by imprisonment, not extending beyond the session, any person not a member who shall be guilty of a contempt by any disorderly behavior in its presence or who shall rescue or attempt to rescue any person arrested by order of either house.

Paragraph IX. *Privilege of members.* The members of both houses shall be free from arrest during sessions of the General Assembly, or committee meetings thereof, and in going thereto or returning therefrom, except for treason, felony, or breach of the peace. No member shall be liable to answer in any other place for anything spoken in either house or in any committee meeting of either house.

Paragraph X. *Elections by either house.* All elections by either house of the General Assembly shall be by recorded vote, and the vote shall appear on the respective journal of each house.

Paragraph XI. *Open meetings.* The sessions of the General Assembly and all standing committee meetings thereof shall be open to the public. Either house may by rule provide for exceptions to this requirement.

Section V
Enactment of Laws

Paragraph I. *Journals and laws.* Each house shall keep and publish after its adjournment a journal of its proceedings. The original journals shall be the sole, official records of the proceedings of each house and shall be preserved as provided by law. The General Assembly shall provide for the publication of the laws passed at each session.

Paragraph II. *Bills for revenue.* All bills for raising revenue, or appropriating money, shall originate in the House of Representatives.

Paragraph III. *One subject matter expressed.* No bill shall pass which refers to more than one subject matter or contains matter different from what is expressed in the title thereof.

Paragraph IV. *Statutes and sections of Code, how amended.* No law or section of the Code shall be amended or repealed by mere reference to its title or to the number of the section of the Code; but the amending or repealing Act shall distinctly describe the law or Code section to be amended or repealed as well as the alteration to be made.

Paragraph V. *Majority of members to pass bill.* No bill shall become law unless it shall receive a majority of the votes of all the members to which each house is entitled, and such vote shall so appear on the journal of each house.

Paragraph VI. *When roll-call vote taken.* In either house, when ordered by the presiding officer or at the desire of one-fifth of the members present or a lesser number if so provided by the rules of either house, a roll-call vote on any question shall be taken and shall be entered on the journal. The yeas and nays in each house shall be recorded and entered on the journal upon the passage or rejection of any bill or resolution appropriating money and whenever the Constitution requires a vote of two-thirds of either or both houses for the passage of a bill or resolution.

Paragraph VII. *Reading of general bills.* The title of every general bill and of every resolution intended to have the effect of general law or to amend this Constitution or to propose a new Constitution shall be read three times and on three separate days in each house before such bill or resolution shall be voted upon; and the third reading of such bill and resolution shall be in their entirety when ordered by the presiding officer or by a majority of the members voting on such question in either house.

Paragraph VIII. *Procedure for considering local legislation.* The General Assembly may provide by law for the procedure for considering local legislation.

The title of every local bill and every resolution intended to have the effect of local law shall be read at least once before such bill or resolution shall be voted upon; and no such bill or resolution shall be voted upon prior to the second day following the day of introduction.

Paragraph IX. *Advertisement of notice to introduce local legislation.* The General Assembly shall provide by law for the advertisement of notice of intention to introduce local bills.

Paragraph X. *Acts signed.* All Acts shall be signed by the President of the Senate and the Speaker of the House of Representatives.

Paragraph XI. *Signature of Governor.* No provision in this Constitution for a two-thirds' vote of both houses of the General Assembly shall be construed to waive the necessity for the signature of the Governor as in any other case, except in the case of the two-thirds' vote required to override the veto or to submit proposed constitutional amendments or a proposal for a new Constitution.

Paragraph XII. *Rejected bills.* No bill or resolution intended to have the effect of law which shall have been rejected by either house shall again be proposed during the same regular or special session under the same or any other title without the consent of two-thirds of the house by which the same was rejected.

Paragraph XIII. *Approval, veto, and override of veto of bills and resolutions.*

(a) All bills and all resolutions which have been passed by the General Assembly intended to have the effect of law shall become law if the Governor approves or fails to veto the same within six days from the date any such bill or resolution is transmitted to the Governor unless the General Assembly adjourns sine die or adjourns for more than 40 days prior to the expiration of said six days. In the case of such adjournment sine die or of such adjournment for more than 40 days, the same shall become law if approved or not vetoed by the Governor within 40 days from the date of any such adjournment.

(b) During sessions of the General Assembly or during any period of adjournment of a session of the General Assembly, no bill or resolution shall be transmitted to the Governor after passage except upon request of the Governor or upon order of two-thirds of the membership of each house. A local bill which is required by the Constitution to have a referendum election conducted before it shall become effective shall be transmitted immediately to the Governor when ordered by the presiding officer of the house wherein the bill shall have originated or upon order of two-thirds of the membership of such house.

(c) The Governor shall have the duty to transmit any vetoed bill or resolution, together with the reasons for such veto, to the presiding officer of the house wherein it originated within three days from the date of veto if the General Assembly is in session on the date of transmission. If the General Assembly adjourns sine die or adjourns for more than 40 days, the Governor shall transmit any vetoed bill or resolution, together with the reasons for such veto, to the presiding officer of the house wherein it originated within 60 days of the date of such adjournment.

(d) During sessions of the General Assembly, any vetoed bill or resolution may upon receipt be immediately considered by the house wherein it originated for the purpose of overriding the veto. If two-thirds of the members to which such house is entitled vote to override the veto of the Governor, the same shall be immediately transmitted to the other house where it shall be immediately considered. Upon the vote to override the veto by two-thirds of the members to which such other house is entitled, such bill or resolution shall become law. All bills and resolutions vetoed during the last three days of the session and not considered for the purpose of overriding the veto and all bills and resolutions vetoed after the General Assembly has adjourned sine die may be considered at the next session of the General Assembly for the purpose of overriding the veto in the manner herein provided. If either house shall fail to override the Governor's veto, neither house shall again consider such bill or resolution for the purpose of overriding such veto.

(e) The Governor may approve any appropriation and veto any other appropriation in the same bill, and any appropriation vetoed shall not become law unless such veto is overridden in the manner herein provided.

Paragraph XIV. *Jointly sponsored bills and resolutions.* The General Assembly may provide by law for the joint sponsorship of bills and resolutions.

Section VI.
Exercise of Powers

Paragraph I. *General Powers.* The General Assembly shall have the power to make all laws not inconsistent with this Constitution, and not repugnant to the Constitution of the United States, which it shall deem necessary and proper for the welfare of the state.

Paragraph II. *Specific powers.*

(a) Without limitation of the powers granted under Paragraph I, the General Assembly shall have the power to provide by law for:

(1) Restrictions upon land use in order to protect and preserve the natural resources, environment, and vital areas of this state.

(2) A militia and for the trial by courts-martial and nonjudicial punishment of its members, the discipline of whom, when not in federal service, shall be in accordance with law and the directives of the Governor acting as commander in chief.

(3) The participation by the state and political subdivisions and instrumentalities of the state in federal programs and the compliance with laws relating thereto, including but not limited to the powers, which may be exercised to the extent and in the manner necessary

to effect such participation and compliance, to tax, to expend public money, to condemn property, and to zone property.

(4) The continuity of state and local governments in periods of emergency resulting from disasters caused by enemy attack including but not limited to the suspension of all constitutional legislative rules during such emergency.

(5) The participation by the state with any county, municipality, nonprofit organization, or any combination thereof in the operation of any of the facilities operated by such agencies for the purpose of encouraging and promoting tourism in this state.

(6) The control and regulation of outdoor advertising devices adjacent to federal aid interstate and primary highways and for the acquisition of property or interest therein for such purposes and may exercise the powers of taxation and provide for the expenditure of public funds in connection therewith.

(b) The General Assembly shall have the power to implement the provisions of Article I, Section III, Paragraph I (2.); Article IV, Section VIII, Paragraph II; Article IV, Section VIII, Paragraph III; and Article X, Section II, Paragraph XII of the Constitution of 1976 in force and effect on June 30, 1983; and all laws heretofore adopted thereunder and valid at the time of their enactment shall continue in force and effect until modified or repealed.

(c) The distribution of tractors, farm equipment, heavy equipment, new motor vehicles, and parts therefor in the State of Georgia vitally affects the general economy of the state and the public interest and public welfare. Notwithstanding the provisions of Article I, Section I, Paragraphs I, II, and III or Article III, Section VI, Paragraph V(c) of this Constitution, the General Assembly in the exercise of its police power shall be authorized to regulate tractor, farm equipment, heavy equipment, and new motor vehicle manufacturers, distributors, dealers, and their representatives doing business in Georgia, including agreements among such parties, in order to prevent frauds, unfair business practices, unfair methods of competition, impositions, and other abuses upon its citizens. Any law enacted by the General Assembly shall not impair the obligation of an existing contract but may apply with respect to the renewal of such a contract after the effective date of such law.

Paragraph III. *Powers not to be abridged.* The General Assembly shall not abridge its powers under this Constitution. No law enacted by the General Assembly shall be construed to limit its powers.

Paragraph IV. *Limitations on special legislation.*

(a) Laws of a general nature shall have uniform operation throughout this state and no local or special law shall be enacted in any case for which provision has been made by an existing general law, except that the General Assembly may by general law authorize local governments by local ordinance or resolution to exercise police powers which do not conflict with general laws.

(b) No population bill, as the General Assembly shall define by general law, shall be passed. No bill using classification by population as a means of determining the applicability of any bill or law to any political subdivision or group of political subdivisions may expressly or impliedly amend, modify, supersede, or repeal the general law defining a population bill.

(c) No special law relating to the rights or status of private persons shall be enacted.

Paragraph V. *Specific limitations.*

(a) The General Assembly shall not have the power to grant incorporation to private persons but shall provide by general law the manner in which private corporate powers and privileges may be granted.

(b) The General Assembly shall not forgive the forfeiture of the charter of any corporation existing on August 13, 1945, nor shall it grant any benefit to or permit any amendment to the charter of any corporation except upon the condition that the acceptance thereof shall operate as a novation of the charter and that such corporation shall thereafter hold its charter subject to the provisions of this Constitution.

(c) (1) The General Assembly shall not have the power to authorize any contract or agreement which may have the effect of or which is intended to have the effect of encouraging a monopoly, which is hereby declared to be unlawful and void. Except as otherwise provided in subparagraph (c)(2) of this Paragraph, the General Assembly shall not have the power to authorize any contract or agreement which may have the effect of or which is intended to have the effect of defeating or lessening competition, which is hereby declared to be unlawful and void.

(2) The General Assembly shall have the power to authorize and provide by general law for judicial enforcement of contracts or agreements restricting or regulating competitive activities between or among:
(A) Employers and employees;
(B) Distributors and manufacturers;
(C) Lessors and lessees;
(D) Partnerships and partners;
(E) Franchisors and franchisees;
(F) Sellers and purchasers of a business or commercial enterprise; or
(G) Two or more employers.

(3) The authority granted to the General Assembly in subparagraph (c) (2) of this Paragraph shall include the authority to grant to courts by general law the power to limit the duration, geographic area, and scope of prohibited activities provided in a contract or agreement restricting or regulating competitive activities to render such contract

or agreement reasonable under the circumstances for which it was made. (d) The General Assembly shall not have the power to regulate or fix charges of Public utilities owned or operated by any county or municipality of this state, except as authorized by this Constitution.

(e) No municipal or county authority which is authorized to construct, improve, or maintain any road or street on behalf of, pursuant to a contract with, or through the use of taxes or other revenues of a county or municipal corporation shall be created by any local Act or pursuant to any general Act nor shall any law specifically relating to any such authority be amended unless the creation of such authority or the amendment of such law is conditioned upon the approval of a majority of the qualified voters of the county or municipal corporation affected voting in a referendum thereon. This subparagraph shall not apply to or affect any state authority.

Paragraph VI. *Gratuities.*

(a) Except as otherwise provided in the Constitution, (1) the General Assembly shall not have the power to grant any donation or gratuity or to forgive any debt or obligation owing to the public, and (2) the General Assembly shall not grant or authorize extra compensation to any public officer, agent, or contractor after the service has

(b) All laws heretofore adopted under Article III, Section VIII, Paragraph XII of the Constitution of 1976 in force and effect on June 30, 1983, shall continue in force and effect and may be amended if such amendments are consistent with the authority granted to the General Assembly by such provisions of said Constitution.

(c) The General Assembly may provide by law and may expend or authorize the expenditure of public funds for a health insurance plan or program for persons and the spouses and dependent children of persons who are retired former employees of public schools or public school systems of this state.

(d) The General Assembly may provide by law for indemnification with respect to licensed emergency management rescue specialists who are or have been killed or permanently disabled in the line of duty on or after January 1, 1991, and publicly employed emergency medical technicians who are or have been killed or permanently disabled in the line of duty on or after January 1, 1987.

(e) (1) The General Assembly may provide by law for a program of indemnification with respect to the death or permanent disability of any law enforcement officer, fireman, prison guard, or publicly employed emergency medical technician who is or at any time in the past was killed or permanently disabled in the line of duty. Funds shall be appropriated as necessary for payment of such indemnification or for the purchase of insurance for such indemnification or both.

(2) The General Assembly may provide by law for a program of compensation for injuries incurred by law enforcement officers and

firemen in the line of duty. A law enforcement officer who becomes physically disabled, but not permanently disabled, as a result of a physical injury incurred in the line of duty and caused by a willful act of violence and a fireman who becomes physically disabled, but not permanently disabled, as a result of a physical injury incurred in the line of duty while fighting a fire shall be entitled to receive monthly compensation from the state in an amount equal to any such person's regular compensation for the period of time that the law enforcement officer or fireman is physically unable to perform the duties of his or her employment; provided, however, that such benefits provided in this subparagraph shall not be granted for more than a total of 12 months for injuries resulting from a single incident. A law enforcement officer or fireman shall be required to submit to a state agency satisfactory evidence of such disability. Benefits made available under this subparagraph shall be subordinate to workers' compensation benefits, disability and other compensation benefits from an employer which the law enforcement officer or fireman is awarded and shall be limited to the difference between the amount of workers' compensation benefits, disability and other compensation benefits actually paid and the amount of the law enforcement officer's or fireman's regular compensation. Any law enforcement officer or fireman who receives indemnification under subparagraph (1) of this subparagraph (e) shall not be entitled to any compensation under this subparagraph.

(f) The General Assembly is authorized to provide by law for compensating. Innocent victims of crimes which occur on and after July 1, 1989. The General Assembly is authorized to define the types of victims eligible to receive compensation and to vary the amounts of compensation according to need. The General Assembly shall be authorized to allocate certain funds, to appropriate funds, to provide for a continuing fund, or to provide for any combination thereof for the purpose of compensating innocent victims of crime and for the administration of any laws enacted for such purpose.

(g) The General Assembly may provide by law for indemnification with respect to public school teachers, administrators, and employees who are killed or permanently disabled by an act of violence in the line of duty, a nonlapsing indemnification fund for such purposes, and dedication of revenue from special and distinctive motor vehicle license plates honoring Georgia educators to such fund.

(g) The General Assembly may provide by law for a program of indemnification with respect to the death or permanent disability of any state highway employee who is or at any time in the past was killed or permanently disabled in the line of duty. Funds shall be appropriated as necessary for payment of such indemnification or for the purchase of insurance for such indemnification or both.

Paragraph VII. *Regulation of alcoholic beverages.* The State of Georgia shall have full and complete authority to regulate alcoholic beverages and to regulate, restrict, or prohibit activities involving alcoholic beverages. This regulatory authority of the state shall include all such regulatory authority as is permitted to the states under the Twenty- First Amendment to the United States Constitution. This regulatory authority of the state is specifically delegated to the counties and municipalities of the state for the purpose of regulating, restricting, or prohibiting the exhibition of nudity, partial nudity, or depictions of nudity in connection with the sale or consumption of alcoholic beverages; and such delegated regulatory authority may be exercised by the adoption and enforcement of regulatory ordinances by the counties and municipalities of this state. A general law exercising such regulatory authority shall control over conflicting provisions of any local ordinance but shall not preempt any local ordinance provisions not in direct conflict with general law.

Section VII
Impeachment

Paragraph I. *Power to impeach.* The House of Representatives shall have the sole power to vote impeachment charges against any executive or judicial officer of this state or any member of the General Assembly.

Paragraph II. *Trial of impeachments.* The Senate shall have the sole power to try impeachments. When sitting for that purpose, the Senators shall be on oath, or affirmation, and shall be presided over by the Chief Justice of the Supreme Court. Should the Chief Justice be disqualified, then the Presiding Justice shall preside. Should the Presiding Justice be disqualified, then the Senate shall select a Justice of the Supreme Court to preside. No person shall be convicted without concurrence of two-thirds of the members to which the Senate is entitled.

Paragraph III. *Judgments in impeachment.* In cases of impeachment, judgments shall not extend further than removal from office and disqualification to hold and enjoy any office of honor, trust, or profit within this state or to receive a pension therefrom, but no such judgment shall relieve any party from any criminal or civil liability.

Section VIII
Insurance Regulations

Paragraph I. *Regulation of insurance.* Provision shall be made by law for the regulation of insurance.

Paragraph II. *Issuance of licenses.* Insurance licenses shall be issued by the Commissioner of Insurance as required by law.

Section IX
Appropriations

Paragraph I. *Public money, how drawn.* No money shall be drawn from the treasury except by appropriation made by law.

Paragraph II. *Preparation, submission, and enactments of general appropriations bill.*

(a) The Governor shall submit to the General Assembly within five days after its convening in regular session each year a budget message and a budget report, accompanied by a draft of a general appropriations bill, in such form and manner as may be prescribed by statute, which shall provide for the appropriation of the funds necessary to operate all the various departments and agencies and to meet the current expenses of the state for the next fiscal year.

(b) The General Assembly shall annually appropriate those state and federal funds necessary to operate all the various departments and agencies. To the extent that federal funds received by the state for any program, project, activity, purpose, or expenditure are changed by federal authority or exceed the amount or amounts appropriated in the general appropriations Act or supplementary appropriation Act or Acts, or are not anticipated, such excess, changed or unanticipated federal funds are hereby continually appropriated for the purposes authorized and directed by the federal government in making the grant. In those instances where the conditions under which the federal funds have been made available do not provide otherwise, federal funds shall first be used to replace state funds that were appropriated to supplant federal funds in the same state fiscal year. The fiscal year of the state shall commence on the first day of July of each year and terminate on the thirtieth of June following.

(c) The General Assembly shall by general law provide for the regulation and management of the finance and fiscal administration of the state.

Paragraph III. *General appropriations bill.* The general appropriations bill shall embrace nothing except appropriations fixed by previous laws; the ordinary expenses of the executive, legislative, and judicial departments of the government; payment of the public debt and interest thereon; and for support of the public institutions and educational interests of the state. All other appropriations shall be made by separate bills, each embracing but one subject.

Paragraph IV. *General appropriations Act.*

(a) Each general appropriations Act, now of force or hereafter adopted with such amendments as are adopted from time to time, shall continue in force and effect for the next fiscal year after adoption and it shall then expire, except for the mandatory appropriations required by this Constitution and those required to meet contractual obligations authorized by this Constitution and the continued appropriation of federal grants.

(b) The General Assembly shall not appropriate funds for any given fiscal year which, in aggregate, exceed a sum equal to the amount of unappropriated surplus expected to have accrued in the state treasury at the beginning of the fiscal year together with an amount not greater than the total treasury receipts from existing revenue sources anticipated to be collected in the fiscal year, less refunds, as estimated in the budget report and amendments thereto. Supplementary appropriations, if any, shall be made in the manner provided in Paragraph V of this section of the Constitution; but in no event shall a supplementary appropriations Act continue in force and effect beyond the expiration of the general appropriations Act in effect when such supplementary appropriations Act was adopted and approved.

(c)   All appropriated state funds, except for the mandatory appropriations required by this Constitution, remaining unexpended and not contractually obligated at the expiration of such general appropriations Act shall lapse.

(d)   Funds appropriated to or received by the State Housing Trust Fund for the Homeless shall not be subject to the provisions of Article III, Section IX, Paragraph IV(c), relative to the lapsing of funds, and may be expended for programs of purely public charity for the homeless, including programs involving the participation of churches and religious institutions, notwithstanding the provisions of Article I, Section II, Paragraph VII.

Paragraph V.   *Other or supplementary appropriations.* In addition to the appropriations made by the general appropriations Act and amendments thereto, the General Assembly may make additional appropriations by Acts, which shall be known as supplementary appropriation Acts, provided no such supplementary appropriation shall be available unless there is an unappropriated surplus in the state treasury or the revenue necessary to pay such appropriation shall have been provided by a tax laid for such purpose and collected into the general fund of the state treasury. Neither house shall pass a supplementary appropriation bill until the general appropriations Act shall have been finally adopted by both houses and approved by the Governor.

Paragraph VI.   *Appropriations to be for specific sums.*

(a)   Except as hereinafter provided, the appropriation for each department, officer, bureau, board, commission, agency, or institution for which appropriation is made shall be for a specific sum of money; and no appropriation shall allocate to any object the proceeds of any particular tax or fund or a part or percentage thereof.

(b)   An amount equal to all money derived from motor fuel taxes received by the state in each of the immediately preceding fiscal years, less the amount of refunds, rebates, and collection costs authorized by law, is hereby appropriated for the fiscal year beginning July 1, of each year following, for all activities incident to providing and maintaining an adequate system of public roads and bridges in this state, as authorized by laws enacted by the General Assembly of Georgia, and for grants to counties by law authorizing road construction and maintenance, as provided by law authorizing such grants. Said sum is hereby appropriated for, and shall be available for, the aforesaid purposes regardless of whether the General Assembly enacts a general appropriations Act; and said sum need not be specifically stated in any general appropriations Act passed by the General Assembly in order to be available for such purposes. However, this shall not preclude the General Assembly from appropriating for such purposes an amount greater than the sum specified above for such purposes. The expenditure of such funds shall be subject to all the rules, regulations, and restrictions imposed on the expenditure of appropriations by provisions of the Constitution and laws of this state, unless such provisions are in conflict with the provisions of this paragraph. And provided, however, that the proceeds of the tax hereby appropriated shall not be subject to budgetary reduction. In the event of invasion of this state by land, sea, or air or in case of a major catastrophe so proclaimed by the Governor, said funds may be utilized for defense or relief purposes on the executive order of the Governor.

(c) A trust fund for use in the reimbursement of a portion of an employer's workers' compensation expenses resulting to an employee from the combination of a previous disability with subsequent injury incurred in employment may be provided for by law. As authorized by law, revenues raised for purposes of the fund may be paid into and disbursed from the trust without being subject to the limitations of subparagraph (a) of this Paragraph or of Article VII, Section III, Paragraph II.

(d) As provided by law, additional penalties may be assessed in any case in which any court in this state imposes a fine or orders the forfeiture of any bond in the nature of the penalty for all offenses against the criminal and traffic laws of this state or of the political subdivisions of this state. The proceeds derived from such additional penalty assessments may be allocated for the specific purpose of meeting any and all costs, or any portion of the cost, of providing training to law enforcement officers and to prosecuting officials.

(e) The General Assembly may by general law approved by a three-fifths' vote of both houses designate any part or all of the proceeds of any state tax now or hereafter levied and collected on alcoholic beverages to be used for prevention, education, and treatment relating to alcohol and drug abuse.

(f) The General Assembly is authorized to provide by law for the creation of a State Children's Trust Fund from which funds shall be disbursed for child abuse and neglect prevention programs. The General Assembly is authorized to appropriate moneys to such fund and such moneys paid into the fund shall not be subject to the provisions of Article III, Section IX, Paragraph IV(c), relative to the lapsing of funds.

(g) The General Assembly is authorized to provide by law for the creation of a Seed-Capital Fund from which funds shall be disbursed at the direction of the Advanced Technology Development Center of the University System of Georgia to provide equity and other capital to small, young, entrepreneurial firms engaged in innovative work in the areas of technology, manufacturing, or agriculture. Funds shall be disbursed in the form of loans or investments which shall provide for repayment, rents, dividends, royalties, or other forms of return on investments as provided by law. Moneys received from returns on loans or investments shall be deposited in the Seed-Capital Fund for further disbursement. The General Assembly is authorized to appropriate moneys to such fund and such moneys paid into the fund shall not be subject to the provisions of Article III, Section IX, Paragraph IV(c) relative to the lapsing of funds. The General Assembly shall be authorized to provide by law for any matters relating to the purpose or provisions of this subparagraph.

(h)   The General Assembly is authorized to provide by general law for additional penalties or fees in any case in any court in this state in which a person is adjudged guilty of an offense against the criminal or traffic laws of this state or an ordinance of a political subdivision of this state. The General Assembly is authorized to provide by general law for the allocation of such additional penalties or fees for the construction, operation, and staffing of jails, correctional institutions, and detention facilities by counties.

(i)   The General Assembly is authorized to provide by general law for the creation of an Indigent Care Trust Fund. Any hospital, hospital authority, county, or municipality is authorized to contribute or transfer moneys to the fund and any other person or entity specified by the General Assembly may also contribute to the fund. The General Assembly may provide by general law for the dedication and deposit of revenues raised from specified sources for the purposes of the fund into the fund. Moneys in the fund shall be exclusively used for primary health care programs for medically indigent citizens and children of this state, for expansion of Medicaid eligibility and services, or for programs to support rural and other health care providers, primarily hospitals, who disproportionately serve the medically indigent. Any other appropriation from the Indigent Care Trust Fund shall be void. Contributions and revenues deposited to the fund shall not lapse and shall not be subject to the limitations of subparagraph (a) of this Paragraph or of Article VII, Section III, Paragraph II. Contributions in the fund which are not appropriated as required by this subparagraph shall be refunded pro rata to the contributors thereof, as provided by the General Assembly.

(j)   The General Assembly is authorized to provide by general law for the creation of an emerging crops fund from which to pay interest on loans made to farmers to enable such farmers to produce certain crops on Georgia farms and thereby promote economic development. The General Assembly is authorized to appropriate moneys to such fund and moneys so appropriated shall not be subject to the provisions of Article III, Section IX, Paragraph IV(c), relative to the lapsing of appropriated funds. Interest on loans made to farmers shall be paid from such fund pursuant to such terms, conditions, and requirements as the General Assembly shall provide by general law. The General Assembly may provide by general law for the administration of such fund by such state agency or public authority as the General Assembly shall determine.

(k)   The General Assembly is authorized to provide by general law for additional penalties or fees in any case in any court in this state in which a person is adjudged guilty of an offense involving driving under the influence of alcohol or drugs. The General Assembly is authorized to provide by general law for the allocation of such additional penalties or fees to the Brain and Spinal Injury Trust Fund, as provided by law, for the specified purpose of meeting any and all costs, or any portion of the costs, of providing care and rehabilitative services to citizens of the state who have survived neurotrauma with head or spinal cord injuries. Moneys appropriated for such purposes shall not lapse. The General Assembly may provide by general law for the administration of such fund by such authority as the General Assembly shall determine.

(l) The General Assembly is authorized to provide by general law for the creation of a roadside enhancement and beautification fund from which funds shall be disbursed for enhancement and beautification of public rights of way; for allocation and dedication of revenue from tree and other vegetation trimming or removal permit fees, other related assessments, and special and distinctive wildflower motor vehicle license plate fees to such fund; that moneys paid into the fund shall not lapse, the provisions of Article III, Section IX, Paragraph IV(c) notwithstanding; and for any matters relating to the purpose or provisions of this subparagraph. An Act creating such fund and making such provisions effective January 1, 1999, or later may originate or have originated in the Senate or the House of Representatives.

(m) There shall be within the Department of Agriculture a dog and cat reproductive sterilization support program to control dog and cat overpopulation and thereby reduce the number of animals housed and killed in animal shelters, which program shall be administered by the Commissioner of Agriculture. In order to fund the program, there shall be issued beginning in 2003 specially designed license plates promoting the program. The General Assembly shall provide by law for the issuance of such license plates and for dedication of certain revenue derived from fees for such plates to the support of the program. All such dedicated revenue derived from special license plate fees, any funds appropriated to the department for such purposes, and any voluntary contributions or other funds made available to the department for such purposes and all interest thereon shall be deposited in a special fund for support of the program, shall not be used for any purpose other than support of the program, and shall not lapse. The General Assembly may provide by law for all matters necessary or appropriate to the implementation of this paragraph.

(n) The General Assembly may provide by law for the issuance and renewal of special motor vehicle license plates that motor vehicle owners may optionally purchase and renew for additional fees. The General Assembly may provide for all or a portion of the net revenue, as defined by the General Assembly, derived from the additional fees charged for any such special license plate to be dedicated to an agency, fund, or nonprofit corporation to implement or support programs related to the nature of the special license plate, as intended by the authorizing statute. Any dedication of funds enacted pursuant to the authority of this subparagraph may be in whole or in part for the ultimate use of a nonprofit corporation, without limitation by Article III, Section VI, Paragraph VI, if the General Assembly determines that the license plate program and such appropriation will benefit both the state and the nonprofit corporation. Any law enacted pursuant to the authority of this subparagraph may provide that funds dedicated pursuant to such law shall not lapse as otherwise required by Article III, Section IX, Paragraph IV(c). Any law enacted pursuant to the authority of this subparagraph shall be required to receive a two thirds' majority vote in both the Senate and the House of Representatives.

Paragraph VII. *Appropriations void, when.* Any appropriation made in conflict with any of the foregoing provisions shall be void.

Section X
Retirement Systems

Paragraph I. *Expenditure of public funds authorized.* Public funds may be expended for the purpose of paying benefits and other costs of retirement and pension systems for public officers and employees and their beneficiaries.

Paragraph II. *Increasing benefits authorized.* Public funds may be expended for the purpose of increasing benefits being paid pursuant to any retirement or pension system wholly or partially supported from public funds.

Paragraph III. *Retirement systems covering employees of county boards of education.* Notwithstanding Article IX, Section II, Paragraph III(a)(14), the authority to establish or modify heretofore existing local retirement systems covering employees of county boards of education shall continue to be vested in the General Assembly.

Paragraph IV. *Firemen's Pension System.* The powers of taxation may be exercised by the state through the General Assembly and the counties and municipalities for the purpose of paying pensions and other benefits and costs under a firemen's pension system or systems. The taxes so levied may be collected by such firemen's pension system or systems and disbursed therefrom by authority of the General Assembly for the purposes therein authorized.

Paragraph V. *Funding standards.* It shall be the duty of the General Assembly to enact legislation to define funding standards which will assure the actuarial soundness of any retirement or pension system supported wholly or partially from public funds and to control legislative procedures so that no bill or resolution creating or amending any such retirement or pension system shall be passed by the General Assembly without concurrent provisions for funding in accordance with the defined funding standards.

Paragraph V-A. *Limitation on involuntary separation benefits for Governor of the State of Georgia.* Any other provisions of this Constitution to the contrary notwithstanding, no past, present, or future Governor of the State of Georgia who ceases or ceased to hold office as Governor for any reason, except for medical disability, shall receive a retirement benefit based on involuntary separation from employment as a result of ceasing to hold office as Governor. The provisions of any law in conflict with this Paragraph are null and void effective January 1, 1985.

Paragraph VI. *Involuntary separation; part-time service.*

(a) Any public retirement or pension system provided for by law in existence prior to January 1, 1985, may be changed by the General Assembly for any one or more of the following purposes:

(1) To redefine involuntary separation from employment; or

(2) To provide additional or revise existing limitations or restrictions on the right to qualify for a retirement benefit based on involuntary separation from employment.

(b) The General Assembly by law may define or redefine part-time service, including but not limited to service as a member of the General Assembly, for the purposes of any public retirement or pension system presently existing or created in the future and may limit or restrict the use of such part-time service as creditable service under any such retirement or pension system.

(c) Any law enacted by the General Assembly pursuant to subparagraph (a) or (b) of this Paragraph may affect persons who are members of public retirement or pension systems on January 1, 1985, and who became members at any time prior to that date.

(d) Any law enacted by the General Assembly pursuant to subparagraph (a) or (b) of this Paragraph shall not be subject to any law controlling legislative procedures for the consideration of retirement or pension bills, including, but not limited to, any limitations on the sessions of the General Assembly at which retirement or pension bills may be introduced.

(e) No public retirement or pension system created on or after January 1, 1985, shall grant any person whose retirement is based on involuntary separation from employment a retirement or pension benefit more favorable than the retirement or pension benefit granted to a person whose separation from employment is voluntary.

Article IV
Constitutional Boards and Commissions

Section I
Public Service Commission

Paragraph I. *Public Service Commission.*

(a) There shall be a Public Service Commission for the regulation of utilities which shall consist of five members who shall be elected by the people. The Commissioners in office on June 30, 1983, shall serve until December 31 after the general election at which the successor of each member is elected. Thereafter, all succeeding terms of members shall be for six years. Members shall serve until their successors are elected and qualified. A chairman shall be selected by the members of the commission from its membership.

(b)   The commission shall be vested with such jurisdiction, powers, and duties as provided by law.

(c)   The filling of vacancies and manner and time of election of members of the commission shall be as provided by law.

Section II
State Board of Pardons and Paroles

Paragraph I. *State Board of Pardons and Paroles.* There shall be a State Board of Pardons and Paroles which shall consist of five members appointed by the Governor, subject to confirmation by the Senate. The members of the board in office on June 30, 1983, shall serve out the remainder of their respective terms, provided that the expiration date of the term of any such member shall be December 31 of the year in which the member's term expires. As each term of office expires, the Governor shall appoint a successor as herein provided. All such terms of members shall be for seven years. A chairman shall be selected by the members of the board from its membership.

Paragraph II. *Powers and authority.*

(a)   Except as otherwise provided in this Paragraph, the State Board of Pardons and Paroles shall be vested with the power of executive clemency, including the powers to grant reprieves, pardons, and paroles; to commute penalties; to remove disabilities imposed by law; and to remit any part of a sentence for any offense against the state after conviction.

(b)   (1)   When a sentence of death is commuted to life imprisonment, the board shall not have the authority to grant a pardon to the convicted person until such person has served at least 25 years in the penitentiary; and such person shall not become eligible for parole at any time prior to serving at least 25 years in the penitentiary.

(2)   The General Assembly may by general law approved by two-thirds of the members elected to each branch of the General Assembly in a roll-call vote provide for minimum mandatory sentences and for sentences which are required to be served in their entirety for persons convicted of armed robbery, kidnapping, rape, aggravated child molestation, aggravated sodomy, or aggravated sexual battery and, when so provided by such Act, the board shall not have the authority to consider such persons for pardon, parole, or commutation during that portion of the sentence.

(3)   The General Assembly may by general law approved by two-thirds of the members elected to each branch of the General Assembly in a roll-call vote provide for the imposition of sentences of life without parole for persons convicted of murder and for persons who having been previously convicted of murder, armed robbery, kidnapping, rape, aggravated child molestation, aggravated sodomy, or aggravated sexual battery or having been previously convicted under the laws of any other state or of the United States of a crime which if committed

in this state would be one of those offenses and who after such previous conviction subsequently commits and is convicted of one of those offenses and, when so provided by such Act, the board shall not have the authority to consider such persons for pardon, parole, or commutation from any portion of such sentence.

(4)   Any general law previously enacted by the General Assembly providing for life without parole or for mandatory service of sentences without suspension, probation, or parole is hereby ratified and approved but such provisions shall be subject to amendment or repeal by general law.

(c)   Notwithstanding the provisions of subparagraph (b) of this Paragraph, the General Assembly, by law, may prohibit the board from granting and may prescribe the terms and conditions for the board's granting a pardon or parole to:

(1)   Any person incarcerated for a second or subsequent time for any offense for which such person could have been sentenced to life imprisonment; and

(2)   Any person who has received consecutive life sentences as the result of offenses occurring during the same series of acts.

(d)   The chairman of the board, or any other member designated by the board, may suspend the execution of a sentence of death until the full board shall have an opportunity to hear the application of the convicted person for any relief within the power of the board.

(e)   Notwithstanding any other provisions of this Paragraph, the State Board of Pardons and Paroles shall have the authority to pardon any person convicted of a crime who is subsequently determined to be innocent of said crime or to issue a medical reprieve to an entirely incapacitated person suffering a progressively debilitating terminal illness or parole any person who is age 62 or older.

Section III.
State Personnel Board

Paragraph I. *State Personnel Board.*

(a)   There shall be a State Personnel Board which shall consist of five members appointed by the Governor, subject to confirmation by the Senate. The members of the board in office on June 30, 1983, shall serve out the remainder of their respective terms. As each term of office expires, the Governor shall appoint a successor as herein provided. All such terms of members shall be for five years. Members shall serve until their successors are appointed and qualified. A member of the State Personnel Board may not be employed in any other capacity in state government. A chairman shall be selected by the members of the board from its membership.

(b) The board shall provide policy direction for a State Merit System of Personnel Administration and may be vested with such additional powers and duties as provided by law. State personnel shall be selected on the basis of merit as provided by law.

Paragraph II. *Veterans' preference.* Any veteran who has served as a member of the armed forces of the United States during the period of a war or armed conflict in which any branch of the armed forces of the United States engaged, whether under United States command or otherwise, and was honorably discharged therefrom, shall be given such veterans preference in any civil service program established in state government as may be provided by law. Any such law must provide at least ten points to a veteran having at least a 10 percent service connected disability as rated and certified by the Veterans Administration, and all other such veterans shall be entitled to at least five points.

Section IV.
State Transportation Board

Paragraph I. *State Transportation Board; commissioner.*

(a) There shall be a State Transportation Board composed of as many members as there are congressional districts in the state. The member of the board from each congressional district shall be elected by a majority vote of the members of the House of Representatives and Senate whose respective districts are embraced or partly embraced within such congressional district meeting in caucus. The members of the board in office on June 30, 1983, shall serve out the remainder of their respective terms. The General Assembly shall provide by law the procedure for the election of members and for filling vacancies on the board. Members shall serve for terms of five years and until their successors are elected and qualified.

(b) The State Transportation Board shall select a commissioner of transportation, who shall be the chief executive officer of the Department of Transportation and who shall have such powers and duties as provided by law.

Section V
Veteran Service Board

Paragraph I. *Veterans Service Board; commissioner.*

(a) There shall be a State Department of Veterans Service and Veterans Service Board which shall consist of seven members appointed by the Governor, subject to confirmation by the Senate. The members in office on June 30, 1983, shall serve out the remainder of their respective terms. As each term of office expires, the Governor shall appoint a successor as herein provided. All such terms of members shall be for seven years. Members shall serve until their successors are appointed and qualified.

(b) The board shall appoint a commissioner who shall be the executive officer of the department. All members of the board and the commissioner shall be veterans of some war or armed conflict in which the United States has engaged. The board shall have such control, duties, powers, and jurisdiction of the State Department of Veterans Service as shall be provided by law.

Section VI
Board of Natural Resources

Paragraph I. *Board of Natural Resources.*

(a) There shall be a Board of Natural Resources which shall consist of one member from each congressional district in the state and five members from the state at large, one of whom must be from one of the following named counties: Chatham, Bryan, Liberty, McIntosh, Glynn, or Camden. All members shall be appointed by the Governor, subject to confirmation by the Senate. The members of the board in office on June 30, 1983, shall serve out the remainder of their respective terms. As each term of office expires, the Governor shall appoint a successor as herein provided. All such terms of members shall be for seven years. Members shall serve until their successors are appointed and qualified. Insofar as it is practicable, the members of the board shall be representative of all areas and functions encompassed within the Department of Natural Resources.

(b) The board shall have such powers and duties as provided by law.

Section VII.
Qualifications, Compensation, Removal from Office and Powers and Duties of Members of Constitutional Boards and Commissions

Paragraph I. *Qualifications, compensation, and removal from office.* The qualifications, compensation, and removal from office of members of constitutional boards and commissions provided for in this article shall be as provided by law.

Paragraph II. *Powers and duties.* The powers and duties of members of constitutional boards and commissions provided for in this article, except the Board of Pardons and Paroles, shall be as provided by law.

Article V
Executive Branch

Section I
Election of Governor and Lieutenant Governor

Paragraph I. *Governor: term of office; compensation and allowances.* There shall be a Governor who shall hold office for a term of four years and until a successor shall be chosen and qualified. Persons holding the office of Governor may succeed themselves for one four-year term of office. Persons who have held the office of

Governor and have succeeded themselves as hereinbefore provided shall not again be eligible to be elected to that office until after the expiration of four years from the conclusion of their term as Governor. The compensation and allowances of the Governor shall be as provided by law.

Paragraph II. *Election for Governor.* An election for Governor shall be held on Tuesday after the first Monday in November of 1986, and the Governor-elect shall be installed in office at the next session of the General Assembly. An election for Governor shall take place quadrennially thereafter on said date unless another date be fixed by the General Assembly. Said election shall be held at the places of holding general elections in the several counties of this state, in the manner prescribed for the election of members of the General Assembly, and the electors shall be the same.

Paragraph III. *Lieutenant Governor.* There shall be a Lieutenant Governor, who shall be elected at the same time, for the same term, and in the same manner as the Governor. The Lieutenant Governor shall be the President of the Senate and shall have such executive duties as prescribed by the Governor and as may be prescribed by law not inconsistent with the powers of the Governor or other provisions of this Constitution. The compensation and allowances of the Lieutenant Governor shall be as provided by law.

Paragraph IV. *Qualifications of Governor and Lieutenant Governor.* No person shall be eligible for election to the office of Governor or Lieutenant Governor unless such person shall have been a citizen of the United States 15 years and a legal resident of the state six years immediately preceding the election and shall have attained the age of 30 years by the date of assuming office.

Paragraph V. *Succession to executive power.*

(a)   In case of the temporary disability of the Governor as determined in the manner provided in Section IV of this article, the Lieutenant Governor shall exercise the powers and duties of the Governor and receive the same compensation as the Governor until such time as the temporary disability of the Governor ends.

(b)   In case of the death, resignation, or permanent disability of the Governor or the Governor-elect, the Lieutenant Governor or the Lieutenant Governor-elect, upon becoming the Lieutenant Governor, shall become the Governor until a successor shall be elected and qualified as hereinafter provided. A successor to serve for the unexpired term shall be elected at the next general election; but, if such death, resignation, or permanent disability shall occur within 30 days of the next general election or if the term will expire within 90 days after the next general election, the Lieutenant Governor shall become Governor for the unexpired term. No person shall be elected or appointed to the office of Lieutenant Governor for the unexpired term in the event the Lieutenant Governor shall become Governor as herein provided.

(c)   In case of the death, resignation, or permanent disability of both the Governor or the Governor-elect and the Lieutenant Governor or the Lieutenant Governor-elect or in case of the death, resignation, or permanent disability of the Governor and there shall be no Lieutenant Governor, the Speaker of the House of Representatives shall exercise the powers and duties of the Governor until the election and qualification of a Governor at a special election, which shall be held within 90 days from the date on which the Speaker of the House of Representatives shall have assumed the powers and duties of the Governor, and the person elected shall serve out the unexpired term.

Paragraph VI. *Oath of office.* The Governor and Lieutenant Governor shall, before entering on the duties of office, take such oath or affirmation as prescribed by law.

Section II
Duties and Powers of Governor

Paragraph I. *Executive powers.* The chief executive powers shall be vested in the Governor. The other executive officers shall have such powers as may be prescribed by this Constitution and by law.

Paragraph II. *Law enforcement.* The Governor shall take care that the laws are faithfully executed and shall be the conservator of the peace throughout the state.

Paragraph III. *Commander in chief.* The Governor shall be the commander in chief of the military forces of this state..

Paragraph IV. *Veto power.* Except as otherwise provided in this Constitution, before any bill or resolution shall become law, the Governor shall have the right to review such bill or resolution intended to have the effect of law which has been passed by the General Assembly. The Governor may veto, approve, or take no action on any such bill or resolution. In the event the Governor vetoes any such bill or resolution, the General Assembly may, by a two-thirds' vote, override such veto as provided in Article III of this Constitution.

Paragraph V. *Writs of election.* The Governor shall issue writs of election to fill all vacancies that may occur in the Senate and in the House of Representatives.

Paragraph VI. *Information and recommendations to the General Assembly.* At the beginning of each regular session and from time to time, the Governor may give the General Assembly information on the state of the state and recommend to its consideration such measures as the Governor may deem necessary or expedient.

Paragraph VII. *Special sessions of the General Assembly.*

(a) The Governor may convene the General Assembly in special session by proclamation which may be amended by the Governor prior to the convening of the special session or amended by the Governor with the approval of three-fifths of the members of each house after the special session has convened; but no laws shall be enacted at any such special session except those which relate to the purposes stated in the proclamation or in any amendment thereto.

(b) The Governor shall convene the General Assembly in special session for all purposes whenever three-fifths of the members to which each house is entitled certify to the Governor in writing, with a copy to the Secretary of State, that in their opinion an emergency exists in the affairs of the state. The General Assembly may convene itself if, after receiving such certification, the Governor fails to do so within three days, excluding Sundays.

(c) Special sessions of the General Assembly shall be limited to a period of 40 days unless extended by three-fifths' vote of each house and approved by the Governor or unless at the expiration of such period an impeachment trial of some officer of state government is pending, in which event the House shall adjourn and the Senate shall remain in session until such trial is completed.

Paragraph VIII. *Filling vacancies.*

(a) When any public office shall become vacant by death, resignation, or otherwise, the Governor shall promptly fill such vacancy unless otherwise provided by this Constitution or by law; and persons so appointed shall serve for the unexpired term unless otherwise provided by this Constitution or by law.

(b) In case of the death or withdrawal of a person who received a majority of votes cast in an election for the office of Secretary of State, Attorney General, State School Superintendent, Commissioner of Insurance, Commissioner of Agriculture, or Commissioner of Labor, the Governor elected at the same election, upon becoming Governor, shall have the power to fill such office by appointing, subject to the confirmation of the Senate, an individual to serve until the next general election and until a successor for the balance of the unexpired term shall have been elected and qualified.

Paragraph IX. *Appointments by Governor.* The Governor shall make such appointments as are authorized by this Constitution or by law. If a person whose confirmation is required by the Senate is once rejected by the Senate, that person shall not be renominated by the Governor for appointment to the same office until the expiration of a period of one year from the date of such rejection.

Paragraph X. *Information from officers and employees.* The Governor may require information in writing from constitutional officers and all other officers and employees of the executive branch on any subject relating to the duties of their respective offices or employment.

Section III
Other Elected Executive Officers

Paragraph I. *Other executive officers, how elected.* The **Secretary of State, Attorney General, State School Superintendent, Commissioner of Insurance, Commissioner of Agriculture, and Commissioner of Labor** shall be elected in the manner prescribed for the election of members of the General Assembly and the electors shall be the same. Such executive officers shall be elected at the same time and hold their offices for the same term as the Governor.

Paragraph II. *Qualifications.*

(a) No person shall be eligible to the office of the Secretary of State, Attorney General, State School Superintendent, Commissioner of Insurance, Commissioner of Agriculture, or Commissioner of Labor unless such person shall have been a citizen of the United States for ten years and a legal resident of the state for four years immediately preceding election or appointment and shall have attained the age of 25 years by the date of assuming office. All of said officers shall take such oath and give bond and security, as prescribed by law, for the faithful discharge of their duties.

(b) No person shall be Attorney General unless such person shall have been an active-status member of the State Bar of Georgia for seven years.

Paragraph III. *Powers, duties, compensation, and allowances of other executive officers.* Except as otherwise provided in this Constitution, the General Assembly shall prescribe the powers, duties, compensation, and allowances of the above executive officers and provide assistance and expenses necessary for the operation of the department of each.

Paragraph IV. *Attorney General; duties.* The Attorney General shall act as the legal advisor of the executive department, shall represent the state in the Supreme Court in all capital felonies *and in all civil and criminal cases in any court when required by the Governor,* and shall perform such other duties as shall be required by law.

Section IV
Disability of Executive Officers

Paragraph I. *"Elected constitutional executive officer," how defined.* As used in this section, the term "elected constitutional executive officer" means the Governor, the Lieutenant Governor, the Secretary of State, the Attorney General, the State School Superintendent, the Commissioner of Insurance, the Commissioner of Agriculture, and the Commissioner of Labor.

Paragraph II. *Procedure for determining disability.* Upon a petition of any four of the elected constitutional executive officers to the Supreme Court of Georgia that another elected constitutional executive officer is unable to perform the duties of office because of a physical or mental disability, the Supreme Court shall by appropriate rule provide for a speedy and public hearing on such matter, including notice of the nature and cause of the accusation, process for obtaining witnesses, and the assistance of counsel. Evidence at such hearing shall include testimony from not fewer than three qualified physicians in private practice, one of whom must be a psychiatrist.

Paragraph III. *Effect of determination of disability.* If, after hearing the evidence on disability, the Supreme Court determines that there is a disability and that such disability is permanent, the office shall be declared vacant and the successor to that office shall be chosen as provided in this Constitution or the laws enacted in pursuance thereof. If it is determined that the disability is not permanent, the Supreme Court shall determine when the disability has ended and when the officer shall resume the exercise of the powers of office. During the period of temporary disability, the powers of such office shall be exercised as provided by law.

Article VI
Judicial Branch

Section I.
Judicial Powers

Paragraph I. *Judicial power of the state.* The judicial power of the state shall be vested exclusively in the following *classes of courts*: **magistrate courts, probate courts, juvenile courts, state courts, superior courts, Court of Appeals, and Supreme Court.**

Magistrate courts, probate courts, juvenile courts, and state courts shall be courts of limited jurisdiction.

In addition, the General Assembly may establish or authorize the establishment of municipal courts and may authorize administrative agencies to exercise quasi-judicial powers.

Municipal courts shall have jurisdiction over ordinance violations and such other jurisdiction as provided by law. Except as provided in this paragraph and in Section X, municipal courts, county recorder's courts and civil courts in existence on June 30, 1983, and administrative agencies shall not be subject to the provisions of this article.

The General Assembly shall have the authority to confer "by law" jurisdiction upon municipal courts to try state offenses.

Paragraph II. *Unified judicial system.* All courts of the state shall comprise a unified judicial system.

Paragraph III. *Judges; exercise of power outside own court; scope of term "judge."* Provided the judge is otherwise qualified, a judge may exercise judicial power in any court upon the request and with the consent of the judges of that court and of the judge's own court under rules prescribed by law. The term "judge," as used in this article, shall include Justices, judges, senior judges, magistrates, and every other such judicial office of whatever name existing or created.

Paragraph IV. *Exercise of judicial power.* Each court may exercise such powers as necessary in aid of its jurisdiction or to protect or effectuate its judgments; but only the superior and appellate courts shall have the power to issue process in the nature of mandamus, prohibition, specific performance, quo warranto, and injunction. Each superior court, state court, and other courts of record may grant new trials on legal grounds.

Paragraph V. *Uniformity of jurisdiction, powers, etc.* Except as otherwise provided in this Constitution, the courts of each class shall have uniform jurisdiction, powers, rules of practice and procedure, and selection, qualifications, terms, and discipline of judges. The provisions of this Paragraph shall be effected by law within 24 months of the effective date of this Constitution.

Paragraph VI. *Judicial circuits; courts in each county; court sessions.* The state shall be divided into judicial circuits, each of which shall consist of not less than one county. Each county shall have at least one superior court, magistrate court, a probate court, and, where needed, a state court and a juvenile court. The General Assembly may provide by law that the judge of the probate court may also serve as the judge of the magistrate court. In the absence of a state court or a juvenile court, the superior court shall exercise that jurisdiction. Superior courts shall hold court at least twice each year in each county.

Paragraph VII. *Judicial circuits, courts, and judgeships, law changed.* The General Assembly may abolish, create, consolidate, or modify judicial circuits and courts and judgeships; but no circuit shall consist of less than one county.

Paragraph VIII. *Transfer of cases.* Any court shall transfer to the appropriate court in the state any civil case in which it determines that jurisdiction or venue lies elsewhere.

Paragraph IX. *Rules of evidence; law prescribed.* All rules of evidence shall be as prescribed by law.

Paragraph X. *Authorization for pilot projects.*

The General Assembly may by general law approved by a two-thirds majority of the members of each house enact legislation providing for, as pilot programs of limited duration, courts which are not uniform within their classes in jurisdiction, powers, rules of practice and procedure, and selection, qualifications, terms, and discipline of judges for such pilot courts and other matters relative thereto.

Such legislation shall name the political subdivision, judicial circuit, and existing courts affected and may, in addition to any other power, grant to such court created as a pilot program the power to issue process in the nature of mandamus, prohibition, specific performance, quo warranto, and injunction.

The General Assembly shall provide by general law for a procedure for submitting proposed legislation relating to such pilot programs to the Judicial Council of Georgia or its successor. Legislation enacted pursuant to this Paragraph shall not deny equal protection of the laws to any person in violation of Article I, Section I, Paragraph II of this Constitution.

Section II
Venue

Paragraph I. *Divorce cases.* Divorce cases shall be tried in the county where the defendant resides, if a resident of this state; if the defendant is not a resident of this state, then in the county in which the plaintiff resides; provided, however, a divorce case may be tried in the county of residence of the plaintiff if the defendant has moved from that same county within six months from the date of the filing of the divorce action and said county was the site of the marital domicile at the time of the separation of the parties, and provided, further, that any person who has been a resident of any United States army post or military reservation within the State of Georgia for one year next preceding the filing of the petition may bring an action for divorce in any county adjacent to said United States army post or military reservation.

Paragraph II. *Land titles.* Cases respecting titles to land shall be tried in the county where the land lies, except where a single tract is divided by a county line, in which case the superior court of either county shall have jurisdiction.

Paragraph III. *Equity cases.* Equity cases shall be tried in the county where a defendant resides against whom substantial relief is prayed.

Paragraph IV. *Suits against joint obligors, copartners, etc.* Suits against joint obligors, joint tort-feasors, joint promisors, copartners, or joint trespassers residing in different counties may be tried in either county.

Paragraph V. *Suits against maker, endorser, etc.* Suits against the maker and endorser of promissory notes, or drawer, acceptor, and endorser of foreign or inland bills of exchange, or like instruments, residing in different counties, shall be tried in the county where the maker or acceptor resides.

Paragraph VI. *All other cases.* All other civil cases, except juvenile court cases as may otherwise be provided by the Juvenile Court Code of Georgia, shall be tried in the county where the defendant resides; venue as to corporations, foreign and domestic, shall be as provided by law; and all criminal cases shall be tried in the county where the crime was committed, except cases in the superior courts where the judge is satisfied that an impartial jury cannot be obtained in such county.

Paragraph VII. *Venue in third-party practice.* The General Assembly may provide by law that venue is proper in a county other than the county of residence of a person or entity impleaded into a pending civil case by a defending party who contends that such person or entity is or may be liable to said defending party for all or part of the claim against said defending party.

Paragraph VIII. *Power to change venue.* The power to change the venue in civil and criminal cases shall be vested in the superior courts to be exercised in such manner as has been, or shall be, provided by law.

Section III.
Classes of Courts of Limited Jurisdiction

Paragraph I. *Jurisdiction of classes of courts of limited jurisdiction.* The **magistrate, juvenile, and state courts** shall have uniform jurisdiction as provided by law. Probate courts shall have such jurisdiction as now or hereafter provided by law, without regard to uniformity.

Section IV.
Superior Courts

Paragraph I. *Jurisdiction of superior courts.* The superior courts shall have jurisdiction in all cases, except as otherwise provided in this Constitution. They shall have exclusive jurisdiction over trials in felony cases, except in the case of juvenile offenders as provided by law; in cases respecting title to land; in divorce cases; and in equity cases. The superior courts shall have such appellate jurisdiction, either alone or by circuit or district, as may be provided by law.

Section V
Court of Appeals

Paragraph I. *Composition of Court of Appeals; Chief Judge.* The Court of Appeals shall consist of not less than nine Judges who shall elect from among themselves a Chief Judge.

Paragraph II. *Panels as prescribed.* The Court of Appeals may sit in panels of not less than three Judges as prescribed by law or, if none, by its rules.

Paragraph III. *Jurisdiction of Court of Appeals; decisions binding.* The Court of Appeals shall be a court of review and shall exercise appellate and certiorari jurisdiction in all cases not reserved to the Supreme Court or conferred on other courts by law. The decisions of the Court of Appeals insofar as not in conflict with those of the Supreme

Court shall bind all courts except the Supreme Court as precedents.

Paragraph IV. *Certification of question to Supreme Court.* The Court of Appeals may certify a question to the Supreme Court for instruction, to which it shall then be bound.

Paragraph V. *Equal division of court.* In the event of an equal division of the Judges when sitting as a body, the case shall be immediately transmitted to the Supreme Court.

Section VI
Supreme Court

Paragraph I. *Composition of Supreme Court; Chief Justice; Presiding Justice; quorum; substitute judges.* The Supreme Court shall consist of not more than **nine Justices** who shall elect from among themselves a Chief Justice as the chief presiding and administrative officer of the court and a Presiding Justice to serve if the Chief Justice is absent or is disqualified. A majority shall be necessary to hear and determine cases. If a Justice is disqualified in any case, a substitute judge may be designated by the remaining Justices to serve.

Paragraph II. *Exclusive appellate jurisdiction of Supreme Court.* The Supreme Court shall be a court of review and shall exercise exclusive appellate jurisdiction in the following cases:

(1) All cases involving the construction of a treaty or of the Constitution of the State of Georgia or of the United States and all cases in which the constitutionality of a law, ordinance, or constitutional provision has been drawn in question; and

(2) All cases of election contest.

Paragraph III. *General appellate jurisdiction of Supreme Court.* Unless otherwise provided by law, the Supreme Court shall have appellate jurisdiction of the following classes of cases:

(1) Cases involving title to land;

(2) All equity cases;

(3) All cases involving wills;

(4) All habeas corpus cases;

(5) All cases involving extraordinary remedies;

(6) All divorce and alimony cases;

(7) All cases certified to it by the Court of Appeals; and

(8) All cases in which a sentence of death was imposed or could be imposed. Review of all cases shall be as provided by law.

Paragraph IV. *Jurisdiction over questions of law from state appellate or federal district or appellate courts.* The Supreme Court shall have jurisdiction and authority to answer any question of law from any state appellate or federal district or appellate court.

Paragraph V. *Review of cases in Court of Appeals.* The Supreme Court may review by certiorari cases in the Court of Appeals which are of gravity or great public importance.

Paragraph VI. *Decisions of Supreme Court binding.* The decisions of the Supreme Court shall bind all other courts as precedents.

Section VII.
Selection, Term, Compensation and Discipline of Judges

Paragraph I. *Election; term of office.* All *superior court* and *state court* judges shall be elected on a nonpartisan basis for a term of four years. All Justices of the *Supreme Court* and the Judges of the *Court of Appeals* shall be elected on a nonpartisan basis for a term of six years. The terms of all judges thus elected shall begin the next January 1 after their election. All other judges shall continue to be selected in the manner and for the term they were selected on June 30, 1983, until otherwise provided by local law.

Paragraph II. *Qualifications.*

(a) Appellate and superior court judges shall have been admitted to practice law for seven years.

(b) State court judges shall have been admitted to practice law for seven years, provided that this requirement shall be five years in the case of state court judges elected or appointed in the year 2000 or earlier. Juvenile court judges shall have been admitted to practice law for five years.

(c) Probate and magistrate judges shall have such qualifications as provided law serve

(d) All judges shall reside in the geographical area in which they are selected to

(e) The General Assembly may provide by law for additional qualifications,

Including, but not limited to, minimum residency requirements.

Paragraph III. *Vacancies.* Vacancies shall be filled by appointment of the Governor except as otherwise provided by law in the magistrate, probate, and juvenile courts.

Paragraph IV. *Period of service of appointees.* An appointee to an elective office shall serve until a successor is duly selected and qualified and until January 1 of the year following the next general election which is more than six months after such person's appointment.

Paragraph V. *Compensation and allowances of judges.* All judges shall receive compensation and allowances as provided by law; county supplements are hereby continued and may be granted or changed by the General Assembly. County governing authorities which had the authority on June 30, 1983, to make county supplements shall continue to have such authority under this Constitution. An incumbent's salary, allowance, or supplement shall not be decreased during the incumbent's term of office.

Paragraph VI. *Judicial Qualifications Commission; power; composition.* The power to discipline, remove, and cause involuntary retirement of judges shall be vested in the Judicial Qualifications Commission. It shall consist of seven members, as follows:

(1) Two judges of any court of record, selected by the Supreme Court;

(2) Three members of the State Bar of Georgia who shall have been active status members of the state bar for at least ten years and who shall be elected by the board of governors of the state bar; and

(3) Two citizens, neither of whom shall be a member of the state bar, who shall be appointed by the Governor.

Paragraph VII. *Discipline, removal, and involuntary retirement of judges.*

(a) Any judge may be removed, suspended, or otherwise disciplined for willful misconduct in office, or for willful and persistent failure to perform the duties of office, or for habitual intemperance, or for conviction of a crime involving moral turpitude, or for conduct prejudicial to the administration of justice which brings the judicial office into disrepute. Any judge may be retired for disability which constitutes a serious and likely permanent interference with the performance of the duties of office. The Supreme Court shall adopt rules of implementation.

(b) (1) Upon indictment for a felony by a grand jury of this state or by a grand jury of the United States of any judge, the Attorney General or district attorney shall transmit a certified copy of the indictment to the Judicial Qualifications Commission.

The commission shall, subject to subparagraph (b)(2) of this Paragraph, review the indictment, and, if it determines that the indictment relates to and adversely affects the administration of the office of the indicted judge and that the rights and interests of the public are adversely affected thereby, the commission shall suspend the judge immediately and without further action pending the final disposition of the case or until the expiration of the judge's term of office, whichever occurs first.

During the term of office to which such judge was elected and in which the indictment occurred, if a nolle prosequi is entered, if the public official is acquitted, or if after conviction the conviction is later overturned as a result of any direct appeal or application for a writ of certiorari, the judge shall be immediately reinstated to the office from which he was suspended. While a judge is suspended under this subparagraph and until initial conviction by the trial court, the judge shall continue to receive the compensation from his office. After initial conviction by the trial court, the judge shall not be entitled to receive the compensation from his office. If the judge is reinstated to office, he shall be entitled to receive any compensation withheld under the provisions of this subparagraph. For the duration of any suspension under this subparagraph, the Governor shall appoint a replacement judge. Upon a final conviction with no appeal or review pending, the office shall be declared vacant and a successor to that office shall be chosen as provided in this Constitution or the laws enacted in pursuance thereof.

(2) The commission shall not review the indictment for a period of 14 days from the day the indictment is received. This period of time may be extended by the commission. During this period of time, the indicted judge may, in writing, authorize the commission to suspend him from office. Any such voluntary suspension shall be subject to the same conditions for review, reinstatement, or declaration of vacancy as are provided in this subparagraph for a non-voluntary suspension.

(3) After any suspension is imposed under this subparagraph, the suspended judge may petition the commission for a review. If

the commission determines that the judge should no longer be suspended, he shall immediately be reinstated to office.

(4) The findings and records of the commission and the fact that the public official has or has not been suspended shall not be admissible in evidence in any court for any purpose. The findings and records of the commission shall not be open to the public.

(5) The provisions of this subparagraph shall not apply to any indictment handed down prior to January 1, 1985

(6) If a judge who is suspended from office under the provisions of this subparagraph is not first tried at the next regular or special term following the indictment, the suspension shall be terminated and the judge shall be reinstated to office. The judge shall not be reinstated under this provision if he is not so tried based on a continuance granted upon a motion made only by the defendant.

(c) Upon initial conviction of any judge for any felony in a trial court of this state or the United States, regardless of whether the judge has been suspended previously under subparagraph (b) of this Paragraph, such judge shall be immediately and without further action suspended from office. While a judge is suspended from office under this subparagraph, he shall not be entitled to receive the compensation from his office. If the conviction is later overturned as a result of any direct appeal or application for a writ of certiorari, the judge shall be immediately reinstated to the office from which he was suspended and shall be entitled to receive any compensation withheld under the provisions of this subparagraph.

For the duration of any suspension under this subparagraph, the Governor shall appoint a replacement judge. Upon a final conviction with no appeal or review pending, the office shall be declared vacant and a successor to that office shall be chosen as provided in this Constitution or the laws enacted in pursuance thereof. The provisions of this subparagraph shall not apply to any conviction rendered prior to January 1, 1987.

Paragraph VIII. *Due process; review by Supreme Court.* No action shall be taken against a judge except after hearing and in accordance with due process of law. No removal or involuntary retirement shall occur except upon order of the Supreme Court after review.

Section VIII
District Attorneys

Paragraph I. *District attorneys; vacancies; qualifications; compensation; duties; immunity.*

(a) There shall be a district attorney for each judicial circuit, who shall be elected circuit-wide for a term of four years. The successors of present and subsequent incumbents shall be elected by the electors of their respective circuits at the general election held immediately preceding the expiration of their respective terms. District attorneys shall serve until their successors are duly elected and qualified. Vacancies shall be filled by appointment of the Governor.

(b) No person shall be a district attorney unless such person shall have been an active-status member of the State Bar of Georgia for three years immediately preceding such person's election.

(c) The district attorneys shall receive such compensation and allowances as provided by law and shall be entitled to receive such local supplements to their compensation and allowances as may be provided by law.

(d) It shall be the duty of the district attorney to represent the state in all criminal cases in the superior court of such district attorney's circuit and in all cases appealed from the superior court and the juvenile courts of that circuit to the Supreme Court and the Court of Appeals and to perform such other duties as shall be required by law.

(e) District attorneys shall enjoy immunity from private suit for actions arising from the performance of their duties.

Paragraph II. *Discipline, removal, and involuntary retirement of district attorneys.* Any district attorney may be disciplined, removed or involuntarily retired as provided by general law.

Section IX
General Provisions

Paragraph I. *Administration of the judicial system; uniform court rules; advice and consent of councils.* The judicial system shall be administered as provided in this Paragraph. Not more than 24 months after the effective date hereof, and from time to time thereafter by amendment, the Supreme Court shall, with the advice and consent of the council of the affected class or classes of trial courts, by order adopt and publish uniform court rules and record-keeping rules which shall provide for the speedy, efficient, and inexpensive resolution of disputes and prosecutions. Each council shall be comprised of all of the judges of the courts of that class.

Paragraph II. *Disposition of cases.* The Supreme Court and the Court of Appeals shall dispose of every case at the term for which it is entered on the court's docket for hearing or at the next term.

Section X
Transaction

Paragraph I. *Effect of ratification.* On the effective date of this article:

(1) Superior courts shall continue as superior courts.

(2) State courts shall continue as state courts.

(3) Probate courts shall continue as probate courts.

(4)   Juvenile courts shall continue as juvenile courts.

(5)   Municipal courts not otherwise named herein, of whatever name, shall continue as and be denominated municipal courts, except that the City Court of Atlanta shall retain its name. Such municipal courts, county recorder's courts, the Civil Courts of Richmond and Bibb counties, and administrative agencies having quasi-judicial powers shall continue with the same jurisdiction as such courts and agencies have on the effective date of this article until otherwise provided by law.

(6)   Justice of the peace courts, small claims courts, and magistrate courts operating on the effective date of this Constitution and the County Court of Echols County shall become and be classified as magistrate courts. The County Court of Baldwin County and the County Court of Putnam County shall become and be classified as state courts, with the same jurisdiction and powers as other state courts.

Paragraph II. *Continuation of judges.* Each judge holding office on the effective date of this article shall continue in office until the expiration of the term of office, as a judge of the court having the same or similar jurisdiction. Each court not named herein shall cease to exist on such date or at the expiration of the term of the incumbent judge, whichever is later; and its jurisdiction shall automatically pass to the new court of the same or similar jurisdiction, in the absence of which court it shall pass to the superior court.

Article VII
Taxation and Finance

Section I
Power of Taxation

Paragraph I. *Taxation; limitations on grants of tax powers.* The state may not suspend or irrevocably give, grant, limit, or restrain the right of taxation and all laws, grants, contracts, and other acts to effect any of these purposes are null and void. Except as otherwise provided in this Constitution, the right of taxation shall always be under the complete control of the state.

Paragraph II. *Taxing power limited.*

(a)   The annual levy of state ad valorem taxes on tangible property for all purposes, except for defending the state in an emergency, shall not exceed one-fourth mill on each dollar of the assessed value of the property.

(b)   So long as the method of taxation in effect on December 31, 1980, for the taxation of shares of stock of banking corporations and other monied capital coming into competition with such banking corporations continues in effect, such shares and other monied capital may be taxed at an annual rate not exceeding five mills on each dollar of the assessed value of the property.

Paragraph III. *Uniformity; classification of property; assessment of agricultural land; utilities.*

(a) All taxes shall be levied and collected under general laws and for public purposes only. Except as otherwise provided in subparagraphs (b), (c), (d), (e), and (f) of this Paragraph, all taxation shall be uniform upon the same class of subjects within the territorial limits of the authority levying the tax.

(b) (1) Except as otherwise provided in this subparagraph (b), classes of subjects for taxation of property shall consist of tangible property and one or more classes of intangible personal property including money; provided, however, that any taxation of intangible personal property may be repealed by general law without approval in a referendum effective for all taxable years beginning on or after January 1, 1996.

(2) Subject to the conditions and limitations specified by law, each of the following types of property may be classified as a separate class of property for ad valorem property tax purposes and different rates, methods, and assessment dates may be provided for such properties:

(A) Trailers.

(B) Mobile homes other than those mobile homes which qualify the owner of the home for a homestead exemption from ad valorem taxation.

(C) Heavy-duty equipment motor vehicles owned by nonresidents and operated in this state.

(3) Motor vehicles may be classified as a separate class of property for ad valorem property tax purposes, and such class may be divided into separate subclasses for ad valorem purposes. The General Assembly may provide by general law for the ad valorem taxation of motor vehicles including, but not limited to, providing for different rates, methods, assessment dates, and taxpayer liability for such class and for each of its subclasses and need not provide for uniformity of taxation with other classes of property or between or within its subclasses. The General Assembly may also determine what portion of any ad valorem tax on motor vehicles shall be retained by the state. As used in this subparagraph, the term "motor vehicles" means all vehicles which are self-propelled.

(c) Tangible real property, but no more than 2,000 acres of any single property owner, which is devoted to bona fide agricultural purposes shall be assessed for ad valorem taxation purposes at 75 percent of the value which other tangible real property is assessed. No property shall be entitled to receive the preferential assessment provided for in this subparagraph if the property which would otherwise receive such assessment would result in any person who has a beneficial interest in such property, including any interest in the nature of stock ownership, receiving the benefit of such preferential assessment as to more than 2,000 acres. No property shall be entitled to receive the preferential assessment provided for in this subparagraph unless the conditions set out below are met:

(1) The property must be owned by:

    (A) (i)   One or more natural or naturalized citizens;

         (ii) An estate of which the devisee or heirs are one or more natural or naturalized citizens; or

         (iii) A trust of which the beneficiaries are one or more natural or naturalized citizens; or

    (B) A family-owned farm corporation, the controlling interest of which is owned by individuals related to each other within the fourth degree of civil reckoning, or which is owned by an estate of which the devisee or heirs are one or more natural or naturalized citizens, or which is owned by a trust of which the beneficiaries are one or more natural or naturalized citizens, and such corporation derived 80 percent or more of its gross income from bona fide agricultural pursuits within this state within the year immediately preceding the year in which eligibility is sought.

(2) The General Assembly shall provide by law:

    (A) For a definition of the term "bona fide agricultural purposes," but such term shall include timber production;

    (B) For additional minimum conditions of eligibility which such properties must meet in order to qualify for the preferential assessment provided for herein, including, but not limited to, the requirement that the owner be required to enter into a covenant with the appropriate taxing authorities to maintain the use of the properties in bona fide agricultural purposes for a period of not less than ten years and for appropriate penalties for the breach of any such covenant.

(3) In addition to the specific conditions set forth in this subparagraph (c), the General Assembly may place further restrictions upon, but may not relax, the conditions of eligibility for the preferential assessment provided for herein.

(d) (1) The General Assembly shall be authorized by general law to establish as a separate class of property for ad valorem tax purposes any tangible real property which is listed in the National Register of Historic Places or in a state historic register authorized by general law. For such purposes, the General Assembly is authorized by general law to establish a program by which certain properties within such class may be assessed for taxes at different rates or valuations in order to encourage the preservation of such historic properties and to assist in the revitalization of historic areas.

(2) The General Assembly shall be authorized by general law to establish as a separate class of property for ad valorem tax purposes any tangible real property on which there have been releases of hazardous waste, constituents, or substances into the environment. For such purposes, the General Assembly is authorized by general law to establish a program by which certain properties within such class may be assessed for taxes at different rates or valuations in order to encourage the cleanup, reuse, and redevelopment of such properties and to assist in the revitalization thereof by encouraging remedial action.

(e) The General Assembly shall provide by general law:

(1) For the definition and methods of assessment and taxation, such methods to include a formula based on current use, annual productivity, and real property sales data, of: "bona fide conservation use property" to include bona fide agricultural and timber land not to exceed 2,000 acres of a single owner; and "bona fide residential transitional property," to include private single-family residential owner occupied property located in transitional developing areas not to exceed five acres of any single owner. Such methods of assessment and taxation shall be subject to the following conditions:

(A) A property owner desiring the benefit of such methods of assessment and taxation shall be required to enter into a covenant to continue the property in bona fide conservation use or bona fide residential transitional use; and

(B) A breach of such covenant within ten years shall result in a recapture of the tax savings resulting from such methods of assessment and taxation and may result in other appropriate penalties;

(2) That standing timber shall be assessed only once, and such assessment shall be made following its harvest or sale and on the basis of its fair market value at the time of harvest or sale. Said assessment shall be two and one-half times the assessed percentage of value fixed by law for other real property taxed under the uniformity provisions of subparagraph (a) of this Paragraph but in no event greater than its fair market value; and for a method of temporary supplementation of the property tax digest of any county if the implementation of this method of taxing timber reduces the tax digest by more than 20 percent, such supplemental assessed value to be assigned to the properties otherwise benefiting from such method of taxing timber.

(f) (1) The General Assembly shall provide by general law for the definition and methods of assessment and taxation, such methods to include a formula based on current use, annual productivity, and real property sales data, of "forest land conservation use property" to include only forest land each tract of which exceeds 200 acres of a qualified owner.

Such methods of assessment and taxation shall be subject to the following conditions:

(A) A qualified owner shall consist of any individual or individuals or any entity registered to do business in this state;

(B) A qualified owner desiring the benefit of such methods of assessment and taxation shall be required to enter into a covenant to continue the property in forest land use;

(C) All contiguous forest land conservation use property of an owner within a county for which forest land conservation use assessment is sought under this subparagraph shall be in a single covenant;

(D) A breach of such covenant within 15 years shall result in a recapture of the tax savings resulting from such methods of assessment and taxation and may result in other appropriate penalties; and

(E) The General Assembly may provide by general law for a limited exception to the 200 acre requirement in the case of a transfer of ownership of all or a part of the forest land conservation use property during a covenant period to another owner qualified to enter into an original forest land conservation use covenant if the original covenant is continued by both such acquiring owner and the transferor for the remainder of the term, in which event no breach of the covenant shall be deemed to have occurred even if the total size of a tract from which the transfer was made is reduced below 200 acres.

(2) No portion of an otherwise eligible tract of forest land conservation use property shall be entitled to receive simultaneously special assessment and taxation under this subparagraph and either subparagraph (c) or (e) of this Paragraph.

(3) (A) The General Assembly shall appropriate an amount for assistance grants to counties, municipalities, and county and independent school districts to offset revenue loss attributable to the implementation of this subparagraph. Such grants shall be made in such manner and shall be subject to such procedures as may be specified by general law.

(B) If the forest land conservation use property is located in a county, municipality, or county or independent school district where forest land conservation use value causes an ad valorem tax revenue reduction of 3 percent or less due to the implementation of this subparagraph, in each taxable year in which such reduction occurs, the assistance grants to the county, each municipality located therein, and the county or independent school districts located therein shall be in an amount equal to 50 percent of the amount of such reduction.

(C) If the forest land conservation use property is located in a county, municipality, or county or independent school district where forest land conservation use value causes an ad valorem tax revenue reduction of more than 3 percent due to the implementation of this subparagraph, in each taxable year in which such reduction occurs, the assistance grants to the county, each municipality located therein, and the county or independent school districts located therein shall be as follows:

    (i) For the first 3 percent of such reduction amount, in an amount equal to 50 percent of the amount of such reduction; and

    (ii) For the remainder of such reduction amount, in an amount equal to 100 percent of the amount of such remaining reduction amount.

(4) Such revenue reduction shall be calculated by utilizing forest land fair market value. For purposes of this subparagraph, forest land fair market value means the 2008 fair market value of the forest land. Such 2008 valuation may increase from one taxable year to the next by a rate equal to the percentage change in the price index for gross output of state and local government from the prior year to the current year as defined by the National Income and Product Accounts and determined by the United States Bureau of Economic Analysis and indicated by the Price Index for Government Consumption Expenditures and General Government Gross Output (Table 3.10.4). Such revenue reduction shall be determined by subtracting the aggregate forest land conservation use value of qualified properties from the aggregate forest land fair market value of qualified properties for the applicable tax year and the resulting amount shall be multiplied by the millage rate of the county, municipality, or county or independent school district.

(5) For purposes of this subparagraph, the forest land conservation use value shall not include the value of the standing timber located on forest land conservation use property.

(g) The General Assembly may provide for a different method and time of returns, assessments, payment, and collection of ad valorem taxes of public utilities, but not on a greater assessed percentage of value or at a higher rate of taxation than other properties, except that property provided for in subparagraph (c), (d), (e), or (f) of this Paragraph.

Section II
Exemptions from ad Valorem Taxation

Paragraph I. *Unauthorized tax exemptions void.* Except as authorized in or pursuant to this Constitution, all laws exempting property from ad valorem taxation are void.

Paragraph II. *Exemptions from taxation of property.*

(a) (1) Except as otherwise provided in this Constitution, no property shall be exempted from ad valorem taxation unless the exemption is approved by two-thirds of the members elected to each branch of the General Assembly in a roll-call vote and by a majority of the qualified electors of the state voting in a referendum thereon.

(2) Homestead exemptions from ad valorem taxation levied by local taxing jurisdictions may be granted by local law conditioned upon approval by a majority of the qualified electors residing within the limits of the local taxing jurisdiction voting in a referendum thereon.

(3) Laws subject to the requirement of a referendum as provided in this subparagraph (a) may originate in either the Senate or the House of Representatives.

(4) The requirements of this subparagraph (a) shall not apply with respect to a law which codifies or recodifies an exemption previously authorized in the Constitution of 1976 or an exemption authorized pursuant to this Constitution.

(b) The grant of any exemption from ad valorem taxation shall be subject to the conditions, limitations, and administrative procedures specified by law.

Paragraph III. *Exemptions which may be authorized locally.*

(a) (1) The governing authority of any county or municipality, subject to the approval of a majority of the qualified electors of such political subdivision voting in a referendum thereon, may exempt from ad valorem taxation, including all such taxation levied for educational purposes and for state purposes, inventories of goods in the process of manufacture or production, and inventories of finished goods.

(2) Exemptions granted pursuant to this subparagraph (a) may only be revoked by a referendum election called and conducted as provided by law. The call for such referendum shall not be issued within five years from the date such exemptions were first granted and, if the results of the election are in favor of the revocation of such exemptions, then such revocation shall be effective only at the end of a five- year period from the date of such referendum.

(3) The implementation, administration, and revocation of the exemptions authorized in this subparagraph

(a) shall be provided for by law. Until otherwise provided by law, the grant of the exemption shall be subject to the same conditions, limitations, definitions, and procedures provided for the grant of such exemption in the Constitution of 1976 on June 30, 1983.

(b) *Repealed.*

Paragraph IV. *Current property tax exemptions preserved.* Those types of exemptions from ad valorem taxation provided for by law on June 30, 1983, are hereby continued in effect as statutory law until otherwise provided for by law. Any law which reduces or repeals any homestead exemption in existence on June 30, 1983, or created thereafter must be approved by two-thirds of the members elected to each branch of the General Assembly in a roll-call vote and by a majority of the qualified electors of the state or the affected local taxing jurisdiction voting in a referendum thereon. Any law which reduces or repeals exemptions granted to religious or burial grounds or institutions of purely public charity must be approved by two-thirds of the members elected to each branch of the General Assembly.

Paragraph V. *Disabled veteran's homestead exemption. Except as otherwise provided in this paragraph, the amount of the homestead exemption granted to disabled veterans shall be the greater of $32,500.00 or the maximum amount which may be granted to a disabled veteran under Section 802 of Title 38 of the United States Code as hereafter amended. Such exemption shall be granted to: those persons eligible for such exemption on June 30, 1983; to disabled American veterans of any war or armed conflict who are disabled due to loss or loss of use of one lower extremity together with the loss or loss of use of one upper extremity which so affects the functions of balance or propulsion as to preclude locomotion without the aid of braces, crutches, canes, or a wheelchair; and to disabled veterans hereafter becoming eligible for assistance in acquiring housing under Section 801 of the United States Code as hereafter amended. The General Assembly may by general law provide for a different amount or a different method of determining the amount of or eligibility for the homestead exemption granted to disabled veterans. Any such law shall be enacted by a simple majority of the votes of all the members to which each house is entitled and may become effective without referendum. Such law may provide that the amount of or eligibility for the exemption shall be determined by reference to laws enacted by the United States Congress.*

Section IIA
Homeowner's Incentive Adjustment

Paragraph I. **State grants; adjustment amount.** *For each taxable year, a homeowner's incentive adjustment may be applied to the return of each taxpayer claiming such state-wide homestead exemption as may be specified by general law. The amount of such adjustment may provide a taxpayer with a benefit equivalent to a homestead exemption of up to $18,000.00 of the assessed value of a taxpayer's homestead or the taxpayer's ad valorem property tax liability on the homestead, whichever is lower. The General Assembly may appropriate such amount each year for grants to local governments and school districts as homeowner tax relief grants. The adjustments and grants authorized by this Paragraph shall be made in such manner and shall be subject to the procedures and conditions as may be specified by general law heretofore or hereafter enacted.*

Section III
Purposes and Methods of State Taxation

Paragraph I. *Taxation; purposes for which powers may be exercised.*

(a) Except as otherwise provided in this Constitution, the power of taxation over the whole state may be exercised for any purpose authorized by law. Any purpose for which the powers of taxation over the whole state could have been exercised on June 30, 1983, shall continue to be a purpose for which such powers may be exercised.

(b) Subject to conditions and limitations as may be provided by law, the power of taxation may be exercised to make grants for tax relief purposes to persons for sales tax paid and not otherwise reimbursed on prescription drugs. Credits or relief provided hereunder may be limited only to such reasonable classifications of taxpayers as may be specified by law.

Paragraph II. *Revenue to be paid into general fund*

(a) Except as otherwise provided in this Constitution, all revenue collected from taxes, fees, and assessments for state purposes, as authorized by revenue measures enacted by the General Assembly, shall be paid into the general fund of the state treasury.

(b) (1) As authorized by law providing for the promotion of any one or more types of agricultural products, fees, assessments, and other charges collected on the sale or processing of agricultural products need not be paid into the general fund of the state treasury. The uniformity requirement of this Article shall be satisfied by the application of the agricultural promotion program upon the affected products.

   (2) As used in this subparagraph, "agricultural products" includes, but is not limited to, registered livestock and livestock products, poultry and poultry products, timber and timber products, fish and seafood, and the products of the farms and forests of this state.

Paragraph III. *Grants to counties and municipalities.* State funds may be granted to counties and municipalities within the state. The grants authorized by this Paragraph shall be made in such manner and form and subject to the procedures and conditions specified by law. The law providing for any such grant may limit the purposes for which the grant funds may be expended.

Section IV
State Debt

Paragraph I. *Purposes for which debt may be incurred.* The state may incur:

(a) Public debt without limit to repel invasion, suppress insurrection, and defend the state in time of war.

(b) Public debt to supply a temporary deficit in the state treasury in any fiscal year created by a delay in collecting the taxes of that year. Such debt shall not exceed, in the aggregate, 5 percent of the total revenue receipts, less refunds, of the state treasury in the fiscal year immediately preceding the year in which such debt is incurred. The debt incurred shall be repaid on or before the last day of the fiscal year in which it is incurred out of taxes levied for that fiscal year. No such debt may be incurred in any fiscal year under the provisions of this subparagraph (b) if there is then outstanding unpaid debt from any previous fiscal year which was incurred to supply a temporary deficit in the state treasury.

(c) General obligation debt to acquire, construct, develop, extend, enlarge, or improve land, waters, property, highways, buildings, structures, equipment, or facilities of the state, its agencies, departments, institutions, and of those state authorities which were created and activated prior to November 8, 1960.

(d) General obligation debt to provide educational facilities for county and independent school systems and to provide public library facilities for county and independent school systems, counties, municipalities, and boards of trustees of public libraries or boards of trustees of public library systems, and, when the construction of such educational or library facilities has been completed, the title to such facilities shall be vested in the respective local boards of education, counties, municipalities, or public library boards of trustees for which such facilities were constructed.

(e) General obligation debt in order to make loans to counties, municipal corporations, political subdivisions, local authorities, and other local government entities for water or sewerage facilities or systems or for regional or multijurisdictional solid waste recycling or solid waste facilities or systems. It shall not be necessary for the state or a state authority to hold title to or otherwise be the owner of such facilities or systems. General obligation debt for these purposes may be authorized and incurred for administration and disbursement by a state authority created and activated before, on, or after November 8, 1960.

(f) Guaranteed revenue debt by guaranteeing the payment of revenue obligations issued by an instrumentality of the state if such revenue obligations are issued to finance:

(1) Toll bridges or toll roads.

(2) Land public transportation facilities or systems.

(3) Water facilities or systems.

(4) Sewage facilities or systems.

(5) Loans to, and loan programs for, citizens of the state for educational purposes.

(6) Regional or multijurisdictional solid waste recycling or solid waste facilities or systems.

Paragraph II. *State general obligation debt and guaranteed revenue debt; limitations.*

(a) As used in this Paragraph and Paragraph III of this section, "annual debt service requirements" means the total principal and interest coming due in any state fiscal year. With regard to any issue of debt incurred wholly or in part on a term basis, "annual debt service requirements" means an amount equal to the total principal and interest payments required to retire such issue in full divided by the number of years from its issue date to its maturity date.

(b) No debt may be incurred under subparagraphs (c), (d), and (e) of Paragraph I of this section or Paragraph V of this section at any time when the highest aggregate annual debt service requirements for the then current year or any subsequent year for outstanding general obligation debt and guaranteed revenue debt, including the proposed debt, and the highest aggregate annual payments for the then current year or any subsequent fiscal year of the state under all contracts then in force to which the provisions of the second paragraph of Article IX, Section VI, Paragraph I(a) of the Constitution of 1976 are applicable, exceed 10 percent of the total revenue receipts, less refunds of the state treasury in the fiscal year immediately preceding the year in which any such debt is to be incurred.

(c) No debt may be incurred under subparagraphs (c) and (d) of Paragraph I of this section at any time when the term of the debt is in excess of 25 years.

(d) No guaranteed revenue debt may be incurred to finance water or sewage treatment facilities or systems when the highest aggregate annual debt service requirements for the then current year or any subsequent fiscal year of the state for outstanding or proposed guaranteed revenue debt for water facilities or systems or sewage facilities or systems exceed 1 percent of the total revenue receipts less refunds, of the state treasury in the fiscal year immediately preceding the year in which any such debt is to be incurred.

(e) The aggregate amount of guaranteed revenue debt incurred to make loans for educational purposes that may be outstanding at any time shall not exceed $18 million, and the aggregate amount of guaranteed revenue debt incurred to purchase, or to lend or deposit against the security of, loans for educational purposes that may be outstanding at any time shall not exceed $72 million.

Paragraph III. *State general obligation debt and guaranteed revenue debt; conditions upon issuance; sinking funds and reserve funds.*

(a) (1) General obligation debt may not be incurred until legislation is enacted stating the purposes, in general or specific terms, for which such issue of debt is to be incurred, specifying the maximum principal amount of such issue and appropriating an amount at least sufficient to pay the highest annual debt service requirements for such issue. All such appropriations for debt service purposes shall not lapse for any reason and shall continue in effect until the debt for which such appropriation was authorized shall have been incurred, but the General Assembly may repeal any such appropriation at any time prior to the incurring of such debt.

The General Assembly shall raise by taxation and appropriate each fiscal year, in addition to the sum necessary to make all payments required under contracts entitled to the protection of the second paragraph of Paragraph I (a), Section VI, Article IX of the constitution of 1976, such amounts as are necessary to pay debt service requirements in such fiscal year on all general obligation debt.

(2) (A) The General Assembly shall appropriate to a special trust fund to be designated "State of Georgia General Obligation Debt Sinking Fund" such amounts as are necessary to pay annual debt service requirements on all general obligation debt. The sinking fund shall be used solely for the retirement of general obligation debt payable from the fund. If for any reason the monies in the sinking fund are insufficient to make, when due, all payments required with respect to such general obligation debt, the first revenues thereafter received in the general fund of the state shall be set aside by the appropriate state fiscal officer to the extent necessary to cure the deficiency and shall be deposited by the fiscal officer into the sinking fund. The appropriate state fiscal officer may be required to set aside and apply such revenues at the suit of any holder of any general obligation debt incurred under this section.

(B) The obligation to make sinking fund deposits as provided in subparagraph (2)(A) shall be subordinate to the obligation imposed upon the fiscal officers of the state pursuant to the provisions of the second paragraph of Paragraph I(a) of Section VI of Article IX of the Constitution of 1976.

(b) (1) Guaranteed revenue debt may not be incurred until legislation has been enacted authorizing the guarantee of the specific issue of revenue obligations then proposed, reciting that the General Assembly has determined such obligations will be self-liquidating over the life of the issue (which determination shall be conclusive), specifying the maximum principal amount of such issue and appropriating an amount at least equal to the highest annual debt service requirements for such issue.

(2) (A) Each appropriation made for the purposes of subparagraph (b) (1) shall be paid upon the issuance of said obligations into a special trust fund to be designated "State of Georgia Guaranteed Revenue Debt Common Reserve Fund" to be held together with all other sums similarly appropriated as a common reserve for

any payments which may be required by virtue of any guarantee entered into in connection with any issue of guaranteed revenue obligations. No appropriations for the benefit of guaranteed revenue debt shall lapse unless repealed prior to the payment of the appropriation into the common reserve fund.

(B) If any payments are required to be made from the common reserve fund to meet debt service requirements on guaranteed revenue obligations by virtue of an insufficiency of revenues, the amount necessary to cure the deficiency shall be paid from the common reserve fund by the appropriate state fiscal officer. Upon any such payment, the common reserve fund shall be reimbursed from the general funds of the state within ten days following the commencement of any fiscal year of the state for any amounts so paid; provided, however, the obligation to make any such reimbursements shall be subordinate to the obligation imposed upon the fiscal officers of the state pursuant to the second paragraph of Paragraph I(a) of Section VI, Article IX of the Constitution of 1976 and shall also be subordinate to the obligation to make sinking fund deposits for the benefit of general obligation debt. The appropriate state fiscal officer may be required to apply such funds as provided in this subparagraph (b) (2) (B) at the suit of any holder of any such guaranteed revenue obligations.

(C) The amount to the credit of the common reserve fund shall at all times be at least equal to the aggregate highest annual debt service requirements on all outstanding guaranteed revenue obligations entitled to the benefit of the fund. If at the end of any fiscal year of the state the fund is in excess of the required amount, the appropriate state fiscal officer, as designated by law, shall transfer the excess amount to the general funds of the state free of said trust.

(c) The funds in the general obligation debt sinking fund and the guaranteed revenue debt common reserve fund shall be as fully invested as is practicable, consistent with the requirements to make current principal and interest payments. Any such investments shall be restricted to obligations constituting direct and general obligations of the United States government or obligations unconditionally guaranteed as to the payment of principal and interest by the United States government, maturing no longer than 12 months from date of purchase.

Paragraph IV. *Certain contracts prohibited.* The state, and all state institutions, departments and agencies of the state are prohibited from entering into any contract, except contracts pertaining to guaranteed revenue debt, with any public agency, public corporation, authority, or similar entity if such contract is intended to constitute security for bonds or other obligations issued by any such public agency, public corporation, or authority and, in the event any contract between the state, or any state institution, department or agency of the state and any public agency, public corporation, authority or similar entity, or any revenues from any such contract, is pledged or assigned as security for the repayment of bonds or other obligations, then and in either such event, the appropriation or expenditure of any funds of the state for the payment of obligations under any such contract shall likewise be prohibited.

Paragraph V. *Refunding of debt.* The state may incur general obligation debt or guaranteed revenue debt to fund or refund any such debt or to fund or refund any obligations issued upon the security of contracts to which the provisions of the second paragraph of Paragraph I(a), Section VI, Article IX of the Constitution of 1976 are applicable.

The issuance of any such debt for the purposes of said funding or refunding shall be subject to the 10 percent limitation in Paragraph II (b) of this section to the same extent as debt incurred under Paragraph I of this section; provided, however, in making such computation the annual debt service requirements and annual contract payments remaining on the debt or obligations being funded or refunded shall not be taken into account.

The issuance of such debt may be accomplished by resolution of the Georgia State Financing and Investment Commission without any action on the part of the General Assembly and any appropriation made or required to be made with respect to the debt or obligation being funded or refunded shall immediately attach and inure to the benefit of the obligations to be issued in connection with such funding or refunding. Debt incurred in connection with any such funding or refunding shall be the same as that originally authorized by the General Assembly, except that general obligation debt may be incurred to fund or refund obligations issued upon the security of contracts to which the provisions of the second paragraph of Paragraph I(a), Section VI, Article IX of the Constitution of 1976 are applicable and the continuing appropriations required to be made under this Constitution shall immediately attach and inure to the benefit of the obligation to be issued in connection with such funding or refunding with the same force and effect as though said obligations so funded or refunded had originally been issued as a general obligation debt authorized hereunder.

The term of a funding or refunding issue pursuant to this Paragraph shall not extend beyond the term of the original debt or obligation and the total interest on the funding or refunding issue shall not exceed the total interest to be paid on such original debt or obligation. The principal amount of any debt issued in connection with such funding or refunding may exceed the principal amount being funded or refunded to the extent necessary to provide for the payment of any premium thereby incurred.

Paragraph VI. *Faith and credit of state pledged debt may be validated.* The full faith, credit, and taxing power of the state are hereby pledged to the payment of all public debt incurred under this article and all such debt and the interest on the debt shall be exempt from taxation. Such debt may be validated by judicial proceedings in the manner provided by law. Such validation shall be incontestable and conclusive.

Paragraph VII. *Georgia State Financing and Investment Commission; duties.*

(a) There shall be a Georgia State Financing and Investment Commission. The commission shall consist of the Governor, the President of the Senate, the

Speaker of the House of Representatives, the State Auditor, the Attorney General, the director, Fiscal Division, Department of Administrative Services, or such other officer as may be designated by law, and the Commissioner of Agriculture. The commission shall be responsible for the issuance of all public debt and for the proper application, as provided by law, of the proceeds of such debt to the purposes for which it is incurred; provided, however, the proceeds from guaranteed revenue obligations shall be paid to the issuer thereof and such proceeds and the application thereof shall be the responsibility of such issuer.

Debt to be incurred at the same time for more than one purpose may be combined in one issue without stating the purpose separately but the proceeds thereof must be allocated, disbursed and used solely in accordance with the original purpose and without exceeding the principal amount authorized for each purpose set forth in the authorization of the General Assembly and to the extent not so used shall be used to purchase and retire public debt.

The commission shall be responsible for the investment of all proceeds to be administered by it and, as provided by law, the income earned on any such investments may be used to pay operating expenses of the commission or placed in a common debt retirement fund and used to purchase and retire any public debt, or any bonds or obligations issued by any public agency, public corporation or authority which are secured by a contract to which the provisions of the second paragraph of Paragraph I(a) of Section VI, Article IX of the Constitution of 1976 are applicable. The commission shall have such additional responsibilities, powers, and duties as are provided by law.

(b) Notwithstanding subparagraph (a) of this Paragraph, proceeds from general obligation debt issued for making loans to local government entities for water or sewerage facilities or systems or for regional or multijurisdictional solid waste recycling or solid waste facilities or systems as provided in Paragraph I(e) of this section shall be paid or transferred to and administered and invested by the unit of state government or state authority made responsible by law for such activities, and the proceeds and investment earnings thereof shall be applied and disbursed by such unit or authority.

Paragraph VIII. *State aid forbidden.* Except as provided in this Constitution, the credit of the state shall not be pledged or loaned to any individual, company, corporation, or association. The state shall not become a joint owner or stockholder in or with any individual, company, association, or corporation.

Paragraph IX. *Construction.* Paragraphs I through VIII of this section are for the purpose of providing an effective method of financing the state's needs and their provisions and any law now or hereafter enacted by the General Assembly in furtherance of their provisions shall be liberally construed to effect such purpose. Insofar as any such provisions or any such law may be inconsistent with any other provisions of this Constitution or of any other law, the provisions of such Paragraphs and laws enacted in furtherance of such Paragraphs shall be controlling; provided, however, the provisions of such Paragraphs shall not be so broadly construed as to cause the same to be unconstitutional and in connection with any such construction such Paragraphs shall be deemed to contain such implied limitations as shall be required to accomplish the foregoing.

Paragraph X. *Assumption of debts forbidden; exceptions.* The state shall not assume the debt, or any part thereof, of any county, municipality, or other political subdivision of the state, unless such debt be contracted to enable the state to repel invasion, suppress civil disorders or insurrection, or defend itself in time of war.

Paragraph XI. *Section not to unlawfully impair contracts or revive obligations previously voided.* The provisions of this section shall not be construed so as to:

(a)   Unlawfully impair the obligation of any contract in effect on June 30, 1983.

(b)   Revive or permit the revival of the obligation of any bond or security declared to be void by the Constitution of 1976 or any previous Constitution of this state.

Paragraph XII. *Multiyear contracts for energy efficiency or conservation improvement.* The General Assembly may by general law authorize state governmental entities to incur debt for the purpose of entering into multiyear contracts for governmental energy efficiency or conservation improvement projects in which payments are guaranteed over the term of the contract by vendors based on the realization of specified savings or revenue gains attributable solely to the improvements; provided, however, that any such contract shall not exceed ten years unless otherwise provided by general law.

Paragraph XIII. *Multiyear rental agreements.* The General Assembly may by general law authorize the State Properties Commission, the Board of Regents of the University System of Georgia, and the Georgia Department of Labor to enter into rental agreements for the possession and use of real property without obligating present funds for the full amount of obligation the state may bear under the full term of any such rental agreement. Any such agreement shall provide for the termination of the agreement in the event of insufficient funds.

Article VIII
Education

Section I
Public Education

Paragraph I. *Public education; free public education prior to college or postsecondary level; support by taxation.* The provision of an adequate public education for the citizens shall be a primary obligation of the State of Georgia. Public education for the citizens prior to the college or postsecondary level shall be free and shall be provided for by taxation, and the General Assembly may by general law provide for the establishment of education policies for such public education. The expense of other public education shall be provided for in such manner and in such amount as may be provided by law.

Section II
State Board of Education

Paragraph I. *State Board of Education.*

(a)   There shall be a State Board of Education which shall consist of one member from each congressional district in the state appointed by the Governor and confirmed by the Senate. The Governor shall not be a member of said board. The ten members in office on June 30, 1983, shall serve out the remainder of their respective terms. As each term of office expires, the Governor shall appoint a successor as herein provided. The terms of office of all members appointed after the effective date of this Constitution shall be for seven years. Members shall serve until their successors are appointed and qualified. In the event of a vacancy on the board by death, resignation, removal, or any reason other than expiration of a member's term, the Governor shall fill such vacancy; and the person so appointed shall serve until confirmed by the Senate and, upon confirmation, shall serve for the unexpired term of office.

(b)   The State Board of Education shall have such powers and duties as provided by law.

(c)   The State Board of Education may accept bequests, donations, grants, and transfers of land, buildings, and other property for the use of the state educational system.

(d)   The qualifications, compensation, and removal from office of the members of the board of education shall be as provided by law.

Section III
State School Superintendent

Paragraph I.   *State School Superintendent.* There shall be a State School Superintendent, who shall be the executive officer of the State Board of Education, elected at the same time and in the same manner and for the same term as that of the Governor. The State School Superintendent shall have such qualifications and shall be paid such compensation as may be fixed by law. No member of the State Board of Education shall be eligible for election as State School Superintendent during the time for which such member shall have been appointed.

Section IV
Board of Regents

Paragraph I. *University System of Georgia; board of regents.*

(a)   There shall be a Board of Regents of the University System of Georgia which shall consist of one member from each congressional district in the state and five additional members from the state at large, appointed by the Governor and confirmed by the Senate. The Governor shall not be a member of said board. The members in office on June 30, 1983, shall serve out the remainder of their respective terms. As each term of office expires, the Governor shall appoint a successor as herein provided. All such terms of members shall be for seven years. Members shall serve until their successors are appointed and qualified. In the event of a vacancy on the board by death, resignation, removal, or any reason other than the expiration of a member's term, the Governor shall fill such vacancy; and the person so appointed shall serve until confirmed by the Senate and, upon confirmation, shall serve for the unexpired term of office.

(b) The board of regents shall have the exclusive authority to create new public colleges, junior colleges, and universities in the State of Georgia, subject to approval by majority vote in the House of Representatives and the Senate. Such vote shall not be required to change the status of a college, institution or university existing on the effective date of this Constitution. The government, control, and management of the University System of Georgia and all of the institutions in said system shall be vested in the Board of Regents of the University System of Georgia.

(c) All appropriations made for the use of any or all institutions in the university system shall be paid to the board of regents in a lump sum, with the power and authority in said board to allocate and distribute the same among the institutions under its control in such way and manner and in such amounts as will further an efficient and economical administration of the university system.

(d) The board of regents may hold, purchase, lease, sell, convey, or otherwise dispose of public property, execute conveyances thereon, and utilize the proceeds arising therefrom; may exercise the power of eminent domain in the manner provided by law; and shall have such other powers and duties as provided by law.

(e The board of regents may accept bequests, donations, grants, and transfers of land, buildings, and other property for the use of the University System of Georgia.

(f) The qualifications, compensation, and removal from office of the members of the board of regents shall be as provided by law.

Section V
Local School Systems

Paragraph I. *School systems continued; consolidation of school systems authorized; new independent school systems prohibited.*

Authority is granted to county and area boards of education to establish and maintain public schools within their limits; provided, however, that the authority provided for in this paragraph shall not diminish any authority of the General Assembly otherwise granted under this article, including the authority to establish special schools as provided for in Article VIII, Section V, Paragraph VII.

Existing county and independent school systems shall be continued, except that the General Assembly may provide by law for the consolidation of two or more county school systems, independent school systems, portions thereof, or any combination thereof into a single county or area school system under the control and management of a county or area board of education, under such terms and conditions as the General Assembly may prescribe; but no such consolidation shall become effective until approved by a majority of the qualified voters voting thereon in each separate school system proposed to be consolidated. No independent school system shall hereafter be established.

Paragraph II. *Boards of education.* Each school system shall be under the management and control of a board of education, the members of which shall be elected as provided by law. School board members shall reside within the territory embraced by the school system and shall have such compensation and additional qualifications as may be provided by law.

Any board of education to which the members are appointed as of December 31, 1992, shall continue as an appointed board of education through December 31, 1993, and the appointed members of such board of education who are in office on December 31, 1992, shall continue in office as members of such appointed board until December 31, 1993, on which date the terms of office of all appointed members shall end.

Paragraph III. *School superintendents.* There shall be a school superintendent of each system appointed by the board of education who shall be the executive officer of the board of education and shall have such qualifications, powers, and duties as provided by general law. Any elected school superintendent in office on January 1, 1993, shall continue to serve out the remainder of his or her respective term of office and shall be replaced by an appointee of the board of education at the expiration of such term.

Paragraph IV. *Reserved.*

Paragraph V. *Power of boards to contract with each other.*

(a)   Any two or more boards of education may contract with each other for the care, education, and transportation of pupils and for such other activities as they may be authorized by law to perform.

(b)   The General Assembly may provide by law for the sharing of facilities or services by and between local boards of education under such joint administrative authority as may be authorized.

Paragraph VI. *Power of boards to accept bequests, donations, grants, and transfers.* The board of education of each school system may accept bequests, donations, grants, and transfers of land, buildings, and other property for the use of such system.

Paragraph VII. *Special schools.*

(a)   The General Assembly may provide by law for the creation of special schools in such areas as may require them and may provide for the participation of local boards of education in the establishment of such schools under such terms and conditions as it may provide; but no bonded indebtedness may be incurred nor a school tax levied for the support of special schools without the approval of the local board of education and a majority of the qualified voters voting thereon in each of the systems affected.

Any special schools shall be operated in conformity with regulations of the State Board of Education pursuant to provisions of law. Special schools may include state charter schools; provided, however, that special schools shall only be public schools. A state charter school under this section shall mean a public school that operates under the terms of a charter between the State Board of Education and a charter petitioner; provided, however, that such state charter schools shall not include private, sectarian, religious, or for profit schools or private educational institutions; provided, further, that this Paragraph shall not be construed to prohibit a local board of education from establishing a local charter school pursuant to Article VIII, Section V, Paragraph I.

The state is authorized to expend state funds for the support and maintenance of special schools in such amount and manner as may be provided by law; provided, however, no deduction shall be made to any state funding which a local school system is otherwise authorized to receive pursuant to general law as a direct result or consequence of the enrollment in a state charter school of a specific student or students who reside within the geographic boundaries of the local school system.

(b) Nothing contained herein shall be construed to affect the authority of local boards of education or of the state to support and maintain special schools created prior to June 30, 1983.

Section VI
Local Taxation for Education

Paragraph I. *Local taxation for education.*

(a) The board of education of each school system shall annually certify to its fiscal authority or authorities a school tax not greater than 20 mills per dollar for the support and maintenance of education. Said fiscal authority or authorities shall annually levy said tax upon the assessed value of all taxable property within the territory served by said school system, provided that the levy made by an area board of education, which levy shall not be greater than 20 mills per dollar, shall be in such amount and within such limits as may be prescribed by local law applicable thereto.

(b) School tax funds shall be expended only for the support and maintenance of public schools, public vocational-technical schools, public education, and activities necessary or incidental thereto, including school lunch purposes.

(c)   The 20 mill limitation provided for in subparagraph (a) of this Paragraph shall not apply to those school systems which are authorized on June 30, 1983, to levy a school tax in excess thereof.

(d)   The method of certification and levy of the school tax provided for in subparagraph (a) of this Paragraph shall not apply to those systems that are authorized on June 30, 1983, to utilize a different method of certification and levy of such tax; but the General Assembly may by law require that such systems be brought into conformity with the method of certification and levy herein provided.

Paragraph II. *Increasing or removing tax rate.* The mill limitation in effect on June 30, 1983, for any school system may be increased or removed by action of the respective boards of education, but only after such action has been approved by a majority of the qualified voters voting thereon in the particular school system to be affected in the manner provided by law.

Paragraph III. *School tax collection reimbursement.* The General Assembly may by general law require local boards of education to reimburse the appropriate governing authority for the collection of school taxes, provided that any rate established may be reduced by local act.

Paragraph IV. *Sales tax for educational purposes.*

(a)   The board of education of each school district in a county in which no independent school district is located may by resolution and the board of education of each county school district and the board of education of each independent school district located within such county may by concurrent resolutions impose, levy, and collect a sales and use tax for educational purposes of such school districts conditioned upon approval by a majority of the qualified voters residing within the limits of the local taxing jurisdiction voting in a referendum thereon.

This tax shall be at the rate of 1 percent and shall be imposed for a period of time not to exceed five years, but in all other respects, except as otherwise provided in this Paragraph, shall correspond to and be levied in the same manner as the tax provided for by Article3 of Chapter 8 of Title 48 of the Official Code of Georgia Annotated, relating to the special county 1 percent sales and use tax, as now or hereafter amended. Proceedings for the reimposition of such tax shall be in the same manner as proceedings for the initial imposition of the tax, but the newly authorized tax shall not be imposed until the expiration of the tax then in effect.

(b)   The purpose or purposes for which the proceeds of the tax are to be used and may be expended include:

(1)   Capital outlay projects for educational purposes;

(2)   The retirement of previously incurred general obligation debt with respect only to capital outlay projects of the school system; provided, however, that the tax authorized under this Paragraph shall only be expended for the purpose authorized under this subparagraph (b)(2)

if all ad valorem property taxes levied or scheduled to be levied prior to the maturity of any such then outstanding general obligation debt to be retired by the proceeds of the tax imposed under this Paragraph shall be reduced by a total amount equal to the total amount of proceeds of the tax imposed under this Paragraph to be applied to retire such bonded indebtedness. In the event of failure to comply with the requirements of this subparagraph (b) (2), as certified by the Department of Revenue, no further funds shall be expended under this subparagraph (b) (2) by such county or independent board of education and all such funds shall be maintained in a separate, restricted account and held solely for the expenditure for future capital outlay projects for educational purposes; or

(3) A combination of the foregoing.

(c) The resolution calling for the imposition of the tax and the ballot question shall each describe:

   (1) The specific capital outlay projects to be funded, or the specific debt to be retired, or both, if applicable;

   (2) The maximum cost of such project or projects and, if applicable, the maximum amount of debt to be retired, which cost and amount of debt shall also be the maximum amount of net proceeds to be raised by the tax; and

   (3) The maximum period of time, to be stated in calendar years or calendar quarters and not to exceed five years.

(d) Nothing in this Paragraph shall prohibit a county and those municipalities located in such county from imposing as additional taxes local sales and use taxes authorized by general law.

(e) The tax imposed pursuant to this Paragraph shall not be subject to and shall not count with respect to any general law limitation regarding the maximum amount of local sales and use taxes which may be levied in any jurisdiction in this state.

(f) The tax imposed pursuant to this Paragraph shall not be subject to any sales and use tax exemption with respect to the sale or use of food and beverages which is imposed by law.

(g) The net proceeds of the tax shall be distributed between the county school district and the independent school districts, or portion thereof, located in such county according to the ratio the student enrollment in each school district, or portion thereof, bears to the total student enrollment of all school districts in the county or upon such other formula for distribution as may be authorized by local law. For purposes of this subparagraph, student enrollment shall be based on the latest FTE count prior to the referendum on imposing the tax.

(h) Excess proceeds of the tax which remain following expenditure of proceeds for authorized projects or purposes for education shall be used solely for the purpose of reducing any indebtedness of the school system. In the event there is no indebtedness, such excess proceeds shall be used by such school system for the purpose of reducing its millage rate in an amount equivalent to the amount of such excess proceeds.

(i) The tax authorized by this Paragraph may be imposed, levied, and collected as provided in this Paragraph without further action by the General Assembly, but the General Assembly shall be authorized by general law to further define and implement its provisions including, but not limited to, the authority to specify the percentage of net proceeds to be allocated among the projects and purposes for which the tax was levied.

(j) (1) Notwithstanding any provision of any constitutional amendment continued in force and effect pursuant to Article XI, Section I, Paragraph IV(a) and except as otherwise provided in subparagraph (j)(2) of this Paragraph, any political subdivision whose ad valorem taxing powers are restricted pursuant to such a constitutional amendment may receive the proceeds of the tax authorized under this Paragraph or of any local sales and use tax authorized by general law, or any combination of such taxes, without any corresponding limitation of its ad valorem taxing powers which would otherwise be required under such constitutional amendment.

(2) The restriction on and limitation of ad valorem taxing powers described in subparagraph (j) (1) of this Paragraph shall remain applicable with respect to proceeds received from the levy of a local sales and use tax specifically authorized by a constitutional amendment in force and effect pursuant to Article XI, Section I, Paragraph IV (a), as opposed to a local sales and use tax authorized by this Paragraph or by general law.

Section VII.
Education Assistance

Paragraph I. *Educational assistance programs authorized.*

(a) Pursuant to laws now or hereafter enacted by the General Assembly, public funds may be expended for any of the following purposes:

(1) To provide grants, scholarships, loans, or other assistance to students and to parents of students for educational purposes.

(2) To provide for a program of guaranteed loans to students and to parents of students for educational purposes and to pay interest, interest subsidies, and fees to lenders on such loans. The General Assembly is authorized to provide such tax exemptions to lenders as shall be deemed advisable in connection with such program.

(3) To match funds now or hereafter available for student assistance pursuant to any federal law.

(4) To provide grants, scholarships, loans, or other assistance to public employees for educational purposes.

(5) To provide for the purchase of loans made to students for educational purposes who have completed a program of study in a field in which critical shortages exist and for cancellation of repayment of such loans, interest, and charges thereon.

(b) Contributions made in support of any educational assistance program now or hereafter established under provisions of this section may be deductible for state income tax purposes as now or hereafter provided by law.

(c) The General Assembly shall be authorized by general law to provide for an education trust fund to assist students and parents of students in financing postsecondary education and to provide for contracts between the fund and purchasers for the advance payment of tuition by each purchaser for a qualified beneficiary to attend a state institution of higher education. Such general law shall provide for such terms, conditions, and limitations as the General Assembly shall deem necessary for the implementation of this subparagraph. Notwithstanding any provision of this Constitution to the contrary, the General Assembly shall be authorized to provide for the guarantee of such contracts with state revenues.

Paragraph II. *Guaranteed revenue debt.* Guaranteed revenue debt may be incurred to provide funds to make loans to students and to parents of students for educational purposes, to purchase loans made to students and to parents of students for educational purposes, or to lend or make deposits of such funds with lenders which shall be secured by loans made to students and to parents of students for educational purposes. Any such debt shall be incurred in accordance with the procedures and requirements of Article VII, Section IV of this Constitution.

Paragraph III. *Public authorities.* Public authorities or public corporations heretofore or hereafter created for such purposes shall be authorized to administer educational assistance programs and, in connection therewith, may exercise such powers as may now or hereafter be provided by law.

Paragraph IV. *Waiver of tuition.* The Board of Regents of the University System of Georgia shall be authorized to establish programs allowing attendance at units of the University System of Georgia without payment of tuition or other fees, but the General Assembly may provide by law for the establishment of any such program for the benefit of elderly citizens of the state.

Article IX.
Counties and Municipal Corporations

Section I. Counties

Paragraph I. *Counties a body corporate and politic.* Each county shall be a body corporate and politic with such governing authority and with such powers and limitations as are provided in this Constitution and as provided by law. The governing authorities of the several counties shall remain as prescribed by law on June 30, 1983, until otherwise provided by law.

Paragraph II. *Number of counties limited; county boundaries and county sites; County consolidation.*

(a) There shall not be more than 159 counties in this state.

(b) The metes and bounds of the several counties and the county sites shall remain as prescribed by law on June 30, 1983, unless changed under the operation of a general law.

(c) The General Assembly may provide by law for the consolidation of two or more counties into one or the division of a county and the merger of portions thereof into other counties under such terms and conditions as it may prescribe; but no such consolidation, division, or merger shall become effective unless approved by a majority of the qualified voters voting thereon in each of the counties proposed to be consolidated, divided, or merged.

Paragraph III. *County officers; election; term; compensation.*

(a) The clerk of the superior court, judge of the probate court, sheriff, tax receiver, tax collector, and tax commissioner, where such office has replaced the tax receiver and tax collector, shall be elected by the qualified voters of their respective counties for terms of four years and shall have such qualifications, powers, and duties as provided by general law.

(b) County officers listed in subparagraph (a) of this Paragraph may be on a fee basis, salary basis, or fee basis supplemented by salary, in such manner as may be directed by law. Minimum compensation for said county officers may be established by the General Assembly by general law. Such minimum compensation may be supplemented by local law or, if such authority is delegated by local law, by action of the county governing authority.

(c) The General Assembly may consolidate the offices of tax receiver and tax collector into the office of tax commissioner.

Paragraph IV. *Civil service systems.* The General Assembly may by general law authorize the establishment by county governing authorities of civil service systems covering county employees or covering county employees and employees of the elected county officers.

Section II.
Home Rule for Counties and Municipalities

Paragraph I. *Home rule for counties.*

(a) The governing authority of each county shall have legislative power to adopt clearly reasonable ordinances, resolutions, or regulations relating to its property, affairs, and local government for which no provision has been made by general law and which is not inconsistent with this Constitution or any local law applicable thereto. Any such local law shall remain in force and effect until amended or repealed as provided in subparagraph (b). This, however, shall not restrict the authority of the General Assembly by general law to further define this power or to broaden, limit, or otherwise regulate the exercise thereof. The General Assembly shall not pass any local law to repeal, modify, or supersede any action taken by a county governing authority under this section except as authorized under subparagraph (c) hereof.

(b) Except as provided in subparagraph (c), a county may, as an incident of its home rule power, amend or repeal the local acts applicable to its governing authority by following either of the procedures hereinafter set forth:

(1) Such local acts may be amended or repealed by a resolution or ordinance duly adopted at two regular consecutive meetings of the county governing authority not less than seven nor more than 60 days apart. A notice containing a synopsis of the proposed amendment or repeal shall be published in the official county organ once a week for three weeks within a period of 60 days immediately preceding its final adoption. Such notice shall state that a copy of the proposed amendment or repeal is on file in the office of the clerk of the superior court of the county for the purpose of examination and inspection by the public. The clerk of the superior court shall furnish anyone, upon written request, a copy of the proposed amendment or repeal. No amendment or repeal hereunder shall be valid to change or repeal an amendment adopted pursuant to a referendum as provided in (2) of this subparagraph or to change or repeal a local act of the General Assembly ratified in a referendum by the electors of such county unless at least 12 months have elapsed after such referendum. No amendment hereunder shall be valid if inconsistent with any provision of this Constitution or if provision has been made therefor by general law.

(2) Amendments to or repeals of such local acts or ordinances, resolutions, or regulations adopted pursuant to subparagraph (a) hereof may be initiated by a petition filed with the judge of the probate court of the county containing, in cases of counties with a population of 5,000 or less, the signatures of at least 25 percent of the electors registered to vote in the last general election; in cases of counties with a population of more than 5,000 but not more than

50,000, at least 20 percent of the electors registered to vote in the last general election; and, in cases of a county with a population of more than 50,000, at least 10 percent of the electors registered to vote in the last general election, which petition shall specifically set forth the exact language of the proposed amendment or repeal.

The judge of the probate court shall determine the validity of such petition within 60 days of its being filed with the judge of the probate court. In the event the judge of the probate court determines that such petition is valid, it shall be his duty to issue the call for an election for the purpose of submitting such amendment or repeal to the registered electors of the county for their approval or rejection. Such call shall be issued not less than ten nor more than 60 days after the date of the filing of the petition. He shall set the date of such election for a day not less than 60 nor more than 90 days after the date of such filing.

The judge of the probate court shall cause a notice of the date of said election to be published in the official organ of the county once a week for three weeks immediately preceding such date. Said notice shall also contain a synopsis of the proposed amendment or repeal and shall state that a copy thereof is on file in the office of the judge of the probate court of the county for the purpose of examination and inspection by the public. The judge of the probate court shall furnish anyone, upon written request, a copy of the proposed amendment or repeal. If more than one-half of the votes cast on such question are for approval of the amendment or repeal, it shall become of full force and effect; otherwise, it shall be void and of no force and effect.

The expense of such election shall be borne by the county, and it shall be the duty of the judge of the probate court to hold and conduct such election. Such election shall be held under the same laws and rules and regulations as govern special elections, except as otherwise provided herein.

It shall be the duty of the judge of the probate court to canvass the returns and declare and certify the result of the election. It shall be his further duty to certify the result thereof to the Secretary of State in accordance with the provisions of subparagraph (g) of this Paragraph.

A referendum on any such amendment or repeal shall not be held more often than once each year. No amendment hereunder shall be valid if inconsistent with any provision of this Constitution or if provision has been made therefor by general law.

In the event that the judge of the probate court determines that such petition was   not valid, he shall cause to be published in explicit detail the reasons why such petition is not valid; provided, however, that, in any proceeding in which the validity of the petition is at issue, the tribunal considering such issue shall not be limited by the reasons assigned. Such publication shall be in the official organ of the county in the week immediately following the date on which such petition is declared to be not valid.

(c) The power granted to counties in subparagraphs (a) and (b) above shall not be construed to extend to the following matters or any other matters which the General Assembly by general law has preempted or may hereafter preempt, but such matters shall be the subject of general law or the subject of local acts of the General Assembly to the extent that the enactment of such local acts is otherwise permitted under this Constitution:

   (1) Action affecting any elective county office, the salaries thereof, or the personnel thereof, except the personnel subject to the jurisdiction of the county governing authority.

   (2) Action affecting the composition, form, procedure for election or appointment, compensation, and expenses and allowances in the nature of compensation of the county governing authority.

   (3) Action defining any criminal offense or providing for criminal punishment.

   (4) Action adopting any form of taxation beyond that authorized by law or by this Constitution.

   (5) Action extending the power of regulation over any business activity regulated by the Georgia Public Service Commission beyond that authorized by local or general law or by this Constitution.

   (6) Action affecting the exercise of the power of eminent domain.

   (7) Action affecting any court or the personnel thereof.

   (8) Action affecting any public school system.

(d) The power granted in subparagraphs (a) and (b) of this Paragraph shall not include the power to take any action affecting the private or civil law governing private or civil relationships, except as is incident to the exercise of an independent governmental power.

(e) Nothing in subparagraphs (a), (b), (c), or (d) shall affect the provisions of subparagraph (f) of this Paragraph.

(f) The governing authority of each county is authorized to fix the salary, compensation, and expenses of those employed by such governing authority and to establish and maintain retirement or pension systems, insurance, workers' compensation, and hospitalization benefits for said employees.

(g) No amendment or revision of any local act made pursuant to subparagraph (b) of this section shall become effective until a copy of such amendment or revision, a copy of the required notice of publication, and an affidavit of a duly authorized representative of the newspaper in which such notice was published to the effect that said notice has been published as provided in said subparagraph has been filed with the Secretary of State. The Secretary of State shall provide for the publication and distribution of all such amendments and revisions at least annually.

Paragraph II. *Home rule for municipalities.* The General Assembly may provide by law for the self-government of municipalities and to that end is expressly given the authority to delegate its power so that matters pertaining to municipalities may be dealt with without the necessity of action by the General Assembly.

Paragraph III. *Supplementary powers.*

(a) In addition to and supplementary of all powers possessed by or conferred upon any county, municipality, or any combination thereof, any county, municipality, or any combination thereof may exercise the following powers and provide the following services:

 (1) Police and fire protection.

 (2) Garbage and solid waste collection and disposal.

 (3) Public health facilities and services, including hospitals, ambulance and emergency rescue services, and animal control.

 (4) Street and road construction and maintenance, including curbs, sidewalks, street lights, and devices to control the flow of traffic on streets and roads constructed by counties and municipalities or any combination thereof.

 (5) Parks, recreational areas, programs, and facilities.

 (6) Storm water and sewage collection and disposal systems.

 (7) Development, storage, treatment, purification, and distribution of water.

 (8) Public housing.

 (9) Public transportation.

 (10) Libraries, archives, and arts and sciences programs and facilities.

 (11) Terminal and dock facilities and parking facilities.

 (12) Codes, including building, housing, plumbing, and electrical codes.

 (13) Air quality control.

 (14) The power to maintain and modify heretofore existing retirement or pension systems, including such systems heretofore created by general laws of local application by population classification, and to continue in effect or modify other benefits heretofore provided as a part of or in addition to such retirement or pension systems and the power to create and maintain retirement or pension systems for any elected or appointed public officers and employees whose compensation is paid in whole or in part from county or municipal funds and for the beneficiaries of such officers and employees.

(b)   Unless otherwise provided by law,

   (1)   No county may exercise any of the powers listed in subparagraph (a) of this Paragraph or provide any service listed therein inside the boundaries of any municipality or any other county except by contract with the municipality or county affected; and

   (2)   No municipality may exercise any of the powers listed in subparagraph (a) of this Paragraph or provide any service listed therein outside its own boundaries except by contract with the county or municipality affected.

(c)   Nothing contained within this Paragraph shall operate to prohibit the General Assembly from enacting general laws relative to the subject matters listed in subparagraph (a) of this Paragraph or to prohibit the General Assembly by general law from regulating, restricting, or limiting the exercise of the powers listed therein; but it may not withdraw any such powers.

(d)   Except as otherwise provided in subparagraph (b) of this Paragraph, the General Assembly shall act upon the subject matters listed in subparagraph (a) of this Paragraph only by general law.

Paragraph IV. *Planning and zoning.* The governing authority of each county and of each municipality may adopt plans and may exercise the power of zoning. This authorization shall not prohibit the General Assembly from enacting general laws establishing procedures for the exercise of such power.

Paragraph V. *Eminent domain.* The governing authority of each county and of each municipality may exercise the power of eminent domain for any public purpose subject to any limitations on the exercise of such power as may be provided by general law.

Notwithstanding the provisions of any local amendment to the Constitution continued in effect pursuant to Article XI, Section I, Paragraph IV or any existing general law, each exercise of eminent domain by a nonelected housing or development authority shall be first approved by the elected governing authority of the county or municipality within which the property is located.

Paragraph VI. *Special districts.* As hereinafter provided in this Paragraph, special districts may be created for the provision of local government services within such districts; and fees, assessments, and taxes may be levied and collected within such districts to pay, wholly or partially, the cost of providing such services therein and to construct and maintain facilities therefor.

Such special districts may be created and fees, assessments, or taxes may be levied and collected therein by any one or more of the following methods:

(a)   By general law which directly creates the districts.

(b)   By general law which requires the creation of districts under conditions specified by such general law.

(c) By municipal or county ordinance or resolution, except that no such ordinance or resolution may supersede a law enacted by the General Assembly pursuant to subparagraphs (a) or (b) of this Paragraph.

Paragraph VII. *Community redevelopment.*

(a) Each condemnation of privately held property for redevelopment purposes must be approved by vote of the elected governing authority of the city within which the property is located, if any, or otherwise by the governing authority of the county within which the property is located. The power of eminent domain shall not be used for redevelopment purposes by any entity, except for public use, as defined by general law.

   (a.1) The General Assembly may authorize any county, municipality, or housing authority to undertake and carry out community redevelopment.

(b) The General Assembly is also authorized to grant to counties or municipalities for redevelopment purposes and in connection with redevelopment programs, as such purposes and programs are defined by general law, the power to issue tax allocation bonds, as defined by such law, and the power to incur other obligations, without either such bonds or obligations constituting debt within the meaning of Section V of this article, and the power to enter into contracts for any period not exceeding 30 years with private persons, firms, corporations, and business entities.

Such general law may authorize the use of county, municipal, and school tax funds, or any combination thereof, to fund such redevelopment purposes and programs, including the payment of debt service on tax allocation bonds, notwithstanding Section VI of Article VIII or any other provision of this Constitution and regardless of whether any county, municipality, or local board of education approved the use of such tax funds for such purposes and programs before January 1, 2009.

No county, municipal, or school tax funds may be used for such purposes and programs without the approval by resolution of the applicable governing body of the county, municipality, or local board of education.

No school tax funds may be used for such purposes and programs except as authorized by general law after January 1, 2009; provided, however, that any school tax funds pledged for the repayment of tax allocation bonds which have been judicially validated pursuant to general law shall continue to be used for such purposes and programs.

Notwithstanding the grant of these powers pursuant to general law, no county or municipality may exercise these powers unless so authorized by local law and unless such powers are exercised in conformity with those terms and conditions for such exercise as established by that local law.

The provisions of any such local law shall conform to those requirements established by general law regarding such powers. No such local law, or any amendment thereto, shall become effective unless approved in a referendum by a majority of the qualified voters voting thereon in the county or municipality directly affected by that local law.

(c) The General Assembly is authorized to provide by general law for the creation of enterprise zones by counties or municipalities, or both. Such law may provide for exemptions, credits, or reductions of any tax or taxes levied within such zones by the state, a county, a municipality, or any combination thereof.

Such exemptions shall be available only to such persons, firms, or corporations which create job opportunities within the enterprise zone for unemployed, low, and moderate income persons in accordance with the standards set forth in such general law. Such general law shall further define enterprise zones so as to limit such tax exemptions, credits, or reductions to persons and geographic areas which are determined to be underdeveloped as evidenced by the unemployment rate and the average personal income in the area when compared to the remainder of the state.

The General Assembly may by general law further define areas qualified for creation of enterprise zones and may provide for all matters relative to the creation, approval, and termination of such zones.

(d) The existence in a community of real property which is maintained in a blighted condition increases the burdens of state and local government by increasing the need for governmental services, including but not limited to social services, public safety services, and code enforcement services.

Rehabilitation of blighted property decreases the need for such governmental services. In recognition of such service needs and in order to encourage community redevelopment, the counties and municipalities of this state are authorized to establish community redevelopment tax incentive programs as authorized in this subparagraph.

A community redevelopment tax incentive program shall be established by ordinance of the county or municipality. Any such program and ordinance shall include the following elements:

(1) The ordinance shall specify ascertainable standards which shall be applied in determining whether property is maintained in a blighted condition. The ordinance shall provide that property shall not be subject to official identification as maintained in a blighted condition and shall not be subject to increased taxation if the property is a dwelling house which is being used as the primary residence of one or more persons; and

(2) The ordinance shall establish a procedure for the official identification of real property in the county or municipality which is maintained in a blighted condition. Such procedure shall include notice to the property owner and the opportunity for a hearing with respect to such determination.

(3) The ordinance shall specify an increased rate of ad valorem taxation to be applied to property which has been officially identified as maintained in a blighted condition. Such increase in the rate of taxation shall be accomplished through application of a factor to the millage rate applied to the property, so that such property shall be taxed at a higher millage rate than the millage rate generally applied in the county or municipality, or otherwise as may be provided by general law.

(4) The ordinance may, but shall not be required to, segregate revenues arising from any increased rate of ad valorem taxation and provide for use of such revenues only for community redevelopment purposes;

(5) The ordinance shall specify ascertainable standards for rehabilitation through remedial actions or redevelopment with which the owner of property may comply in order to have the property removed from identification as maintained in a blighted condition. As used herein, the term "blighted condition" shall include, at a minimum, property that constitutes endangerment to public health or safety;

(6) The ordinance shall specify a decreased rate of ad valorem taxation to be applied for a specified period of time after the county or municipality has accepted a plan submitted by the owner for remedial action or redevelopment of the blighted property and the owner is in compliance with the terms of the plan. Such decrease in the rate of taxation shall be accomplished through application of a factor to the millage rate applied to the property, so that such property shall be taxed at a lower millage rate than the millage rate generally applied in the county or municipality, or otherwise as may be provided by general law.

(7) The ordinance may contain such other matters as are consistent with the intent and provisions of this subparagraph and general law.

Variations in rate of taxation as authorized under this subparagraph shall be a permissible variation in the uniformity of taxation otherwise required. The increase or decrease in rate of taxation accomplished through a change in the otherwise applicable millage rate shall affect only the general millage rate for county or municipal maintenance and operations. A county and one or more municipalities in the county may, but shall not be required to, establish a joint community redevelopment tax incentive program through the adoption of concurrent ordinances.

No Act of the General Assembly shall be required for counties and municipalities to establish community redevelopment tax incentive programs. However, the General Assembly may by general law regulate, restrict, or limit the powers granted to counties and municipalities under this subparagraph.

Paragraph VIII. *Limitation on the taxing power and contributions of counties, municipalities, and political subdivisions.* The General Assembly shall not authorize any county, municipality, or other political subdivision of this state, through taxation, contribution, or otherwise, to appropriate money for or to lend its credit to any person or to any nonpublic corporation or association except for purely charitable purposes.

Paragraph IX. *Immunity of counties, municipalities, and school districts.* The General Assembly may waive the immunity of counties, municipalities, and school districts by law.

Section III.
Intergovernmental Relations

Paragraph I. *Intergovernmental contracts.*

(a)   The state, or any institution, department, or other agency thereof, and any county, municipality, school district, or other political subdivision of the state may contract for any period not exceeding 50 years with each other or with any other public agency, public corporation, or public authority for joint services, for the provision of services, or for the joint or separate use of facilities or equipment; but such contracts must deal with activities, services, or facilities which the contracting parties are authorized by law to undertake or provide. By way of specific instance and not limitation, a mutual undertaking by a local government entity to borrow and an undertaking by the state or a state authority to lend funds from and to one another for water or sewerage facilities or systems or for regional or multijurisdictional solid waste recycling or solid waste facilities or systems pursuant to law shall be a provision for services and an activity within the meaning of this Paragraph.

(b)   Subject to such limitations as may be provided by general law, any county, municipality, or political subdivision thereof may, in connection with any contracts authorized in this Paragraph, convey any existing facilities or equipment to the state or to any public agency, public corporation, or public authority.

(c)   Any county, municipality, or any combination thereof, may contract with any public agency, public corporation, or public authority for the care, maintenance, and hospitalization of its indigent sick and may as a part of such contract agree to pay for the cost of acquisition, construction, modernization, or repairs of necessary land, buildings, and facilities by such public agency, public corporation, or public authority and provide for the payment of such services and the cost to such public agency, public corporation, or public authority of acquisition, construction, modernization, or repair of land, buildings, and facilities from revenues realized by such county, municipality, or any combination thereof from any taxes authorized by this Constitution or revenues derived from any other source.

Paragraph II. *Local government reorganization.*

(a) The General Assembly may provide by law for any matters necessary or convenient to authorize the consolidation of the governmental and corporate powers and functions vested in municipalities with the governmental and corporate powers and functions vested in a county or counties in which such municipalities are located; provided, however, that no such consolidation shall become effective unless separately approved by a majority of the qualified voters of the county or each of the counties and of the municipality or each of the municipalities located within such county or counties containing at least 10 percent of the population of the county in which located voting thereon in such manner as may be prescribed in such law. Such law may provide procedures and requirements for the establishment of charter commissions to draft proposed charters for the consolidated government, and the General Assembly is expressly authorized to delegate its powers to such charter commissions for such purposes so that the governmental consolidation proposed by a charter commission may become effective without the necessity of further action by the General Assembly; or such law may require that the recommendation of any such charter commission be implemented by a subsequent local law.

(b) The General Assembly may provide by general law for alternatives other than governmental consolidation as authorized in subparagraph (a) above for the reorganization of county and municipal governments, including, but not limited to, procedures to establish a single governing body as the governing authority of a county and a municipality or municipalities located within such county or for the redistribution of powers between a county and a municipality or municipalities located within the county. Such law may require the form of governmental reorganization authorized by such law to be approved by the qualified voters directly affected thereby voting in such manner as may be required in such law.

(c) Nothing in this Paragraph shall be construed to limit the authority of the General Assembly to repeal municipal charters without a referendum.

Section IV.
Taxation Power of County and Municipal Governments

Paragraph I. *Power of taxation.*

(a) Except as otherwise provided in this Paragraph, the governing authority of any county, municipality, or combination thereof may exercise the power of taxation as authorized by this Constitution or by general law.

(b) In the absence of a general law:

(1) County governing authorities may be authorized by local law to levy and collect business and occupational license taxes and license fees only in the unincorporated areas of the counties. The General

Assembly may provide that the revenues raised by such tax or fee be spent for the provision of services only in the unincorporated areas of the county.

(2) Municipal governing authorities may be authorized by local law to levy and collect taxes and fees in the corporate limits of the municipalities.

(c) The General Assembly may provide by law for the taxation of insurance companies on the basis of gross direct premiums received from insurance policies within the unincorporated areas of counties. The tax authorized herein may be imposed by the state or by counties or by the state for county purposes as may be provided by law.

The General Assembly may further provide by law for the reduction, only upon taxable property within the unincorporated areas of counties, of the ad valorem tax millage rate for county or county school district purposes or for the reduction of such ad valorem tax millage rate for both such purposes in connection with imposing or authorizing the imposition of the tax authorized herein or in connection with providing for the distribution of the proceeds derived from the tax authorized herein.

Paragraph II. *Power of expenditure.* The governing authority of any county, municipality, or combination thereof may expend public funds to perform any public service or public function as authorized by this Constitution or by law or to perform any other service or function as authorized by this Constitution or by general law.

Paragraph III. *Purposes of taxation; allocation of taxes.* No levy need state the particular purposes for which the same was made nor shall any taxes collected be allocated for any particular purpose, unless otherwise provided by this Constitution or by law.

Paragraph IV. *Tax allocation; regional facilities.* As used in this Paragraph, the term "regional facilities" means industrial parks, business parks, conference centers, convention centers, airports, athletic facilities, recreation facilities, jails or correctional facilities, or other similar or related economic development parks, centers, or facilities or any combination thereof. Notwithstanding any other provision of this Constitution, a county or municipality is authorized to enter into contracts with:

(1) Any county which is contiguous to such county or the county in which such municipality is located;

(2) Any municipality located in such a contiguous county or the same county; or

(3) Any combination thereof. Any such contract may be for the purpose of allocating the proceeds of ad valorem taxes assessed and collected on real property located in such county or municipality with such other counties or municipalities with which the assessing county or municipality has entered into agreements for the development of one or more regional

facilities and the allocation of other revenues generated from such regional facilities.

Any such regional facility may be publicly or privately initiated. The allocation of such tax proceeds and other revenues shall be determined by contract between the affected local governments. Such contract shall provide for the manner of development, operation, and management of the regional facility and the sharing of expenses among the contracting local governments and shall specify the percentage of ad valorem taxes and other revenues to be allocated and the method of allocation to each contracting local government.

Unless otherwise provided by law, such a regional facility will qualify for the greatest dollar amount of income tax credits which may be provided for by general law for any of the counties or municipalities which have entered into an agreement for the development of the regional facility, regardless of the county or municipality in which the business is physically located. The authority granted to counties and municipalities under this Paragraph shall be subject to any conditions, limitations, and restrictions which may be imposed by general law.

Section V
Limitations on Local Debt

Paragraph I. *Debt limitations of counties, municipalities, and other political subdivisions.*

(a) The debt incurred by any county, municipality, or other political subdivision of this state, including debt incurred on behalf of any special district, shall never exceed 10 percent of the assessed value of all taxable property within such county, municipality, or political subdivision; and no such county, municipality, or other political subdivision shall incur any new debt without the assent of a majority of the qualified voters of such county, municipality, or political subdivision voting in an election held for that purpose as provided by law.

(b) Notwithstanding subparagraph (a) of this Paragraph, all local school systems which are authorized by law on June 30, 1983, to incur debt in excess of 10 percent of the assessed value of all taxable property therein shall continue to be authorized to incur such debt.

Paragraph II. *Special district debt.* Any county, municipality, or political subdivision of this state may incur debt on behalf of any special district created pursuant to Paragraph VI of Section II of this article.

Such debt may be incurred on behalf of such special district where the county, municipality, or other political subdivision shall have, at or before the time of incurring such debt, provided for the assessment and collection of an annual tax within the special district sufficient in amount to pay the principal of and interest on such debt within 30 years from the incurrence thereof; and no such county, municipality, or other political subdivision shall incur any debt on behalf of such special district without the assent of a majority of the qualified voters of such special district voting in an election held for that purpose as provided by law.

No such county, municipality, or other political subdivision shall incur any debt on behalf of such special district in an amount which, when taken together with all other debt outstanding incurred by such county, municipality, or political subdivision and on behalf of any such special district, exceeds 10 percent of the assessed value of all taxable property within such county, municipality, or political subdivision.

The proceeds of the tax collected as provided herein shall be placed in a sinking fund to be held on behalf of such special district and used exclusively to pay off the principal of and interest on such debt thereafter maturing.

Such moneys shall be held and kept separate and apart from all other revenues collected and may be invested and reinvested as provided by law.

Paragraph III. *Refunding of outstanding indebtedness.* The governing authority of any county, municipality, or other political subdivision of this state may provide for the refunding of outstanding bonded indebtedness without the necessity of a referendum being held therefor, provided that neither the term of the original debt is extended nor the interest rate of the original debt is increased. The principal amount of any debt issued in connection with such refunding may exceed the principal amount being refunded in order to reduce the total principal and interest payment requirements over the remaining term of the original issue. The proceeds of the refunding issue shall be used solely to retire the original debt. The original debt refunded shall not constitute debt within the meaning of Paragraph I of this section; but the refunding issue shall constitute a debt such as will count against the limitation on debt measured by 10 percent of assessed value of taxable property as expressed in Paragraph I of this section.

Paragraph IV. *Exceptions to debt limitations.* Notwithstanding the debt limitations provided in Paragraph I of this section and without the necessity for a referendum being held therefor, the governing authority of any county, municipality, or other political subdivision of this state may, subject to the conditions and limitations as may be provided by general law:

(1) Accept and use funds granted by and obtain loans from the federal government or any agency thereof pursuant to conditions imposed by federal law.

(2) Incur debt, by way of borrowing from any person, corporation, or association as well as from the state, to pay in whole or in part the cost of property valuation and equalization programs for ad valorem tax purposes.

Paragraph V. *Temporary loans authorized.* The governing authority of any county, municipality, or other political subdivision of this state may incur debt by obtaining temporary loans in each year to pay expenses. The aggregate amount of all such loans shall not exceed 75 percent of the total gross income from taxes collected in the last preceding year. Such loans shall be payable on or before December 31 of the calendar year in which such loan is made. No such loan may be obtained when there is a loan then unpaid obtained in any prior year. No such county, municipality, or other political subdivision of this state shall incur in any one calendar year an aggregate of such temporary loans or other contracts, notes, warrants, or obligations for current expenses in excess of the total anticipated revenue for such calendar year.

Paragraph VI. *Levy of taxes to pay bonds; sinking fund required.* Any county, municipality, or other political subdivision of this state shall at or before the time of incurring bonded indebtedness provide for the assessment and collection of an annual tax sufficient in amount to pay the principal and interest of said debt within 30 years from the incurring of such bonded indebtedness. The proceeds of this tax, together with any other moneys collected for this purpose, shall be placed in a sinking fund to be used exclusively for paying the principal of and interest on such bonded debt. Such moneys shall be held and kept separate and apart from all other revenues collected and may be invested and reinvested as provided by law.

Paragraph VII. *Validity of prior bond issues.* Any and all bond issues validated and issued prior to June 30, 1983, shall continue to be valid.

Section VI.
Revenue Bonds

Paragraph I. *Revenue bonds; general limitations.* Any county, municipality, or other political subdivision of this state may issue revenue bonds as provided by general law. The obligation represented by revenue bonds shall be repayable only out of the revenue derived from the project and shall not be deemed to be a debt of the issuing political subdivision. No such issuing political subdivision shall exercise the power of taxation for the purpose of paying any part of the principal or interest of any such revenue bonds.

Paragraph II. *Revenue bonds; special limitations.* Where revenue bonds are issued by any county, municipality, or other political subdivision of this state in order to buy, construct, extend, operate, or maintain gas or electric generating or distribution systems and necessary appurtenances thereof and the gas or electric generating or distribution system extends beyond the limits of the county in which the municipality or other political subdivision is located, then its services rendered and property located outside said county shall be subject to taxation and regulation in the same manner as are privately owned and operated utilities.

Paragraph III. *Development authorities.* The development of trade, commerce, industry, and employment opportunities being a public purpose vital to the welfare of the people of this state, the General Assembly may create development authorities to promote and further such purposes or may authorize the creation of such an authority by any county or municipality or combination thereof under such uniform terms and conditions as it may deem necessary. The General Assembly may exempt from taxation development authority obligations, properties, activities, or income and may authorize the issuance of revenue bonds by such authorities which shall not constitute an indebtedness of the state within the meaning of Section V of this article.

Paragraph IV. *Validation.* The General Assembly shall provide for the validation of any revenue bonds authorized and shall provide that such validation shall thereafter be incontestable and conclusive.

Paragraph V. *Validity of prior revenue bond issues.* All revenue bonds issued and validated prior to June 30, 1983, shall continue to be valid.

Section VII.
Community Improvement Districts

Paragraph I. *Creation.* The General Assembly may by local law create one or more community improvement districts for any county or municipality or provide for the creation of one or more community improvement districts by any county or municipality.

Paragraph II. *Purposes.* The purpose of a community improvement district shall be the provision of any one or more of the following governmental services and facilities:

(1) Street and road construction and maintenance, including curbs, sidewalks, street lights, and devices to control the flow of traffic on streets and roads.

(2) Parks and recreational areas and facilities.

(3) Storm water and sewage collection and disposal systems.

(4) Development, storage, treatment, purification, and distribution of water.

(5) Public transportation.

(6) Terminal and dock facilities and parking facilities.

(7) Such other services and facilities as may be provided for by general law.

Paragraph III. *Administration.*

(a) Any law creating or providing for the creation of a community improvement district shall designate the governing authority of the municipality or county for which the community improvement district is created as the administrative body or otherwise shall provide for the establishment and membership of an administrative body for the community improvement district. Any such law creating or providing for the creation of an administrative body for the community improvement district other than the municipal or county governing authority shall provide for representation of the governing authority of each county and municipality within which the community improvement district is wholly or partially located on the administrative body of the community improvement district.

(b) Any law creating or providing for the creation of a community improvement district shall provide that the creation of the community improvement district shall be conditioned upon:

(1) The adoption of a resolution consenting to the creation of the community improvement district by:

    (A) The governing authority of the county if the community improvement district is located wholly within the unincorporated area of a county;

    (B) The governing authority of the municipality if the community improvement district is located wholly within the incorporated area of a municipality; or

    (C) The governing authorities of the county and the municipality if the community improvement district is located partially within the unincorporated area of a county and partially within the incorporated area of a municipality; and

(2) Written consent to the creation of the community improvement district by:

    (A) A majority of the owners of real property within the community improvement district which will be subject to taxes, fees, and assessments levied by the administrative body of the community improvement district; and

    (B) The owners of real property within the community improvement district which constitutes at least 75 percent by value of all real property within the community improvement district which will be subject to taxes, fees, and assessments levied by the administrative body of the community improvement district; and for this purpose value shall be determined by the most recent approved county ad valorem tax digest.

(c) The administrative body of each community improvement district may be authorized to levy taxes, fees, and assessments within the community improvement district only on real property used nonresidentially, specifically excluding all property used for residential, agricultural, or forestry purposes and specifically excluding tangible personal property and intangible property. Any tax, fee, or assessment so levied shall not exceed 2 1/2 percent of the assessed value of the real property or such lower limit as may be established by law.

The law creating or providing for the creation of a community improvement district shall provide that taxes, fees, and assessments levied by the administrative body of the community improvement district shall be equitably apportioned among the properties subject to such taxes, fees, and assessments according to the need for governmental services and facilities created by the degree of density of development of each such property.

The law creating or providing for the creation of a community improvement district shall provide that the proceeds of taxes, fees, and assessments levied by the administrative body of the community improvement district shall be used only for the purpose of providing governmental services and facilities which are specially required by the degree of density of development within the community improvement district and not for the purpose of providing those governmental services and facilities provided to the county or municipality as a whole.

Any tax, fee, or assessment so levied shall be collected by the county or municipality for which the community improvement district is created in the same manner as taxes, fees, and assessments levied by such county or municipality. The proceeds of taxes, fees, and assessments so levied, less such fee to cover the costs of collection as may be specified by law, shall be transmitted by the collecting county or municipality to the administrative body of the community improvement district and shall be expended by the administrative body of the community improvement district only for the purposes authorized by this Section.

Paragraph IV. *Debt.* The administrative body of a community improvement district may incur debt, as authorized by law, without regard to the requirements of Section V of this Article, which debt shall be backed by the full faith, credit, and taxing power of the community improvement district but shall not be an obligation of the State of Georgia or any other unit of government of the State of Georgia other than the community improvement district.

Paragraph V. *Cooperation with local governments.* The services and facilities provided pursuant to this Section shall be provided for in a cooperation agreement executed jointly by the administrative body and the governing authority of the county or municipality for which the community improvement district is created. The provisions of this section shall in no way limit the authority of any county or municipality to provide services or facilities within any community improvement district; and any county or municipality shall retain full and complete authority and control over any of its facilities located within a community improvement district. Said control shall include but not be limited to the modification of, access to, and degree and type of services provided through or by facilities of the municipality or county. Nothing contained in this Section shall be construed to limit or preempt the application of any governmental laws, ordinances, resolutions, or regulations to any community improvement district or the services or facilities provided therein.

Paragraph VI. *Regulation by general law.* The General Assembly by general law may regulate, restrict, and limit the creation of community improvement districts and the exercise of the powers of administrative bodies of community improvement districts.

Article X
Amendments to the Constitution

Section I. Constitution, How, Amended

Paragraph I. *Proposals to amend the Constitution; new Constitution.* Amendments to this Constitution or a new Constitution may be proposed by the General Assembly or by a constitutional convention, as provided in this article. Only amendments which are of general and uniform applicability throughout the state shall be proposed, passed, or submitted to the people.

Paragraph II. *Proposals by the General Assembly; submission to the people.* A proposal by the General Assembly to amend this Constitution or to provide for a new Constitution shall originate as a resolution in either the Senate or the House of Representatives and, if approved by two-thirds of the members to which each house is entitled in a roll-call vote entered on their respective journals, shall be submitted to the electors of the entire state at the next general election which is held in the even-numbered years. A summary of such proposal shall be prepared by the Attorney General, the Legislative Counsel, and the Secretary of State and shall be published in the official organ of each county and, if deemed advisable by the "Constitutional Amendments Publication Board," in not more than 20 other newspapers in the state designated by such board which meet the qualifications for being selected as the official organ of a county. Said board shall be composed of the Governor, the Lieutenant Governor, and the Speaker of the House of Representatives. Such summary shall be published once each week for three consecutive weeks immediately preceding the day of the general election at which such proposal is to be submitted. The language to be used in submitting a proposed amendment or a new Constitution shall be in such words as the General Assembly may provide in the resolution or, in the absence thereof, in such language as the Governor may prescribe. A copy of the entire proposed amendment or of a new Constitution shall be filed in the office of the judge of the probate court of each county and shall be available for public inspection; and the summary of the proposal shall so indicate. The General Assembly is hereby authorized to provide by law for additional matters relative to the publication and distribution of proposed amendments and summaries not in conflict with the provisions of this Paragraph.

If such proposal is ratified by a majority of the electors qualified to vote for members of the General Assembly voting thereon in such general election, such proposal shall become a part of this Constitution or shall become a new Constitution, as the case may be. Any proposal so approved shall take effect as provided in Paragraph VI of this article. When more than one amendment is submitted at the same time, they shall be so submitted as to enable the electors to vote on each amendment separately, provided that one or more new articles or related changes in one or more articles may be submitted as a single amendment.

Paragraph III. *Repeal or amendment of proposal.* Any proposal by the General Assembly to amend this Constitution or for a new Constitution may be amended or repealed by the same General Assembly which adopted such proposal by the affirmative vote of two-thirds of the members to which each house is entitled in a roll-call vote entered on their respective journals, if such action is taken at least two months prior to the date of the election at which such proposal is to be submitted to the people.

Paragraph IV. *Constitutional convention; how called.* No convention of the people shall be called by the General Assembly to amend this Constitution or to propose a new Constitution, unless by the concurrence of two-thirds of the members to which each house of the General Assembly is entitled. The representation in said convention shall be based on population as near as practicable. A proposal by the convention to amend this Constitution or for a new Constitution shall be advertised, submitted to, and ratified by the people in the same manner provided for advertisement, submission, and ratification of proposals to amend the Constitution by the General Assembly. The General Assembly is hereby authorized to provide the procedure by which a convention is to be called and under which such convention shall operate and for other matters relative to such constitutional convention.

Paragraph V. *Veto not permitted.* The Governor shall not have the right to veto any proposal by the General Assembly or by a convention to amend this Constitution or to provide a new Constitution.

Paragraph VI. *Effective date of amendments or of a new Constitution.* Unless the amendment or the new Constitution itself or the resolution proposing the amendment or the new Constitution shall provide otherwise, an amendment to this Constitution or a new Constitution shall become effective on the first day of January following its ratification.

Article XI
Miscellaneous Provisions

Section I
Miscellaneous Provisions

Paragraph I. *Continuation of officers, boards, commissions, and authorities.*

(a) Except as otherwise provided in this Constitution, the officers of the state and all political subdivisions thereof in office on June 30, 1983, shall continue in the exercise of their functions and duties, subject to the provisions of laws applicable thereto and subject to the provisions of this Constitution.

(b) All boards, commissions, and authorities specifically named in the Constitution of 1976 which are not specifically named in this Constitution shall remain as statutory boards, commissions, and authorities; and all constitutional and statutory provisions relating thereto in force and effect on June 30, 1983, shall remain in force and effect as statutory law unless and until changed by the General Assembly.

Paragraph II. *Preservation of existing laws; judicial review.* All laws in force and effect on June 30, 1983, not inconsistent with this Constitution shall remain in force and effect; but such laws may be amended or repealed and shall be subject to judicial decision as to their validity when passed and to any limitations imposed by their own terms.

Paragraph III. *Proceedings of courts and administrative tribunals confirmed.* All judgments, decrees, orders, and other proceedings of the several courts and administrative tribunals of this state, heretofore made within the limits of their several jurisdictions, are hereby ratified and affirmed, subject only to reversal or modification in the manner provided by law.

Paragraph IV. *Continuation of certain constitutional amendments for a period of four years.*

(a) The following amendments to the Constitutions of 1877, 1945, and 1976 shall continue in force and effect as part of this Constitution until July 1, 1987, at which time said amendments shall be repealed and shall be deleted as a part of this Constitution unless any such amendment shall be specifically continued in force and effect without amendment either by a local law enacted prior to July 1, 1987, with or without a referendum as provided by law, or by an ordinance or resolution duly adopted prior to July 1, 1987, by the local governing authority in the manner provided for the adoption of home rule amendments to its charter or local act: (1) amendments to the Constitution of 1877 and the Constitution of 1945 which were continued in force and effect as a part of the Constitution of 1976 pursuant to the provisions of Article XIII, Section I, Paragraph II of the Constitution of 1976 which are in force and effect on the effective date of this Constitution; (2) amendments to the Constitution of 1976 which were ratified as general amendments but which by their terms applied principally to a particular political subdivision or subdivisions which are in force and effect on the effective date of this Constitution; (3) amendments to the Constitution of 1976 which were ratified not as general amendments which are in force and effect on the effective date of this Constitution; and (4) amendments to the Constitution of 1976 of the type provided for in the immediately preceding two subparagraphs (2) and (3) of this Paragraph which were ratified at the same time this Constitution was ratified.

(b) Any amendment which is continued in force and effect after July 1, 1987, pursuant to the provisions of subparagraph (a) of this Paragraph shall be continued in force and effect as a part of this Constitution, except that such amendment may thereafter be repealed but may not be amended. The repeal of any such amendment shall be accomplished by local Act of the General Assembly, the effectiveness of which shall be conditioned on its approval by a majority of the qualified voters voting thereon in each of the particular political subdivisions affected by the amendment.

(c) All laws enacted pursuant to those amendments to the Constitution which are not continued in force and effect pursuant to subparagraph (a) of this Paragraph shall be repealed on July 1, 1987. All laws validly enacted on, before, or after July 1, 1987, and pursuant to the specific authorization of an amendment continued in force and effect pursuant to the provisions of subparagraph (a) of this Paragraph shall be legal, valid, and constitutional under this Constitution. Nothing in this subparagraph (c) shall be construed to revive any law not in force and effect on June 30, 1987.

(d) Notwithstanding the provisions of subparagraphs (a) and (b), the following amendments to the Constitutions of 1877 and 1945 shall be continued in force as a part of this Constitution: amendments to the Constitution of 1877 and the Constitution of 1945 which created or authorized the creation of metropolitan rapid transit authorities, port authorities, and industrial areas and which were continued in force as a part of the Constitution of 1976 pursuant to the provisions of Article XIII, Section I, Paragraph II of the Constitution of 1976 and which are in force on the effective date of this Constitution.

(e) Any person owning property in an industrial area described in subparagraph (d) of this Paragraph may voluntarily remove the property from the industrial area by filing a certificate to that effect with the clerk of the superior court for the county in which the property is located. Once the certificate is filed, the property described in the certificate, together with all public streets and public rights of way within the property, abutting the property, or connecting the property to property outside the industrial area, shall no longer be in the industrial area and shall upon the filing of the certificate be annexed to the city which provides water service to the property, or if no city provides water service shall be annexed to the city providing fire service as provided under the constitutional amendments that created such industrial areas described in subparagraph (d) of this Paragraph. The filing of a certificate shall be irrevocable and shall bind the owners, their heirs, and their assigns. The term "owner" includes anyone with a legal or equitable ownership in property but does not include a beneficiary of any trust or a partner in any partnership owning an interest in the property or anyone owning an easement right in the property.

Paragraph V. *Special commission created.* Amendments to the Constitution of 1976 which were determined to be general and which were submitted to and ratified by the people of the entire state at the same time this Constitution was ratified shall be incorporated and made a part of this Constitution as provided in this Paragraph. There is hereby created a commission to be composed of the Governor, the President of the Senate, the Speaker of the House of Representatives, the Attorney General, and the Legislative Counsel, which is hereby authorized and directed to incorporate such amendments into this Constitution at the places deemed most appropriate to the commission. The commission shall make only such changes in the language of this Constitution and of such amendments as are necessary to incorporate properly such amendments into this Constitution and shall complete its duties prior to July 1, 1983. The commission shall deliver to the Secretary of State this Constitution with those amendments incorporated therein, and such document shall be the Constitution of the State of Georgia. In order that the commission may perform its duties, this Paragraph shall become effective as soon as it has been officially determined that this Constitution has been ratified. The commission shall stand abolished upon the completion of its duties.

Paragraph VI. *Effective date.* Except as provided in Paragraph V of this section, this Constitution shall become effective on July 1, 1983; and, except as otherwise provided in this Constitution, all previous Constitutions and all amendments thereto shall thereupon stand repealed.

Table of Amendments			
Year	Proposed General	Ratified General	Rejected General
1984	11	10	1
1986	9	8	1
1988	15	6	9
1990	9	8	1
1992	8	7	1
1994	6	5	1
1996	5	4	1
1998	5	4	1
2000	7	6	1
2002	6	4	2
2004	2	2	0
2006	3	3	0
2008	3	3	0
2010	5	5	0
2012	2	2	0
TOTAL	96	77	19
Total number of amendments ratified through 2012			

Bibliography

Books and Publications

ACCG, *1995 Survey of County Governments.*

Allen, L. M. (1989). "Civil Service Reform Act of 1978" in Vol. 11 *Encyclopedia USA.* Gulf Breeze, FL: Academic International Press.

Ammons, D. N., & Campbell, R. W. (1993). "County Government Structures" in Weeks, J. Devereaux and Hardy, Paul T., eds. *Handbook for Georgia County Commissioners.* Athens: Carl Vinson Institute of Government, University of Georgia.

Argyle, N. J. (1991). *New Federalism and Public Mass Transit: The Case of SCAT.* Discussion Paper 91-6. Atlanta GA: Institute of Public Administration, Georgia State University.

Banks, C. L. *"Councilmembers marched to the Capitol in protest of unfunded mandates"* in *Council Contact* (In-house publication of the Atlanta City Council), Winter, 1994.

Barber, J. D. (1965). *The Lawmakers.* New Haven: Yale University Press.

Barber, J. D. (1972). *The Presidential Character: Predicting Performance in the White House.* Englewood Cliffs, NJ: Prentice Hall.

Barber, J. D. (1973). *The Lawmakers: Recruitment and Adaptation to Legislative Life.* Clinton, MA: The Colonial Press, Inc.

Black, E. & M. Black. (2002). *The Rise of Southern Republicans.* Cambridge, Mass: Harvard University Press.

Breeden, K. H., (2003). *Foundations and Defining Principles of Georgia's Technical College System: Business Partnerships, Customer Focus, Quality, and Innovations for the Future.* Atlanta: Georgia Department of Technical and Adult Education.

Bullock, C. S. III. (1991). *The Georgia Political Almanac: The General Assembly.* Decatur, GA: Cornerstone Publications.

Bullock, C. S. III. (1993). *The Partisan, Racial and Gender Makeup of Georgia County Offices, Public Policy Research Series.* Carl Vinson Institute of Government: The University of Georgia.

Burke, Edmund. (1967). "Address to the Electorate at Bristol" in *The Works of Edmund Burke.* New York: Harper.

Busbee, G. D. (1981). *Proposed Constitution of the State of Georgia.* Atlanta, GA: Select Committee on Constitutional Revision, Georgia General Assembly.

Carson, E.A. (2015). *Prisoners in 2014.* Washington, D.C.: Bureau of Justice Statistics.

Christianberry, G. A. Jr. (1991). "The Facts: The Department of Administration" in *Georgia State Telephone Directory.* Atlanta, GA: Office of the Secretary of State, January.

Chung, J. (2014). *Felony Disenfranchisement: A Primer.* Washington, D.C.: The Sentencing Project.

Cooper, P. J. (1988). *Public Law and Public Administration.* Englewood Cliffs, NJ: Prentice Hall.

Crutchfield, J. A. (1990). *The Georgia Almanac and Book of Facts 1989–1990.* Nashville, TN: Rutledge Hill Press.

Current, R. N., Williams, T. H., Fredal, Frank, & Brinkley, Alan. (1983). *A Survey of American History.* 6th ed. New York: Alfred A. Knopf.

Dahl, Robert. (1967). *Pluralist Democracy in the United States.* Chicago, IL: Rand McNally.

Dahl, Robert. (2000). *On Democracy.* New Haven, CT: Yale University Press, 2000.

Deal, Nathan, & Alford, D. D. (2015). *The Governor's Budget Report, Fiscal Year 2013*, page 13. Internet:http://opb.georgia.gov/sites/opb.georgia.gov/files/related_files/document/Governors%20Budget%20Report%20FY%202014.pdf

Dye, T. R. (1997). *Politics in States and Communities.* 9th ed. Englewood Cliffs, NJ: Prentice-Hall.

Elza, J. L. (1991). "Teaching Research Skills in Administrative Law" in the *Preceedings of the 14th National Teaching Public Administration Conference.* Knoxville, TN: American Society of Public Administration.

Elazar, D. J. (1984). *American Federalism: A View from the States.* 5th ed. New York: Thomas Y. Crowell Company.

Elazar, D. J., & Grodzin, Morton. (1966). *The American System.* Chicago, IL: Rand-McNally Press.

Eldersveld, S. J. (1964). *Political Parties: A Behavioral Analysis.* Chicago, IL: Rand-McNally.

Ellinger, K. W. (1997). An Analysis of Voter Turnout in Georgia's Presidential Elections 1960–96: Proposals for Electoral Reform. Paper presented at annual meeting of Georgia Political Science Association, Savannah, GA, February 1997.

Executive Order extending the Governor's Special Council on Criminal Justice Reform, signed by Gov. Nathan Deal on May 24, 2012.

Fleischmann, Arnold, Pierannunzi, Carol. (1997). *Politics in Georgia.* Athens: UGA Press.

"Georgia 2010–2030 Population Projection," The Governor's Office of Planning and Budget, Performance Management Office March 10, 2010.

Friedman, Barry. (1991). *Regulations in the Reagan Era: New Procedures, New Results.* Unpublished Ph.D. Dissertation at the University of Connecticut.

Froman, Jr. Lewis A. (Dec. 196). "Some Effects of Interest Group Strength in State Politics," *The American Political Science Review,* Vol. 60, No. 4 pp. 952–962.

Gifis, S. H. (1973). *Law Dictionary,* 5th ed. New York, Hauppauge: Barrons Educational Series Inc.

Gifis, S. H. (2003). *Dictionary,* 5th ed. New York, Hauppauge: Barrons Educational Series Inc.

Gray, Virginia, & Eisinger, Peter. (1997). *American States and Cities.* New York: Longman.

Gray, Virginia, & Jacob, Herbert. (1996). *Politics in the American States: A Comparative Analysis.* 6th ed. Washington, D.C.: CQ Press.

Grodzin, Morton, & Elazar, D. J. (1966). *The American System.* Chicago, IL: Rand-McNally Press.

Hanson, L. H. (2003). *City of Valdosta Georgia Annual Budget. FY 2003.* Valdosta, GA: Office of the City Manager.

Hardy (see Weeks and Hardy, Handbook for Georgia Mayors and Council members, 1993).

Hardy, Oliver. (1982). *The Georgia History Book.* Athens, GA: Carl Vinson Institute of Government, University of Georgia.

Henry, Nicholas. (1987). "Report on Evaluation of the 50 State Legislatures" in *Governing at the Grass Roots.* 3rd ed. Englewood Cliffs, NJ: Prentice-Hall.

Hepburn, L. R. (1987). "Politics and Government" in *Contemporary Georgia.* Athens, GA: Carl Vinson Institute of Government, University of Georgia.

Hiott, Perry, & Dobbs, Chris. (2015). Georgia's City Governments, *New Georgia Encyclopedia,* last updated November 12, 2015.

Holder v. Hall (No. 91202, 1994).

Hy, Ronn, & Saeger, R. T. (1976). "The Nature and Role of Political Parties" in *Mississippi Government and Politics in Transition,* edited by David M. Landry and Joseph B. Parker. Dubuque, IA: Kendall/Hunt Publishing Company.

Jackson, E. L. and Stakes, M. E. (1988). *Handbook of Georgia State Agencies.* Athens, GA: Carl Vinson Institute of Government, University of Georgia.

Jackson, E. L. (1975) The Handbook of Georgia State Agencies. Athens, Georgia: Institute of Government, University of Georgia.

Joiner, O. H. (1979). *A History of Public Education in Georgia, 1734–1976.* Columbia, SC: R. B. Bryan Co.

Katz, Robert. N. (1986). "The History of the Georgia Bill of Rights," *Georgia State University Law Review* 3 (fall-winter 1986).

Lasswell, Harold. (1936). *Who Gets What, When and How?* New York: McGraw-Hill.

Lauth, T. P., & Reese, C. C. (1993). *"The Line-Item Veto in Georgia: Incidence and Fiscal Effects."* A scholarly paper presented at the Annual Meeting of the Georgia Political Science Association, Savannah, GA, February 25–27, 1993.

Lehan, E. A. (1984). *Budgetmaking: A Workbook of Public Budgeting Theory and Practice.* New York: St. Martin's Press.

Lewis, Eugene. (1977). *American Politics in a Bureaucratic Age: Citizens, Constituents, Clients and Victims.* Cambridge, Mass.: Winthrop Publishing Inc.

Locke, John. *Two Treatises of Government,* any edition.

Love, Margaret C. (2007). *Relief from the Collateral Consequences of a Criminal Conviction.*

LWV. (1991). League of Women Voters of Georgia, Inc. *The Georgia Government.* Atlanta, GA: The League of Women Voters of Georgia, Inc.

Machiavelli, Niccolo. (1952). *The Prince.* Translated by Luigi Ricci, Introduction by Christian Gauss. New York: Mentor Books.

Madison, James, Hamilton, Alexander, & Jay, John. (1961). *The Federalist Papers.* New York: New American Library.

Maitland, F. W. (1962). *The Forms of Action at Common Law.* Cambridge University Press.

NAACP v. Billups, U.S., 129 S.Ct. 2770, 174 L.Ed.2d 271 (2009).

Nachmias, David, & Rosenbloom, D. H. (1980). *Bureaucratic Government USA.* New York: St. Martin's Press.

Nice, D. C. (1987). *Federalism—The Politics of Intergovernmental Relations.* NY: St. Martin's Press.

OLC. (1991). *Office of the Legislative Council, Official Code of Georgia, Annotated.* Charlottesville, Va.: The Michie Company.

OLC. (1991). *The Pocket Part.* The Michie Company.

Orr, Dorothy. (1950). *A History of Education in Georgia.* Chapel Hill: University of North Carolina Press.

Orwell, G.(Eric Arthur Blair). (1949), 1984. Signet Classic Secker & Warburg.

Parenti, Michael. (1988). *Democracy for the Few,* 5th ed. Boston: St. Martin's Press.

Pew Center on the States. (2013). *Public Safety in Oregon.* Washington, D.C.: The Pew Charitable Trusts, May 28, 2013.

Phinizy Spalding and Edwin L. Jackson. (1988). *James Edward Oglethorpe: A New Look at Georgia's Founder* (Athens: Carl Vinson Institute of Government, University of Georgia.

Phinizy Spalding and Harvey H. Jackson, eds. (1989). *Oglethorpe in Perspective: Georgia's Founder after Two Hundred Years* (Tuscaloosa: University of Alabama Press.

Pound, M. B., & Saye, A. B. (1971). *Handbook on the Constitutions of the United States and Georgia.* 9th ed. Athens, Ga.: Department of Political Science, University of Georgia.

Report of the Special Council on Criminal Justice Reform for Georgians, December 2012.

Rousseau, J. J. (1978). *Du Contrat Social.* St. Martin's Press.

Saeger, R. T., & Hy, Ronn. (1976). "The Nature and Role of Political Parties" in *Mississippi Government and Politics in Transition,* edited by D.M. Landry and J.B. Parker. Dubuque, IA: Kendall/Hunt Publishing Company.

Smith, E. C. (1979). *Constitution of the United States, with Case Summaries.* New York: Harper and Row, Publishers.

Thomas, W. R., & Prather, J. E. (1993). *"Race, Politics and redistricting in Georgia: Analysis of the 1992 Congressional Election"* a scholarly paper presented at the Annual Meeting of the Georgia Political Science Association, Savannah, Georgia, February 25–27, 1993.

Tocqueville, Alexis de. *Democracy in America.* New York: Knopf.

Tuck, S. G. N. (2001). *Beyond Atlanta: The Struggle for Racial Equality in Georgia, 1940–1980.* Athens: University of Georgia Press.

Uggen, C., Shannon, S., & Manza, J. (2012). *State-Level Estimates of Felon Disenfranchisement in the United States, 2010.* Washington, D.C.: The Sentencing Project.

Walmsley, R. (2015). World Prison Brief. London: Institute for Criminal Policy Research. Available online: http://www.prisonstudies.org/world-prison-brief.

Weber, Max. (1958). *From Max Weber: Essays in Political Sociology,* edited by H.H. Gerth, and C. Wright Mills. New York: Oxford University Press.

Weber, Max. (1961). *Basic Concepts in Sociology.* New York: Citadel, 1913, or see Amitai etzioni, ed. *Complex Organizations.* New York: Holt, 1961 at pp. 4–14.

Weeks, J. D., & Hardy, P. T., eds. (1993). *Handbook for Georgia Mayors and Council Members.* Athens: Carl Vinson Institute of Government, UGA.

Wilson, J. Q. (1992). *American Government: Institutions and Policies.* Lexington, Mass.: D.C. Heath & Company.

Wilson, J. Q., Editor. (1980). *The Politics of Regulation.* New York: Basic Books, Inc.

Winder, D. W. (1991). "The Powers of the Attorneys General: A Quantitative Assessment" in Vol. 19, *Southeastern Political Review.*

Winder, D. W. (1993). *"Governor Miller Drops Proposal to Change the Georgia State Flag for 1993"* in *Comparative State Politics* Vol. 14 (June 1993).

Wolfe, W.H. (1991). *Decatur County, Georgia: Past and Present*. Roswell, GA: Historical Publications.

Journals and Newspapers

2015 Building a Grad Nation Report, "Progress and Challenge in Ending the High School Dropout Epidemic" *released annually, by the Alliance for Excellent Education, America's Promise Alliance, Civic Enterprises, and the Everyone Graduates Center at Johns Hopkins University, May* 12, 2015. Retrieved April 20, 2016, from http://www.gradnation.org/report/2015-building-grad-nation-report.

AJ/AC. (02–21–1992). Editorial. "Miller's Roads to Glory" in the *Atlanta Journal/Atlanta Constitution*. (February 21, 1992) at A12.

AJ/AC. Jan. 13, (1994). *"A Greener Year for State Spending"* in the *Atlanta Journal/Atlanta Constitution*, at p. E4.

AJC, 1/12/11. The Atlanta Journal Constitution (AJC Jan 12 2011-02-17) "Deal warns of cuts, promises progress in first State of the State" Jan. 12, 2011

AJC, 2/13/11. *http://www.ajc.com/news/content/metro/stories/2009/02/02/perdue_st.*

AJC, 2/13/11. *http://www.ajc.com/news/nation-world/georgia-says-stimulus-funds.*

American Bar Association, "How-to" Series to Help the Community, the Bench and the Bar Implement Change in the Justice System," June 2008. Retrieved April 17, 2016, from http://www.americanbar.org/content/dam/aba/migrated/JusticeCenter/Justice/PublicDocuments/judicial_selection_roadmap.authcheckdam.pdf.

American Judicature Society, "Judicial Merit Selection: Current Status," 2011. Retrieved April 17, 2016, from http://www.judicialselection.us/uploads/documents/Judicial_Merit_Charts_0FC20225EC6C2.pdf.

Anthony, Susan B. (1873). "Woman's Rights to the Suffrage" A speech delivered in 1873, Her Arrested, Trial and Conviction for voting in the 1872 presidential election. Retrieved from http://www.nationalcenter.org/AnthonySuffrage.html.

"Annual Estimates of the Resident Population for Incorporated Places". Retrieved April 13, 2016, from census.gov.

Associated Press. (01–01–1992). "Who Should Draw State's Districts?" *Valdosta Daily Times*. (Valdosta, GA: January 1, 1992) at 5-A.

Associated Press. (02–23–1992). Paulding Ponders County Manager. *Florida Times-Union, Georgia Section.* (Dallas, Georgia: AP, February 23, 1992) at B4.

Associated Press. (03–29–1992). "300-pound Woman Sues in Bus Arrest" in the *Florida Times-Union, Georgia Section.* (Atlanta, GA: AP, March 29, 1992) at B8.

Associated Press. (04–29–1992). "Busted Bingo Players Pledge to Change Law" in the *Florida Times-Union, Georgia Section.* (Lavonia, Georgia: AP, April 29, 1992) at A1.

Associated Press. (1993). "Bowers: Murphy threatened child protection funding" in the *Tifton Gazette,* October 5, 1993.

Associated Press. (1993). "Atlanta's archbishop urges support for voucher law" in the *Florida Times-Union,* October 19, 1993.

Associated Press. (1993). "State would need big-time bucks to take over Georgia education costs" in the *Tifton Gazette,* November 15, 1993.

Associated Press. (1994). "Gov. gives lawmakers new agenda as he prepares for re-election bid" in the *Tifton Gazette,* January 1, 1994.

Associated Press. (1994). *"Weeping Murphy growls over guide dog coverage"* in the *Tifton Gazette,* February 23, 1994.

Associated Press. (1994). *"How will Georgia House be ruled after Speaker Murphy"* in the *Tifton Gazette,* March 28, 1994.

The Atlanta Journal Constitution (AJC Jan 12 2011-02-17) "Deal warns of cuts, promises progress in first State of the State." Jan. 12, 2011.

Beasley, Dorothy T. (1985) "The Georgia Bill of Rights: Dead or Alive?" *Emory Law Journal* 34.

Beer, Samuel H. (1978). "Federalism, Nationalism and Democracy in America" in *American Political Science Review.* (March, 1978).

Bergstrom. Retrieved September 29, 2010, from http://lake.typepad. com/on-the-lake-front/2010/09/brad-bergstrom-unsubstantiated-assertions-are-not-facts.html.

Blackmon, Douglas A. (1993). *"Council avoids risk, supports stadium"* in the *Atlanta Journal/Atlanta Constitution,* March 2, 1993.

Blau, Max. 2014. A blog site: @maxblau at http://clatl.com.

Bratcher, Stewart D. (2005). *Georgia Bill of Rights,* The New Georgia Encyclopedia, *Georgia Humanities Council. Retrieved January 31, 2011, from http://www.georgiaencyclopedia.org/nge/Article.jsp?id=h-3015.*

Bratcher, S. D. (2005). *Georgia Bill of Rights,* The New Georgia Encyclopedia, *Georgia Humanities Council.* Retrieved March 15, 2016, from: http://m.georgiaencyclopedia.org/articles/government-politics/georgia-bill-rights.

Census. 2011 Statistical Abstract of the United States. http://www.census. gov/library/publications/2011/compendia/statab/131ed.html.

The Committee for the Study of the American Electorate, United States Presidential Elections 2004, https://www.gwu.edu/~action/2004/ electrte.html.

Common Cause/Georgia v. Billups, 406 F.Supp.2d 1326, 1369–1370, 1377 (N.D.Ga.2005).

Common Cause/Georgia v. Billups, 439 F.Supp.2d 1294, 1351, 1360 (N.D.Ga.2006) ("Common Cause/Ga. II ").

Common Cause/Georgia v. Billups, 504 F.Supp.2d 1333, 1340(30) (N.D.Ga.2007) ("Common Cause/Ga. III ").

Common Cause/Georgia v. Billups, 554 F.3d 1340, 1355(III) (A) (11th Cir.2009). ("Common Cause/Ga. IV").

Cook, Rhonda. (10–14–1991). "Backlog of State Inmates Is Growing" in the *Atlanta Journal/Atlanta Constitution* (October 14, 1991), at D1.

Cook, Rhonda. (04–02–1992). "Feds Play 'Partisan Politics' with Re-districting, Miller says" in the *Atlanta Journal/Atlanta Constitution* (April 2, 1992) at D3.

Cook, Rhonda, & Hendricks, Gary. (01–22–1992). "Black vote was 'minimalized,' so redistricting starts again today." *The Atlanta Journal/ The Atlanta Constitution* (Wednesday, January 22, 1992) at A1, A8.

Deeptha Thattai. *A History of Public Education in the United States.* Retrieved from: http://www.academia.edu/5177440/A_history_of_ public_education_in_the_United_States.

Delk, Glenn. (1993). "School choice law is common sense" in the *Atlanta Journal/Atlanta Constitution,* September 26, 1993.

Democratic Party of Georgia, Inc. v Perdue Case No. S10A1517 (GA Sup. Ct., March 7, 2011).

Digby, M. F. 2004. Capitol Budgeting and State Debt. New Georgia Encyclopedia. A project of the Georgia Humanities Council, in partnership with the University of Georgia Press, the University System of Georgia/GALILEO, and the Office of the Governor. Retrieved from *http://dlg.galileo.usg.edu.*

Ebel, Carol. "William Stephens (1671–1753)." New Georgia Encyclopedia. 15 January 2015. Web. 15 April 2016.

Faler, Brian. "A Polling Sight: Record Turnout," November 5, 2004, Washington Post, p. A07.

Fayette FrontPage. http://fayettefrontpage.blogspot.com/ Flags that have Flown Over Georgia. http://georgiainfo.galileo.usg.edu/flags/.

Froman, L. L. (1985). "Some Effects of Interest Group Strength in State Politics" in *American Journal of Political Science* Vol. 29 (February).

"Georgia 2010–2030 Population Projection," The Governor's Office of Planning and Budget, Performance Management Office March 10, 2010.

Georgia Budget & Policy Institute. 2015. *Georgia Budget Primer 2016.*
Retrieved from http://gbpi.org/georgia.

Georgia Code, Title 36 "Local Government Provisions Applicable to the
Establishment of municipal court;..." Section 36, 32, 1–40 (2010).
[O.C.G.A. 36-32-1-40 (2010)].

The Georgia Department of Corrections (GDC) "The Friday Report About
Adult Offenders in Georgia's prisons." http://www.dcor.state.ga.us/
Research/FridayReport.pdf, April 8, 2014.

The Georgia Department of Corrections, Annual Report FY2014, http://
www.dcor.state.ga.us/AboutGDC/AgencyOverview/pdf/Annual_
Report_FY14.pdf.

The Georgia Department of Education, "Georgia Wins Race to the Top."
Retrieved August 24, 2010, from http://sonnyperdue.georgia.gov/00/
press/detail/0%2c2668%2c78006749_161911047_162431828%2c00.
html.

Georgia Lottery for Education Act. O.C.G.A. §§50-27-1–50-27-34, 1992

Georgia Peace Officer Standards and Training Council v. Mullis, 281 S.E.2d
569 (Ga. 1981). Official Code of Georgia Annotated.

Georgia State Office of Planning and Budget. 2009. Budget in Brief,
Amended FY 2008 and FY 2009, p. 14.

Gibson, J. L. (1985). "Whither the Local Parties?" *American Journal of
Political Science* Vol. 29 (February).

Gold, S. D. (1990). "Demystifying Those Scary Statistics" in *State
Legislatures* (May/June).

The Governor Policy Report, 2015/16, Office of Budget and Planning, opb.
georgia.gov.

Grillo, Jerry. (2009). "How Low Can They Go?" Retrieved December 2009,
from *http://www.georgiatrend.com/cover-story/12_09_education.shtml.*

Haines, Errin. Originally reported in the Athens Banner-Herald. Retrieved
January 25, 2011, from *http://onlineathens.com/stories/012511/new_
775802352.shtml.*

Harvey, Steve. (04–01–1992). "$8.2 Billion Budget OK'ed on Eve of
Adjournment" in *The Atlanta Journal/The Atlanta Constitution* (April
1, 1992), at A1 and A8.

Hinton, Kendra. (2011). Placement of Amendments within Constitution.
http://www.publiceye.org/magazine/v19n3/carter_wallace.html.
The voter ID bill has both pros and cons. http://lubbockonline.com/
editorials/2011-12-04/our-view-voter-id-law-battle-wastes-energy-
while-pros-cons-are-questionable.

Kirchner, Joan. (AP 2–12–1998). "Few Select Groups in the Running for
Georgia Sales Tax Exemptions" in the *Valdosta Daily Times.* Valdosta,
GA: February 12, 1998, at 3-A.

LoMonte, Frank. (04–02–1992). "Miller Proclaims Session a Success" in the Georgia Section of the *Florida Times-Union* (April 2, 1992) Georgia Section.

LoMonte, Frank. (04–02–1992). "Zell Miller to Sign New Ethics Bill Monday" in the Georgia Section of the *Florida Times-Union,* (April 2, 1992) Georgia Section.

Maitland F. W. (1962). The Forms of Action at Common Law. Cambridge University Press. *Perdue v. Baker.* 2003. SO3A1154 Supreme Court of Georgia.

Mewborn, D. S. (2009). Public Education (PreK–12, *New Georgia Encyclopedia,* Georgia Humanities Council. Retrieved from *http://www.georgiaencyclopedia.org/nge/Article.jsp?id=h-2619.*

Miller, Zell. Feb. 24, (1994). "House Embraces Tax Cut" in the *Atlanta Journal/Atlanta Constitution,* at p. A1.

Morris v. Hartsfield, 197 S.E. 251 (Ga. 1938).

O'Connor, Robert, & Swift, Nick, "U.S. Local Government and Mayors of largest Cities"*10 November 2015.* Retrieved April 13, 2016, from http://www.citymayors.com/mayors/us-mayors.html.

OCGA § 21–2–417 (2005).

OCGA § 21–2–417.1. (2006).

The Office of the Attorney General of the State of Georgia, "Attorney General Olens' Statement on Supreme Court Marriage Ruling." Retrieved March 4, 2016, from http://law.ga.gov/press-releases/2015-06-29/attorney-general-olens%E2%80%99-statement-supreme-court-marriage-ruling, June 26, 2015.

The Office of the Attorney General of the State of Georgia, http://www.georgia.gov/02/ago/home/0,2705,87670814,00.html, assessed February 1, 2011).

Office of Communications, Office of the Governor of the State of Georgia, "Governor Perdue Signs $17.9 Billion Fiscal Year 2011 Budget." Retrieved June 8, 2010, from http://sonnyperdue.georgia.gov/00/press/detail/0,2668,78006749_160096907_160266268,00.html.

Office of the Governor, "Deal signs second edition of criminal justice reform" http://gov.georgia.gov/press-releases/2013-04-25/deal-signs-second-edition-criminal-justice-reform, April 25, 2013.

Osinski, Bill. (1994). "Law has towns fighting Oblivion" in *The Atlanta Journal/Atlanta Constitution,* 03–28–94, p. B6.

Parker, J. F. (1993). "Business owners worry about bus disruption" in *Atlanta Journal/Atlanta Constitution,* August 29, 1993.

Paulk, Harold. (2002). Melvin Thompson (1903–1980). New Georgia Encyclopedia. A project of the Georgia Humanities Council, in partnership with the University of Georgia Press, the University System of Georgia/GALILEO, and the Office of the Governor. Retrieved from *http://dlg.galileo.usg.edu.*

Perdue v. Baker. 2003. SO3A1154 Supreme Court of Georgia.

Perdue, Sonny. Press Release, Governor Perdue, Chief Justice Sears Resolve DA Funding Crisis. Retrieved June 7, 2007, from *http://sonnyperdue.georgia.gov/00/press/detail/0%2c2668%2c78006749_83473563_83473198%2c00.html.*

Pettys, Dick. (06-26-1990). "Lobbying a Thriving Business in Georgia, Even IF IT Is Illegal" in the *Brunswick News* (June 26, 1990).

Pettys, Dick. Governor: "Two-strikes law changes currently on hold," *Associated Press,* January 04, 2005. Retrieved April 15, 2016, from http://onlineathens.com/stories/010405/new_20050104023.shtml#.VxDpwkfVteU.

Rankin, Bill. (1993). "Top judges say they need a pay increase" in the *Atlanta Journal/Atlanta Constitution,* December 07, 1993.

Salter, Sallye. (1993). "Nearby merchants excited about project" in *Atlanta Journal/Atlanta Constitution,* August 29, 1993.

Salzer, James. (1994). "State Flag Supporters Fire Angry Volley" in *Savannah Morning News,* 2–25–94, Morris News Service.

Seabrook, Charles. (1993). "State Lawmakers debate impact of reprimand" in *Atlanta Journal/Atlanta Constitution,* Jan. 14, 1993.

Sheinin, Aaron Gould "Republicans pull redistricting work into the Capitol," http://www.ajc.com/news/news/local-govt-politics/republicans-pull-redistricting-work-into-the-capit/nQqMf/ Friday, Feb. 4, 2011.

Sherman, Mark. (1992). "Primary change boosts Ga.'s profile" in *The Atlanta Journal/The Atlanta Constitution* (January 22, 1992) page A1.

Shipp, Bill. (2005). VDT, "Of Fuzzy Images and Perdue," October 13, 2005, p. 6A.

Staff Report. (1992). "Status of Major Bills in Legislature" in *The Atlanta Journal/The Atlanta Constitution* (April 1, 1992) at A1 and A8.

Swift, James. (2016). "Georgia Gov. Deal Signs Law Establishing New Juvenile Justice Reform Commission." *Juvenile Justice Information Exchange* April 26, 2013 (JJIE), http://jjie.org/georgia-gov-deal-signs-law-establishing-new-juvenile-justice-reform-commission/, April 14, 2016.

Tuck, Stephen. (2004). "Civil Rights Movement." *New Georgia Encyclopedia.* Updated 04 March 2016. Web. 11 July 2016.

U.S. Census Bureau. 2012 Census of Governments.

U. S. Debt Clock, Georgia. 02/17/11, 9:57pm EST. Retrieved from *http://www.usdebtclock.org.*

Vickers, R. J. (1994). "Friends and contributors all" in the *Atlanta Journal/Atlanta Constitution,* January 2, 1994.

WALB News. 03-06-11. *http://www.walb.com/Global/story.asp?S=14075512.*

Walston, Charles, & Cook, Rhonda. (1992). "Blame the Legislature, not Justice, Brooks says" in *The Atlanta Journal/The Atlanta Constitution* (January 22, 1992) at A-8.

Watson, Tom. (1993). "Gay fight unfolds in Georgia" in *USA Today,* August 23, 1993.

Weinman, Melissa. "Brookhaven residents vote to create new city" on July 31, 2012. Retrieved April 13, 2016, from http://www.reporternewspapers.net/2012/07/31/breaking-brookhaven-resident-vote-to-create-new-city/.

Whitt, Richard. (1994). "Study commissions: Where bills go to die" in the *Atlanta Journal/Atlanta Constitution,* January 10, 1994.

Wooten, Jim. (1993). "I give up in the war on lottery" in the *Atlanta Journal/Atlanta Constitution,* September 26, 1993.

The World Almanac and Book of Facts. (2002). Mahwah, NJ: World Almanac Books.

World Almanac and Book of Facts. (2010). Sarah Johnson (Ed.) Infobase Publishing.

Yarbrough, Dick. (2011). "Bad Weather Doesn't Alter Political Landscape," January 22, 2011. *Valdosta Daily Times,* p. 6A.

Yarbrough, Dick. (2011). "Ralston Could Have Gone to Power Springs," *The Valdosta Daily Times,* p. 6A, February 19, 2011.

Zanardi, David. (1994). *"Experts say mega-school is unwise"* in the *Tifton Gazette* (September 17, 1993).

Index